Poets and Politics

CRITICAL CONDITIONS: FIELD DAY ESSAYS AND MONOGRAPHS

Edited by Seamus Deane

Critical Conditions: Field Day Essays

Poets and Politics

Continuity and Reaction in Irish Poetry, 1558–1625

Marc Caball

CORK UNIVERSITY PRESS
in association with
FIELD DAY

First published in 1998 by
Cork University Press
Cork
Ireland

British Library Cataloguing in Publication Data

A CIP catalogue record for this book is available from the British Library.

ISBN 1-85918-162-7

Typesetting by Red Barn Publishing, Skeagh, Skibbereen, Co. Cork

Printed by ColourBooks, Baldoyle, Co. Dublin

CONTENTS

ACKNOWLEDGEMENTS

During the course of preparing the doctoral dissertation on which this book is based, I was fortunate to have been supervised by two historians of distinction and exemplary scholarship: Dr Brendan Bradshaw, S.M., and Professor Thomas Charles-Edwards. My work has benefited immeasurably from their insights and criticisms. In his capacity as external examiner, Professor Breandán Ó Buachalla was kind enough to comment in detail on the original thesis. Dr Katharine Simms read a draft of the present book and I have greatly profited from her expertise. Of course, it goes without saying that I am solely responsible for any errors of detail and stylistic infelicities which remain. In an age of relentless academic specialisation, I am especially privileged to have been introduced by Professor D. Ellis Evans, FBA, to the broader vista of medieval and early modern Celtic civilisation. More generally, I am indebted to many people for encouragement, advice and suggestions while researching and writing this study: Mishtooni Bose, Professor Ann Dooley, Nicolas Jacobs, John McCafferty, Hiram Morgan, Máire Ní Bháin, Professor Máirín Ní Dhonnchadha, Éamonn Ó Ciardha, Canon Oliver O'Donovan, Mary O'Dowd, Pádraig Ó Macháin, Professor Máirtín Ó Murchú, Michelle O Riordan, Micheal O'Siadhail, Ciarán Parker, Brian Young. On a practical level, I am pleased to record my gratitude to the Trustees of the Sir John Rhys Fund for electing me to a studentship at Jesus College, Oxford, and to the School of Celtic Studies at the Dublin Institute for Advanced Studies for awarding me a research scholarship. My thanks are also due to Sara Wilbourne of Cork University Press and Seamus Deane in his role as editor of the Field Day Critical Conditions series for so readily agreeing to publish my work. This book is dedicated to Carol Baxter in gratitude for her constant support and encouragement.

A note on translations and nomenclature

I have generally reproduced translations which accompany critical editions of poems. Occasionally for purposes of clarity and style, I have emended existing translations and indicated my intervention in the relevant footnotes. Where material has not previously been translated, I have provided English versions in all cases. The personal names of Gaelic literati are given in their Irish form. In the case of the Gaelic political élite, I have for the most part used the anglicised forms cited in T.W. Moody, F.X. Martin and F.J. Byrne (eds.), *A new history of Ireland* III (Oxford, 1976).

INTRODUCTION

Early modern Ireland witnessed an epic struggle between an aggrandising English state and the indigenous Gaelic polity which was characterised by a network of regional magnates and local lords. By the early seventeenth century, this protracted conflict had resulted in the effective destruction of élite Gaelic society and the ancient culture it enshrined. A dearth of historical evidence and the bias of posterity have often ensured that the history of vanquished peoples has been obscured or misunderstood. Gaelic Ireland has proved no exception in this regard. Fortunately, however, the survival of an extensive range of contemporary poems composed by the bardic intellectual élite offers a fascinating means of reconstructing Gaelic attitudes to the cataclysm which overtook their world at this period. While bardic poets chronicled the progressive enfeeblement of Gaelic society with acuity, they also initiated a major reassessment of communal identity by way of reaction to crown expansionism. Although early modern bardic poets can be said to have been the last custodians of high Gaelic culture, they also, somewhat ironically, played a central role in the creation of a modern Irish sense of nationality.

This study is intended as a contribution to 'Ireland's scanty conceptual repertoire'.[1] More specifically, it is an analysis of the ideologies and *mentalités* discernible in bardic poetry composed during the reigns of Elizabeth I and James I (1558–1625).[2] In a period which had significant long-term implications for the future of Gaelic society and of Ireland in general, the reaction of the Gaelic intellectual élite to the process of New English conquest, subsequent colonial consolidation and ancillary religious reform is of great historical importance, particularly if the precise significance of this momentous change is to be understood in its appropriate political and cultural context. While important advances have been made in the delineation of ideological developments and shifts among the so-called Old English community, descendants of the twelfth-century Anglo-Norman colonists, and the incoming New English settlers, Gaelic intellectual responses to social and political ferment remain the focus of vigorous and controversial historiographical discussion.[3] It is commonly agreed that the elucidation of indigenous perceptions of conquest and colonisation can be mainly advanced through study of the most important extant Gaelic source: bardic poetry.[4] Composed by a professional caste broadly between 1250 and 1650, bardic poetry was intimately linked to aristocratic society and, as such, reflects the ideological priorities and aspirations not only of the bardic clerisy, but also of the Gaelic and gaelicised Anglo-Norman élite.

1

It has been reliably estimated that just over two thousand poems from the classical bardic period have survived in manuscripts. A higher proportion of the extant poetry belongs to the end of the bardic era and over a thousand poems date from 1566 onwards.[5] This legacy is greatly enriched by several family poem-books or *duanaireadha*. These family poem-books are complemented by composite manuscript collections, particularly important examples of which include the 'Book of O'Donnell's Daughter' (probably begun in the later part of the reign of James I), the 'Book of O'Conor Don' (1631) and the O'Gara manuscript (*c.* 1655–9).[6] These family or seigneurial poem-books constitute an immediately convenient forum in which to analyse the bardic outlook. It seems that the traditional legitimatory genres of eulogy and elegy secured ready inclusion in poem-books. More often than not, compositions of a personal or idiosyncratic nature owe their preservation to other miscellaneous manuscript sources. Therefore, for example, if a poet composed a piece responding exclusively to aspects of Elizabethan encroachment, it may well have been unlikely to have been included in a lord's *duanaire* because of its non-traditional focus. Conversely, if a poet composed a eulogy, interspersed with topical commentary, its chances of being recorded in a poem-book were probably much greater.[7] Most poems, however, are individual survivals and they provide a valuable counterbalance to the evidence offered by the material in family poem-books.

Bardic poetry cannot be separated from its ideological and historical background in the Gaelic polity and its nuanced interpretation requires an understanding of the role of the poet in society.[8] Briefly stated, it is clear that the primary professional function of *fileadha* was to provide political and social validation for the ascendant élite. Invoking a series of motifs and conventions sanctioned by long usage, bardic poets established the validity of a ruling or potential lord before fellow noblemen and the inhabitants of his territories. In this sense, the poetry projects the key ideological precepts which underpinned conventional notions of lordship and its exercise. The evidence from the ultimate phase of bardic composition demonstrates that the *fileadha* were closely involved in the political affairs of Gaelic lordships and were no doubt in a position of some influence. In a piece entitled 'Mór an t-ainm ollamh flatha', Eochaidh Ó hEódhusa (ob. 1612) drew the attention of Hugh Maguire (ob. 1600), lord of Fermanagh, to the quasi-diplomatic duties of a lord's poet:[9]

> Dlighidh bhós beagán ainbhreath,
> rún flatha, fonn comhroighneach,
> a thogha go tolaigh shíth,
> dola a gcoraibh do choigcrích.

> He (the lord's poet) is entitled to
> some excessive demands; to a lord's counsel;

to prime lands; to be selected to attend a
peace parley; to go surety for an alien territory.

The idea that a poet might enjoy access to the counsels of his patron and perhaps even assume an active diplomatic role as emissary or political mediator is confirmed by contemporary sources.

Around 1597–8 the west Munster *fileadh* Cú Chonnacht Ó Dálaigh composed a poem beginning 'Cionnas do fhúigfinnse Aodh', where he describes his trepidation at the prospect of leaving his erstwhile benefactor, Hugh Roe O'Donnell (ob. 1602) of *Tír Conaill*, in order to return to his native locality in Kerry. In a fascinating reversal of narrative roles, the poet allows the English authorities a direct voice in the piece. Dwelling on his own fear of imprisonment, Ó Dálaigh has the English state their case against him. In his portrayal, the 'English' perception of the poet is that of an agitator encouraging O'Donnell and his people to resist English overlordship ('do-bheir i nGaoidhealaibh gomh 's neimh ré saoirfhearaibh Saxan').[10] This key text provides direct evidence of Ó Dálaigh's understanding of the central role a poet might play in the political affairs of a Gaelic lordship. Further corroboration of the potential for bardic political influence is found in a letter addressed to Sir Robert Cecil in 1602 by the Munster nobleman Florence MacCarthy Reagh (ob. *c.* 1641). MacCarthy identifies two groups as having particular status in Irish society, priests and poets. He goes so far as to suggest that some of the *fileadha* might be employed in the service of the crown, for he declares that, among the Irish, only the priests and poets were 'of greatest ability, and authority to persuade that country gentlemen; which of all other sorts, and sexes, doth most distaste and mislike the State and government of England'. MacCarthy claims, however, that such was the hostility of the Catholic clergy to the crown authorities, that only the *fileadha* could be trusted with official business, and even then, the poets' primary loyalty was to their patrons.[11] Insights revealed by Ó hEódhusa, Ó Dálaigh and MacCarthy indicate that the poets enjoyed unrivalled access to the political élite, and depending on the particular individuals, were strategically positioned to influence the political outlook of their patrons and associates.[12] When Giolla Riabhach Ó Cléirigh congratulated Cú Chonnacht Maguire (ob. 1589) and the nobles of Fermanagh on their extensive knowledge of the bardic art ('do-chuaidh ar chléir ccomhadhaigh buain fá t'fhéin a n-ealadhain'), he was, perhaps unwittingly, highlighting both the dominant role of the *fileadha* in the articulation of Gaelic political ideology and their almost symbiotic relationship with the seigneurial élite.[13]

Modern Celtic scholarship, partly in response to prevailing political orthodoxies, has until recently tended to emphasise the supposedly archaic aspects of medieval and early modern Gaelic society. In contrast, current historical research has begun to reveal a picture of a less static world which eschews the notion of an unyielding and monolithic culture.[14] The sixteenth century, in particular, has been shown to have been receptive to renaissance ideas to an extent considered unlikely by previous generations of scholars.[15] Although the full impact of renaissance influence on Gaelic literature in the sixteenth and seventeenth centuries is yet to be explored systematically, it is certain that the native learned class was not unmindful of developments in Europe.[16] A modernising tendency which emerges among some of the nobility is likely to have been connected with the appearance of elements of humanist thought in Gaelic literature. A well-stocked library such as that, for instance, of Gerald Fitzgerald (ob. 1534), ninth earl of Kildare, which in 1525–6 contained material in Irish, French, English and Latin, may well have served as a fruitful conduit between Irish and continental scholarship.[17] Of course, both the literati and the aristocracy were also exposed to new trends and developments by means of overseas commercial and ecclesiastical links.

Given that bardic poetry bears the distinctive imprint of a venerable and conservative poetic tradition, it is not surprising that the poetry's conventional characteristics should have been highlighted by modern scholars to the neglect of consideration of external parallels or influences.[18] Yet it is clear that what may have been a fairly widespread knowledge of Latin among the *fileadha* allowed them potentially unrestricted access to contemporary European intellectual and scholarly trends. Such was his competence in Latin that one poet, Donnchadh Ó Cobhthaigh (*fl.*1584), even tried his hand, with some success, at verse composition in the language.[19] Many allusions and exempla of classical provenance bear testimony to bardic familiarity with Latin scholarship.[20] Indeed, not only were many poets conversant with classical literature, recent research suggests that some among their number were acquainted with contemporary literature in English. It has been demonstrated that aspects of the work of two poets, Eochaidh Ó hEódhusa and Cearbhall Ó Dálaigh, bear the impress of English literary culture.[21] Despite the dearth of immediately direct evidence, it may be assumed that at least some of the *fileadha*, whether by means of literary interchange or foreign travel, had been introduced to humanist learning.[22] It is probably no coincidence that just as the new continental attitudes had begun to percolate into Ireland, poetic innovators – Ó hEódhusa, Fearghal Óg Mac an Bhaird, and Eoghan Ruadh Mac an Bhaird, for example – started to leave their own individual mark on the bardic corpus.

More importantly, the bardic institution was also capable of generating internal dynamism. Much of the poetry's scope for historical rationalisation may be attributed to the pseudo-historical compilation, which, in its various recensions, is known as *Lebor Gabála* ('The Book of Conquests'). This work was of fundamental importance in the traditional explanation of the origins of the *Gaoidhil* and the successive prehistoric invasions of Ireland which culminated in Gaelic supremacy. With its elaborate portrayal of the evolution of Gaelic ascendancy, it constituted the central historiographical component of bardic ideology.[23] Aspects of the communal origin-legend, when appropriately manipulated by bardic poets, were transformed into potent political propaganda. While the *Lebor Gabála* provided historical validation for the presence of the *Gaoidhil* in Ireland, it took, of course, no account of the arrival of the two major post-Gaelic influxes, the Anglo-Normans in the later twelfth century and the New English in the early modern period.

The literati considered the precedent of the successive invasions of Ireland as outlined in the *Lebor Gabála* to possess an exemplary power of validation. Therefore, while the medieval Anglo-Norman colonists and their descendants occupied no place in the schema of the *Lebor Gabála*, the learned class could resourcefully reassure the progeny of the twelfth-century invasion that their presence on the island was indeed legitimate in terms of an extension of the traditional validatory mechanism. They achieved this by pointing to the example of the several prehistoric peoples who had invaded the country and established their position by virtue of the sword, until, in turn, they too were displaced by the superior martial strength of newcomers ('Fearann cloidhimh críoch Bhanbha').[24] However, the alternative application of the *Lebor Gabála* paradigm, as the German settler Mathew De Renzy warned the lord deputy in *c.* 1617, enabled the Gaelic Irish to employ it to justify and assert their historic social and political hegemony in Ireland. Of course, the implication of this latter approach was the putative inculturation of non-Gaelic ethnic groups by the dominant culture in Ireland.[25]

Although the contractual focus of bardic composition was inevitably local in scope, centred on the aspirations and ambitions of a given lord or territory, the linguistic and ideological framework within which the *fileadha* operated was predicated on a pan-insular basis. The use of a standardised prescriptive literary medium from the twelfth century onwards ensured a practical communicative advantage in the articulation of bardic ideologies which was free from the geographical limitations imposed by localised dialectal custom.[26] The poets wielded a linguistic medium which was intelligible and sociologically meaningful throughout the Gaelic realms in Ireland and Scotland. Such communicative facility was further advantaged by the essentially oral and scribal mode of Gaelic literary activity.[27] As a result of adverse social and political conditions, contemporary print culture made no extended impact on the transmission and conservation of literature in Irish.[28] Yet the largely communal oral delivery of bardic poetry may well have guaranteed its practitioners a broader audience than printed books could ever have aspired to reach.[29] This factor suggests that the ideological impact of bardic composition was confined not just to the higher echelons of society but may well have exercised a wider influence. The use of a fixed classical Gaelic dialect was complemented by the fact that the poets drew from a common conceptual store of legend, genealogy and pseudo-history. It has already been noted that the *Gaoidhil* possessed an acute historical and ethnic consciousness based on the phased occupational schema documented in the *Lebor Gabála*. In addition to this self-consciously elaborate notion of ethnic sensibility, mention should also be made of the early modern implications of the topos of the female personification of Ireland's sovereignty. While the *Lebor Gabála* schema promoted Gaelic ethnic suzerainty, the imagery of the female embodiment of sovereignty sustained awareness of a primordial insular territorial integrity. Its origins reaching back to antiquity, the idea of *Éire's* personified sovereignty must surely have developed in application and tone over the course of the centuries.[30] Although its poetic invocation may well have been largely conventional by the sixteenth century, the ongoing deployment of the theme indicates the extent to which the bardic mindset was pan-insular in outlook and application. Crucially, therefore, while the New English met with no effective centralised opposition to the piecemeal extension of the crown's writ throughout an island whose political organisation was dominated by a handful of regional potentates and an array of local lords, this cannot be taken to mean that the literati engaged with Tudor and Stuart aggrandisement in strictly localised political circumstances. Although the *fileadha* functioned within the dynastic power structures of the Gaelic polity, their cultural tradition was neither local nor provincial in aspirational or interpretative terms. The testimony of both *Lebor Gabála* and the sovereignty motif illustrate how the poets were conceptually equipped to engage with the challenges posed by colonial expansionism.

In acknowledging the reigns of Elizabeth and James as a period of critical significance in the history of Gaelic literature and culture, literary scholars have long recognised a tendency towards innovation in bardic poetry at this juncture. The shadow of the battle of Kinsale and the flight of the northern earls to the continent, traditional historiographical markers in the supposedly rapid demise of élite Gaelic society, appear to have convinced some scholars that inchoate literary development was in effect immediately truncated by extremely adverse socio-political conditions. It was to this notion of nascent bardic reassessment, halted by the negative force of political circumstance, that two distinguished modern scholars of bardic poetry were committed. James Carney summed up the view which he shared with a pioneering predecessor in this field:[31]

> Eleanor Knott, speaking to me over a decade ago about Ó hEoghusa, remarked that, if the Irish had not collapsed politically at this time and had the literature of the Irish upper-classes continued to develop Ó hEoghusa would be the beginning of a new tradition rather than the end of the old. This is also my opinion.

The present study argues that the Elizabethan and Jacobean periods certainly witnessed ideological innovation in the work of bardic poets. However, contrary to the reading advanced by Carney and Knott that the prospect of sustained and developed innovation was brought to naught by the apparent paralysis of the bardic institution, it will be demonstrated in this work that the tradition was transformed rather than overwhelmed. This transformation took place in the context of the impressive modernisation of Gaelic literature which occurred broadly during the last three decades of the sixteenth century and the first quarter of the seventeenth century. While the corporate bardic institution was in protracted professional decline, Gaelic poetry and prose blossomed in the stimulating warmth of the renaissance. Although the bardic institution itself decayed, many bardic themes and motifs were destined to flourish in the poetry of the gifted non-professional literati who came to inherit much of the thematic stock-in-trade of the bardic order. The endurance of these motifs and themes is proof of a traditional literature selectively moulded to cope with radically altered social and political conditions.

By the time James VI, King of Scotland, acceded to the English throne in 1603 the viability of the corporate bardic apparatus was threatened by a number of pressures, none of which was to diminish in effect. The New English conquest and the imposition of common law in Ireland early in the sixteenth century subverted, indeed obviated the need for bardic political legitimation among the already considerably-weakened Gaelic and gaelicised grandees. The progressive degradation of the poetry's key function was not solely responsible, however, for the straitened circumstances of the bardic institution. Increased literacy among the nobles, no doubt facilitated by the availability of printed books, further undermined the cultural dominance traditionally exercised by the poets in Gaelic society.[32] While there is substantial evidence of amateur poetic practice in Irish in the later middle ages, a trend towards non-professional composition of poetry was facilitated from the reign of Elizabeth onwards, by burgeoning upper-class literacy and the humanist literary tradition.[33] In effect, by the beginning of the seventeenth century the retention of the medieval bardic system was no longer tenable in a society transformed by conquest, renaissance and counter-reformation.

The present work is a contribution to the historiographical debate centring on what early modern literature in Irish, bardic poetry in particular, reveals of the responses of the Gaelic literati to the impact of colonial consolidation. Since its initiation in 1978 with the publication of Brendan Bradshaw's study of poems in the *Leabhar Branach*, the debate has been characterised by two contrasting interpretative schemas. Highlighting the advances made in the reconstruction of the intellectual worlds of the Old and New English communities, Bradshaw's analysis of poems addressed to Hugh McShane (ob. 1579) and Fiach McHugh O'Byrne (ob. 1597) of *Gabhal Raghnuill* in Wicklow sought to address an historiographical imbalance by identifying aspects of Gaelic perception of contemporary political developments. Acknowledging the primarily professional quality of many of the poems in the O'Byrne collection, he argued, nonetheless, that a handful of works illustrated a crucial ideological refocusing among *fileadha*. Emphasising a shift from the limited local political concerns of classical bardic composition, he discerned evidence of an emergent political dynamic supporting the articulation of a national political consciousness and the creation of the image of the Gaelic lord as a national political figure.[34] This positive reading of bardic material was complemented by the conclusions drawn by Breandán Ó Buachalla in his work on the Gaelic literati and their incorporation of the Stuarts within the Gaelic ideological pantheon. Taking the celebratory bardic poems composed by Eochaidh Ó hEódhusa and Fearghal Óg Mac an Bhaird on James's accession to the English throne as emblematic of his overall thesis, Ó Buachalla, like Brendan Bradshaw, argued the case for an essentially resourceful bardic political paradigm at this period. Generally, Gaelic responses to the political and social conditions of James I's reign were as complex and diverse as the period itself, with the reaction of individual poets ranging from optimism to despair depending on the compositional circumstances.[35] He maintained that the manipulation of James's distant Gaelic ancestry was a significant example of reshaping by the literati of their political ideology to adapt to new challenges. James's reign is portrayed as a vital stage in the development and enunciation of an Irish national consciousness informed by a common Gaelic and gaelicised Anglo-Norman allegiance to counter-reformation Catholicism and a realisation of ethno-cultural mutuality encouraged by social oppositions consequent on New English aggrandisement. Ó Buachalla highlighted the importance of counter-reformation thinking and especially the influence of the theological polemicists operating from the Irish Franciscan College at Louvain in the articulation of a common idea of Irish nationality. He further developed the broader European background to Irish responses to conquest and colonisation by stressing how the frequent Gaelic and gaelicised Anglo-Norman invocation of the concept of divine providence to account for group misfortune was a common and widely-accepted feature of European theological and political debate at the time. The influence of the counter-reformation movement and the impact of providentialist notions of causation caution against viewing Gaelic intellectual and cultural activity in exceptional or singular terms and demonstrate its links with continental developments.[36]

Tom Dunne's analysis of Gaelic poetry composed in the period extending from the last decades of the sixteenth century to the death of Aodhagán Ó Rathaille in 1729 sought to rebut Brendan Bradshaw's reading of the O'Byrne bardic material and, in doing so, he may be said to have laid the basis for an interpretative stance in opposition to that of Bradshaw and subsequently Ó Buachalla. In contradistinction to Bradshaw, Dunne argued that the political focus of bardic poetry was rigidly local and as a result ill-equipped to register the impact of overarching military, constitutional and religious processes. He denied the emergence of a Gaelic national consciousness arguing that fundamental constitutive elements of politicised nationality developing contemporaneously in other European countries, factors such as common notions of nation, identity and sovereignty, were apparently absent or defective in the Gaelic case.[37] While admitting that Gaelic Ireland possessed important unifying features in terms of homogenised expressions of culture, religion and law, it allegedly lacked a communal political identity. On the basis of the evidence marshalled in favour of his argument, Dunne claimed there was no meaningful or relevant bardic response to conquest and colonisation. Incapable of transcending local professional allegiances, bardic poets, he said, remained wedded to an archaic ideology which was effectively 'tribal' in scope and indifferent to the articulation of an inclusive political identity.[38]

Nicholas Canny re-echoed Tom Dunne's conclusions in an examination of the themes of politics and religion in Gaelic literature in the period 1580 to 1750. He too took issue with Brendan Bradshaw's argument for an emergent national consciousness and stressed what he saw as the overwhelmingly localised focus of bardic composition. Emphasising the importance of professional learned families within the structure of Gaelic society, he claimed that their loyalties remained determinedly personal and dynastic. The most telling instance of what he saw as Gaelic political myopia was in his opinion the apparent indifference of the bardic class to the implications and challenges posed by the Protestant reformation. Politically also, Canny saw no readiness or ability among bardic poets to distinguish between internal Gaelic seigneurial feuds and the struggle between individual Gaelic lords and the English crown.[39] Unlike Dunne, however, he identified a process of fundamental ideological realignment on the part of the literati as a result of counter-reformation influence from the beginning of the seventeenth century onwards. Traditional and apparently outmoded bardic precepts were replaced by political and religious assumptions which, although often inconsistent, were of a recognisably modern and European character. Although Gaelic lords had been conscious of the propaganda and strategic value of associating with the counter-reformation movement at least as early as the Nine Years War (1594–1603), this link bore sustained cultural and political results in the aftermath of Elizabeth's death. Prolonged Gaelic exposure to counter-reformation Catholicism on mainland Europe, especially among Gaelic scholars and clerics who had followed in the wake of the exiled northern Gaelic lords, proved decisive. A sense of missionary endeavour revitalised literature in Irish while also expanding the range of literary genres customary to the language. Significantly, this new phase of counter-reformation Gaelic Catholicism was directed by priests, scholars and littérateurs of both Gaelic and Anglo-Norman stock. In seeking to articulate and advance their religious agenda, the agents of the Irish counter-reformation were also contributing to the growth of an inclusive political awareness among Ireland's seigneurial élite.[40] In effect, Canny saw no basis for assuming the existence of an internal dynamic within the bardic mindset ready to grapple with non-traditional political challenges. It was only when Gaelic culture came into contact with the modernising thrust of the counter-reformation that Gaelic political and religious consciousness could be said, he argued, to have joined the European mainstream and to have become recognisably modern and, by implication, realistic in its assessment of externally-generated developments.

Bernadette Cunningham echoed Nicholas Canny's argument that the Gaelic literati were unable to distinguish between conflict with a centralising English administration and the internecine feuding characteristic of warring Gaelic dynasts. She argued that bardic poetry of the sixteenth and early seventeenth centuries manifests no awareness of the presence of an intrusive power and, in fact, bardic ideology remains inwardly-focused and committed to a world view underpinned by a conventional social paradigm.[41] Indeed, the poets apparently remain preoccupied with their own interests and only react to events in so far as they impinge on their professional status and financial well-being. Thus, for example, she argued that bardic responses to the flight of the northern earls were mediated solely in personal terms and most certainly reveal no trace of a national political perspective among the poets.[42] The alleged provincialism of the bardic outlook reflected the decentralised political framework of Gaelic Ireland and since the provision of a unified response to non-traditional political situations, such as the establishment of New English authority, formed no part of conventional bardic functions, modern scholars would, she said, find no evidence of reaction to New English influences in Gaelic poetry composed prior to 1640.[43] Bernadette Cunningham, like Nicholas Canny, stressed the modernising impact of the counter-reformation and she suggested that continental influences were operative in the development of an Irish national identity in the seventeenth century.[44] In attributing the genesis of a recognisably modern Irish national identity to continental influences, she also excluded the possibility of an internally-sourced Gaelic intellectual momentum capable of contextualising and responding to early modern change.

Joep Leerssen's portrayal of late medieval and early modern Gaelic society as a basically static phenomenon, supposedly too closely attached to historical precedent to allow the evolution of meaningful social and cultural accommodation to change, set the interpretative keynote for his approach to bardic poetry and what evidence it yielded concerning concepts of ethnic identity. Advancing the decentralised political pattern of Gaelic Ireland as the appropriate context in which to discuss the work of bardic poets, Leerssen accordingly considered their *oeuvre* permeated by an archaic political consciousness of limited local relevance. He argued that bardic poetry was politically timeless and suggested that the poets' supposed inability to differentiate between historical and contemporary political considerations resulted in a self-conscious and stilted antiquarianism.[45] While acknowledging the pan-insular homogeneity of élite Gaelic culture, Leerssen nonetheless opted to highlight the apparently dominant factional and localised rationale of the bardic outlook. No 'national Gaelic stance', he felt, was evident in the poetry and the poets reacted to the consolidation of New English suzerainty in terms of professional self-interest and grievance. In fact, he was unable to discern traces of an intellectual shift of focus in Gaelic discourse until at least as late as the 1650s and even then he argued that it was not until the reign of James II that a tangible sense of national consciousness emerged among Irish Catholics.[46]

Like Joep Leerssen, Ann Dooley in a study of *Iomarbhágh na bhfileadh* ('The contention of the bards' *c.* 1616–7), a bardic debate centring on the respective merits of the two historic geographical divisions of Ireland, also acknowledged the binary composition of bardic ideology, at once national and local in focus. Yet she interpreted the role of the debate's instigator, Tadhg Mac Bruaideadha, in essentially negative terms, seeing in his action an affirmation of the apparent inadequacy of the conventional bardic world view in the context of early seventeenth-century colonial Ireland. She cited Mac Bruaideadha's adherence to the interests of the anglophile fourth earl of Thomond (ob. 1624) as evidence of a generalised rupture in the bardic tradition and symptomatic of the irrelevance of the transcendental and universal emphasis of élite Gaelic culture.[47]

Michelle O Riordan's monograph study of bardic *mentalités* in the late sixteenth and early seventeenth centuries is undoubtedly the most comprehensively-argued depiction of a bardic mindset allegedly characterised by its inflexible obsession with form and custom and unwilling to engage critically with innovation or deviation from normative precepts. O Riordan argued that a static bardic ideological continuum extended from the thirteenth to the seventeenth centuries. Drawing largely from material preserved in poem-books, she advocated a continuity of meaning in theme and motif over a period of some four hundred years, irrespective of social and political variables. She identified an apparently inherent bardic ability to adapt within the parameters of their repertoire to prevailing political and contractual constraints, principally by means of acquiescence in what she termed the *fait accompli*.[48] Conventional bardic themes such as the female personification of Ireland's sovereignty, the formulaic idealisation of the traits of an actual or aspiring lord, and the facility with which Anglo-Norman patrons were incorporated within the ambit of bardic practice, maintained a fixed significance in both a pre- and post-Tudor conquest context. While highlighting continuity in the primary focus of activity, the provision of ideological sanction for the Gaelic and gaelicised élite, she discerned no evidence of a coherent response to contemporary social and political circumstances. O Riordan concluded that the bardic caste was incapable of transcending its own supposedly self-defining and self-limiting discursive boundaries.[49] She also examined the work of the non-professional successors to the *fileadha*, littérateurs such as Céitinn, Feiritéar, Haicéad, Carthún, Ó Duincín and the work of the poets collected together in Cecile O'Rahilly's *Five seventeenth-century political poems*. On the basis of the evident thematic continuity between *fileadha* and their literary heirs, she argued that the new generation was also motivated by the same timeless conceptual rationale supposedly emblematic of bardic discourse. Michelle O Riordan emphatically denied the poets any role in the articulation of an Irish national consciousness, particularly given what she interpreted as the immutable antiquity of bardic themes and concerns, which were all apparently quite unsusceptible to contemporaneous reordering of nuance or figurative range.[50]

The weight of current historiographical opinion is evidently firmly committed to viewing early modern bardic *mentalités* as effectively antiquarian or outmoded in contemporary political terms. Intellectually programmed in a hermetic medieval mode and fixated on individual privilege and personal loyalties, the poets were allegedly unable or unwilling to adduce coherent interpretative strategies applicable to evolving social and political circumstances. This notion of monolithic bardic rigidity is challenged in the present work. Instead, it is proposed that bardic activity during this critical phase can more accurately be portrayed as binary in focus, incorporating strands of innovation within a largely traditional professional paradigm. Following in the wake of Brendan Bradshaw's and Breandán Ó Buachalla's pioneering identification of a dynamic element in the bardic mindset, it is argued that the poetry is characterised by both ideological reaction and continuity. Indeed, bardic thematic continuity should not be automatically equated with political conservatism given that bardic conceits and motifs must surely have conveyed variable meanings to different people at different times.[51] Although it may never be possible to recreate the contemporary polysemic grammar of bardic practice, it is evident from the extant material that bardic *mentalités* were considerably more fluid than current historical and literary scholarship generally admits. It is demonstrated in this study that the final phase of classical bardic composition witnessed a radical re-evaluation of long-established concepts of ethnic and cultural identity in direct response to the establishment and consolidation of Anglo-Saxon authority.

Mindful of certain important interpretative constraints imposed by contractual obligations and the manuscript context in which poems have been recorded, the analysis of a representative selection of poetic material undertaken here is unambiguous in its illustration of the cogent formulation of responses to contemporary challenges. While continuing where possible to fulfil largely formulaic contractual duties, *fileadha* developed a pattern of communal projection and explication. Far from demonstrating a passive and self-interested acquiescence in the *status quo*, bardic poets articulated a providentialist causation of group misfortune which was in turn complemented by the invocation of the idea of repentance resulting in communal liberation. They also initiated the re-evaluation of Gaelic modes of self-representation and self-perception which for centuries had been determined by the canonical schema outlined in the *Lebor Gabála*. The formal ideological incorporation of the gaelicised Anglo-Normans within a common framework of cultural, religious and ethnic expression marked the emergence of an innovative and inclusive concept of Irish identity (*Éireannaigh*). The potential for political dissent consequent on this fundamental shift in communal self-definition in the context of the intrusion of crown authority need hardly be overstressed. The new sense of politicised nationality may be said to have been tripartite in composition given its constituent elements of common allegiance to Tridentine Catholicism, loyalty to Gaelic cultural mores and consciousness of insular territorial integrity. The latter factor was the logical outcome of the early modern bardic revitalisation of the conventional motif of Ireland's territorial sovereignty in personified form. Furthermore, an overriding awareness of Gaelic cultural integrity resulted in a missionary zeal to inculturate newcomers within a Gaelic representational framework. The more or less continuous hostility of the crown administration to bardic poets testifies to the real threat posed to English colonial aspirations by an intellectual élite manipulating a thematic canon intelligible within a pan-insular context. The bardic projection of an inclusive Irish identity was of enduring significance in the long-term history of Anglo-Irish relations. This study seeks to restore to the *fileadha* their rightful place in the story of the development of Irish national consciousness and to redress the historiographical imbalance which has erroneously characterised their world view as obscurantist and arcane. Bardic poetry is a rich and fascinating historical source and the light it sheds on the responses of the vanquished to conquest and colonisation is well worth the labour of sustained examination.

CONTINUITY AND REACTION IN
TWO POEM-BOOKS

In this chapter a selection of material from the poem-books of Cú Chonnacht Maguire (ob. 1589) and Cormac O'Hara (ob. 1612) is examined to provide an insight into social and cultural factors determining the nature of a lord's poem-book. This evidence reflects the milieu in which these collections took shape and illustrates how bardic poets were centrally engaged in the articulation of an ideology of Gaelic lordship. The evidence they provide for cultural and political history must be interpreted in relation to the constraints of their particular format and circumstances of composition and preservation.[1] The material in poem-books was, by and large, the product of a conventional outlook and the relationship between poet and patron was mediated at two levels. When a bardic poet contracted to compose praise poetry for his patron, he was providing a political and cultural service in return for payment or reward in kind. The second mode of interaction was both cultural and ideological in scope. The *fileadh* invoked and reworked as the occasion demanded the richly-allusive symbolism of tradition to provide a backdrop of communal legitimation for his patron. Any attempt to draw on the evidence of the poem-books to explore Gaelic responses to the Tudor reconquest and ensuing Stuart colonial consolidation must bear this primary function in mind. These poems served to underpin a venerable and common ideology in a tradition-centred polity. Scholars who fault the absence of a choreographed analysis of crown expansionism in the *duanaireadha* poems misunderstand their functional agenda.[2]

In the main, the conceptual response of *fileadha* to conquest and colonisation is not found in professional work represented in family poem-books. Rather, scholars must look to individually preserved and in compositional terms *ad hoc* pieces, produced on an informal basis and not subject to the requirements of contractual constraints. Yet, the overtly functional nature of the poem-books does not invalidate their significance as historical source-material. Although the *duanaireadha* provide no evidence of extensive Gaelic intellectual reappraisal in the face of unprecedented political upheaval, they, nonetheless, highlight a cultural continuity which is as important a reflection of Gaelic *mentalités* as the evidence of changing perceptions found in poems extant in composite manuscripts. It is argued in this chapter that poets exploited the flexibility of the conventional bardic format to present a response to crown aggrandisement within the ideological parameters of professional discourse.

This introduction to the Maguire and O'Hara poems begins with an outline of the careers of both men and a review of each lord's poem-book. Maguire is effectively identifiable with Elizabethan Ireland, while in contrast, the lordship of O'Hara straddled the reigns of both Elizabeth I and James I. The tone of Cú Chonnacht Maguire's lordship in Fermanagh was set by the circumstances of his accession. In September 1566 Maguire's brother Seaán died while attempting to regain his territory from Shane O'Neill (ob. 1567), head of one of the two leading northern Gaelic families.[3] Cú Chonnacht's attempts to take possession of his inheritance were facilitated by the murder of Shane O'Neill at the hands of the MacDonnells in the year following the death of his brother.[4] While the demise of Shane cleared the way for Cú Chonnacht to assert control over Fermanagh, his reign as lord of the Maguires was to be overshadowed by O'Neill attempts to claim hegemony over his territory. The new head of the O'Neills, Turlough Luineach, was to demand or seek tribute from Maguire on several occasions.[5] Cú Chonnacht's policy of exploiting Turlough Luineach and the English administration as much as possible for his own ends forms a major theme in the history of his lordship.[6] Caught between the superior power of O'Neill in Tyrone and that of the English in the Pale, Maguire seems to have made use of either side, as circumstances dictated, in his bid to maintain a measure of autonomy in Fermanagh.

In April 1585 Cú Chonnacht was present in Dublin for the opening of Sir John Perrot's Parliament.[7] In June of the same year he made a very significant gesture of submission to the crown. In a manner somewhat reminiscent of the composition of Connacht enacted during that summer, Maguire surrendered his land to the crown with the intention of having it regranted to him. This move guaranteed him the security of having validated his position vis-à-vis the Dublin administration.[8] The following year he journeyed to Dublin to receive a royal pardon and the regrant of Fermanagh from lord deputy Perrot.[9] However, Maguire never quite managed to elude the influence of O'Neill. In 1587 the English administration confirmed Turlough Luineach as superior lord over Maguire and Fermanagh. Henceforth, Maguire was to be considered as an uirrí (vassal lord) of O'Neill.[10] It can only have been minor compensation when the Dublin authorities awarded Maguire, in the same year, a commission to exercise martial law in Fermanagh.[11] Cú Chonnacht died in 1589.[12]

Cormac O'Hara was a figure of less important political significance than Maguire. The O'Hara territory of Leyney in south-west Sligo was one of six sub-lordships presided over by O'Connor Sligo.[13] Divided into two branches, the senior O'Hara Buidhe took the leading role in the family's affairs.[14] The date and circumstances of Cormac's accession to the lordship are obscure. It is clear from what Tadhg Dall Ó hUiginn says that Cormac's father Cian and his brother, Tadhg, had both been lords of Leyney. However, there had been an interlude when Conn, son of Ruaidhrí, had held the lordship.[15] Conn seems to have been a powerful figure within Leyney until his death in 1581.[16] The situation is further complicated by the fact that it is known that Cormac

O'Hara was appointed seneschal of Leyney in 1578, while his brother Brian was confirmed as *tánaiste* or heir-apparent.[17] This information, when considered in the context of numerous allusions in the poems in the O'Hara compilation, suggests that Cormac experienced protracted difficulty in taking control of the lordship.[18] What may be understood from the confusing picture which the evidence presents is that Cormac was probably a youth at the time of his brother's death in 1560 and that his claim on the lordship was usurped by Conn O'Hara. In the meantime, Cormac struggled to assert his control of Leyney, winning English recognition in 1578 but not obtaining complete mastery until Conn was killed in 1581.

An important event in Cormac's career, so far as the records show, seems to have been his acceptance of the provincial fiscal agreement known as the composition of Connacht.[19] Perhaps in recognition of his acquiescence, Cormac, along with several of his kinsmen, was pardoned by the crown in June 1586.[20] It is significant that Cormac appears to have abandoned his policy of loyalty to the English administration when he took part in the Connacht rebellion of 1595–6.[21] Cormac's decision to throw in his lot with the insurgents may have been influenced by the draconian rule of Sir Richard Bingham as president of Connacht. Bingham had ordered the execution of Cormac's brother Brian in 1586.[22] Another more immediate factor in O'Hara's decision must have been the fraudulent activities of Richard Boyle in Leyney. Boyle, the deputy-escheator in Ireland since 1590, was empowered to seek out and establish the queen's title to concealed lands. He used his position to defraud landowners by falsely alleging concealment and obtaining verdicts for the crown from corrupt juries. He in turn outmanoeuvred grantees of concealed land by compelling them to sell him their shares in grants of concealment. In addition, he defrauded the crown by undervaluing land found to be concealed and by allowing it to pass into his ownership. Boyle helped himself to lands in Leyney through such means in 1594.[23]

The surrender of the Spanish expeditionary force at Kinsale in 1602 and O'Neill's submission to Lord Mountjoy in March of 1603 must have encouraged Cormac to seek terms from the English authorities. In any event, he, along with several other O'Haras, received a pardon from King James I in April 1603.[24] Surely mindful of Richard Boyle's land fraud in 1594, Cormac made careful legal preparations for the continued possession of family lands by his sons Tadhg and Cormac Óg after his death.[25] Cormac died in 1612, having completed the legal arrangements for his sons' inheritance in the previous year.[26] Cormac was succeeded by his son Tadhg. The latter, who died in 1616, followed his father's example in making detailed legal provision for continued O'Hara ownership of the lands in Leyney.[27] It is also likely that Tadhg arranged for his sons to be brought up in the Anglican faith.[28] It was due to the foresight of Cormac and Tadhg that the O'Haras were among the few élite Gaelic families to emerge relatively intact from the prolonged process of Tudor reconquest and Stuart colonisation.

Having located Maguire and O'Hara within their historical contexts, some general remarks about their respective poem-books are necessary.[29] The Maguire poem-book contains twenty-four pieces dedicated to Cú Chonnacht. Given that all the poets represented addressed the ruling Maguire, the poems may be safely dated to within the chronological framework of Cú Chonnacht's lordship (1566–89).[30] These compositions, with two exceptions, are eulogies extolling Maguire's supposed virtues.[31] A scribal note on folio 2a by a Cú Mhumhan Ó Cléirigh has been interpreted by David Greene, who edited the poems addressed to Cú Chonnacht, as evidence for ascribing responsibility to Ó Cléirigh for compilation of the material pertaining to Maguire.[32]

The O'Hara poem-book has been in the possession of the O'Hara family since work on its compilation was begun in 1597.[33] While the bulk of the work is the product of one scribe, Tuathal Ó hUiginn, several other hands also appear. Ó hUiginn identified himself in a postscript to the anonymous poem 'Gabh mo chosaoid, a Chormuic'.[34] A contemporary reference on page five of the manuscript states that the compilation was begun in the same year as a military encounter between the English and O'Donnell at Assaroe. Fortunately, these events in Donegal are mentioned by Sir Conyers Clifford in a letter to the lord deputy. This allows scholars to date the greater part of the poem-book to 1597.[35] Twenty-three of the thirty-eight poems in the *duanaire* are addressed to Cormac O'Hara.[36]

This chapter's central objective is to examine a range of poems from the Maguire and O'Hara poem-books. Firstly, a selection of poems is discussed as evidence of ideological continuity. In this review, the focus is on two areas in particular, the ideology of lordship and images of bardic self-perception. Secondly, a range of poems is assessed for evidence which illuminates shades of change and reassessment in bardic political awareness. This analysis is conducted with three considerations in mind, each of which is informed by a guiding theme of bardic divergence from convention. In essence, change is highlighted within the poetry in this approach as it reflects evolving ideas of lordship, ethnic sensibility and Gaelic cultural consciousness.

The bardic poet provided his patron with social and political validation by means of a variety of poetic conventions. Central to this process of endorsement was the concept of the ruler who possessed the desired qualities of an aspiring or actual lord. A Gaelic lord could be expected to embody certain traits and virtues and in order to accommodate a subject within the formulaic mould of lordship, the poet emphasised a nobleman's supposed possession of conventional physical and mental attributes. For instance, the ideologically-sanctioned lord was brave, handsome and a generous patron of the poets. The reign of any such validated lord resulted in great fertility of nature. A recurrent theme in the Maguire and O'Hara poems is that of the generosity of Cú Chonnacht and Cormac to the poets. The *fileadha* emphasised that patrons received from them an essential attribute in exchange for patronage: fame. The complementary concepts of generosity and fame are discussed here as sample aspects of the formulaic bardic perception of lordship.

The piece beginning 'Fiodhbhaidh a chéile clú deise' is a standard example of the eulogist at work. Its author Tadhg Dall Ó hUiginn (ob. 1591) praises the aristocratic demeanour of Cormac O'Hara and his brother Brian (ob. 1586).[37] The usual formulaic descriptions are adduced, both men are fierce warriors, generous and admired by women. Importantly, it is Cormac as head of the family rather than Brian who imposes tribute. Moreover, the poet unambiguously identifies the source of nature's fecundity: Cormac's lordship. Ó hUiginn dwelled particularly on what are presented as the most admirable elements in both men's characters: liberality to the poets and martial valour. The theme of O'Hara generosity is introduced in the first quatrain. Their unstinting nature is noted and by implication he suggests they deserve respect accordingly ('dáil a gcruidh ní choigill siad . . . tamhoin do thoill umhla iad').[38] In stanza six he mentions the generosity of the O'Haras in general to the poets. Once the poets finished with Cormac they went directly to Brian's household. Having fulfilled his obligations to Brian, the poet now concentrates the discussion on Cormac's presumed largesse. This strategy is motivated by the necessity not to have Cormac overshadowed by his brother and the poem's validatory aim obscured. The overall consequence of Cormac's patronage is the acquisition of fame and because of this, he is the object of intense bardic attention:[39]

> Tú, a Chormuic, dod chor a n-iongnadh
> ó aoss tiomchoil na dtrí rann;
> ní chleacht sí do dhol a ndiamhair,
> ní bhí an sgol dot iarroidh and.

> Thou Cormac, art celebrated by those who travel
> the three continents; the schools are not accustomed to thy
> going into obscurity, they do not seek
> thee there.

The author does not elaborate on why he assumed that O'Hara deserved such a degree of fame, rather acceptance of self-evident communal values is presumed. The legitimate lord follows etiquette in any event, Tadhg Dall implied, making it unnecessary to offer explanations of why certain courses of action are either desirable or required.

Such stereotypical perception of the Gaelic grandee is also very marked in Maguire's poem-book. In 'Manchaigh riamh 'na Róimh oinigh', a poem of anonymous composition, the author portrayed Cú Chonnacht as a champion of generosity.[40] Not surprisingly, the poet congratulated Maguire on his particular liberality to the *fileadha*.[41] The poem follows the standard course of praising Maguire's heroic traits and alludes to his supposedly prominent standing within the province of Ulster. The author is specific in his identification of fame as the end product of a lord's generosity. The latter quality ensured that a lord's name lived on after he died and when his material wealth would have long since disappeared ('buan an clú, caiter an crodh').[42] While the tone of this poem is quite conventional, there are some curious references in quatrains eight and nine. At this point, the poet declares that generosity (*eineach*) had been taken away from the Gaelic literati and subjected to foreign aggression:[43]

> A-tá an t-eineach a nglas Ghall
> ó éigsibh Éirionn tamall.

> Generosity has been taken for a time from the poets of Ireland
> into the fetters of foreigners.

Appropriately enough, Cú Chonnacht's intervention ameliorated the situation. Maguire, maintains the author, has removed the prison fetters from the poets ('do réidhigh a nglas ngoghaing').[44] By his actions, Cú Chonnacht had re-established the integrity of generosity. These allusions may refer to the intermittent repressive measures taken by the crown authorities against the *fileadha* during the Tudor period.[45] A more detailed investigation of bardic attitudes to English expansion is undertaken later in the chapter.

Giolla Riabhach Ó Cléirigh also celebrated seigneurial largesse and patronage in two poems he composed for Maguire.[46] 'Craobh eoluis teisd tigherna' and 'Díon Fódla a bhfeis rídhamhna' were conceived in the standard bardic mode of validatory eulogy.[47] In 'Díon Fódla a bhfeis rídhamhna', Ó Cléirigh depicted Maguire as the spouse of Ireland, a partner in possession of various apposite traits such as bravery, generosity, kindness and good name.[48] His 'Craobh eoluis teisd tigherna' notes that a name for generosity would ensure popularity for a lord among poets, while the immediate effect of such popularity results in Maguire being subject to numerous bardic visitations:[49]

> Craobh eoluis teisd tigherna
> teisd dana cóir comhumhla.

> The fame of a lord, to which all should defer,
> is a signpost.

The poet introduces several references to Maguire's patronage and to how the *fileadha* profited as a result. A vivid picture is painted of poets seeking out Cú Chonnacht's company, exchanging their original sponsors for his patronage and in the process placing great pressure on his material resources. Of course, Maguire is represented as responding as the legitimate lord always did in such circumstances, making light of the burden the *fileadha* had placed on him:[50]

> Sgol cháich ort ní hionaithbhir
> gé atá a dtol do roidheithbhir;
> do chliar féin ní fuirighther
> le riar do chléir choimhighthigh.

> You are to be blamed if other people's poets
> wish to hurry away; your own poets' satisfaction
> is not delayed by granting the desires of your
> visiting poets.

It is evident from this material that the bardic perception of lordship in relation to patronage is a constant in the Maguire and O'Hara poems. These compositions are informed and motivated by one overarching common objective: legitimation of seigneurial aspirations. Although composed against a background of critical political and cultural change, the poems continued to embody the medieval Gaelic concept of sanctioned lordship. This brief examination of bardic mediation of the theme of patronage illustrates how in this instance bardic poets worked to guidelines designed for a quasi-feudal society.

Another useful approach to the task of defining bardic cultural continuity in the early modern period is to look at the poets' self-image in the overall context of Gaelic society. The *fileadha* had occupied an important place in the social hierarchy since the thirteenth century and clearly many of the considerations which historically shaped their self-perception remained relevant in the sixteenth-century bardic sense of cultural and vocational integrity. Recent research has drawn attention to the evolving nature of the Gaelic polity, traditionally regarded as a static monolith.[51] The extent to which poets adapted their self-image to accommodate a changing socio-political environment is an essential consideration in the study of bardic responses to early modern upheaval. Bearing in mind the influences which determined the timbre of the *dánta* or poems ultimately destined for a family poem-book, it is very likely that such material accurately mirrors bardic self-perception in the last three decades of the sixteenth century. The Maguire and O'Hara collections present an interesting choice of poems illustrative of bardic self-awareness. Among the poems composed for Cú Chonnacht Maguire there is an example of a relatively uncommon bardic genre, an apology and reconciliation poem. In 'Uaibhreach mise ar Mhág Uidhir', Fearghal Óg Mac an Bhaird apologises to Maguire for having thrown a goblet of wine at his face in a fit of pique.[52] Mac an Bhaird expresses his regret at this unfortunate outburst of pride ('guais an t-uabhar d'athuighidh'), compounded by the fact that the hapless Cú Chonnacht had been a most hospitable host:[53]

> Nír thuill sé féin a fagháil,
> a bhfuair uaimsi d'esanáir;
> íoc do sa díoth nach derna,
> ag so críoch na cinnemhna.

> He did not deserve the dishonour which
> he got from me; he paid for the crime
> which he had not committed – such is the
> ordinance of fate.

In fact, the warm reception which he received was all the more remarkable given that he was a visiting poet (*file cuarta*). Indeed, Mac an Bhaird regrets that he was not *ollamh* (chief poet) to Maguire ('nír mé, far-íor, a ollamh').[54] Evidently, he was sufficiently confident of his status to approach Maguire with a proposal for reconciliation. The poet's expectation of success was such that he managed to poke some gentle fun at his earlier behaviour. Fearghal Óg declares that he wished to pour another draught on Maguire; however, on this occasion, it is a libation of praise rather than wine ('Anois ar a chruth chorcra dáilfiod mo dheoch aghmolta').[55] So it is with full confidence that Fearghal Óg says he will make restitution through the medium of eulogy ('mur luagh sa digh do doirtedh').[56] The sweet sound of praise will dispel any lingering resentment on Maguire's part ('budh réidh mar sin a ghruadh geal').[57] This poem is remarkable as much for its implicit assumptions as for its crafted lyricism. Mac an Bhaird pinpoints the source of bardic authority: even the mere promise of praise poetry is sufficiently enticing to regain the favour of Maguire. The poet enjoyed his status because of the influence which conventional bardic eulogy wielded in a given ideological context.

A poem by Maguire's *ollamh*, Eochaidh Ó hEódhusa (ob. 1612), is a classic exposition of the bardic communal role and of the poet's relationship with his patron.[58] Composing in the mid-1580s, he presents a very traditional image of his function. The central theme focuses on Eochaidh's determination to become a fully-fledged bardic poet before he formally undertakes his duties as *ollamh* to Maguire. Ó hEódhusa is adamant that only a poet with a comprehensive training is qualified to carry out the primary requirement of his profession. Once he has undergone the necessary bardic formation, he can begin to eulogise his patron with confidence. The concept of praise is a critical consideration in the poem:[59]

> Anois gur dherbhus mo dhán
> fada meisi, a mheic Shiobhán,
> a rélta chorcra chnuic Bhregh,
> gan molta dhuit do dhéinemh.

> Bright star of the hill of Bregia,
> son of Siobhán,
> I have been a long time without making praises to
> you, until I perfected my art.

Standard conventions and metaphors are invoked throughout the piece. Cú Chonnacht, for instance, is portrayed as a possible spouse for Ireland and as an unstinting supporter of the literati. Of course, all such attributes were inherent to the generalised bardic formulation of praise. The main interest of the piece rests in the author's conceptualisation of 'praise' (*moladh*) as the essence of the bardic vocation and, in this respect, the poem is a concise encapsulation of a corporate *raison d'être*.

The premise of eulogy's primacy is echoed in a poem composed by Ó hEódhusa's rival for the post of *ollamh* to Maguire. 'Gabh m'égnach, a Chú Chonnacht' was presented by Conchubhar Crón Ó Dálaigh in an opening bid to become Maguire's chief poet. He had been poet to the Desmond Fitzgeralds in his native west Munster. Following the deaths of his three most important patrons, James Fitzmaurice (ob. 1579), John of Desmond (ob. 1582) and his brother Gerald, earl of Desmond (ob. 1583), Ó Dálaigh had apparently migrated northwards in search of a new patron.[60] From what has been said above about Ó hEódhusa, it is clear that Ó Dálaigh was unsuccessful in his candidacy for the Maguire post. Although the factors which inspired its composition were primarily political, the poem itself is apolitical and conventional in outlook. Ó Dálaigh's late patrons had been major players in the Munster rebellion of 1579–83. One of them, James Fitzmaurice, had been influenced in his actions by a counter-reformation agenda, while Gerald of Desmond may have been driven to revolt by an outdated desire to retain the feudal authority of his ancestors in the south-west. Clearly, Fitzmaurice's motivation was politically complex and influenced by the broader European political climate.[61] 'Gabh m'égnach, a Chú Chonnacht' evidences no trace of the poet's involvement with the ideologically-conscious Fitzmaurice or of his documented support for Gerald of Desmond. The author recounts that he had endured great misfortune following the elimination of his three noble patrons, yet no attempt is made to situate these deaths or their implications in a larger political context. Ó Dálaigh's approach suggests little or no awareness of an externally-powered challenge to the Gaelic polity. It is not obvious if the poet grasped the implications for Gaelic society of the expansion and consolidation of crown suzerainty. Interpreting the evidence which 'Gabh m'égnach, a Chú Chonnacht' presents, it might seem not. It also reveals a poet hidebound by the corporate constraints of the bardic institution. Although Ó Dálaigh touched on the causes of his unemployment, the constraint of professional need ensured his concentration on the primary purpose of acquiring a new patron. In other words, 'Gabh m'égnach, a Chú Chonnacht' is basically a composition in which a vocational proposition is developed according to conventional bardic criteria and as such is hardly a bardic exercise in which reflective political analysis can be reasonably anticipated.

The fact that Conchubhar now seeks a new master following the demise of his three patrons is a key idea in the poem ('ac súr chéile do charfuinn').[62] Ó Dálaigh, invoking the conventional bardic terminology of patronage, describes himself as the spouse/partner of his former patrons ('mo thrí chéile chumuindse').[63] The metaphor of lover is employed to describe his desired relationship with Maguire ('gabhuim libhsi mur lendán').[64] He seeks the privileges (anáir) which were an ollamh's entitlement and he pleads with Maguire not to deal with him as a poet simply doing his customary rounds but rather to accord him a position in his household ('gabh lind mar bhar bhfilidh féin').[65] This vocational approach is underscored by his boast that he would provide him with the best of poetry in return for patronage ('sgoth ar n-éigsi red ghruaidh ghil').[66] In effect, the poem is an emphatic reiteration of the classical bardic grammar of corporate projection. It reveals an outlook apparently unconcerned with adapting to evolving social and political conditions.

A similar sense of bardic self-perception is evident in three poems composed by Írial Ó hUiginn and extant in the O'Hara poem-book.[67] After a long career as a peripatetic poet in both Scotland and Ireland, Írial had secured the post of ollamh to Cormac. 'Ceanglam re chéile, a Chormuic' appears to be the earliest surviving piece Ó hUiginn composed for Cormac. In this poem, he calls on Cormac to join him in an enduring pact of friendship ('ceanglam cunnradh neamhmheallta').[68] In a manner reminiscent of Conchubhar Crón Ó Dálaigh, he deployed the emotive and occasionally sentimental terminology of the poet/patron nexus to stress the depth of the intimate professional relationship which he hoped to experience with O'Hara. For instance, the poet assures Cormac of his professional devotion ('leat tol mo chroidhe, a Chormoic') and it is stated that their amity should be mutually affectionate ('bíodh ar searc rer-oile and').[69] Írial makes the customary promise to devote his finest poetry to Cormac in return for the latter's grace and favour ('budh leat díoghrais mo dhána').[70] Unfortunately, the stability and permanence which Ó hUiginn sought in 'Ceanglam re chéile, a Chormuic' was to prove elusive. In 'Ag so chugad, a Chormuic', he speaks of reconciliation with O'Hara following an apparent disagreement. In fact, the poem was not Írial's first attempt to regain his patron's favour ('roimhe ad cheann do-chuaidh meise').[71] In an appeal to historical precedent, Írial compared his predicament to that of several famous fileadha who had also become estranged from their patrons. Significantly, all of them were eventually reconciled with their erstwhile benefactors. All such ancient poetic rapprochements were to serve as an example for Cormac.

No reconciliation followed, for by the time Cormac had married Caitilín O'Reilly, Írial seems to have been in a state of penury.[72] In the poem 'Cionnaim a-nois cia ar gcara', he is reduced to supplicating O'Hara for the gift of a horse. Ó hUiginn adduces a standard proposition with the declaration that if Cormac were to make him this present, its value would prove trifling in comparison to the fame accruing to O'Hara as a result:[73]

> Girre ná sin saoghul h'eich
> buaini an laoidh 's ní mar leithbhreith;
> cóir iarruidh séad ar a son
> dá chéad bliaghoin do-bhéradh.

> Shorter shall thy horse's life be than that of any poem to thee
> which will live longer, and this is no biassed judgment;
> it is right for me to ask for wealth in return for a gift
> that will bring thee two hundred years of life.

Írial intended composing a eulogy for O'Hara which would fulfil his stated aim. It is interesting that in this context he made a vague but sufficiently menacing allusion to Cormac's evasion of satire if he were to make such a gift to the poet ('do bhreith ghealghruadh gan ghoradh').[74] The dominant theme throughout the poem is the desirability of bardic eulogy which ensures a vibrant reputation for a patron long after death ('dán na suadh ní sochaimhthe').[75] It is not clear how credible this argument would have been in the 1580s. Presumably, the traditionalist world-view embodied in these poems still enjoyed a widespread, if perhaps diminishing, currency in later sixteenth-century Gaelic society.

The preceding review of thematic continuity in bardic expressions of lordship and self-image underlines the functional focus of these poem-books which were compiled during a period of accelerated cultural and political development. Michelle O Riordan has argued that the obvious conventionalism of much of the corpus should be interpreted as evidence of the allegedly apolitical and evasive quality of Gaelic assessment of conquest and colonisation.[76] This reading, however, rests on assumptions too readily taken for granted. Adherence to tradition may in itself have been a strategic response to chaotic socio-political factors. In fact, an emphasis on cultural integrity may have been, in part at least, predicated as a valorisation of communal mores. Other readings of the ingrained traditionalism evident in these poems are also possible. In 1585 both Maguire and O'Hara made formal submission of their lands to the crown in return for their regrant and royal pardons. The formal recognition by Gaelic leaders of an external power's supreme authority must have implicitly undermined both the validity and orthodoxy of the indigenous concept of lordship. As already demonstrated, a lord's rule was metaphorically sanctioned by the notion of his marriage to the female sovereignty figure of the territory in question. By reason of their formal acquiescence in the dominion of the Tudor monarchy and by admission of its legal right to make official grant to them of land held by their families for centuries, the status of lords like O'Hara and Maguire must surely have been attenuated if not compromised within the prescriptive context of normative convention. Accordingly, it is possible to argue that men such as O'Hara and Maguire viewed praise poetry as a form of social and political redress. In fact, patronage of the *fileadha* must have been partly motivated by a need to cloak the increasingly non-traditional basis of the lords' authority within the protective folds of bardic validation. Once more, it should be remembered that the poem-books are by their very essence instruments of contemporary local propaganda.

While this chapter's central thesis proposes that the poem-books are models of cultural continuity, it is also argued that a number of poems in both the Maguire and O'Hara collections manifest elements of political mediation of crown expansion. Aspects of bardic response to extraneous cultural and political factors are discussed within the framework of three general rubrics. Thus far the emphasis has been on continuity in the ideology of lordship and the bardic institution's corporate image within Gaelic society. The remainder of the chapter concentrates on determining shifting perceptions of lordship and sifts the evidence for internal reordering of cultural priorities. The third strand in the analysis concerns consciousness of the English presence in Ireland.

Fearghal Óg Mac an Bhaird composed two poems for Cú Chonnacht which are noteworthy for their singular ambiguity of inference. At first glance the pieces, 'Leath re Fódla fuil Uidhir' and 'Brath lendáin ac Leic Lughaidh', seem to be conventional eulogies of the lord of Fermanagh and the Maguires.[77] Outwardly, Mac an Bhaird follows the standard bardic course of proclaiming his subject a fitting spouse for the sovereignty figure Éire. In both poems, the apparent eligibility of Maguire for marital union is emphasised by an elaborate but formulaic account of his seigneurial credentials. Accordingly, Cú Chonnacht is depicted as possessing all the necessary virtues to sustain and to validate his aspiration to be seen as the embodiment of sovereignty. Importantly, he is presented as a fierce warrior and an implacable reiver. On the other hand, he is also a man characterised by kindness and by an incontrovertible sense of justice. Mac an Bhaird's flattering portrayal of the Maguires is a distinctive feature of both poems. He highlights their renown, liberality and warlike mien. Yet a close reading of the two poems, in particular, 'Leath re Fódla fuil Uidhir' reveals some apparently deliberate equivocation on the part of the author in his presentation of the traditional concept of lordship. The ambiguity arises in Mac an Bhaird's treatment of the sovereignty motif and in his emphasis on what might be termed an Ulster dimension. One suggestion to account for the equivocal nature of Mac an Bhaird's deployment of the sovereignty conceit may be that he sought to impart a more realistic and relevant political significance to the convention. His resolute emphasis on an Ulster dimension may likewise be a reflection of the dominant political influence of Gaelic factions in the north of Ireland.

Mac an Bhaird presents the Maguires as the foremost choice of Ireland in the opening stanza of 'Leath re Fódla fuil Uidhir'. Immediately, the reader is conscious of the abstract quality of the poet's formulation. It is noted that the Maguires ('crú Uidhir') had always been the choice (rogha) of Ireland. The suggestion that the Maguires might constitute a pan-insular force is approached more vaguely in the next stanza. Here the poet simply observes that every king of Ulster ('gach rí tarla ar Fhiadh Emhna') had won the support of Ireland (Banbha). The nature of Mac an Bhaird's argument in stanza three is at once convoluted and intriguing. It opens with the remark that Maguire met no opposition in Ireland and that Ulster was the equivalent of

Ireland in any event ('is leth re hÉirind Ulaigh'). In the final *leathrann*, Mac an Bhaird implied that the situation described in his opening lines would prevail unless Maguire considered it more important that Ireland should assume her appropriate guise ('a ccló chubhaidh').[78] It is not immediately obvious what the poet meant when he spoke of Ireland's 'cló cubhaidh'. The first two lines in this quatrain may be a formal acknowledgment of convention which subsequently allows the poet to venture a subtle and somewhat opaque political reference in the last two lines. Ostensibly, the poem was predicated as an affirmation of Maguire's right to Ireland. Yet by his almost immediate allusion to the possibility of Ireland enjoying another more 'appropriate' state, the author undermined the cogency of the sovereignty motif.

Mac an Bhaird further refined the notion of a royal union between *Éire* and Maguire while also extending the potential for ambiguity. He appears to contradict himself in quatrain twelve when he declares that Maguire has put *Éire* under tribute ('fá chomhaidh') and that he is a suitable spouse for the country ('céile cubhaidh'). Mac an Bhaird underscored the image of Maguire's control of Ireland with the implication in quatrain sixteen that he had effected his conquest by force of arms. Yet, in quatrain twenty-one the poet presents Maguire's supposed preeminent status as willingly embraced by Ireland ('toghthoir tú le Clár Criomhthuin'). The same idea is repeated in the next stanza where the poet notes that the chosen kings ('ríoghraidh thoghtha') of Ireland yielded tribute to Maguire's five stewards ('cóig maoraibh').[79] The reference to five stewards echoes the five historic provinces of Ireland. This interpretation is confirmed in quatrain twenty-seven when Mac an Bhaird speaks of how easy it would be for Maguire to take control of Ireland ('Críoch Gaoidheal do léim luidhe') and how in turn the five hosts (i.e., the *Gaoidhil*) would be suitably grateful ('cóic slóigh ag breith a bhuidhe').[80] This sort of imagery suggests that he envisaged Maguire's suzerainty extending throughout the island. Reference to Maguire supremacy in the context of *Éire*, *Críoch Gaoidheal* and the *cóic slóigh* highlights the all-island context of this posited overlordship.

The theme of 'Brath lendáin ac Leic Lughaidh' mirrors that of 'Leath re Fódla fuil Uidhir'. The opening line at once introduces the prospect of nuptial union between the sovereignty figure and Cú Chonnacht. Leac Lughaidh was a stone at Tara which reputedly had the power to proclaim the rightful king.[81] This lapidary prophet had recognised in the lord of Fermanagh a legitimate king and thus Ireland had again found a worthy mate ('gébhaidh sí arís le haoinfher'). The poet offers conventional remarks regarding Maguire's physical and mental attributes and his imposition of tribute on Ireland. Whereas in 'Leath re Fódla fuil Uidhir' Maguire's claim to the overlordship of Ireland was delineated primarily in terms of a moral and passive ascendancy, in 'Brath lendáin ac Leic Lughaidh' the basis of Cú Chonnacht's power is distinctly martial. Accordingly, the poet depicts Ireland as having fallen victim to the valour of Maguire ('mur do-ní Éire d'fhaghail').[82] This poem contains the same element of ambiguity and thematic manipulation discernible in 'Leath re Fódla fuil Uidhir'. While it is stated that Maguire's right to Ireland is by virtue of a conveniently vague military charter ('cairt cloidhimh'), Mac an Bhaird maintains in quatrain nine that although Maguire had not been tested in battle he nonetheless dominates Ireland:[83]

> Nír dearbhadh é a ngrian ghábhaidh,
> 's do tsáraigh sé Fhiadh Éimhir.

> He has not been proven in the field of
> battle and yet he has overcome Ireland.

The notion of Maguire's passivity is re-echoed a number of times. Even when Maguire adopted a sedentary posture, opted to remain on his couch and chose to refrain from warfare the island was still his for the taking ('budh libh amhlaidh Clár Conghail'). In quatrain twenty-four he advises Maguire to forget any thought he may have had of plundering Ireland since the island had already passed to the chosen candidate ('Críoch Bhanbha riamh ag roghain').[84] In both poems, Mac an Bhaird was elusive and abstract in his deployment of the sovereignty motif. He used the theme, it seems, to draw attention to Maguire's putative pan-insular status. The poet made an apparently unrealistic claim for Cú Chonnacht when he cast him as the potential spouse of Ireland. By virtue of his seigneurial attributes, Mac an Bhaird argues that Maguire could aspire to a position of primacy in Ireland. The poet's use of this conceit in the context of Maguire is, of course, not unique. A standard element in the bardic process of validation was the use of the sovereignty motif to upgrade the status of even the most inconsequential Gaelic lord. Mac an Bhaird's treatment of the topos differed from the conventional bardic usage in that he subtly highlighted the impracticality of the motif in the case of Maguire by ambiguity and prevarication.

Occasionally, Fearghal Óg Mac an Bhaird eschewed subtlety in favour of outright equivocation. He undermined the sovereignty motif's coherence by means of the deliberate archaism of components of his argument. References playing on the old concept of the five provinces must have been self-evidently obsolete in this period. Use of the word rí (king) to describe Cú Chonnacht's position within the Gaelic polity was certainly outmoded. In both poems Maguire was described as king of the river Erne ('rí Éirne').[85] In both he was portrayed as a potential lord of Ireland in the context of specific reference to his status as a 'king' ('rí chinidh Chuinn', 'rí fhréimhe hUidhir').[86] In her monograph on the evolving structures of the Gaelic polity in the later middle ages, Katharine Simms drew attention to the archaism of the concept of rí by the sixteenth century and she argued that from the late fourteenth century onwards rí was gradually supplanted in usage and in theory by dominus or tighearna.[87] In fact, Mac an Bhaird introduced a premeditated note of antiquarianism by employing the term *rí*. The rather arcane quality of Mac an Bhaird's approach in 'Leath re Fódla fuil Uidhir' is further emphasised by allusion to Maguire's rights over Connacht and the Boyne/Bregia area.[88] In quatrain eighteen the poet refers to Maguire's supposed right to dominate Connacht:[89]

> Let Cruacha tiar a ttiomna
> mur na tuatha um Fhiadh Emhna
> budh saor soin ar fher t'fhoghla,
> teagh gan comhla a Moigh Mhedhbha.

> Cruacha in the west is destined to be yours,
> like the territories around Ulster;
> in Connacht a house without a door (i.e., with an open doorway)
> would be secure from a man who would plunder you.

It is not immediately apparent how to decode Mac an Bhaird's allusion to Maguire's claim to Cruacha in Roscommon, the traditional capital of Connacht. It is possible he may have in mind a genealogical link between the Maguires and the legendary kings of Connacht. Indeed, the Maguires traditionally boasted descent from Eochaidh Doimhlein, whose brother Fiachaidh Sraibhthine was grandfather of Eochaidh Muighmheadhón, progenitor of the *Connachta*.[90]

Similarly obscure is the poet's basis or authority for stating that the Maguires were the legitimate power in the Boyne region ('séla a ccairti ar Bhóinn mbiligh').[91] At first sight, it seems difficult to reconcile this assertion with geographical and political actuality. On further enquiry, however, it is probable that Fearghal Óg is once more indulging his recondite knowledge of genealogy. A prose text edited by Eleanor Knott in her edition of the poetry of Tadhg Dall Ó hUiginn offers a plausible resolution of the problem. The Maguires traced their descent from Colla Dhá Chríoch, one of the three sons ('na Colla') of Eochaidh Doimhlein. The text concerns the privileges bestowed on the Collas by Muireadhach Tíreach on their return from Scotland. Here it is stated that the four noblest rivers in Ulster were to form the boundaries of the Collas's territories, that is the Boyne, the Bann, the Erne and the Finn.[92] This legendary demarcation of Colla land probably encouraged Mac an Bhaird to refer to Cú Chonnacht Maguire's rights in the vicinity of the Boyne. In any event, this sort of learned allusion must have added to the opaque presentation in 'Leath re Fódla fuil Uidhir'.

A sense of an Ulster dimension or provincial affiliation is evident in both poems. In 'Leath re Fódla fuil Uidhir', Mac an Bhaird invoked Maguire's position as an Ulster lord to reflect indirectly the province's supposed regional supremacy in Ireland and he manipulated the conventional eulogy genre to articulate themes of obvious personal concern. Fearghal Óg's juxtaposition of Maguire with the northern province is admittedly vague. The implication that

Maguire and Ulster were indivisible allows for a degree of political and poetic creativity. In suggesting that Maguire and his family were coterminous with Ulster, Mac an Bhaird was enabled to use what was ostensibly a praise poem for Cú Chonnacht as a platform for a brand of provincial consciousness. The equation of Maguire with Ulster offers a tantalising glimpse of Mac an Bhaird's political outlook at the time of composition. Obviously concerned to highlight Ulster's apparent primacy, he claimed that the most powerful ruler within the province had traditionally been recognised by the entire island:[93]

> 'na leth riamh do bhí Banbha
> gach rí tarla ar Fhiadh Emhna.

> Ireland has always sided with every king who
> came to power in Ulster.

The constraints engendered by the requirements of a seigneurial poem-book mean that Mac an Bhaird's thesis must, perforce, remain rather elusive. The equation of Ulster with Ireland in the third quatrain ('is leth re hÉirind Ulaigh') also appears obscure. In the light of what has been said already about Mac an Bhaird's manipulation of bardic formulae it acquires interpretative significance. The ambiguity of the Maguire/Ulster comparison was confirmed when Fearghal Óg raised the question of the Maguires' ('aicme Uidhir') right to ascendancy over the Boyne area and also when he elaborated on his argument with the declaration that the host of Aileach controlled Ireland ('le fóir Oiligh Fiadh Fuinidh'). Equivocation in the poet's use of tags like 'fóir Oiligh', 'rí chinidh Chuinn' and 'Crú Cuind' centred on a range of potential inferences. In their general usage these applied to the whole of Ulster, while a more specific contextualisation by the poet had them refer to Cú Chonnacht and the Maguires.[94] A close reading of 'Leath re Fódla fuil Uidhir' and 'Brath lendáin ac Leic Lughaidh' supports two conclusions. First, Mac an Bhaird sought to refocus presentation of the sovereignty motif. Second, he presented Ulster as the dominant region in Ireland and it is implied that the province and by extension its élite should exert a corresponding political hegemony on a pan-insular basis. Interestingly, there is some other evidence which illuminates Fearghal Óg's political outlook. It is known that Mac an Bhaird spent some time in Scotland around the year 1581. From the evidence of a poem he composed about his visit to that country, it is clear that he was unhappy with the influence of the Protestant reform movement there, lamenting the proscription of the Mass and eucharist in particular.[95] The testimony of the two poems already discussed, and that of another of his compositions in Maguire's poem-book, supports the conclusion that Mac an Bhaird questioned aspects of the contemporary relevance of traditional Gaelic political organisation and that he attempted to posit the emergence of an alternative indigenous political focus in Ireland.

In 'Cia re bhfuil Éiri ac anmhuin?', Mac an Bhaird articulated political observation in a more accessible fashion. Like the two poems examined above, this piece is superficially a eulogy for Cú Chonnacht. Significantly, however, it contains an elaborate mixture of pungent political commentary and traditional convention. As in 'Leath re Fódla fuil Uidhir' and 'Brath lendáin ac Leic Lughaidh', Mac an Bhaird subverted and manipulated convention for his own purposes. The entirely orthodox theme concerns Maguire's impeccable credentials to become the spouse of Éire ('céile Cláir Dá Thí').[96] In the customary mode, Mac an Bhaird recommended Maguire as the best spouse for Ireland, significantly now alone and deserted. In adverting to the causes of the island's metaphorical abandonment, he is clearly responding to the prevailing political situation. His concern for the lack of a centralised Gaelic political dynamic is evident in an emphasis on the fact that the country lacked a recognised supreme native overlord:[97]

> Cia re bhfuil Éiri ac anmhuin?
> mó is righin dá ríoghdhamhnaibh,
> críoch na n-iath linnte leabhar,
> gan triath innti d'áitiughadh.
>
> For whom is Ireland waiting? Claimants
> to her throne are slow to appear, for
> no lord inhabits her, the country of the
> wide territories with warm lakes.

Mac an Bhaird notes that Ireland was the only land among the venerable countries of Europe ('fedh seinEorpa') without a high-king ('gan airdrígh'). This situation had obtained since Donnchadh, son of Brian Bóraimhe, died while on pilgrimage in Rome in 1065.[98] Following the departure of Donnchadh, Ireland never again had a crowned overlord ('triath coróna'):[99]

> A nÉirinn na n-es ttana
> ní raibhe a ndiaigh Dhonchadha
> – ní tuar onóra d'Iath Bhregh
> – triath coróna dár creidedh.
>
> In Ireland of the shallow streams there
> was not a crowned lord who won
> acknowledgment after Donnchadh – it is
> not an omen of honour for Ireland.

The implication of the phrase 'triath coróna' requires consideration. The coronation ceremony never played a part in the Gaelic ritual of inauguration and the concept of a crowned king is not native to the Gaelic tradition. References to Donnchadh, son of a famed high-king, and the medieval idea of the crowned king suggest that Mac an Bhaird regretted that a dominant ruling house had failed to evolve towards a centralised monarchy. As the theme of 'Cia re bhfuil Éiri ac anmhuin?' concerns the absence of a pan-insular leader, it seems that Mac an Bhaird perceived Ireland as a potentially unitary political entity.[100] As well as the loss of Donnchadh, Fearghal Óg reckoned that Ireland suffered other disadvantages. In consequence of Ruadhán's curse on Tara, the supreme lordship of Ireland had remained vacant ('tug folamh Ráith ríghFhéilim'). However, the allusion to Ruadhán is by way of preface to Mac an Bhaird's identification of the particular problems affecting the country. The content of quatrains eight and nine illustrates his perception of English aggrandisement in Ireland. The Gaelic Irish were fighting for survival in their own land:[101]

Cuid eile d'anbhuain Fhódla
Gaoidhil uatha d'fhurfhógra
– cnuic thoghtha bhraoinindsi Bhregh,
tolcha taoibhmhillsi Taillten.

Cuid eile d'fháth a horchra:
Gaoidhil is Goill danortha,
gach neach díbh ag cor 'na cend
– an tír do thogh an Táilgeand.

Another disability of Ireland is that the Irish
are being warned off from the chosen hills of the
watery island of Bregh, from the sweetsided hillocks
of Taillte.

Another part of the cause of her sorrow is the
Irish and barbarous foreigners all fighting for
her – the land chosen by Patrick!

The preceding analysis of poems by Mac an Bhaird illustrates how he subverted and redirected some central ideological assumptions underpinning the medieval Gaelic polity. Even though he worked within the ambit of formulaic constraints imposed by the rationale of eulogy, Mac an Bhaird moulded convention to articulate aspects of his political outlook. His mindset, as exemplified in these poems, is characterised by two particular concerns: the absence of an all-island overlord in Ireland and Ulster's posited regional ascendancy. By means of ambiguity and equivocation, the poet exploited the sovereignty motif to stress the absence of native centralised political direction in Ireland, while using it so theoretically in the case of Maguire as to render its actual application to him academic. In effect, Mac an Bhaird enterprised a re-evaluation of Gaelic lordship. The analysis of Ireland's afflictions in 'Cia re bhfuil Éiri ac anmhuin?' indicates that his assessment came in response to English expansionism. With regard to his advocacy of Ulster dominance, it is possible Mac an Bhaird calculated that the only coherent sponsors of the development of pan-Gaelic solidarity in the face of Tudor expansionism could be Ireland's most powerful Gaelic families: the O'Donnells and O'Neills of Ulster.

If the work of Fearghal Óg Mac an Bhaird reveals evolving political perceptions, the poem-books also evidence divergence from established bardic priorities. The prominence of conventional bardic self-perception in the *duanaireadha* has been noted earlier in the chapter. The picture which emerges from this study shows bardic poets in the Maguire and O'Hara poem-books to have been largely vocationally-oriented in outlook. In contrast, several poems in the O'Hara *duanaire* indicate that poets recognised the implications posed for the bardic profession by crown expansion. From the reign of King Henry VIII onwards the crown authorities had been more or less resolute in their hostility to the native learned orders. Given this history of official intolerance of the poets, it is reasonable to assume that by the 1580s echoes of professional and social vulnerability would be evident in their work. It must be said at once that the poems contained in the O'Hara and Maguire poem-books reflect, for the most part, no shadow of the threat confronting the bardic institution. Yet there are exceptions to the dominant pattern. Three poems in the O'Hara collection offer proof of bardic consciousness of a cultural milieu in a state of flux.

In a poem entitled 'Maith an ceanduighe Cormac' Tadhg Dall Ó hUiginn praised Cormac for his patronage of poets. Tadhg Dall invoked the standard bardic argument in such circumstances when he declared that the fame accruing to O'Hara on foot of his largesse to the *fileadha* would ensure a reputation for him long after his material wealth had declined into insignificance (' 's pudh buain na molta ar marthoin').[102] He depicted Cormac as an able merchant who had reaped a handsome profit from his dealings with the poets ('maith an ceanduighe Cormac'). What Cormac spent on the purchase of praise poetry was nothing in comparison to the profit which he would reap from his investment:[103]

> Maith an ceannuighe an fear fuair
> ar bhréig ndiomolaidh ndiombuain
> díoghrais mholta buain bhaluidh
> a n-uair obtha dh'ealadhuin.

> A good merchant is he who got in return for
> a worthless, transitory figment the sincerest
> of fragrant, lasting panegyric at a time when
> art was being rejected.

At this point he injects a note of doubt and uncertainty into the poem. While the fundamental objective was to praise Cormac by reference to his actions and patronage of *fileadha*, Tadhg Dall contrasts Cormac's generosity to the poets with an apparently more prevalent negative attitude to the bardic art. In a quite exaggerated statement, Ó hUiginn declares that O'Hara was alone among the Irish in commissioning poetry from the poets ('oirne ag iaroidh ealaghna'). However, Tadhg Dall used overstatement to good effect. Having obtained the audience's attention, he proceeds in quatrains fifteen, sixteen and seventeen to outline a more convincing case for a decline in the popularity of bardic poetry among Gaelic grandees. Again, Ó hUiginn notes the generosity of O'Hara in his dealings with poets. When poetry was to be had most cheaply ('as sé an uair as saoire soin') and only a few sought it (' 's as teirce a-tá gá iarroigh'), that was the time when the finest bardic compositions were to be truly appreciated ('énuair as chára a charrthoin'). Tadhg Dall unambiguously stresses the contemporary significance of his sentiments. In quatrain seventeen he declares that poetry was not so highly valued at the time he was composing ('ó a-tá in dán neamhdhaor a-niodh'). Given that the demand for praise poetry was hardly acute, Tadhg Dall observes that Cormac would receive a substantial number of eulogies ('biaidh lón nach éidir dh'áireamh') from various poets.[104] He reverts to the theme of declining interest in bardic work in quatrain forty-three. In the preceding quatrain, Tadhg Dall again lauded Cormac's generosity to the poets and remarked that his largesse would be well repaid by the lasting good fortune of the O'Haras ('go lá an bhráich biaidh ar marthain'). He draws a further conclusion in the following quatrain where it is suggested that it was all the more appropriate that Cormac should contribute to the upkeep of the bardic institution ('feirdi an tráth tug dá aire, riar éigeas Fhóid Laoghaire'), considering its unhappy predicament. Now that the literati ('éigeas Fhóid Laoghaire') no longer enjoyed unequivocal public esteem ('cion gach aonduine ar ndol dí') they resembled a flock without a shepherd ('crodh gan aodhuire an éigse').[105]

This theme of bardic retrenchment is further discussed in a poem composed for Cormac by Maol Mhuire Ó an Cháinte.[106] In 'Mithidh déanamh cuairte ag Cormac' the poet laments the time that had elapsed since his last visit to Cormac ('fad na treimhsi a-tú 'n-a fhéagmhois'). Despite their separation, Ó an Cháinte continues to hold his erstwhile patron in affection ('a ghrádh um chridhe do caomhnadh'). The poet is anxious to record the reason for his prolonged absence and he directs Cormac to note his excuse for not having sojourned with him ('tuigeadh féin an fáth fá bhfoilim, feadh treimhsi gan triall dá fhios').[107] He had not set out for O'Hara because of his fear of possible assault by English troops:[108]

> Beantor sind le sluaghoibh Danar
> gur uamhan linn aghoidh air.
>
> I am being attacked by the troops of the
> English and thus I am afraid to visit him.

He adds an interesting twist to his remarks by stating that since the Gaelic Irish were now driving the English out of Ireland ('ó a-táid Gaoidhil do ghuth éinfhir ag athchor Ghall nguirt na bhFionn') he wished to visit O'Hara. A historical parallel to Maol Muire Ó an Cháinte's story is found in a letter which dates from the year 1589. In August of that year, Conaire Ó Mailchonaire wrote to the earl of Thomond to complain about what he considered his wrongful imprisonment by the English authorities. He denied vehemently the charge brought against him, namely, that he had composed a poem for O'Rourke ('co nderna sé dán d'O Ruairc'). Supposedly on the point of execution, Ó Mailchonaire just managed to escape his gaolers' clutches and escaped to freedom ('dobi sé acu chum a churtha chum báis nóco tucc Dia glés dó ar élódh'). He emphasised that none of his family were poets, on the contrary, they followed a profession sanctioned by the crown administration, that of chronicler:[109]

> Et ata fhios agaibhsi, a thigherna, nach re dán
> dobi aenduine do chloinn I Mailchonaire riam acht
> risan eladhain atá molta eiter Gallaib agus
> Gaodhalaib .i. croinicecht.

> And you know, my lord,
> that no member of the Ó Mailchonaire family has ever been a poet,
> rather, they practise the art approved of
> by both the Irish and English, namely history.

Ó Mailchonaire's graphic illustration of the official attitude to the *fileadha* contradicts the assumption that Ó an Cháinte was simply indulging a metaphoric stratagem to advance a convincing excuse for his absence from Cormac.

A third and anonymous poem from the O'Hara poem-book also contains evidence of bardic awakening to adverse external developments impinging on the status of the literati. In 'Gabh mo chosaoid, a Chormuic' an unrecorded poet laments that Gaelic nobles were turning away from patronage of traditional scholarship.[110] The poet is specific in his charge against the nobility whom he claimed had abandoned the *fileadha* ('tugsad uaisle cláir Chonnla cúl rinn in t-aois ealodhna'). Inquiring allusively if this was the time or hour to vilify the poets ('in tráth nó in uair dá égnach'), he particularises the accusation by stating that the O'Donnells and O'Neills had rejected poetry:[111]

> Clann nDálaigh is daghfhuil Néill
> do-chuadar uile dh'éinmhéin
> a ghéag nach bhfaghair folamh,
> a n-aghaidh na healadhan.

> O ever fruitful branch,
> Dálach's and Niall's good race
> have all leagued against poetry.

The poet proceeds to appeal to O'Hara for assistance ('doid as cóir ar ccobhairni'), declaring it unacceptable that *fileadha* were without status or due deference ('ní cóir gan fhéagain oroinn'). In support of this request, he remarks that he had yet to compose a poem for O'Hara ('ní dán daoibh do dhearphamoir'), thus placing the onus on his addressee to commission a piece.[112]

It appears from what Tadhg Dall Ó hUiginn, Maol Muire Ó an Cháinte and this anonymous poet say that bardic corporate status was subject to some degree of pressure. These poems may manifest the initial stages of a consciousness among the poets that their privileged social and professional position was no longer automatically guaranteed or indeed secure from external opposition. The poems contain no real discussion of why the bardic élite had supposedly experienced diminished prestige. Yet the three O'Hara poems highlight two developments obvious, if not immediately explicable, to their authors. Tadhg Dall Ó hUiginn's 'Maith an ceanduighe Cormac' and the anonymous 'Gabh mo chosaoid, a Chormuic' ascribe the decline in bardic poetry's popularity to the supposed indifference of the seigneurial class. Of course, it is not possible to determine comparative demand for bardic poetry in one period above another during the approximate chronological span 1200–1650 and there is no precise means of investigating these claims. Certainly, the accusation in 'Gabh mo chosaoid, a Chormuic' that the O'Donnells and the O'Neills had forsaken their patronage of bardic poetry appears quite exaggerated. Hugh O'Donnell was the lord of *Tír Conaill* during most of the period when 'Gabh mo chosaoid, a Chormuic' was composed, presumably sometime between 1581 and 1597. Hugh succeeded his brother as head of Ceinéal Conaill in 1566 and he ruled until replaced by his son in 1592. Evidently a fairly active patron of the poets, his section of the O'Donnell poem-book contains eighteen poems.[113] On the other hand, Maol Muire Ó an Cháinte's 'Mithidh déanamh cuairte ag Cormac' hints at the pressure applied to the Gaelic and gaelicised élite to discontinue bardic patronage.[114] Maol Muire is blunt in his identification of English hostility to the poets. On the whole, these three poems are indicative of a reassessment of conventional notions of professional integrity. This questioning of the traditional ethos was largely the result of official crown opposition to the bardic order.

This chapter's third and final section considers aspects of the general consciousness of the English presence discernible in two particular poems. They are 'Ag so an chomuirce, a Chormoic' by Tadhg Dall Ó hUiginn, from the O'Hara poem-book, and Giolla Riabhach Ó Cléirigh's 'Buaidh n-egna ar Fhréimh ríoghUidhir', preserved in the Maguire collection. It appears that Tadhg Dall composed his poem against the background of the taxation settlement known as the composition of Connacht undertaken by Sir John Perrot in 1585. On this basis, Eleanor Knott dated the poem to sometime between 1584 and 1585.[115] In this piece the poet seeks the protection of Cormac, declaring that new regulations imposed by the English required him to do so ('ní ghabhuid ó neach fá nimh gan bheith dó ag urrodh éigin'). He makes it clear that he was not *ollamh* to O'Hara, so this was not a reason for selecting Cormac as his guarantor ('ní har bheith am ollamh aguibh'). Rather, he had chosen the lord of Leyney because both the English and Irish approved of his rule. The inhabitants of each territory were being summoned together by the English and required to supply personal information to the authorities and to indicate where they resided. All this material was duly recorded 'in a large, clean roll or parchment' ('a nglanrolla mhór mheamruim').[116] Ó hUiginn probably had little choice in the matter of naming his overlord. As he lived in Leyney, he may have been obliged to link himself with the local seigneur for taxation and administration purposes. In typical bardic fashion, Tadhg Dall was not slow to point to the benefits likely to come O'Hara's way if he agreed to act as his sponsor. Cormac could expect poems in praise of his ancestry if he granted the author's request. This poem illustrates a poet seeking the aid of a local overlord in the face of new political and administrative circumstances. Yet it is difficult to determine how the composition of Connacht, an agreement which concerned the Gaelic and Anglo-Norman political élite, would have affected Ó hUiginn. Although he was an important personage within the structures of Gaelic society, his status would have hardly merited individual attention with regard to the terms of a composition which essentially aimed to regulate fiscal matters and also sought to strengthen the English-created office of Connacht's presidency. The inquisition taken before provincial president Sir Richard Bingham and Sir Nicholas White in Sligo on 22 September, 1585, concerned the baronies of the county and the major divisions of land within each barony. The indenture signed on the following day was an agreement concerning the English crown and the landed Sligo élite. While Cormac O'Hara was required to give an account of his position in Leyney, it is unlikely that less important tenants within the barony would have been in contact with the surveyors.[117]

If the poem was a response to the composition of Connacht, Ó hUiginn has certainly interpreted the agreement in a distinctly self-referential manner. Tadhg Dall makes some intriguing references to his own predicament at the outset. He advises Cormac that it was fitting to support him in every just cause but he was also to back the poet in the event of wrong-doing or injustice on the latter's part. Ó hUiginn states that he was in constant danger because of gossip that had been circulated about him. It is not easy to determine whether these allusions relate to the main argument put forward by Tadhg Dall within the poem or whether he is touching on another matter. If this last scenario is considered, it may be assumed that knowledge of his position was known to his listeners and would not have required detailed explanation:[118]

> A-tú a mbeol ghuaisi do ghnáth
> re ndeachaidh oroinn d'iomráth

gan neach do-ní dísle dhamh
muna thí dhíbhse a dheunamh.

I am continually in the jaws of danger,
because of all the gossip that has been
made about me, having no one to protect
me, unless thou canst undertake it.

Of course, the danger to which Tadhg Dall alludes possibly reflects the
anti-bardic measures promulgated by the crown authorities and probably
mirrors the apprehension expressed by Maol Muire Ó an Cháinte in 'Mithidh
déanamh cuairte ag Cormac'. In 'Ag so an chomuirce, a Chormuic', Tadhg
Dall attempts to accommodate new politico-administrative structures. While
obviously aware of these evolving considerations, he offers no immediate
solution to his problem. Beyond seeking the help of Cormac, he ventured no
other interpretative strategy in this poem to assess factors impinging on the
projection and cultivation of the bardic art. He notes that Cormac had been
accepted as a lawful ruler by both the Gaelic Irish and the English ('do aomh-
sad Gaoidhil is Goill . . . rí fíréanda do rádh ribh').[119] As far as he was concerned, it appears that Cormac was a good choice for a poet seeking
protection. In summary, Tadhg Dall's 'Ag so an chomuirce, a Chormoic' illustrates his sensitivity and vulnerability to crown administrative intrusion and
presents an outlook mindful of the administrative implications posed by a
centralising regime. Indeed, the malleable tenor of his engagement with English administrative dictates is evident in Ó hUiginn's choice of outward conformity as opposed to overt resistance.

Several informative references appear in the poem entitled 'Buaidh n-egna
ar Fhréimh ríoghUidhir' preserved in the Maguire manuscript. Stern ascribed
this poem to Giolla Riabhach Ó Cléirigh, although the poem is acephalous in
the Copenhagen manuscript.[120] Once more the poet pursued the uniform
course of lauding Maguire for his unstinting support of the *fileadha* and of
course he highlights his lordly virtues. Naturally enough, Cú Chonnacht's
character traits mean that he is an entirely suitable object for *Éire's* affections.
The poem's principal interest centres on a number of allusions to the English
and their relationship with Maguire. In quatrain eleven, the poet praises the
martial vigour of Maguire in battle and observes that the English were reluctant to become entangled in a military encounter with Cú Chonnacht ('col do
ghliaidh ac Gallshaxoibh a ndiaigh na Con Connachtsin'). This is continued
in the following quatrain when the author describes the devastating effects of
Maguire's heroic temperament: a covering of grass over an English homestead
('barr feoir tar gruaidh gallbhaile'). The notion of Maguire as a raider of English settlements is repeated again in quatrain twenty-two, here he is portrayed
as a plunderer of such establishments ('d'éis braite bairr ghallbhaile').[121] However, a curious twist in the poet's treatment of the English becomes apparent

in quatrain thirty-two. At this point, the poet makes an intriguing claim on Maguire's behalf: it was because of Cú Chonnacht that the English were no longer seen as vulnerable newcomers throughout Ireland and, thanks to him also, they no longer endured attack:[122]

> Ní Goill iad ón imbeirtsin
> fá iath Floind dá bhfannfhaicsin;
> fiú riar an Chon Connachtsin
> gan cor gliadh ar GhallShaxaibh.

> From that treatment they are no longer foreigners,
> seen weak throughout the land of Ireland; as a
> result of the administration of that Cú Chonnacht
> the English are no longer attacked.

These conflicting opinions on Maguire's relationship with the English seem difficult to reconcile with the historical record. Indeed, attempts to read the poem within too rigid a framework of historical empiricism entail a flawed understanding of its internal logic. It is more instructive to approach the poem's evidence as reflective of an aspect of Gaelic responses to Tudor aggrandisement. The claims ventured by its anonymous author should not be construed as factual commentary. Indeed, it is more convincing to interpret the statements made regarding Maguire's supposed attitude to the English in terms of ideological rather than historical reconciliation. The documentary record attests that Maguire was obliged to recognise the overlordship of the English authorities. This poem manipulates tradition to present Maguire's submission to the external overlordship of the crown in a purely formal context of validation and sanction. Initially, Maguire is depicted as the military peer, if not superior, of the English settlers. Yet the crucial actuality of Maguire's predicament is touched on fleetingly in quatrain thirty-two. Here Maguire's submission to the English administration is turned around with the implication that the English are reliant on Maguire for their welfare in Ireland. 'Buaidh n-egna ar Fhréimh ríoghUidhir' and Tadhg Dall Ó hUiginn's 'Ag so an chomuirce, a Chormoic' represent two expressions of Gaelic consciousness of the Elizabethan presence. Each poem, in its peculiarly allusive way, is an effort to come to grips with that situation and each response to expanding English hegemony is characterised by a degree of intellectual ambivalence to ambiguous and shifting political pressures.

Certainly, the ideological character of the Maguire and O'Hara poem-books is best described as predominantly traditional in tone and expression. Evidently, the functional nature of the poem-book ensured that it served more as a source of conventional sanction than as a forum for innovation. However, it is possible that this traditionalism was occasionally itself a strategic response to the cultural and political implications of the Tudor presence.[123]

The approach adopted in this chapter has been to acknowledge the conventional seam in the poem-books while concurrently exploring intellectual potential for reaction and innovation. In this manner, aspects of bardic response have been analysed from three points of scrutiny: shifting views of lordship, evolving cultural perceptions and bardic consciousness of English intrusion. The foregoing discussion demonstrates evidence of response under these three headings and illustrates how this reaction centres on the bardic re-evaluation of political and social perceptions in relation to Gaelic society and the cumulative trauma of Gaelic engagement with the Elizabethans.

A PATTERN ESTABLISHED
1558–1603

As far back as 1729, the Scottish antiquarian Thomas Innes argued that bardic poetry's communal focus vitiated its potential as a reliable historical source.[1] This perception continues to influence the interpretative approach of contemporary scholars to the poetry. The critical consideration in this particular reading centres on the fact that bardic poets composed panegyrics and eulogies in exchange for financial reward. Automatic bardic thematic manipulation and consequent distortion of the historical record is presumed as a result. While praise poetry's inevitable subjectivity must, of course, be reckoned with constantly, it should also be remembered that the poets constituted a professional cohort acutely conscious of its collective status. The primary focus of bardic practice ensured that the fortunes of the poets were linked to the patronage of ascendant Gaelic magnates and lords. The assumption that bardic assessment of colonial aggrandisement is invariably influenced by the norms of professional praise poetry is challenged in the present and following chapters. The preceding chapter illustrated how the generally localised and dynastic political scope of the family poem-book results in a somewhat opaque source for the reconstruction of bardic analyses of expansionary English activity. The material examined in this chapter is drawn from a wider and more representative base than that of the family poem-books already discussed. Working within the chronological framework of Elizabeth's reign, this chapter focuses on evidence, selected without regional or dynastic bias, preserved in seigneurial *duanaireadha* and in composite manuscripts. In effect, it is proposed to elaborate on and to offer a more detailed account of the evolving bardic mindset fleetingly glimpsed in some of the Maguire and O'Hara poems.

The analytical procedure adopted for the following discussion is structured around three general headings: politics, culture and religion. Although the rubric division is thematic, analysis of poems within each of the three divisions is undertaken on a chronological basis. An evidential prototype for the selection of this tripartite interpretative framework is provided by a poem composed around 1542–3, almost fifteen years prior to the accession of Queen Elizabeth I in 1558. Elements of bardic reaction to Tudor aggrandisement, both political and social, find preliminary expression in the anonymous piece entitled 'Fúbún fúibh, a shluagh Gaoidheal'. It is among the earliest extant Gaelic compositions illustrating the process by which the consolidation of crown influence during the later sixteenth and early seventeenth centuries provoked a commensurate bardic political response. 'Fúbún fúibh,

a shluagh Gaoidheal', as the title suggests, berates some leading Gaelic families for their alleged supine acquiescence in English political influence and
their acceptance of English cultural habits.[2] The charged political tone of the
piece is immediately apparent in the opening stanza when the Gaelic élite is
accused of passively accepting crown encroachment on their lands ('Goill ag
comhroinn bhur gcríche; re sluagh síthe bhur samhail').[3] If the opening
reproach is vague by reason of its unilateral inclusivity ('sluagh Gaoidheal'),
the poet is more specific in the second and following stanzas about the focus
of his accusation. Among those to incur his displeasure were the MacCarthys
of west Munster, the O'Briens of Thomond and the Leinster nobility in general ('cóigeadh gnímhéachtach Laighean'). His condemnation of supposed
Gaelic malleability becomes more concrete when two contemporary Ulster
lords are berated for their failure to stand against the thrust of English expansion. Conn Bacach O'Neill (ob. 1559), styled O'Neill of *Aileach* and *Eamhain*
in the poem ('Ó Néill Oiligh is Eamhna'), had foolishly exchanged his Gaelic
designation for an English title ('tugsad ar iarlacht Uladh ríoghacht go
humhal aimhghlic').[4] Similarly, it is maintained that Manus O'Donnell (ob.
1563), once noted for his warlike mien, had failed to come to the aid of Ireland ('-d'Éirinn fá mór an t-amghar – do mheath Maghnas Ó Domhnaill').[5] It
is not obvious what the poet meant when he spoke of O'Donnell having
failed Ireland ('do mheath'). O'Donnell, a renowned patron of Gaelic scholarship, could hardly be credibly accused of cultural disaffection, the allega-
tion seems more likely to have been political in substance. Like O'Neill,
Manus had also petitioned King Henry VIII for a crown title. Although
O'Neill was created earl of Tyrone in 1542, it was not until the reign of King
James I that an earldom was bestowed on an O'Donnell of *Tír Conaill*.[6]

The author of 'Fúbún fúibh, a shluagh Gaoidheal' was mainly preoccupied
with the perceived factional interests of the Gaelic élite in the face of what he
presents as the pan-insular as opposed to local implications of the crown's
ambitions. If the poet saw the challenge posed by King Henry's administration
as mainly a question of political power and its control, he was also aware of
incipient cultural tension. In the penultimate stanza a remarkable measure of
political insight is manifest when he touches on two issues which were to
become increasingly critical themes in the course of Ireland's history, religion
and culture:[7]

> Fúbún fán ngunna ngallghlas,
> fúbún fán slabhra mbuidhe,
> fúbún fán gcúirt gan Bhéarla
> fúbún séana Mheic Mhuire.

> Shame on the grey foreign gun, shame on
> the golden chain, shame on the court without
> the language of the poets (Irish law?),
> shameful is the denial of Mary's son.

In a fascinating collocation of imagery, he alludes to what may have seemed the most immediately disturbing signs of Tudor penetration of the Gaelic heartlands. The first two lines of the quatrain coming after the stanza devoted to Manus O'Donnell surely refer back to the subject of the preceding lines. As the poem's editor Brian Ó Cuív observed, O'Donnell was promised artillery by King James V of Scotland in 1537 ('gunna gallghlas') and, in 1542, O'Donnell requested a gold chain ('slabhra buidhe') from Henry VIII, while later in the same year Conn Bacach received a gold chain from the monarch on his submission in London. Therefore, the image of the *slabhra buidhe* would have had definite connotations of submission to and acquiescence in English dominion. While the allusion to the 'cúirt gan Bhéarla' is not immediately intelligible, one suggestion appears to offer a solution to its troubled interpretation for both linguistic and historical reasons. If *Béarla* is an ellipsis for 'Béarla na bhfileadh' ('the poetic language'), then the image of 'cúirt gan Bhéarla' implies that the author feared the blandishments of the English authorities might possibly encourage the Gaelic nobility to abandon their adherence to indigenous culture, in particular their patronage of the poets. The imagery of a destitute Gaelic learned class becomes a relatively common theme in poetry composed especially after the flight of the Ulster magnates to the continent in 1607. However, its early modern pedigree is to be traced to its preliminary expression in 'Fúbún fúibh, a shluagh Gaoidheal'. The theme continues to be invoked during the Elizabethan period, culminating finally with the exile or collapse of the leading aristocratic Gaelic houses. The line which runs 'fúbún séana Mheic Mhuire' ('shameful is the denial of Mary's son') appears to contain a reference to Henry's breach with Rome. Brian Ó Cuív is surely correct in reading 'séana Mheic Mhuire' as an allusion to the Gaelic lords' renunciation of papal authority and their acceptance of the oath of supremacy.[8] Significantly, this is an early example of Gaelic consciousness of the Protestant reformation. In a manner akin to the projection of the image of a besieged bardic institution, the poets' responses to the question of religious dissension and allegiance were further developed in the Elizabethan period, although in the case of this theme to a much lesser degree of conceptual refinement.

Bardic Engagement with Political Change, 1558–1603

In 1566 the turbulent Shane O'Neill was murdered by the MacDonnells of Antrim, to whom in desperation he had fled for assistance following his defeat by O'Donnell at Farsetmore. His successor as lord of the O'Neills, Turlough Luineach, proved no less resourceful but rather more enduring. Turlough Luineach managed, by and large, to wield control over the O'Neill territory until his death in 1595. The early years of Turlough Luineach's lordship were dominated by two developments: the unsuccessful colonising schemes of Sir Thomas Smith and his son, Thomas, in Clandeboye and the Ards in 1572–3, and a similar venture in 1573, when Walter Devereux, earl of Essex, arrived in Ireland with a plan to colonise most of Antrim. Essex was no more successful in his aims than the Smiths and his proposed colony soon came to a disorderly end. The aspiring settlers were opposed both by the Gaelic Irish and the Scots. Turlough Luineach, in particular, was entrenched in his opposition to the implementation and success of Essex's project.[9]

The anonymous poem, 'An sluagh sidhe so i nEamhuin?', seems to date to the period 1574–5 when Essex engaged in intermittent hostilities against Turlough Luineach.[10] This piece, dedicated to O'Neill, casts him in the role of opponent of the English. The poem is structured around a hosting of troops supplied by the leading Gaelic families in Ulster and convened under O'Neill's direction. The event described in the poem may well have been imaginary and unconnected with an actual occurrence. In fact, the poet may have availed of this device to highlight the desirability of an Ulster Gaelic military force united under Turlough Luineach's command. The poem's visionary quality is at once evident in the opening couplet when the poet inquires rhetorically if it was a fairy host which he saw before him in *Eamhuin* or Navan Fort ('An sluagh sidhe so i nEamhuin do-chíu lán do lúithghreadhaibh?').[11] The choice of Navan Fort as the location of this martial hosting reinforces the notion of Ulster cohesion discernible in the poem. It is an instructive choice given that Navan Fort possessed particular significance because of its former status as capital of the ancient province of Ulster. The poet makes it clear that his allegory relates more to actuality than to abstract topographical antiquarianism, in spite of its deceptively ethereal *mise en scène*. While the hosting is certainly otherworldly in form ('ní sluagh sídhe acht ar fhaicsin'), its true purpose, however, was to wage war ('sluagh adhnaidh an eissíodha').[12] The poem's author proceeds to give a more detailed account of this levy assembled around O'Neill like a wall of axes ('fál tuagh um chodhnach ua gCuinn'). Among those assembled in support of the lord of Tyrone were the MacDonnells, the O'Cahans, the Clandeboye O'Neills (Clann Aodha Buidhe) and contingents from prominent northern families such as Magennis, MacMahon, O'Reilly and Maguire.[13] In a further step away from the poem's initial note of abstraction, the author anchored his case firmly to contemporary events when he disclosed the reason for this assembly:[14]

> Críoch a sinnser i nglas gall
> ciall cruinnighthe na Saorchlann;
> cuimhneach le triath a dtionóil
> cuibhreach ar iath Eiriomhóin.

> That the land of their ancestors is under foreign oppression
> is the reason for the gathering of the noble families,
> the lord of their assembly remembers
> that the land of Ireland is fettered.

The poet elaborated on the image of Turlough Luineach as Ireland's defender by recounting an exemplum to offer supporting evidence of previous and similar actions in the island's history and mythology. In a manner similar to Turlough Luineach at the time of the poem's composition, it was Lugh who in times past defended Ireland against the depredations of the legendary Balar ('cosmhuil ag cosnamh Banbha').[15] Indeed, Lugh was so successful in routing Balar that nobody among the invader's force survived to tell the tale ('Fear sgél ní theurno dha thoigh do shluagh Bhalair 'na bheathoigh').[16] The contemporary usurpers of the land must be told that O'Neill is arrayed against them, presupposing they are even capable of enduring his onslaught ('Agsin chugaibh, a chath gall, má tá agaibh a fhulang, Ó Néill do char an chatha'). O'Neill is poised to avenge some of the wrongs inflicted on the *Gaoidhil* by foreign invaders in the past, especially the death of Brian Bóraimhe at Clontarf and the defeat of Brian O'Neill at Downpatrick in 1260.[17]

Brian Ó Gnímh's "Na Bhrían táinig Aodh Eanghach' is another poem which must be read in the context of the colonial ambitions of Smith and Essex in the early 1570s. Ó Gnímh composed this piece for Brian O'Neill (ob. 1574), lord of Clandeboye and a resolute opponent of the activities of Smith and Essex. As soon as Smith had landed in Ireland in 1572, he met with armed opposition from Brian and, during the years 1573–4, the latter opposed Essex in a similar fashion. However, in 1574 Brian O'Neill submitted to Essex and later in the same year was lured by Essex's guile to his eventual death in Dublin.[18] As the opening line of Ó Gnímh's poem suggests, O'Neill (ob. 1574) is represented by means of the imagery associated with the mythical liberator of Ireland and stock heroic character, Aodh Eanghach.[19] The composition's central theme suggests that O'Neill was both entitled to be and actually was a spouse worthy of Ireland. Indeed, the sovereignty figure is invoked to sanction Brian's position ('Do thogh an Bhanbha ar mBríainne'). The assumption that Brian had won the right to take possession of Ireland ('Críoch Bhanbha id sheilbh fa shéula') was, in practical terms, unrealistic and this suggests consideration of a possible allegorical meaning to an otherwise unremarkable conceit.[20] Ó Gnímh employs a standard element in the bardic process of validation to adduce ideological endorsement for his subject. The poem's central premise encourages Brian to resist foreign hegemonic claims, illustrating that he did so in the knowledge that he was operating within the recognised and sanctioned parameters of Gaelic ideology. What is important about the proposed union of O'Neill and Ireland is not so much the obvious theoretical nature of the suggestion but rather the political validity which the conceit's invocation enshrined in a Gaelic framework. The core warning which Ó Gnímh conveyed to Brian and a wider communal audience was one of alert vigilance with regard to English aggrandisement. Given the emphasis on Brian's active profile among the Gaelic Irish ('Brian ag brosdadh na nGaoidheal') and his possession of political imprimatur, it is not surprising to find Ó Gnímh declaring that Brian and his followers had subverted English designs on the land of Ireland:[21]

> Slegh arsaidh do ghoir gualoinn
> Saxoin da ngoin le a géirrinn
> báidhter le crann thonn dtírim
> sgríbhinn gall ar fhonn Fhéidhlim.

> An ancient spear which burns a shoulder,
> its sharp point wounds Saxons, a dry
> wave of spears submerges the foreign
> claim to Ireland.

The reference to the English claim to Irish land ('sgríbhinn gall ar fhonn Fhéidhlim') is significant in the context of what is known about Brian O'Neill's opposition to two colonising ventures where it was attempted to implement such acquisitive designs.

The inference that the *Gaoidhil* might suffer the loss of their lands is echoed in a poem probably composed early in the 1570s by Uilliam Óg Mac an Bhaird (ob. 1576).[22] Mac an Bhaird's reason for composing 'Gaoidhil meallta nó mac Néill' for Turlough Luineach O'Neill stemmed from his fear that the Gaelic nobility were being outwitted by English stratagems. He compared the Gaelic Irish to bees who have been lured from their hives by means of artifice, and who once drawn out into the open, find that their assailants intend making off with their cache of honey. In much the same way, according to the poet, the Gaelic Irish endure the diminution of their patrimony through Anglo-Saxon guile:[23]

> Mar soin do-níd gasraidh Ghall
> re Gaoidhealaibh Guirt Fhreamhann,
> na fir fhlathamhla ó Lios Bhreagh,
> dá sgrios d'atharrdha a n-aithreadh.

> It is in this manner that the English host
> deals with the *Gaoidhil* of Ireland, the princely
> men of Lios Bhreagh are being driven from the
> native land of their ancestors.

The English seduce the Gaelic élite with luxury goods: feather quilts, red wines and bright new mantles among other items. In Mac an Bhaird's opinion the desire of the Gaelic Irish to obtain such merchandise ('áille a séad feabhas a bhfleadh, sanntaighid maicne Mhíleadh') resulted in their being duped by the English ('mealltair Gaoidhil le Galloibh'). The poet invoked a traditional metaphor to describe the Gaelic élite's predicament, they resembled the salmon who had been lured to his capture by the promise of the bait ('Mar bhréagas baoite an dubháin an t-eo is é ar a iongabháil').[24]

In the much the same vein as the preceding poems, Tadhg Dall Ó hUiginn's 'Fearann cloidhimh críoch Bhanbha' reveals something of the tension manifested by the Gaelic literati in the face of the consolidation of Elizabethan authority. In this piece, which was composed sometime between 1571 and

1580 for Seaán, the Lower MacWilliam (1571–80), the poet engages with a re-evaluation of Gaelic ethnic assumptions. Ó hUiginn argues that Ireland is effectively sword land ('fearann cloidhimh') and this means that the island will inevitably be in the possession of the strongest contender for its domination. In the past, various groups had invaded and held the island, until they in turn were displaced by newcomers of superior military strength. Ó hUiginn mentioned the *Fir Bolg,* the *Tuatha Dé Danonn* and the *Gaoidhil* as having occupied and controlled Ireland in succession. Up to this point, Tadhg Dall followed the orthodox Gaelic reading of prehistory, which assumed the primacy of the *Gaoidhil* at the summit of a pyramid formed by successive invading peoples.[25] However, he obviously sought to extend this ethnic schema further in order to include the descendants of the Anglo-Norman colonial settlers of 1169 and after. Tadhg Dall aimed to assure the Lower MacWilliam, an Anglo-Norman de Burgo, that he was as legitimate an inhabitant of Ireland as a *Gaedheal.* With this purpose in mind, he reformulated the conventional Gaelic ethnic paradigm to take account of the Anglo-Norman community. Interestingly, Ó hUiginn subdivides the Anglo-Norman influx into three distinct contingents, reflecting the supposed origins of some of the leading Anglo-Norman dynasties in Ireland. He mentions adventurers from three lands ('teaguid tar tuinn teóra cath'): France, Greece and England.[26] Among these newcomers were the de Burgos and they had since acquired their own share of the land of Ireland.

Yet, Tadhg Dall is aware that the de Burgos risk the charge of remaining foreigners in Ireland. To refute any such accusation, he poses a simple but effective question:[27]

> Gi bé adéaradh gur deóraidh
> Búrcaigh na mbeart n-inleóghain –
> faghar d'fhuil Ghaoidhil nó Ghoill
> nach fuil 'na aoighidh agoinn.

> Gi bé adeir nách dleaghar dháibh
> a gcuid féin d'Éirinn d'fhagháil –
> cia san ghurt bhraonnuaidhe bhinn
> nách lucht aonuaire d'Éirinn?

> Should any say that the Burkes of lion-like
> prowess are strangers – let one of the blood
> of *Gaedheal* or *Gall* be found who is not a sojourner
> among us.

> Should any say they deserve not to receive
> their share of Ireland –
> who in the sweet dew-glistening field
> are more than visitors to the land?

In any case, observed Tadhg Dall, the de Burgos were here to stay and determined to maintain control of their land like any Gaelic family and accordingly deserving of respect ('oireachta dan cóir creideamh'). The de Burgos were not to be induced to leave the island, for their right of residence was predicated on long and venerable occupation of land in Ireland ('dul uatha ag Éirinn ní fhuil').[28] This poem has been cited as a classic example of bardic hypocrisy and insincerity. To the uncritical eye, it apparently presents a picture of Tadhg Dall turning his back on the *Gaoidhil* and providing political validation for the scion of a medieval colonial dynasty.[29] This sort of cursory reading fails to take account of the historical context of its composition. Ó hUiginn did not deny the supremacy of the Gaelic presence in Ireland. If anything, he consolidated the premise of Gaelic dominion by adding another layer to the invasion model. Realising the impracticality of the exclusive nature of Gaelic aspirations to unique cultural and political hegemony in Ireland, he sought to codify the ideological status of the community which had been marginalised in the context of the formal Gaelic world view: the gaelicised descendants of the Anglo-Norman colonists. The poet aimed at effecting ethnic coalescence among both historic communities on the basis of language and culture. Tadhg Dall's presentation of the Gaelic and Anglo-Norman Irish as joint heirs to Ireland's land finds expression in a simple but meaningful gesture. At the end of the poem, composed for a de Burgo, the poet appended a quatrain in praise of Conn O'Donnell (ob. 1583), the son of An Calbhach (ob. 1566), Gaelic lord of *Tír Conaill*. Crucially, the relaxation of self-conscious ethnic differences adumbrated here by Ó hUiginn was to become an important factor in the reformulation of Gaelic political attitudes in the period covered by the present study. Moreover, the perception of ethnic mutuality emerging among the Gaelic literati was complemented by a corresponding realignment of attitudes among intellectuals of Anglo-Norman background.

Two other poems by Tadhg Dall Ó hUiginn reveal more of his innovative political outlook. The poem, 'T'aire riot, a Riocaird Óig', was composed for another member of the Lower MacWilliam sept. On this occasion, Tadhg addressed Ricard Óg, son of Ricard (ob. 1571), a former lord of the family. Ricard Óg was hanged in 1586 on the orders of Sir Richard Bingham, lord president of Connacht.[30] Apparently, Tadhg Dall had heard talk about Ricard accepting an English title. The immediate political or administrative background to this poem is unclear. Eleanor Knott has conjectured that Ricard Óg was offered either the sheriffship of Mayo or a seneschalship.[31] In any case, the poet was horrified that Ricard Óg should even consider adopting an English title at the expense of his customary appellation. He advised Ricard to keep his original name ('San riocht i rabhabhair riamh bí id Riocard mhac Mheic Uilliam').[32] In doing so, Tadhg Dall made a number of revealing observations why Ricard should avoid taking a foreign title ('ainm allmhardha'). Listing the advantages and disadvantages associated with the acceptance of a crown title, he argues that the traditional descriptive mode of 'Riocard mhac Mheic Uilliam' had been to its bearer's benefit in a number of ways. Riocard had derived from it authority ('lais do-chuabhair i gcéimibh'), support and wealth ('a mhaoin do bheith ar biseach, a phosd cothaighthe is sé sin').[33] In other words, the poet is saying that Ricard's title had underwritten his patrimony, emblematic as it was of the sanctioned integrity of his overlordship in the family territories. Ricard Óg owed everything to his possession of the traditional designation and accordingly he would do well to retain it:[34]

> Mar sin nár dhealoighthe dhoit
> ret ainm ngnáth, red ghníomh n-ordhruic,
> ris gach mbuaidh dá mbíoth oraibh,
> ós uaidh fríoth a bhfuarabhair.

> Even thus it were not for thee to part from
> thy wonted title, thy well-known deeds, with
> every triumph that thou hadst of old, since
> from it was got all that thou didst win.

Tadhg Dall was direct and unambiguous in stating the case against acceptance of a foreign title. He noted that possession of a foreign designation would not benefit his subject should he assume a position of power in Ireland ('níorbh fhiú dhuit, a dhreach shéaghoinn, ainm allmhardha dá rádh ruibh'). In his use of this approach, the poet was probably referring to the possibility of Ricard Óg becoming head of his sept in the context of the allegorical schema of sovereignty's espousal. More fundamentally, the poet claimed that unless he renounced the new title he risked losing his patrimony ('cóir car an athanma ar ais suil rabh h'athardha it éagmais'). Because Ricard Óg had exchanged his indelible ancestral name for a foreign appellation ('ainm síor ar ainm n-iasachta') he had caused a rift to open between himself and Tadhg Dall ('fá bhfuil sionn éadána ort').[35] One of the poem's chief interests lies in its author's equation of authentic and successful political power with possession of a traditional title. Given the sentiments expressed in 'Fearann cloidhimh críoch Bhanbha', it is no surprise to find Ó hUiginn recommending a title which was essentially Gaelic ('Riocard mhac Mheic Uilliam'), even though the bearer was of Anglo-Norman stock. Using the complementary evidence of both poems, it is clear that Ó hUiginn envisaged a common insular identity encompassing the Gaelic and gaelicised Anglo-Norman communities, united by a common culture and standing together in opposition to the intrusion of foreign socio-political modes of expression.

In the poem, 'D'fhior chogaidh comhailtear síothcháin', Ó hUiginn provides a fuller insight to his political outlook.[36] This poem was dedicated to Brian na Múrtha O'Rourke (ob. 1591) and seems likely to date to around 1588. During this period O'Rourke incurred the wrath of Sir Richard Bingham for the assistance he had afforded survivors of armada wrecks off the north-west coast and, later, for allowing an effigy of Queen Elizabeth to be made and publicly reviled. In 1590 O'Rourke was forced to flee his territory and he crossed over to Scotland in the following year. However, he was immediately handed over to the English government by King James VI and subsequently hanged at Tyburn.[37] Although the poem is addressed to O'Rourke of west *Bréifne*, Tadhg Dall situated his opening remarks in an all-island context. In the first ten quatrains, he expressed anxiety about the political predicament confronting the *Gaoidhil*, a collective descriptive term used by Ó hUiginn without prejudice to the Anglo-Norman community as will be clear from the preceding analysis. Only a warrior could achieve peace for Ireland, he argues, because the English would never retreat voluntarily to a state of passivity ('Ní fhuighid síad síodh ó Ghallaibh, Gaoidhil na ngníomh gcathardha'). In any case, it seemed evident to the English that the Gaelic Irish were ill-prepared to stand against them ('do-chíthear dhóibh – truagh mar tharla – sluagh Banbha gan bharánta'). Although the Gaelic Irish yearned for war, the English had already begun to destroy the nobility ('Beag nách deachsad go díoth n-éinfhir uaisle fola fionnGhaoidhil'). The *Gaoidhil* are being driven to the island's extremities, while English troops occupy the very centre of Ireland ('Siad dá gcur i gciomhsaibh Banbha, buidhne Ghall 'na glémheadhón').[38] The Gaelic Irish had fallen prey to an invading force because they were poorly resourced militarily ('Ar a loige do lucht cogaidh') and this deficiency had been compounded by the fact that they were without effective leadership ('truagh nách faghaid lucht a laoidhidh a hucht aoinfhir oirbheartaigh').[39] Crucially, Ó hUiginn considers it the task of the literati to proffer political counsel because the *Gaoidhil* were hindered by a lack of direction arising from defective leadership. In this particular case, he maintains that the poets should urge the men of Ireland to declare war on the invaders:[40]

> Mór an neamhchuid do neach éigin
> d'éigsibh an fhuinn ghealtholchaigh
> gan a rádh re fearaibh Fódla
> deabhaidh d'fhógra ar eachtronnchaibh.

> Great unfriendliness were it did none of the
> poets of the bright-knolled land say to the
> men of *Fódla* that they should declare war upon
> the foreigners.

Throughout the remainder of the poem, Ó hUiginn addresses O'Rourke directly and advises him regarding an appropriate response to this externally-driven threat to Ireland. He envisages a situation in which Ireland would be united behind O'Rourke in his attempts to defeat the crown's forces ('leis ón tuinn chalaidh go' chéile raghaidh Éire ar aonchogadh'). The country would suffer much in the ensuing war with castles deserted, crops ravaged and famine. However, once O'Rourke had proved his mettle on the field of battle, the English would wish to seek terms of peace ('na Goill ó chrích iathbhuig Almhan iarrfuid snadhmadh síothchána'). Even in this case, Ó hUiginn warned Brian na Múrtha to exercise due caution to avoid being duped by their apparently conciliatory overtures ('Ná meallaid le millsi briathar Brian mhac Briain ó Bhréifneachaibh').[41]

Having warned O'Rourke of English guile, Ó hUiginn underlined the presumption that Brian would enjoy widespread support among the *Gaoidhil* for his campaign against a common enemy. Brian could particularly count on the support of those families related to his mother, Gráinne, daughter of Manus O'Donnell (ob. 1563) ('Beid na fréamha ó bhfuil a mháthair fá mhac Briain'). Once Brian assembled his army, the poet considers the capture of Dublin his logical priority ('Ríoghraidh Ghaoidheal gluaisfid ainnséin go hÁth Cliath don chéidiarraidh'). Of course, the idea of sacking Dublin, the centre of Tudor administration, would have carried with it the affective symbolism of a resurgent Gaelic polity. He further stresses that any success in an onslaught against the English would only be achieved with great loss of life on both sides ('budh iomdha marbh Goill is Gaoidhil').[42] Ó hUiginn provides a summary encapsulation of his political outlook in quatrain sixty-eight, a declaration which may also be taken as a statement of the dominant theme in this poem:[43]

> Muidhfidh ainnséin ar fhóir Saxan
> ré síol Ghaoidhil ghéirreannaigh,
> nách bia do shíor ón ágh d'fhógra
> ós chlár Fhódla acht Éireannaigh.

> Then will the Saxon tribe be vanquished by
> the seed of keen-weaponed *Gaoidhil*, so that
> from the proclamation of war there will never
> be any save Irishmen over the land of *Fódla*.

On the basis of an analysis of three poems by Ó hUiginn, it is possible to speak of his innovative political agenda. He was obviously concerned to advocate ethnic cohesion between the *Gaoidhil* and the gaelicised Anglo-Normans and he sought to highlight the negative implications for both communities of the English presence in Ireland. The poet envisaged a common and inclusive Irish front (*Éireannaigh*) resisting Tudor expansion by means of force.

The motif of malevolent English guile also appears in a poem entitled 'Fuath gach fir fuidheall a thuaighe' composed by Tuileagna Ruadh Ó Maolchonaire for Feagh McHugh O'Byrne (ob. 1597). Feagh McHugh succeeded his father, Hugh McShane O'Byrne, as lord of *Gabhal Raghnuill* in Wicklow in 1579. Feagh had achieved prominence as a result of the part he played, in association with the Viscount Baltinglass, in the Leinster rising of 1580.[44] O'Byrne won special renown for his defeat of the lord deputy, Lord Grey de Wilton, at Glenmalure.

The poem may date to 1581 when Feagh submitted to the Dublin administration. The poet warned O'Byrne to be especially vigilant now that he alone among the Gaelic nobility of Leinster retained a measure of autonomy ('ós cionn do chinn tarla an tuagh'). While O'Byrne had weathered the negative attentions of the crown authorities ('Ní chluinim gan chlaoi ó Ghalluibh, a ngné threisi acht tusa a-mháin'), he was not to doubt that no one man alone could deal with the English ('ní gníomh aoinfhir righe rú').[45] Surely, remarked Ó Maolchonaire, Feagh did not think that the English would readily forget the humiliation he had brought on them ('Cionnus tuigios tusa, a Fhiacha, d'éis ar ionnarbais d'fhóir Ghall . . . nách biadh cuimhne ar fhalaidh ann?'). The English will not accept peace easily ('fá shíoth riamh is duilghe Danair') and the author accordingly invokes divine protection for Feagh in the face of their dangerous pride ('Dia mór dot anacol ortha, uabhar is cniocht chloinne Gall').[46]

A salient feature of these poems is their shared consciousness of an intrusive foreign presence in Ireland. Bardic poets tend to differ in their formulation of political responses to the extension of the crown's writ. It is evident from 'D'fhior chogaidh comhailtear síothcháin' that Tadhg Dall considered a concerted plan of military action a desirable reaction to this explicit challenge to Gaelic autonomy. Other poets, while no less hostile to the New English, were prepared to manipulate their presence and view them as a counterweight to be exploited for dynastic ends. This approach is adopted by Maolmuire Mac an Bhaird in a poem of counsel he composed for Hugh Roe O'Donnell (ob. 1602), when the latter was held captive at Dublin Castle in 1590.[47] In 'Iomchair th'atuirse, a Aodh Ruaidh' Mac an Bhaird advised his young addressee to bear with his imprisonment and to endure the inconvenience patiently ('tug, a mheic, foighide it ulc'). Hugh Roe was not the first Gaelic Irishman to suffer incarceration at the hands of foreigners ('ar láimh ghlanshluaighidh Ghall'). The English were in Ireland to stay ('Timcheall cheannais críche Fáil beid Goill go deireadh ndomhnáin') and, in any case, hostility between *Gaill* and *Gaoidhil* had long prevailed ('Ríoghradh Ghall, Gaoidhil Bhanbha riamh go fóill ag freasabhra').[48] The O'Donnells were noteworthy for their conciliatory attitude to the English in the past ('Níor chaith aoinneach riamh romhaibh . . . fiú an orchair in aghaidh Ghoill') and as a result O'Donnell should take advantage of this political credit. It will have been for his own good, as well as in their interest, that the English had detained Hugh Roe in Dublin ('Ar mhaith riotsa agus riú féin rugsad Goill do ghnúis soilléir . . . go hÁth ndaoineach nDuibhlinne'). He had been taken to Dublin to learn the art of temperate lordship ('dod mhúnadh i modhaibh ríogh'). Once Hugh had become conversant with the precepts of enlightened rule ('go beith d'airrdhibh inríodha'), the English would allow him to resume dominion over his family territories ('Léigfid Goill do ghnúis míolla . . . ós chrích gcnóbhuidhe Conaill').[49] It may be argued that in this instance the poet would have been obliged to express pro-English sentiments by reason of O'Donnell's captivity in Dublin. Had Mac an Bhaird deliberately antagonised the authorities, Hugh's delicate position might have been further imperilled. Indeed, a certain amount of self-interest on the part of the poet may also be discerned. He may well have recommended a course of political moderation to Hugh to facilitate his release from Dublin Castle. It is clear from what he says that near anarchy obtained in *Tír Conaill* in the absence of effective political direction. With the return of Hugh Roe to his territories, firm stewardship might once again be expected. At this point, he reveals a personal interest in the restoration of law and order in the O'Donnell lordship. Due to the unsettled conditions, the literati, among other groups, had been driven from their hereditary lands ('Atáid th'éigis is t'ollaimh . . . i dtalmhaibh nár dhúthchais dáibh').[50] Significantly, just some four years later, Maolmuire seems to have modified his views concerning the English in Ireland.

In 'A dhúin thíos atá it éanar', Mac an Bhaird addressed the ruins of Donegal Castle, which had been dismantled by Hugh Roe in 1595 to prevent a strategic bulwark falling into the hands of a crown garrison.[51] The poem follows a conventional path until quatrain twenty when the poet injects a note of displeasure with Hugh. While he had so far mourned the demise of the old castle, he now, quite explicitly, assigns responsibility for its destruction to O'Donnell ('Ó Domhnaill Ruadh, do rí féin, de tháinig . . . lot do mhúir, toghail do thuir').[52] Although he softened this indictment in the following quatrains, Hugh Roe's actions appear to have annoyed him more than it would have been diplomatic to admit. By way of explanation of O'Donnell's demolition of the castle, Mac an Bhaird observes that his behaviour had resulted from fear of an English force seizing the fortress ('d'eagla Dubhghall ndanardha . . . do dhul d'áitreabhadh ionnad'). The threat implicit in the name of Donegal (*Dún na nGall* or 'fortress of the foreigners') becoming a reality caused O'Donnell to act as he had ('D'eagla go n-aibeórthaoi sin, 'Dún na nGall', ribh dá-ríribh').[53] Given the very limited range of choices, dismantlement by O'Donnell was preferable to occupation by the English ('Do dhíobhadh leis Ó nDomhnaill fearr dhuitse ná Danarghoill'). More generally, the poet depicts the English presence in Ireland as a disease in need of a skilled doctor; the physician he had in mind was, not surprisingly, Hugh Roe ('An easláinte is iad na Goill, 's is é an deighliaigh Ó Domhnaill').[54]

Advocacy of resistance to crown hegemony is a distinctive feature of bardic poetry composed during the 1590s. The violent death of the earl of Desmond in 1583 signalled the end of any popular attempt to counter Tudor influence in Munster, while the implementation of the composition of Connacht in 1585 appeared to set a seal on English administrative control in the western province. It is hardly coincidental that the manifestation of more strident attitudes in the poetry in the last decade of the sixteenth century took place against the background of Gaelic military assertiveness during the Nine Years War. The bardic call to resistance seems to have been generalised in intention and not to have applied solely to powerful Gaelic magnates such as O'Neill and O'Donnell. One finds, for instance, a distinguished poet such as

Fearghal Óg Mac an Bhaird recommending a minor nobleman like Philip O'Reilly (ob. 1596) as a potential succour of Ireland ('Tusa, a Philib Phuirt Teamhra, bheanfus di-si a doimheanma').[55]

Opposition to English suzerainty is also a dominant theme in two poems composed during the 1590s preserved in the poem-books of Feagh O'Byrne and his son, Féilim. Although Feagh O'Byrne had been pardoned by the English authorities in 1581 for his involvement in the Leinster rebellion, the semi-feudal and seigneurial style of his rule so close to Dublin was a constant and uncomfortable reminder to the Elizabethan administration of its more or less tenuous hold over the island. When Hugh Roe O'Donnell made his second and successful escape from Dublin Castle in 1591, it was with the help of O'Byrne that he managed to make his way northwards. O'Byrne's open support for the rebellious earl of Tyrone finally forced the lord deputy, Sir William Russell, to launch a surprise attack on Feagh in his mountain fastness in Wicklow in May of 1597. O'Byrne was executed and his quartered body sent to Dublin. Following the death of his father, Féilim went northwards to serve under O'Neill's command. Later in the same year, he returned to Glenmalure and with a force supplied by the earl of Tyrone, he engaged in open confrontation with the English administration. However, with the appointment in 1600 of Lord Mountjoy as lord deputy, and of Sir George Carew as president of Munster in the same year the English position was greatly strengthened. In December 1600 Mountjoy drove Féilim out of the O'Byrne homestead at Ballinacor and subsequently burned the house and adjoining countryside. Finally, the defeat of the Irish at Kinsale in 1601 spelled the end of O'Byrne autonomy in *Gabhal Raghnuill*.[56]

In the poem 'Ésga an oinigh fán aird toir' Feagh O'Byrne is portrayed as a moon rising in the east who will come to the aid of a beleaguered Ireland ('Ré cabartha Chláir Gaoidhiol').[57] Conventional imagery is employed to present Feagh as a potential spouse of *Éire* ('Éire ar a thí ó tharla'). In this case, the poet Domhnall Ó hUiginn unambiguously depicts the country as subject to foreign dominion. It was time the *Gaoidhil* roused themselves to reclaim their patrimony ('A n-oighriocht is dóibh dleaghair do ghabháil ar Gaoidhealuibh'), namely Irish land occupied by the English ('fonn Banbha do bhaoi ag Galluibh').[58] By way of a traditional analogy for the present unfortunate state of the country, he recounts the story of Balar's oppression of Ireland in the past ('Sgél oirdheirc arar cóir cion fríoth liom ar leatrom Gaoidhiol'). Like Lugh Lámhfhada, Feagh would become his people's saviour.[59] Refining his depiction of Feagh as a messianic Gaelic liberator, Ó hUiginn alludes to an old prophecy which predicted Gaelic victory over the foreigners ('Do thairngir fáidh fada ó shoin treise Gaoidhiol ar Ghalloibh'). He implies that Feagh would defeat the invaders ('Mac Aodha bhloghas bearnaidh, do-clos sin a seinleabhraibh') and because of this, the English of the Pale had better pay careful attention to his movements ('Ná cluinid Goill guirt Midhe . . . triall ar Fhiachaidh go Bóinn Breagh').[60]

The poem beginning 'Dia libh, a laochruidh Gaoidhiol' is an aggressive denunciation of English aspirations in Ireland and it urges the Gaelic Irish to resist and to overthrow Elizabethan hegemony.[61] While the poet, Aonghus Ó Dálaigh, ostensibly addresses the men of *Gabhal Raghnuill*, and although the poem is extant in Feagh's collection, it is as much directed at the wider Gaelic community as the O'Byrnes. It appears that the author considered the O'Byrnes a receptive audience for his stirring exhortation, a reasonable assumption given their record of resolute opposition to crown authority in south Leinster.[62] A dramatic and clarion call to arms is made in the opening quatrain:[63]

> Dia libh, a laochruidh Gaoidhiol!
> ná cluintior claoiteacht oraibh;
> riamh níor thuilliobhair masla
> a n-am catha iná cogaidh.

> God be with the heroes of the *Gaoidhil*!
> let not defeatism be reported of you,
> you have never earned reproach in time
> of battle or war.

The poet went on to urge the Gaelic Irish to fight for what he obviously regarded as the most important asset at risk as a result of English expansion – land:[64]

> Déntar libh coinghleic calma,
> a bhuidhion armghlan fhaoiltioch,
> fá cheann bhar bhfearuinn dúthchais,
> puirt úrghoirt innsi Gaoidhiol.

> Let you, joyful and bright weaponed company,
> struggle bravely for your native land,
> homesteads of the fair field of the
> island of the *Gaoidhil*.

The claim that the English had taken control of land in Ireland is highlighted in quatrain four when Ó Dálaigh once more urges the *Gaoidhil* to engage in arms the foreigners who occupied their ancestral lands ('Fearr bheith . . . ag seilg troda ar fhéin eachtrann 'gá bhfuil fearann bhar sinnsear').[65] In the introductory stanzas Ó Dálaigh calls on the *Gaoidhil* to flock to the standard of rebellion. No sooner had he begun to call on them to initiate a campaign of resistance than he presented his audience with an overview of the state of affairs prevailing in Ireland. He accuses the Gaelic Irish of having acquiesced in English overlordship. It was not because of any inherent military weakness on the part of their nobility that they had proved so passive in the face of English aggrandisement:[66]

Ní tacha lúidh ná lámhaigh
tug oruibh, ágbhaidh Banbha,
beith díbh urramach umhal
do mhearshluagh gusmhar ghallda.

It is no lack of support in vigour or
firepower that has caused you, young men
of Ireland, to be passive and submissive
before the pushing and powerful English mob.

In Ó Dálaigh's estimation, God had willed that the Irish should not stand united ('Acht nách deóin le Dia, a Éire, sibh le chéile do chongnamh') and were it not for this disunity, the London administration would not have consolidated so easily in Ireland ('ní bheith bhar mbuadh a n-éinfheacht ag sluagh críoch léidmheach Lonndan').[67] The idea that God had intervened in the country's political destiny, with resulting misfortune for the *Gaoidhil*, becomes a relatively common theme in bardic poetry, especially in the reign of James VI and I. This poem provides an early example of a providentialist explication of political evolution which was increasingly adduced to account for communal crisis.

It troubled the poet to think that Gaelic nobles were considered by the crown authorities as no better than common outlaws or 'wood-kerns' ('s nách goirthior dhíobh 'na ndúthchus acht ceithearn chúthail choilleadh'), who had been driven to the most remote and inaccessible regions, while the English occupied the fertile land ('s fonn mín an Chláir-si Críomhthuin ag feadhain fhíochmhair eachtronn').[68] The dire predicament which confronts the *Gaoidhil* ('s a liacht námha ar tí a ngona') causes Ó Dálaigh to experience a fretful and disturbed sleep ('do-bheir orm codladh corrach'). He would only relax when he knew that the warriors of Leinster, presumably the O'Byrnes, had dealt a final fatal blow to the foreigners ('bídh m'aigne suilbhir subhach').[69] Nonetheless, he cannot avoid confronting the reality of the situation. The *Gaoidhil* are being decimated by the foreigners who had come across the sea ('na Goill-si tig tar tonnmhuir do chomhloit gasradh Gaoidhiol'). Especially depressing for Ó Dálaigh is the fact that even the O'Byrnes were no longer safe in their once secluded valley of Glenmalure ('méd a nguaisi san ghleann-so do chuir mo mheanma a míneart').[70]

The third O'Byrne poem to be considered was composed by Fearghal Mac Eochadha for Féilim, Feagh's son and successor as lord of *Gabhal Raghnuill*. The poem concerns his proclamation as a rebel and it may possibly date from 1598, when Féilim was named as one of the leaders of the rising in Leinster.[71] While the political outlook in 'Ésga an oinigh fán aird toir' and 'Dia libh, a laochruidh Gaoidhiol' is vehemently opposed to English consolidation and confrontationalist in tone, Mac Eochadha in 'Égcóir do fógradh Féilim' is ambivalent and non-committal in his approach to the English. In a series of alternating quatrains, he dispenses advice to Féilim which is both pro- and anti-war in turn. Although he expresses regret that Féilim had been outlawed ('toisc dá ttáinig daoirchréidhim'), and though it grieved him that the latter is obliged to lead the life of a hunted criminal ('Mairg fá deara a dhul ar cheilt, mairg bél do bhrosd a dhíbeirt'), the poem suggests that Mac Eochadha considered a campaign of resistance against the English futile. Admittedly, Féilim had been unique among the great figures in the Gaelic historical tradition in obtaining help for his cause in Ireland itself. For instance, O'Byrne had secured support from the Ulstermen ('s fuair Féilim ó fhéin Uladh a nÉirinn féin fuasguladh').[72] Mac Eochadha contrasts his subject with Dermot Mac-Murrough, a figure infamous in popular historical tradition because of his involvement in the coming of the Anglo-Normans in 1169. In this obscure comparison, it is claimed that MacMurrough succeeded in claiming land in Ireland only because he received outside support ('Ní dheachaidh Diarmuid na nGall a seilbh coda na comhrann d'iath Banbha acht lé neart a-noir'). Crucially, Féilim still held complete sway in his patrimony ('atá th'athardha ar th'ionchoibh'), and given that no part of *Gabhal Raghnuill* had been occupied by the English ('ó nách fuil fód fá Ghalluibh d'fhearann aoinmheic Raghnallaigh'), he suggests that O'Byrne avoid open confrontation with the authorities.[73] He continues with a convoluted discussion about whether Féilim should decide on peace or war, yet he is more convincing in his argument for a cessation of hostilities. Towards the close of 'Égcóir do fógradh Féilim', Mac Eochadha stresses that Féilim had undertaken his due share of martial duty ('is lór dhuit a ndearnobhair do chreachthurnamh Chláir Dá Thí') and, in any case, he was not to rely on the possibility of obtaining aid from Ulster ('fir na slimchiabh, sluaigh Uladh, imchian uaibh a n-anaghal').[74] While his reasoning is opaque and often labyrinthine, Mac Eochadha appears to be moving away from the simple anti-English stance evident in the two poems composed for Feagh O'Byrne. The complexity of the poem may reflect the poet's intellectual difficulties in adapting the bardic political paradigm to an enforced transformation of Gaelic notions of autonomy. Though Mac Eochadha proposes a policy of appeasement to Féilim, he ensures, by alluding to his supposed achievements, that such a course would involve no loss of face for O'Byrne in traditional terms.

A poem for Hugh Roe O'Donnell composed sometime during the period 1597–8 illustrates its author's reading of the implications of the inherently politicised bardic communal role. This piece beginning 'Cionnas do fhúigfinnse Aodh' was composed by Cú Chonnacht Ó Dálaigh on the occasion of his proposed leave-taking of O'Donnell to return to his native west Munster.[75] The introductory stanzas are conventional in their treatment; while the poet hoped to make his way home, affection for Hugh Roe would make any such move difficult. In stanzas five and six, Ó Dálaigh introduces a theme which dominates the remainder of the poem. If he were to head south, he feared interception by English forces and arraignment for various crimes:[76]

> Saoilim go gcuirfidhe im cheann
> dom thír dhúthchais dá ndigheam
> (má atá a rochtain i ndán dhamh)
> a lán d'fholtaibh gan ionnramh.

> I think that were I to go to my
> country – if I am destined to reach
> it – I would be accused of many
> reckless offences.

The English would charge him most immediately with having spent time in Ulster with O'Donnell, a well-known enemy of the Dublin administration ('Is sé adéarthaoi arís rinne Aodh Ruadh díobhadh Duibhlinne . . . gurbh é m'aonchara d'Ultaibh'). He realises that if he were to find himself in such a situation he might deny the patronage granted him by Hugh ('go séanfainn méid mo mhoirne ó ghéig mhéarchuirr Mhodhairne').[77] In fact, Ó Dálaigh was certain that more charges against him would follow – the English would surely seize the opportunity presented by his incarceration to confront him with what they considered crimes committed by bardic poets in general ('maith chreidim go gcuirfidis níos mó im cheann do choiribh'). He has his inquisitors speak directly in that part of the poem where the English enumerate supposed bardic transgressions. In fact, this fascinating section illustrates a poet listing the crimes with which he feared the authorities might charge him. Ó Dálaigh's personal preamble to this litany establishes the tone of the ensuing quatrains:[78]

> Adéardaois más díobh meise,
> aos cuma mo cheirdise
> do-bheir i nGaoidhealaibh gomh
> 's neimh ré saoirfhearaibh Saxan.

> They would say, if it is the case that I
> belong to those practitioners of my art
> who excite bitterness in Irishmen and
> enmity against Saxon nobles.

The central consideration unifying the various charges levelled against bardic poets by the English is that they perceived them as constituting an influential grouping which, by a variety of means, encouraged the *Gaoidhil* in violent opposition to their suzerainty. It is of note that Ó Dálaigh has his interlocutors speak in an all-island as opposed to regional context. In the opening stanza of his roll-call of bardic 'misdemeanours', Ó Dálaigh places a most significant charge in the mouths of the English, a sentiment destined to become a rallying cry for later generations of nationalists:[79]

> Maoidhid orra uaisle a sean;
> reacaid re macaibh Míleadh

Banbha gurab dóibh dleaghair,
labhra ar nach cóir creideamhain.

They extol the nobility of their forefathers
to the descendants of *Míl*. They declare to them
that Ireland is their due inheritance – words that
ought not to be believed.

In effect, Ó Dálaigh delineates the nucleus of a political programme by presenting it as the antithesis of the English viewpoint outlined in the 'accusations' against him. The 'English' claimed that among the devices employed by bardic poets to foment unrest within Irish Gaelic ranks was their practice of disseminating knowledge of ancestral dynasts among audiences ('luadh ar a ríoghaibh reampa'). In addition, poets also prophesied calamity and war ('tairngire an uilc 's an eissídh') with the intention of setting the *Gaoidhil* against the English ('d'ionnlach Gall re Gaoidhealaibh').[80] This poem affords a unique view of a *fileadh* formulating a coherent political response to conquest within a referential framework defined by ethnic sensibility and consciousness of the potency of bardic political influence in the face of external challenge.

The English interlocutors focus their attention on Ó Dálaigh in particular. On the assumption that he resembled other bardic poets ('Sibhse féin mar gach fear dhíobh'), it followed that he too was intent on glorifying Gaelic misdeeds ('báidh leat móradh a míghníomh') and encouraging more turmoil ('gríosadh olc is dot airrdhibh').[81] An account is given of occasions when Ó Dálaigh accompanied Hugh Roe on military hostings and the more explicit references seem to date these expeditions to between 1595 and 1598. To conclude this indictment, the 'English' held Cú Chonnacht guilty of far more than the actual charges just outlined ('Lia th'fholta ioná a n-éilighthir'). For reasons such as those outlined, Cú Chonnacht questioned the feasibility of passing through the crown's jurisdiction ('cia dár dholta fa a ndlighthibh?'). In truth, he would meet with misfortune if he left Hugh Roe for the subjugated south of Ireland ('olc uaras má imthighim go Leith Mogha is daor ndlighthe – dola ó Aodh ar imirche').[82] He establishes a dichotomy between an Ulster under Gaelic control and the south of Ireland subject to foreign suzerainty. 'Cionnas do fhúigfinnse Aodh' is curious in so far as Ó Dálaigh makes no attempt to advise O'Donnell with regard to the English presence; rather he chronicles somewhat impassively the misdeeds for which he believed the English held him responsible. While the poem provides an unparalleled insight into bardic self-perception *vis-à-vis* crown hegemony in the late 1590s, it also presents a picture of an author convinced that the English were not to be easily dislodged from Ireland. He appears to envisage a situation in which the Dublin administration dominated the south and the Gaelic Irish maintained a measure of autonomy in Ulster.

While the evidence suggests that some bardic poets saw opposition as the sole guarantee of Gaelic dominion in the early and middle years of the 1590s, it seems that by the last years of the sixteenth century bardic attitudes had become more uncertain and fragmented. Eochaidh Ó hEódhusa in the poem beginning 'Fód codarsna críoch Bhanbha' wrestled with the problem of interpreting Irish history in the light of continuous strife on the island. Ostensibly composed in praise of the martial attributes of Conor MacDermot (ob. *c.* 1607) of Moylurg, the poem operates at two discursive levels. At first glance, Ó hEódhusa appears to follow conventional eulogistic practice when he lauds MacDermot's prowess. Concurrently, however, in his comments on the nature of the perpetual warfare in Ireland, he reflects on contemporary events and attempts to formulate an appropriate political response. There is no extant evidence on which to base a precise date for the piece, nonetheless, it was certainly composed sometime between 1595 and 1600.[83] Ó hEódhusa argues that there had always been turmoil and warfare in Ireland, in fact this discord invariably stemmed from the protracted attempts of the *Gaoidhil* and the English to acquire exclusive mastery of the island:[84]

> Meinic a-niodh 's a-nallain
> miosgais chroidhe ag cniocht Ghallaibh
> do chloinn mhéirsheing Ghaoidhil Ghlais
> fa Éirinn bhfaoilidh bhfoltchais.

> Often, both now and in the past,
> have the English knights had hatred in their hearts
> for the slender-fingered children of *Gaoidheal Glas*,
> because of Ireland of the pleasing and elaborate foliage.

It may be assumed that when Ó hEódhusa alluded to the foreigners who had previously fought for domination in Ireland, he had the medieval Anglo-Norman colonists in mind. Such conflict had resulted in numerous deaths on both sides ('Iomdha leacht Ghoill is Ghaoidhil'), yet many worthy deeds had been enterprised ('iomdha éacht do b'ionmhaoidhimh'). Mutual hatred caused the *Gaoidhil* and the English to ravage the island ('Ríoghraidh Ghall, Gaoidhil Bhanbha, gnáth leo lot na hathardha, re gomh croidhe dá chéile'). Given that the New English subjected MacDermot to almost constant onslaught, Connacht was particularly affected by despoliation ('Ní choisgid aonlá d'fhoghail Goill Fhódla d'fhuath Chonchobhair'). Yet Conor's prowess as a warrior ensured that he avenged all wrongs inflicted on him ('bídh amhlaidh ar fhuath na nGall faghlaidh a dtuath 'n-a dtiomchall').[85] Ó hEódhusa feels that Ireland had been and was then subject to great strife over the vexed question of Gaelic versus English ascendancy. He appears to accept the logic of the premise that warfare was endemic on the island. Having acquiesced in the proposed inevitability of Anglo-Irish conflict, Ó hEódhusa does not attempt to debate the question any further. Such hostility strikes him as axiomatic in the island's political landscape. Accordingly, the reasons underlying ethnic conflict, the validity or otherwise of English ambitions in Ireland, the appropriateness of Gaelic reactions to crown aggrandisement are all issues remarkable by their absence from the poem. He accepts without comment Ireland's turbulent political climate and provides no analytical review of the factors or considerations determining his gloomy prognosis.

The four remaining poems which are examined here illustrate aspects of the acute intellectual flux which characterises the bardic institution in the last years of the sixteenth century. In 'Fréamha an chogaidh críoch Laighion', Giolla Íosa Ó Dálaigh urges Féilim O'Byrne and his brother Réamonn to resist English encroachment. Ó Dálaigh begins by alluding to the key role the province of Leinster had played in efforts to frustrate Tudor expansion ('Dí táinig cogadh Gall ré Gaoidhioluibh'). From the arrival of the Anglo-Normans onwards, the province had known only occasional peace ('níor shaoghlaigh síothcháin acht seal fá fhaobhruibh líochláir Laighean'), and moreover the *Gaoidhil* had suffered at the hands of recent newcomers:[86]

> Mar sin dóibh (díochra an pudhar)
> dá n-athchur, dá n-uathaghadh,
> lé fíorShaghsuibh bonn frí bonn
> fán bhfonn síodharsuidh slatchorr.

> Thus were they dispossessed and diminished
> in numbers (vehement the misfortune) by the
> true English, who were united upon the ancient,
> wonderful, tapering-branched land.

Fortunately, two individuals had managed to survive this process of attrition, Féilim and Réamonn O'Byrne, both of whom were ready to aid the Leinster *Gaoidhil* ('Mairid d'fhuidheall na healta dias fhóirfios a hairmearta').[87] Having established the military credentials of both men, Giolla Íosa devotes space, over a series of six quatrains, to general comments on Glenmalure ('Fríoth daingion dá ndearnsad bun, dá ngoirthear Gleann Mo Luradh'). An exemplum is introduced which recounts the story of Lugh Mheann's two sons, Fiacha and Eacha. Apparently, both sons had approached their father in search of an inheritance. Their demands, however, were met with rebuttal by Lugh Mheann, who instead advised them to do as he had done in his youth; for Lugh had won his land by the vigour of his hand ('Fríoth liom-sa a los mo láimhe').[88] Ó Dálaigh makes it clear that he had retold this story with the aim of providing an analogy for the O'Byrne brothers so that they could begin the task of securing their patrimony by force of arms.

An internal reference in 'Fréamha an chogaidh críoch Laighion' suggests that the poem was composed in 1600. While the evidence of this composition might be taken to imply that O'Byrne was resolute in his defiance of crown authority, the historical record presents a quite different picture. In September 1600 Féilim made at least a temporary submission to the government when he applied to the earl of Ormond for a month's grace. By December of that year the lord deputy, Mountjoy, had driven O'Byrne out of the family homestead at Ballinacor. Féilim and his brother Réamonn then sued for peace, obtaining a pardon in March 1601. Yet by July, both men had reneged upon their agreement with the Dublin authorities and were in open revolt. The defeat of the Irish forces at Kinsale in December 1601 spelled an end to the volatile policy of Féilim vis-à-vis the crown administration.[89] Interpreted in the light of extant historical data, Ó Dálaigh's poem appears an unconvincing response, in political terms at least, to the situation facing the O'Byrnes in the period 1600–1. The poet seems preoccupied with extolling the topographical merits of Glenmalure and illustrating his bardic scholarship by allusion to an obscure exemplum. He provides neither an intelligible nor cogent analysis of the O'Byrne predicament. By means of a pseudo-historical analogy, the poet certainly endorses a policy of opposition to the English. The feasibility or likely success of such a proposition are passed over, however, in favour of apparently abstract antiquarian scholarship.

Mathghamhain Ó hUiginn's poem beginning 'Créd do choisc cogadh Laighean' dates to sometime between the accession of Féilim O'Byrne as lord of *Gabhal Raghnuill* in 1597 and the battle of Kinsale in 1601.[90] The fact that the poet seems to have composed the piece while Féilim was avoiding active engagement in hostilities may suggest a date during the period 1600–1 when O'Byrne sought peace terms on at least two occasions. Like 'Fréamha an chogaidh críoch Laighion', it appears to be an attempt to encourage Féilim to continue military resistance against the English administration, a path which it seems Féilim had temporarily abandoned at the time of composition. Ó hUiginn ventures some conventional observations about the past military record of the O'Byrnes. Significantly, he implies displeasure with the peace made with the English ('an umhla nua-sa a-niugh'). According to him, O'Byrne and his family would now devote their time to peaceful domestic pursuits ('barrbhuain bu-dheacht a ndícheall'). It is obvious that Ó hUiginn is not satisfied with the notion of a passive Féilim attending to his domestic duties. He develops a succinct train of thought which suggests that Féilim could only remain true to his heritage by openly seeking war. He dwells with deliberate relish on O'Byrne's past record of military action, portraying him as the quintessential Gaelic hero ('Ní choigleadh a chrú a gcathaibh').[91] Having demonstrated O'Byrne's military prowess, he introduces an allegorical, but vivid, exemplum as another consideration in his argument for a renewal of hostilities. In summary, this apologue describes an island containing two factions, one of snakes, the other of lions. In the poet's opinion this schema represents the situation in Ireland where the English correspond to the snakes ('na nathracha Goill Ghuirt Breagh') while the Leinster warriors (more precisely the men of *Gabhal Raghnuill*?) under Féilim's direction are to be equated with the lions ('na leómhain laochruidh Laighean . . . is é an flaithleómhan Féilim'). Yet he effects a deft transition to actuality by depicting the O'Byrnes' stance at the time of composition:[92]

Ní thaobhaid Laighnigh lot Goill,
ní thógbhuid airm dá n-ealchoing;
ortha féin do chló a gconfaidh
ón ló as réidh do Raghnallchaibh.

The Leinstermen undertake not to plunder the English,
they abstain from taking weapons from their rack;
since the men of *Gabhal Raghnuill* are inclined to peace
they subdue their rage.

While Mathghamhain Ó hUiginn does not directly criticise O'Byrne for having submitted to the crown's writ, he manages by subtle juxtaposition of imagery to imply unhappiness with Féilim's course of action. The quatrain mentioned already, coming immediately after the exemplum concerning lions and snakes, represents an admonishment of O'Byrne for lethargy of spirit. The concerted process of insinuation evident in the poem reaches a climax with the poet's claim that if the English antagonise Hugh Roe O'Donnell again hostilities are inevitable:[93]

Giodh eadh trá, dá ngríosdais Goill
fearg ar-ís ar Ua nDomhnuill,
mór bhfear dárbh athfhabhairt soin;
ceadh acht athadhoint fhalaigh?

However, if the English again arouse
the anger of O'Donnell, this will be
a renewed tempering for many men,
what is that but a rekindling of enmity?

Once the spark had been ignited, the ensuing fire of rebellion would prove difficult to extinguish:[94]

An teine ó théid a ttreisi,
deacair eadráin oirthei-si.

Once the fire becomes vigorous,
it is difficult to bring it under control.

To cap his argument, Ó hUiginn devotes a number of quatrains to persuading O'Byrne that if he were to stand against the English he would not find himself lacking for support among the Gaelic Irish. In 'Créd do choisc cogadh

Laighean', Ó hUiginn displays a clarity of purpose absent in 'Fréamha an chogaidh críoch Laighion'. While both poems seek to persuade Féilim O'Byrne of the legitimacy of active opposition to the crown's dominion, Ó hUiginn succeeds in presenting his message with a subtlety and sophistication absent in Giolla Íosa's poem. Of course, both pieces must be read against the historical background of O'Byrne's uncertain course of action in the period 1600–1. An unusual element in the poems is a consciousness of localised Leinster affiliation. At first glance, the poets' heightening of regional aware-ness may seem anomalous given the pan-insular context of the challenge to Gaelic Ireland's cultural and political integrity. It may well be that they sought to fashion a wider political agenda on the basis of the application of a local strategic awareness with all-island implications.

The last two poems under consideration here were composed for Hugh Roe O'Donnell in 1602, the first on his departure for Spain, while the second is an elegy composed on his death in that country. Following the defeat of the Irish at Kinsale in December 1601, Hugh Roe visited Spain with the intention of persuading King Philip III to send reinforcements to enable a resumption of hostilities. However, O'Donnell died in Simancas in September 1602 before accomplishing his mission. Eoghan Ruadh Mac an Bhaird composed the piece beginning 'Rob soruidh t'eachtra, a Aodh Ruaidh' as a type of bardic *bon voy-age* for O'Donnell. At the time of its composition, the lord of *Tír Conaill* seems to have already set off on his journey.[95] An interesting aspect of both 'Rob soruidh t'eachtra, a Aodh Ruaidh' and Fearghal Óg Mac an Bhaird's 'Teasda Éire san Easbáinn' centres on the all-island context of the presentation. The beginning of Eoghan Ruadh's poem is a conventional exposition of bardic sen-timent: he wishes O'Donnell a safe journey and good fortune with his Span-ish mission. Nonetheless, he was well aware of the wider implications of Hugh Roe's trip. Gaelic Ireland's well-being depended on the positive out-come of his diplomatic initiative:[96]

> Gá ttú acht as tingheall sláinte
> do thoisg, nó as tuar anbhfáilte,
> gibé thí do thaobh t'eachtra
> do shní, a Aodh, ar n-aigeanta.

> In short thy journey is a pledge of
> health or a presage of sickness;
> whatever comes of thy venture, Hugh,
> it wrings our hearts.

The whole of Ireland, nobility, literati and commoners, anxiously awaited the result of his mission. In view of the fact that O'Donnell had embarked on a venture concerning the relief of the *Gaoidhil*, there were many people wait-ing expectantly in Ireland ('D'furtacht shleachta Gaoidhil Ghlais tar muir ón tráth do thriallais'). The poet is obviously much concerned with Hugh Roe's progress and fate. He juxtaposes his trepidation for O'Donnell with an emphasis on his anxiety regarding Ireland's future. It was not so much Hugh's possible misfortune which grieved him most but rather Ireland's uncertain destiny should O'Donnell perish or his diplomatic initiative founder:[97]

> Inis Chuinn do chleacht leónadh,
> gá ttám as dí theigeómhadh,
> dá ttíste ruibh god rochtain
> tar muir ngríste nguasachtaigh.

> Ireland that has experienced suffering,
> it is she, in short, that would
> feel the blow, if you should be prevented
> from journeying over the raging perilous sea.

Mac an Bhaird points to several figures in the Gaelic tradition who had been in a similar position to that of O'Donnell and who had all failed in their efforts to succour Ireland at the time of direst necessity. Tuathal Teachtmhar, Conghal Cláireineach, Eoghan Mór and Mac Con had all endured deprivation and hardship when they came to the island's aid. In the present case, O'Donnell boarded ship because of Ireland's misfortune ('do dheasgaibh olc na hÉireann'). In this vessel sailing to Spain rested Ireland's hopes for the guarantee of Gaelic political integrity:[98]

> Atá san luingsin tar lear
> oireachas Insi Gaoidheal
> a síodh, a ghuaisbhearta, a glóir,
> díon a huaisleachta, a honóir.

> There are in that ship beyond the sea the
> sovereignty of Ireland, her peace,
> her perilous exploits, her glory,
> the defence of her nobility, her honour.

Eoghan Ruadh must have been sorely grieved in due course to hear the news of Hugh's death some months after his departure from Ireland. Fearghal Óg Mac an Bhaird's 'Teasda Éire san Easbáinn' is an elegy on a grand scale for both O'Donnell and Gaelic Ireland.[99] In a manner similar to that of 'Rob soruidh t'eachtra, a Aodh Ruaidh' the poet mourns the loss of a pan-insular Gaelic leader as much as a regional magnate. Indeed, at various stages in the poem, O'Donnell and Ireland are portrayed as synonymous ('Uainn don Easbáinn d'fhagháil bháis do-chuaidh Fódla, fáth dóláis'). Hugh Roe died before he could secure Ireland's sovereignty ('Níor hanadh tuir Tholcha Fáil re flaitheas Éirionn d'fhagháil') and now, tragically, Ireland was dominated by foreigners ('danair indte in gach éntaobh'). Moreover, on the passing of O'Donnell it could be said that no part of Ireland belonged to the *Gaoidhil*:[100]

> Ag Gaoidhealaibh go nua a-nois
> d'éis mheic Aodha meic Mhaghnuis
> ní fhuil cuid do Chathraigh Fhloinn;
> marthain duid a Í Dhomhnoill!

> Now, of late, after the son of Hugh
> son of Maghnas, no part of Ireland
> is in the possession of the *Gaoidhil*.
> Hail to you, O'Donnell!

Hugh had spent ten years attempting to unify Ireland in the face of foreign aggression ('do mhian uamchobhra Éirenn'). Now that he had died, Ireland was merely a lifeless image ('Íomhaigh gan anam Éire'), a country cast adrift like a vessel without steering equipment ('Arthrach gan sdiúir Banbha Breagh'). In sum, it had been Hugh's devotion to his native land which ultimately resulted in his death abroad ('Aodh Ó Domhnaill Dhúin na bhFionn don Easbáinn d'fhurtocht Éirionn').[101]

The evidence presented here illustrates bardic consciousness of a non-indigenous and aggressive ethnic presence in Ireland. In general, it may be said that the sentiments expressed with regard to external socio-political intrusion advocate a strategic oppositional process to the crown's actual and aspirational status. As might be expected in the context of colonial consolidation, poets in differing compositional circumstances were not encompassed by a hermetic intellectual homogeneity and individual practitioners diverged in terms of reactive assessments of the implications of ethno-political dissension. Overall, the corpus reveals bardic perception of a high degree of elemental political and cultural conflict inherent in Gaelic and New English encounters. In 'Teasda Éire san Easbáinn', Fearghal Óg Mac an Bhaird echoes this notion of a binary ethnic conflict which figures in many poems composed during Elizabeth's reign and he also anticipates themes which are emblematic of Jacobean bardic poetry. The sense of communal disaster and the notion of stoic anticipation evident in 'Teasda Éire san Easbáinn' become common elements in the final phase of classical bardic composition. In addition to a dynamic presentation of politicised nationality, a current of strategic ambivalence, reflecting the tangled complexities of the Gaelic polity's predicament at this juncture, runs through poetry dating from the late Elizabethan period. Evidently, some poets articulated forceful and decisive responses to the crown's challenge to Gaelic society. Yet, reactions among the Gaelic intelligentsia were not uniform in their decoding of socio-political crisis. If some poets advocated confrontationalist attitudes, others appear disposed to suggest a course of manipulative containment or appeasement. While the retrospective verdict of popular Irish historical consciousness has generally tended to favour the militant tradition, it should be emphasised that in this context the discursive duality of the bardic approach is significant in historiographical terms. The complementary diversity of the collective bardic assessment is a telling indication of a classically homogeneous intellectual élite mediating a fundamental reordering of political priorities. Had the *fileadha* responded to change with monolithic uniformity, it would have underscored the continuity of the medieval mindset. The coherent duality of response visible in the poetry was made possible by the dynamism of an élite experiencing a modernising transformation.

Bardic Interpretation of Cultural Flux, 1558–1603

It is indicative of Gaelic/Anglo-Norman ethnic coalescence that an early statement of Irish cultural patriotism in the Elizabethan period occurs in two poems composed not by a bardic poet, but by an Oxford-educated nobleman of Anglo-Norman background. Uilliam Nuinseann (*anglice* William Nugent) was the son of Richard Nugent (ob. 1559), eighth baron of Delvin in Meath. By all accounts, the family was wholly immersed in the Gaelic cultural idiom. Uilliam's brother Sir Christopher, ninth baron of Delvin, compiled a primer of Irish for Queen Elizabeth when she expressed an interest in learning the rudiments of the language. Notwithstanding their Anglo-Norman origins and English education, both brothers were implicated in Viscount Baltinglass's uprising in Leinster in the summer of 1580. Following the imprisonment of Christopher in Dublin on suspicion of complicity in the Baltinglass affair, Uilliam in protest and frustration led a separate, although short-lived, revolt against the Dublin administration, which drew support from both Anglo-Norman Palesmen and Gaelic families such as the O'Reillys and O'Connors. During the greater part of 1581, Nuinseann engaged in intermittent and somewhat desultory skirmishes with English forces in and around the Pale. By November of the same year, the revolt had more or less petered out with the apprehension and execution of several of Nuinseann's leading lieutenants. Uilliam fled the country in January of the following year and spent the years between 1582 and 1584 in France and Rome in the company of his sometime ally and confidant Brian MacGeoghegan. In Rome, he unsuccessfully sought the papacy's support to mount an invasion of Ireland. Ultimately, however, he returned to Ireland in August 1584 via Scotland where he acquired a small expeditionary force. Following some months of ineffectual manoeuvring, Nuinseann submitted to lord deputy Perrot and made a formal submission at Dublin early in December 1584. Uilliam lived until 1625, and although his lands were not officially restored to him until 1608, he never again played an active role in politics.[102]

Nuinseann's two poems reflect the emergence of a newly-forged Irish patriotic sensibility. 'Diombáidh triall ó thulchaibh Fáil' may date from the time he left Ireland to pursue studies at Oxford where, in 1571, at the age of twenty-one he matriculated as a student at Hart Hall. The content of the second poem appears to indicate its composition in England. In 'Diombáidh triall ó thulchaibh Fáil' he presents a picture of Ireland which is distinctly utopian. Even if moving in the grandest circles in England he claims he would always yearn for his native land:[103]

> Dá bhfaomhadh Dia dhamh tar mh'ais
> rochtain dom dhomhan dúthchais,
> ó Ghallaibh ní ghéabhainn dol
> go clannaibh séaghainn Sacsan.

> Were God to grant me return to my native
> country, I should accept from the *Gaill*
> no offer of visiting families of England's
> nobles.

In 'Fada i n-éagmais inse Fáil', Ireland is depicted in a similarly idyllic light as a land of veritable peace and plenty. On this occasion, however, experience of English life provides Nuinseann with the opportunity to specify what he missed about Ireland. He particularly remembered his native land for its cultural and religious life:[104]

> A haifrinn, a huird chrábhaidh,
> a haos ciúil (mo chompánuigh),
> filidh cláir Ghall a's Ghaoidheal,
> ann is cáir do chommaoidheamh.

> Her Masses, her religious orders, her musicians
> who were my companions, and the poets of that
> land where *Gaill* and *Gaoidhil* dwell: all should
> be included in our enumeration.

It is significant that Nuinseann should describe Ireland as 'clár Ghall a's Ghaoidheal', his use of *Gall* in this instance is evidently in reference to families of Anglo-Norman origin and not to the Elizabethan English. Both poems offer a glimpse of the poet articulating his national identity in the context of what he obviously regards as an alien milieu. It is all the more noteworthy that this formulation of patriotic awareness should come from the pen of an Anglo-Norman grandee who identified instinctively with Gaelic cultural and social norms.

Given that Gaelic cultural expression was an integral element in Nuinseann's patriotic credo, it is worth examining how the formal custodians of the Gaelic high tradition were responding to the introduction into Ireland of a potentially predatory and immediately divergent culture. It is proposed to focus on two general aspects of contemporary bardic cultural awareness: the

poets' consciousness of intrusive cultural alterity and their reaction to an
emergent challenge to bardic corporate integrity. Analysis of the material is
undertaken along thematic lines and arrangement of the evidence under both
headings is more or less chronological. Doighri Ó Dálaigh's poem beginning
'Cia as uaisle do Laighneachuibh?' provides quite early evidence of internal re-
evaluation of conventional Gaelic assumptions and priorities. The fact that it
was composed for Hugh O'Byrne, lord of *Gabhal Raghnuill* from around the
middle of the sixteenth century until his death in 1579, may account for its
sense of urgency. The proximity of the Wicklow O'Byrnes to the nominally-
anglicised Pale area in and around Dublin most likely explains the self-consciously negative filtering of the English presence in poem-books of three
successive O'Byrne lords. It is not recorded precisely when 'Cia as uaisle do
Laighneachuibh?' was composed – an internal reference to the dispossession
of the O'Connors of Offaly suggests a date sometime in the period 1557 to
1579. The poem's narrative centres on the concept of *uaisle* which is generally
translated to English as 'nobility' or 'dignity'. Ó Dálaigh's invocation of the
term, however, implies a more complex semantic range of meaning and sig-
nification. He interprets *uaisle* as a quasi-transcendental quality emblematic of
the aristocratic Gaelic *mentalité*. It is the mark of an authentic Gaelic grandee,
a frame of mind conducive to the cultivation of conventionally heroic Gaelic
virtues. Ó Dálaigh argues that this vital trait had been dismally neglected by
Gaelic noblemen.[105] He identifies one of the key elements of *uaisle* as patronage of the poets and with the candidature of Hugh O'Byrne uppermost in
mind he asks rhetorically who is most popular with them ('cia as oirdhiorca
ag deaghscoluibh in gach aonchóigeadh d'Éirinn?').

While O'Byrne admirably fulfilled the duties of a conventional Gaelic
seigneur, some of his fellow noblemen had allegedly reneged on the social
code enshrined in *uaisle* at a time of crisis, presumably a reference to crown
legislative pressure for the reform of miscellaneous Gaelic political and cultural practices:[106]

> An uaisle do thréigiodar
> Gaoidhil Fhódla acht a aicme;
> a n-aimsir an éigiontuis
> gnáth an fíorchara d'aithne.
>
> Mac Seaáin as fíorchara
> don uaisle a n-am na héigne;
> lé do ghabh an ríoghmhac-sa
> 's fir Éirionn d'éis a tréigthe.
>
> The *Gaoidhil* of Ireland,
> with the exception of [Hugh's] family,
> have deserted nobility; in time of emergency
> the true friend is usually recognised.

> The son of Seaán is a true friend to nobility
> in a time of difficulty, this noble scion sided
> with it [nobility] when the men of Ireland
> had abandoned it.

The poet presents the concept of nobility in much the same way as *Éire* is personified in metaphorical terms. Another concept which appears synonymous with *uaisle* in the poet's thematic grammar is *eineach* or literally 'honour'. According to Ó Dálaigh, the men of Munster, Connacht and Ulster had failed in their guardianship of *uaisle*, while in Leinster only the O'Byrnes, led by the redoubtable Hugh, remained faithful to established values and the cultural autonomy which they epitomised. Indeed, in Leinster itself the Molloys and the O'Melaghlins were no better than commoners, lacking appreciation of the arts of music or traditional hosting and hospitality ('mar an aicme anuasail gan chion ar cheól ná ar chongháir'). Moreover, the crown administration had expelled the O'Connors of Offaly from their lands ('Danair nó gur dhíbriodar sliocht roghlan Rosa Failghe'), while also subduing the senior branch of the O'Byrnes and the Kavanaghs ('Branuigh agus Caomhánuigh claoitior uile go haoinfhear').[107] Hugh O'Byrne alone stood against the rising tide of English domination and refused to betray *uaisle* and all that it symbolised:[108]

> Mac Seaáin an t-aoinfhear-soin
> nach tug a chlaoi do Ghallaibh;
> le huaisle do Ghaoidhioluibh
> anois acht Aodh ní faghair.

> The son of Seaán is the one man
> who did not give his submission to the English;
> only Hugh among the *Gaoidhil*
> is now to be found standing with nobility.

Employing the image of a feminine representation of the concept, Ó Dálaigh described *uaisle* travelling around Ireland in search of a partner until she met O'Byrne ('Do bhí an uaisle a n-aontumha . . . go rochtain an Aodha-so').[109] A definitive reading of the poem is not facilitated by the fact that it cannot be precisely dated. Its certain composition prior to 1579 cautions against literal acceptance of the poet's claim that the Gaelic élite had reneged on the values encapsulated in the concept of *uaisle*, with only O'Byrne's loyalty supposedly remaining unquestioned. It is most appropriately interpreted as a reflection of the pressure applied to the Gaelic political hierarchy by the crown administration to accommodate the former's outlook and behaviour to anglicised norms. Their proximity to the Pale must have left the O'Byrnes particularly vulnerable to such legislative and social pressure. Ó Dálaigh may also have aimed in this poem to provide guidance for O'Byrne in an effort to encourage him to minimise English cultural penetration of the lordship.

In 'Bráthair don bhás an doidhbhreas!', Maoilín Óg Mac Bruaideadha
laments his poverty and appeals to the earl of Thomond to alleviate it in an
approach which may not have been entirely serious.[110] The prefatory section
centres on the author's chagrin at finding himself in reduced circumstances.
In stanza ten of the poem, Mac Bruaideadha turned his attention to Conor
O'Brien (ob. 1581), the third earl of Thomond ('triath Fhorghais na bhfonn
lígheal'). He threatens to avenge himself on the earl for supposedly deserting
him ('Dígheóla mé mo thréigean'). He relates a heavily ironic proposal to
blackmail Thomond for support of Gaelic customs forbidden by the authorities. The poem offers a fascinating glimpse of the social and cultural pressures
to which a Gaelic lord was subjected by a centralising administration in the
period of the poem's composition, 1576–9.[111] Mac Bruaideadha initiated his
catalogue of Thomond's apparent lapses in stanza twelve and effects his task
with garrulous abandon: the earl plundered in the usual Gaelic manner ('s a
bheith congháireach creachach'), he honoured those who snubbed English
legislation ('Adéar go dtabhair anóir . . . do dhaoinibh nách díol ceana, i n-
aghaidh reachta an Phrionnsa'). Thomond also apparently cocked a snook at
promulgations concerning ecclesiastical reform, he worshipped religious
images ('adéar go n-adhrann d'íomháigh') and continued to embark on pil-
grimages to holy wells ('adéar go dtéid fá thobar'). As well as snubbing new
ecclesiastical directives, the earl remained a staunch patron of the poets, with,
it would seem, the curious exception of Mac Bruaideadha ('s go n-éistfeadh
dán is duanlaoidh'). Among other Gaelic practices which Thomond had
neglected to discontinue were those of coyne or the demanding of free
upkeep for soldiers and servants in his territory ('Adéar go ndéineann coinn-
mheadh') and the levying of local taxes ('go dtógbhann sreath is sobhadh').[112]
In making a facetious case for blackmail, Mac Bruaideadha reveals much
about the cultural milieu in a western Gaelic lordship in the 1570s. Although
he threatens to publicise Thomond's adherence to officially discredited social
and religious practices, he did so not out of sympathy for decrees laid down
by Dublin. Rather, his motivation is self-interested: supposedly destitute, he
exploited a witty parodic ruse to entice O'Brien to resume his patronage.
Indeed, the fact that a bardic poet might face uncertain material circumstances at this time is quite possibly significant and may suggest reduced
demand for poetic services. Secondly, once Mac Bruaideadha had succeeded
in his objective, he hardly expected Thomond either to take seriously or to act
on the administration's hostility to the Gaelic literati. The implication of his
surely irreverent approach is that even though he ironically invokes the threat
of informing on O'Brien for failing to conform, he obviously did not treat the
effective imposition of crown social and ecclesiastical legislation as imminent.

Laoiseach Mac an Bhaird's 'A fhir ghlacas a ghalldacht' is a subtle and acerbic attack on a Gaelic nobleman who had apparently abandoned the customary apparel of a man of his rank in favour of the latest English court fashions.
The poem appears to date to the reign of Elizabeth.[113] Mac an Bhaird launches

his attack on the poem's target, identified simply as the son of Donnchadh, with an observation on his preference for English *coiffure* over a Gaelic hairstyle. The nobleman, apparently, considered the indigenous style old-fashioned ('Ní modh leatsa an barr buidhe'). In stanza four, Mac an Bhaird introduces a noble called Eoghan Bán, who may have been another son of Donnchadh. Unlike his malleable brother, Eoghan Bán is portrayed as hostile to English ways ('fear nár ghrádhaigh an ghalldacht'), happy to abjure Anglo-Saxon customs in favour of his cultural inheritance ('don ghalldacht ní thug a thoil, an alltacht rug do roghain').[114] Eoghan Bán's introduction allows Mac an Bhaird to use him as a foil against which to set in relief the effeteness of Donnchadh's other son. Eoghan Bán completely rejected the Tudor dandy's distinguishing traits: coat and leggings ('cóta is coisbeirt'), a jewelled spur on his boots ('mionn sbuir ar bhróig bhuataisí'), English-style stockings ('sdocaidhe ar sdair na nGall'), his hair cut in locks ('locaidhe air ní fhágbhann'), an ornamental but ineffective rapier ('ráipér maol nach muirfeadh cuil'), a mantle with gold embroidery ('brat órdha'), an unwieldy golden ring ('fail óir far ghabhtha ghoimh') or a satin scarf extending to the heels ('sgarfa sróill go sálaibh').[115] Moreover, Eoghan Bán, altogether more austere in nature, disdained sleeping in a feather bed ('Dúil a leaba chlúimh ní chuir'), preferring to bed down on a mattress of rushes ('annsa leis luighi ar luachair'). In much the same manner, he would as soon live in an uncomplicated temporary structure made of poles than in a tower with battlements ('teach garbh-shlat ná táille tuir'). Mac an Bhaird brings his account of Eoghan Bán's robust virtues to a climax in the penultimate stanza: what distinguished Eoghan Bán above all else was his constant readiness to engage in battle, especially against foreigners ('s gleic d'iarraidh ar allmhurchaibh'). In effect, Donnchadh's son was in complete contrast to the virile Eoghan Bán:[116]

> Ní hionann is Eóghan Bán
> gáirit 'mad chois ar chlochán
> truagh nach bfacas libh bhar locht
> a fhir ghlacas an ghalldacht.

> How unlike are you to Eoghan Bán–
> they laugh at your foot on the stepping-stone.
> Pity that you have not seen your fault,
> O man who follows English ways.

In this case, the author's contempt for the anglicised deportment of Donnchadh's son is presented more immediately along social rather than political lines. His denunciation of perceived degeneracy reflects no obvious awareness of broader challenges to Gaelic society, especially to the extent that English fashions impinge more acutely on the author's consciousness than on their actual originators. With the adoption of luxurious foreign goods and habits, Donnchadh's son has involuntarily cast himself in an effeminate and supine role. In this poem, Mac an Bhaird portrays passive effeteness as a more pernicious threat to the Gaelic order than direct Tudor aggrandisement. Eoghan Bán represents a vigorous and forceful Gaelic world unsullied by cultural contagion while the attitude of mind exemplified by Donnchadh's son presages its emasculation. The cultural integrity embodied by Eoghan Bán is predicated in the context of a dichotomous contrast with an alien system of values and illustrates a focusing of Gaelic self-perception in response to the intrusion of an oppositional ethnic identity.

On the basis of an analysis of these three poems, it is possible to highlight aspects of the mediation of English cultural influence. Certainly, it emerges that these poets prioritised the defence and cultivation of an élite social code which privileged Gaelic high culture. The perception of English ethnicity and culture is negative and the New English are presented in less than flattering terms. In contrast, Gaelic society is depicted in heroic and bold colours while English identity is conveyed in a constrained manner suggestive of wily decadence. Although it is arguable that the *Gaoidhil* benefited from a remarkably vibrant consciousness of cultural integrity throughout the later middle ages, it is certain that the expansion of Tudor dominion had the effect of underlining the political implications of a sophisticated socio-linguistic awareness while also reinvigorating the traditional Gaelic versus foreigner paradigm. The example of 'A fhir ghlacas a ghalldacht' provides a two-tiered model of ethnocultural dissimilarity where an intrusive Anglo-Saxon system stands in contrast to the unquestioned validity and integrity of Gaelic mores.

The poem beginning 'Cia cheannchus adhmad naoi rann?', composed for Hugh O'Byrne (ob. 1579), provides early evidence of a poet's filtering of crown hostility to the bardic profession. While it is not possible to date the poem exactly, it is tempting to connect it with the instructions regarding the literati and other elements issued to Sir Henry Harrington on his appointment as seneschal of *Críoch Bhranach* and *Gabhal Raghnuill* in April 1578. Harrington was empowered to enforce the following penalties:[117]

> He shall make proclamation that no idle person, vagabond or masterless man, bard, rymor, or other notorious malefactor, remain within the district on pain of whipping after eight days, and of death after twenty days. He shall apprehend those who support such, and seize their goods, certifying the same to the lord deputy.

Read in the light of this decree, the poem acquires particular interest as a commentary on preliminary bardic assessment and re-evaluation when faced with administrative discrimination. The limited geographical range within which Seaán Ó hUiginn locates his theme is an important aspect of the poem. His subject concerns the supposed neglect of bardic patronage by the Leinster élite on foot of the authorities' determination to outlaw the poets. The exposition of his theme is centred on an interrogative premise: 'Who will buy a composition of nine verses?'. Posing the question in the opening stanza, Ó hUiginn 'outlines' the response to it by the leading Gaelic houses of Leinster. Were the senior branch of the O'Byrnes to be asked to invest in poetry, they would reply, somewhat gnomically, that no composition should be heard or paid for until the English had quit the country ('go dul Sagsanach tar sál'). Nor were the O'Tooles willing to commission a poem, even in the case of an obvious bargain, because of their submission to the English 'peace' ('anois ní thiúrdaois bonn bán, go gcuirid suas do shídh Gall ar luach fichead marg do dhán'). He is not any more optimistic of finding a buyer for his work among the Kavanaghs, even though they were formerly unstinting patrons ('Caomhánuigh cérbh fhoraois cliar, ré neach dhíobh ní fhuil mo shúil'). Because of fear of the English, nobody is willing to venture to pay for a poem ('fear ceannuigh adhmuid naoi rann do ghuais Ghall ní haithne dhúin'). Like-wise, the Fitzgeralds and the O'Mores were also unprepared to offer patron-age. There was one place in Leinster, however, where the literati were still greeted with old-style hospitality ('do dearbhadh dúin, deimhin scél, go bhfuil fréamh don einioch ann'). It was with Hugh O'Byrne, a man unswayed by the crown's directives, that Ó hUiginn rested his hopes:[118]

> Fear nach umhal do nós Gall
> Aodh mhac Seaáin is ard gnaoi,
> ós air do chuirios mo chrann
> le hadhmad ocht rann nó naoi.

> Most illustrious Hugh son of Seaán,
> is a man not submissive to English custom,
> it is with him that I have cast my lot,
> with a composition of eight or nine verses.

Ó hUiginn invokes the metaphor of a hound pursuing his quarry to describe his own approach to Hugh with a poetic offering ('leantor lé coin a fiadh féin'). In the final stanza, he repeats his assertion that the élite had turned away from bardic patronage ('ní haithnidh damh thoir ná thiar neach le cean-nach [mo] naoi rann').[119] While the poet provides an eloquent statement of his understanding of how the bardic system operated in Leinster, the modern scholar is obliged to approach Ó hUiginn's evidence with a degree of critical caution. This and other poems suggest that the demand for bardic poetry had diminished. Administrative opposition to bardic poets indirectly emphasises the actual or potential political influence which the English feared they wielded. However, an apparent decline in bardic fortunes cannot be entirely traced to haphazard and often ineffectual crown hostility. More accurately, the latter factor in conjunction with the paralysis of the ideological rationale underpinning Gaelic lordships combined to contribute to long-term bardic decline.

Brian Ó Gnímh's poem, 'Treisi an eagla ioná an andsacht', is a curious piece dealing somewhat opaquely with his desire for *rapprochement* with the MacDonnells of Antrim and which repudiates his former association with the English. The poem has not been precisely dated, though it was composed after 1566, when James MacDonnell of Islay died, and before 1586, when James's sons Domhnall and Alastar were killed. The poem concerns James's children and his brother Somhairle Buidhe MacDonnell and their treatment of the poet. Apparently, a rift had arisen between Ó Gnímh and the MacDonnells because he felt they had not recognised his status as a *fileadh* ('Ní tuicthi liom laithe an óil go mbeinn énlá gan anóir'). It is clear from what Ó Gnímh says that he had abandoned the MacDonnells for a period to sojourn among the English ('ar fheadh na nGall sa gabhoim'), although no hint is divulged as to what role he performed for them, he claims that he had been forced to join their ranks ('Goill dom chur fa chumhangsmacht'). Although Ó Gnímh had mixed with newcomers, he apparently privately despised them, all the while reserving his affection for his erstwhile patrons, the MacDonnells ('Grádh chloinne Colla um chroidhe as fuath Ghall ghuirt Laoghoire').[120]

In the last stanza of the poem, Ó Gnímh fired the ultimate salvo in his bid to rekindle the MacDonnells' favour. His postulated kinship with the family is mentioned with the implication that this bond must act as a cementing agent between the two parties:[121]

> Dúinn araon giodh ionann frémh
> meisi as fhuil Eachoidh Duibhléin
> mo lucht cuil as siad Sacsain
> 's ní hiad an fhuil Eathach soin.

> Though we are both of the same root-stock,
> I and the blood of Eochaidh Doimhléan, it
> is the English who are my kin and not the
> blood of that Eochaidh.

Ó Gnímh's claim to common descent with the MacDonnells, whose origins were traced to Scotland, is corroborated by seventeenth-century genealogical manuscripts. By emphasising his kinship with the MacDonnells, Ó Gnímh is highlighting how inappropriate he considers his association with the English. His central point hinges on the fact that he felt a poet's obvious place was with Gaelic patrons rather than among the English. Like Seaán Ó hUiginn in the poem discussed above, he attempts to negotiate a scenario where the corporate imperatives of the bardic system had begun to falter in a rapidly changing political environment. While the poems are undeniably illustrative of the institutional paralysis enveloping the profession, they also demonstrate an élite wrestling with crisis and formulating a range of responses characterised by an alternation of tradition and innovation. During the reign of King James I, poets, having embarked on a process of reorientation and rejuvenation, were constant in their advocacy of Gaelic cultural integrity. In this instance, Ó Gnímh foreshadows a later more developed bardic insistence on the sovereignty of Gaelic cultural expression. Ironically, a late but nonetheless resourceful re-evaluation by proponents of Gaelic cultural integrity advocated the inculturation of New English settlers and their incorporation within the social ambit of the indigenous population.

Giolla Brighde Ó hEódhusa's 'Slán agaibh, a fhir chumtha' also documents the predicament of a bardic poet in a liminal position. In this poem, composed sometime between 1592 and 1600, Ó hEódhusa bids farewell to an unidentified man called Eoghan on the occasion of the author's decision to forsake his ancestral profession to take holy orders. Distinguished by a lyrical beauty of great sensitivity, the poem's main interest for present purposes centres on the nature of Ó hEódhusa's reflections on the bardic system.[122] Regretting the prospect of leaving Eoghan behind, he explains that the cause of their pending separation arose from his decision to give up poetry for another calling ('Do mheas mé ar mhalairt gceirde – seachna na ngrés nGaoidheilge').[123] He is not retiring as a poet out of dislike for his ancestral vocation ('ní fuath d'ealadhain mh'aithreach') or because the composition of poetry is no longer honoured among the Irish as it once had been ('ná an ghlóir do-gheibhthí dá cionn do neimhthní ó fhóir Éirionn'). This latter observation certainly corroborates the evidence of other poets regarding a decline in bardic patronage. Having discounted the possibility of negative causation, Ó hEódhusa explains his departure:[124]

> Gidh beag ar n-eólas ionnta,
> sduidéar leabhrán léighionnta
> iseadh ro chealg uaibhsi inn –
> an cheard is uaisle aithnim.

> Though our knowledge of them is small,
> it is the study of learned books – the
> most noble profession known to me –
> that has enticed me away from you.

When Ó hEódhusa mentions his intention to begin academic studies, he is, no doubt, referring to his decision to study for the clerical ministry at Douai. In April 1609, he was ordained a Franciscan priest in Louvain. If Ó hEódhusa forsook the call of his ancestral profession in favour of the religious life, the extant evidence demonstrates that he continued to compose poetry in Irish. Once again, the record presents a model of professional retrenchment coexisting with individual ideological reassessment. Ó hEódhusa's significance lies in the fact that he remained loyal to bardic culture, even in his continental exile and that he redirected poetry to non-traditional objectives. For example, when he spoke of the most worthy of trades, namely book learning ('an cheard is uaisle aithnim'), Ó hEódhusa in all probability had theology in mind. This seemingly casual remark indicates that a fundamental intellectual shift had altered the focus of his outlook. By gravitating to the counter-reformation ministry, Ó hEódhusa emphasised his commitment to powerful new ideological priorities.

Mathghamhain Ó hIfearnáin's 'Ceist! cia do cheinneóchadh dán?' is an emotive expression of despair at the decline which he argued had vitiated the bardic institution. It is not unlike 'Cia cheannchus adhmad naoi rann?' in that its author laments diminishing bardic patronage, although, as already noted, Seaán Ó hUiginn at least had the consolation of O'Byrne support. Ó hIfearnáin was a Munster poet, who according to his own account, formerly enjoyed the patronage of the Desmond Fitzgeralds ('Mé im luing cheannaigh ar gcaill laist d'éis Chlann nGearailt do thuill teist').[125] He claims to have toured Munster with the intention of selling a bardic composition but he found no buyer ('do shiobhail mé an Mhumhain leis – ní breis é a-nuraidh ná a-nois'). Not a single groat was offered for his work and he concludes that both the *Gaoidhil* and the English had ignored him ('D'éirneist gémadh beag an bonn, níor chuir fear ná éinbhean ann').[126] As a result of this failure to win support, he argues that he would have been better off financially and in terms of status as a maker of combs ('uaisle dul re déiniomh cíor – gá bríogh d'éinfhior dul re dán?'). Heroes of ancient Ireland like Corc Chaisil and Cian never stinted largesse to the poets, but now that this situation no longer prevailed, it was time to bid farewell to the heroic virtues of the *Gaoidhil* ('slán lé síol Éibhir mon-uar').[127] Moreover with the demise of the Fitzgeralds, Ó hIfearnáin portrays himself as a cargo-less ship. The nature of his grievance seems to indicate again a shrinking demand for bardic poetry. It must be remembered, however, that the poet was dealing with the situation he encountered in Munster in the late 1580s or perhaps the early 1590s. With the suppression of the Desmond rebellion and the ensuing plantation of large tracts of land in the province, poets in the south-west region must have found it difficult to obtain patronage on a par with pre-1579 rates of demand. A likely reduction in levels of support available to bardic poets in Munster at this stage is reflected in the migration to Ulster of poets like Cú Chonnacht and Conchobhar Crón Ó Dálaigh.

Regardless of the travails besetting the bardic profession, the poets never countenanced a challenge to the validity of their status. Fearghal Óg Mac an Bhaird's 'Beannacht siar uaim go hÉirinn' is an idealised evocation of Ireland composed during a sojourn in Scotland in which he sends salutations to Ireland, to various centres in Ulster, to the men of that province and to the men of Munster and Connacht. Interestingly, he describes the earl of Thomond as the last autonomous lord in Munster which implies that the piece was composed sometime after 1583. Having toured the country, Mac an Bhaird focuses on the professional classes and clergy: panegyrists ('lucht dénta na nduan molta'), genealogists ('lucht sgaoilte gég ngeinealaigh'), physicians ('go ríghleaghaibh Fhuinn Fhéilim'), clergy ('go cléirchibh Fhóid Iughoine') and musicians ('go lucht an cheóil charthonaigh') receive, in turn, the poet's best wishes. The poem is essentially a description of what must have been a largely imaginary Gaelic idyll; nonetheless, Mac an Bhaird places his own caste in a distinctive niche in that world.[128] This composition is influenced by the same burgeoning sense of patriotism evident in the poems by Uilliam Nuinseann already discussed. Both authors drew on their experience of foreign cultures to set in relief features they considered characteristic of the island. The poems' emphasis on a Gaelic and Catholic ambience is indicative of the central role which religion and culture now increasingly assumed in the development of a communal mode of politicised self-depiction. Of course, the diasporic consequences of English political consolidation intensified during James's reign and the exile poem genre became a more common element in the extended projection of new and revamped Gaelic ideological priorities.

Bardic Perception of Religious Controversy, 1558–1603

The extant corpus of Elizabethan bardic poetry reveals limited engagement with contemporary ecclesiastical issues. This relative indifference probably results from two factors: the initially ineffectual course and limited public profile of the Protestant reform movement outside larger urban centres and, secondly, what may have been a traditional bardic reluctance to comment on questions of ecclesiastical remit.[129] The Elizabethan administration made little or no effort to provide religious instruction in the majority language. Although Seaán Ó Cearnaigh's *Aibidil Gaoidheilge agus Caiticiosma* ('Irish Primer of Religion') was published in 1571 with the intention of catering for those submissive to the reformed faith and the Queen's authority ('dá gach aon nduine atá umhal do reachd Dia agus na bannríoghan'), it appears to have made little impact. For instance, the Munster settler, Sir William Herbert, seemed unaware of its existence when he wrote to Lord Burghley from his recently-granted estate at Castleisland in 1587 telling him that he had 'caused the Lord's Prayer and the Ten Commandments and the Articles of the Belief, to be translated into Irish'. It was not until 1602–3 that an Irish New Testament finally appeared. Two poets, Maoilín Óg Mac Bruaideadha and Domhnall Óg Ó hUiginn, were among those who helped prepare the translation.[130] Although bardic poets were either reluctant or simply not sufficiently interested to comment on religious dissension, churchmen of Gaelic background were less restrained about expressing opinions in verse regarding the reformation. Of the four poets featured in this section only two were *fileadha*, the other two being clerics skilled in Gaelic versification. The bardic poets, Fearghal Óg Mac an Bhaird and Lochluinn Ó Dálaigh, cannot be said to offer comprehensive analyses of religious controversy. The compositions of the non-professional clerical authors, Eoghan Ó Dubhthaigh and Maolmhuire Ó

hUiginn, are both significant and informative in so far as they reflect an outlook imbued with a counter-reformation dynamic but nonetheless rooted in
the Gaelic tradition.[131]

Eoghan Ó Dubhthaigh's (ob. 1590) 'Léig dod chomhmórtas dúinn' is one
of the earliest extant poems in Irish manifesting elements of counter-reformation influence. Its author, a Franciscan, combines a Marian paean and a corus-
cating diatribe against three figures who had taken Anglican holy orders.
Mathew Seaine, Protestant bishop of Cork (1572–1582/3), Uilliam Ó Cathasaigh, Protestant bishop of Limerick (1571–91) and the infamous Miler
Magrath, apostate archbishop of Cashel (1571–1622) are castigated for their
desertion of the Roman faith and their alleged indifference to the cult of the Virgin. Ó Dubhthaigh was particularly infuriated by Magrath's marriage to Áine Ní
Mheadhra and she suffers her own share of carefully-crafted vituperation. Curiously, he also reproved several bardic poets for what he took to be the overly
secular nature of their poetry. The equation of Anglicanism with the English
presence in Ireland is an especially revealing aspect of this long and multifac-
eted poetic document. In addition to the colonial political implications, he
depicts the established church as an essentially Anglo-Saxon cultural phenomenon. For instance, he portrays its clergy as having come across from England
and he employs English terminology to satirise the immigrant divines:[132]

> An chliar-sa anois tig anall,
> cliar dhall ar a ndeachaidh ceo,
> ní mó leo Muire ná dog,
> dar by God, ní rachaidh leo.

> These clergymen who have come from the
> other side – blind clergy enveloped in
> fog, respect a dog more than Mary. And,
> by heaven, they shall not get away with it.

Furthermore, the author highlights his perception of Protestant deviation
from societal norms in claiming the Anglican bishops and clergy were characterised by their 'seduction' and 'corruption' of justice ('Drong do sheduction
lán do chuir corruption sa chóir'). Moreover, he charged the Anglican clergy
of both English and Irish origin with having drawn misfortune on Ireland
('d'fhág an sonas Éire díbh'). Ó Dubhthaigh pinpoints the Elizabethan administration as the determining factor in the reform movement's progress and
direction and as such he presents the established church as the religious ancillary of a broader colonial enterprise. His perception of this religio-political
nexus is illustrated through a startling image of the Virgin presenting herself
at Dublin Castle only to meet with violent abuse ('ní fhuighe acht dorn ar a
dúid, istigh i gcúirt Átha Cliath'). In contrast, the standing of the wives of the
Anglican episcopate was considerably higher at the castle (''s mná na n-easbog
fá chion ann'). Uilliam Ó Cathasaigh is singled out for his close links with the

settler community and it is claimed he was more conversant with the English regime than with God ('Uilliam Ó Cathasaigh gidh teann ar chlannaibh Gall is ní ar Dhia'). The reformation is presented as a betrayal of the natural course of historical development and Mathew Seaine, for instance, is accused of having 'deserted history' by virtue of his belittlement of the Virgin ('a Mhaighistir Seidhin do thréig stair'). Overall, it is clear that the Anglican clergy were in receipt of seriously-flawed advice ('An chliar abhus 's an chliar thall, ó láimh na comhairle is cam stair').[133]

In a much shorter poem, 'A Bhanbha, is truagh do chor!', Ó Dubhthaigh elaborated on his interlinking of the established church with the crown administration in a politically-conscious attack on the English presence and the aspirations of its ecclesiastical adjunct. The fate of Ireland merits lamentation and he supplicates Jesus to aid the island ('a aoin Mhic Dé, ainic í'). Already overrun by English and Scots newcomers ('Ag siúd sluagh Saxan ad dháil, a Iaith Fáil . . . is fir Alban'), he fears that Ireland will become an inferior replication of England ('Narab tusa Saxa óg, a Bhanbha mhór, is fearr ainm!'). Calling on Ireland to resist Lutheran and Calvinist blandishments ('Cáiptín Lúitér is beag neart 's cáiptín Cailbhín nach ceart glór'), he urges her to follow instead her own 'general' Saint Patrick ('Pádruig do ghénerál féin').[134] Unfortunately, this poem's date of composition is not clear and, if it is the work of Ó Dubhthaigh, 1590 must be taken as its *terminus ante quem*. Despite this chronological uncertainty, 'A Bhanbha, is truagh do chor!' is important in that its author links nationality and allegiance to Roman Catholicism as complementary facets of Irish identity.

The poems of Maolmhuire Ó hUiginn merit attention principally because of their author's status as a prominent Catholic ecclesiastic and his membership of a prestigious bardic family. Although little is recorded about the circumstances of his life and career, the manuscript tradition remembers him as archbishop of Tuam (1586–*c.*1590) and as a brother of the well-known Tadhg Dall Ó hUiginn. Apparently, Maolmhuire died in Antwerp while returning home from Rome.[135] The poem, 'A fhir théid go Fiadh bhFuinidh', is addressed to an unidentified figure who was about to leave the continent for Ireland. It is mainly concerned with idealised praise of Ireland and its natural beauty. Its author, however, reveals aspects of his religio-political outlook. In stanza twelve, he describes Ireland as a country which had not deserted the 'yoke of faith' ('Tír nár thréig a cuing chreidimh'). While such phraseology is evidently the product of counter-reformation attitudes, it appears curious at first that the archbishop should choose to employ the word 'yoke' to characterise loyalty to Catholicism. This image of religious faith as a burden is elaborated in stanza fourteen when Ó hUiginn explained the misfortunes of the *Gaoidhil* as having resulted from divine wrath. Because of overweening pride, they had forfeited God's favour ('Fuilngidh Dia dúthaigh a sean tré anuabhar Mac Míleadh') and consequently by way of condign punishment the country had been overrun by foreigners ('fá rian ainbhfine eachtrann'). Though he interpreted events in the light of providentialist retribution, the author softens the impact of his conclusion somewhat with the assertion that possession of Gaelic ancestry is still worthy of pride ('céim ionmhaoidhimh re a áireamh').[136] In 'Slán uaim don dá aoghaire', Ó hUiginn delineates a considerably more positive and optimistic vista for his compatriots. This piece was addressed to two clergymen in Ireland whose identities are not revealed because of fear for their safety and security. The argument advanced here centres on his belief that assistance was always at hand when circumstances seemed most desperate. Relief invariably follows prolonged oppression ('Tig saoirse i ndiaidh róbhruide') just as fine weather inevitably comes after bad weather ('tar éis dubhaidh tig soineann'), but in the meantime the poet advocates an attitude of patient endurance ('fuilngeam feadh an órlaigh-se'). When help is least expected, God intervenes to aid the desperate ('Tig an uair nách saoilfidhe, grás is cabhair on gCoimdhe') and he was now poised to succour the *Gaoidhil* ('gearr uainn am an fhaoithighe'). Ó hUiginn regarded the Gaelic predicament as a sort of spiritual purgative ('ól na dighe domblasta meinic fhóireas an t-easlán').[137] In both poems he attributes the religious and political turmoil in Ireland to God's anger with the misbehaviour of the *Gaoidhil*. Reflecting Ó Dubhthaigh, he presents Roman Catholicism and Gaelic consciousness as indivisible components of communal identity.

The two remaining poems to be discussed reveal aspects of a bardic response to the Protestant reformation. It is significant that one of these poems resulted from its author's experience in Scotland and this fact underlines the somewhat limited impact of the reformation in Gaelic Ireland and what may be described as the cautious attitude displayed by bardic poets to questions of ecclesiastical contention. In 'Dursan mh'eachtra go hAlbuin', Fearghal Óg Mac an Bhaird laments his decision to travel to Scotland for professional reasons, probably on the occasion of his documented sojourn there in 1581, when he also appears to have composed 'Beannacht siar uaim go hÉirinn'. He complains bitterly about the absence of the eucharist ('ní chaithim corp an Choimdheadh') and the fact that not only Scotland, but other countries also, denied the validity of the fundamental Roman Catholic dogma of transubstantiation ('Mór dtír nach í Alba a-mháin nach creideann fós . . . don bhairgin go mbí 'n-a fuil'). He bewails the banishment of the Catholic clergy and the Mass ('is mé gan ord gan Aifrionn') and were he granted Scotland's riches, he would rather hear the Mass again ('Dá bhfhaghuinn a bhfuil d'argod . . . do b'fhearr aonuair an t-Aifrionn'). He prays to be allowed return home to avoid dying in a country in the grip of heresy ('ó nach faicim é innte an corp diadha doimhillte . . . iarruim gan mh'éag i nAlbain').[138] An idyllic vision of Ireland is presented and, although it is not explicitly stated, Mac an Bhaird implies that at home he could worship freely in accordance with the liturgical rites of the pre-reformation church.

Lochluinn Ó Dálaigh composed 'Uaigneach a-taoi, a theagh na mbráthar' as a celebratory lament for the Franciscan monastery at Multyfarnham which had been put to the torch by crown forces in 1601. While it displays no deep theological concerns, it is interesting in so far as it evidences the author's awareness of a religious foundation and the social aspects of its communal influence. Although other religious orders and communities had been banished, Ó Dálaigh remarks that the community in Multyfarnham had nonetheless managed to maintain its position. Now with the destruction of the friary itself, worship was regretfully neglected ('H'altóra gan earradh gcrábhaidh'), because many people formerly obtained spiritual solace within its environs ('Iomdha coireach ciontadh n-iomdha . . . fuair . . . leas a n-anman, ionnoibhsi'). In the realm of the more strictly temporal, the community had alleviated the plight of the poor ('Iomdha boicht do biathtaoi it orsain') and served as a centre of hospitality for the nobility ('Iomdha cuideachta chlann bhflaitheadh, lé bhfríoth fésda soineamhuil'). The friars were celebrated on account of their scholarship ('ní feas ní 'na aincheas orro d'ailcheas rollo ríghleabhar') and, of course, their piety and charity were well known ('mór a gcrábhadh, deas a ndaonnocht').[139] He depicts a community performing a relevant and beneficial function in the surrounding district and deals with the dissolution of the monastery in terms of its practical quotidian implications. The sacking of the friary is not mediated in the context of the reformation, rather the poet presents its fate as signifying the baneful destruction of a local centre of scholarship and charitable relief. Its demise is definitely not interpreted as an episode in a wider theological and political conflict.

Conclusion

Several influential conceptual developments are discernible in the foregoing survey of poetry dating from the Elizabethan period. Generally, bardic poets articulate a political outlook underpinned by a confident sense of national identity. Of course, individual poets differ in terms of the interpretative emphasis they place on personal responses to the subject of ethnicity and the manipulation and exercise of political power. It is clear also that Tudor aggrandisement was interpreted within a discursive framework of rival and oppositional ethnic identities. Crucially, in the context of the historic Irish communities, the evidence demonstrates that Gaelic notions of communal identity were not overtly exclusivist, and, in fact, formal Gaelic ethno-cultural terms of reference were incrementally amplified to embrace the gaelicised descendants of Anglo-Norman settlers. Bardic poets were greatly facilitated in the projection of shared political assumptions by virtue of professional and ideological mobility within the communicative parameters of a common all-island cultural sphere. Bardic awareness of the challenges posed to the classical Gaelic socio-cultural model, therefore, resulted in the emergence of an oppositional schema predicated on a conflictive Gaelic-English engagement.[140]

It is simplistic to assume that the relative eclipse of the indigenous seigneurial élite both immediately prior to and after 1603 marked the effective termination of the classical bardic tradition's pre-eminent political and social status. In fact, it is now obvious that the bardic institution was not consumed overnight by cataclysm, rather, its decline was essentially a prolonged and no doubt uneven process of attrition. Material presented in this chapter demonstrates that poets had become conscious of a diminution in their status and material prospects at an early stage in Elizabeth's reign. Although the documented evidence of official hostility to the Gaelic literati must be acknowledged, it seems unlikely that contracting patronage of the poets on the part of the élite is to be attributed to unfavourable legislative impact alone. Conventional bardic legitimatory functions were undermined at an elemental level in a society where the exercise of actual political authority was, increasingly, underwritten by alternative ideological and jurisdictional precepts. Indeed, the number of fileadha quite possibly outstripped the demand for their services.[141] This process of vocational retrenchment was not confined to the bardic institution, other Gaelic corporate entities, particularly jurists, appear to have experienced professional decline.[142] Ironically, the Elizabethan period witnessed a contrasting bardic developmental duality and it is possible to delineate the evolution of an acute contemporary bardic political awareness against a background of cumulative institutional degeneration.

Surviving material suggests that the Protestant reformation exercised limited influence on bardic mentalités at this period. This probably resulted not so much from bardic indifference to ecclesiastical dissension but rather was a consequence of the initially-erratic performance of Anglican evangelisation. Indeed, for most of Elizabeth's reign the reformed church maintained next to no presence in the Gaelic heartlands. The poems of Mac an Bhaird and Ó Dálaigh manifest an appreciation of the social role of quasi-medieval Christianity, but they provide no evidence of critical engagement with politicised theological polemics. Crucially, the work of the cleric Ó Dubhthaigh charts the emergence of a concept vital to the transformation of the Gaelic mindset and the formation of an early modern Irish identity. His portrayal of Protestantism as an alien and intrusive English imposition is in implicit contrast to the 'nativeness' of Catholicism. Such cultivation of popular perception of the reformation as the religious arm of hegemonic colonialism was to become a serious obstacle to the advancement of Protestant evangelisation in Ireland.

CONQUEST AND EVALUATION
1603–1612

On 30 March 1603, six days after the death of Queen Elizabeth I, Hugh O'Neill, earl of Tyrone, made formal submission to lord deputy Mountjoy at Mellifont. Tyrone was unaware of the queen's passing as he signed the treaty, for in his anxiousness to conclude an agreement Mountjoy had concealed the news from the Irish side and he had proposed more generous terms than the Ulster leader might otherwise have expected. Tyrone was permitted to remain as the absolute head of the O'Neill lordship and O'Cahan, his chief *uirrí* (vassal lord), was to remain subservient to him. In the light of the decisive defeat of the Irish forces at Kinsale, O'Neill's fate at the hands of the crown authorities was decidedly lenient. In effect, Tyrone had survived defeat to emerge as an entrenched power in Ulster.[1] With regard to the bardic order, Edmund Curtis in his influential *A History of Ireland*, first published in 1936, concluded that Tyrone's acquiescence in the terms of the Mellifont treaty heralded the final curtain-call on the literati's magisterium:[2]

> In the struggle the hereditary poets had thrown real inspiration and passion into their verse, giving a Biblical fervour to their exhortations to the chiefs to save their mother Erin. Now came the violent and sudden ending of the whole Gaelic world.

Curtis's melodramatic depiction of a colonial deluge overtaking the poets vividly exemplifies a later commentator interpreting an historical pattern on the basis of what is, in hindsight at any rate, an apparently explicitly linked chain of events. It will be argued in this chapter that bardic poets did not attach the same significance to the treaty of Mellifont as did Curtis. In fact, the extant poetry reveals that bardic poets continued to manifest a considerable degree of compositional brio and self-confidence. Indeed, the very year which Edmund Curtis postulated as marking the effective dismantlement of the bardic order witnessed a new mood of enthusiasm and optimism among poets. Breandán Ó Buachalla has demonstrated in detail how the literati viewed the accession of a monarch with a Gaelic pedigree to England's throne as a matter of some significance and he has documented the manner in which they interpreted the Stuart accession as an omen propitious to Gaelic renewal.

However, the optimism engendered among bardic poets by James's arrival in London was soon defused by the flight of O'Donnell and O'Neill to a continental exile in September 1607. The response of the poets to the events of

1607 and after was, to a large extent, the climax of a dynamic which powered a refocus of the bardic political outlook clearly reaching back to Elizabeth's reign. In the preceding chapter, it has been demonstrated how poets formulated an inclusive notion of politicised Irish identity and the appearance of counter-reformation influence in Gaelic poetry has been observed. Ironically, the process of bardic conceptual revitalisation continued to develop in tandem with professional decline during James's reign. As will be evident from the historiographical discussion in the first chapter, the case made in this study for bardic dynamism contrasts with interpretations of the poetry advanced by scholars such as Tom Dunne, Bernadette Cunningham, Michelle O Riordan and Joep Leerssen. The latter are, generally, in broad agreement in their emphasis on allegedly outmoded conventionalism in bardic readings of contemporary political developments. The demise or exile of important Gaelic patrons in the first decade of the seventeenth century, essential partners in the cultivation and transmission of high Gaelic culture, and the ensuing Ulster plantation certainly marked the termination of unquestioned bardic primacy in the much attenuated Gaelic polity. Confronted with the peculiar difficulties of post-1607 Ireland, bardic poets consolidated an unprecedented analytical process centring on the interpretation of the causes and effects of the severe diminution in Gaelic autonomy. Their analysis differs, no doubt, from the conclusions of some modern historians, but this contrasting emphasis in no way lessens the importance of bardic poetry as an historical source for Gaelic assessments of colonisation and the political paralysis of the native élite.

As in the previous chapter, this analysis of primary sources will be undertaken on a thematic and broadly chronological basis. In the first section, bardic perceptions of the accession of James Stuart to the English throne are sketched while in sections two and three an attempt is made to determine responses to the political vacuum created by the departure of the earls of Tyrone and Tyrconnell. Twenty-one of the thirty or so poems discussed in this chapter come from three manuscript collections assembled on the continent over a period of approximately fifty years from 1607. All three manuscript compilations duplicate each other's material, probably reflecting the popularity of certain poems among the élite of Gaelic émigré society. Given that the bulk of the evidence comes from manuscript collections compiled and written outside Ireland, it is necessary to consider possible influences on the selection criteria and overall composition of these poem-books. The earliest in date of the manuscripts, 'The Book of O'Donnell's Daughter', is a compilation of material which largely relates to the O'Donnell family. Possibly the property of Nuala O'Donnell, a sister of Hugh Roe (ob. 1602) and Rory (ob. 1608), she took up residence in Louvain around 1613. The presence of several different scribal hands in the manuscript indicates that it was added to from time to time in Flanders. Among those who copied material into the manuscript was the well-known northern poet, Eoghan Ruadh Mac an Bhaird.[3] The second oldest in date of the three manuscripts is known as 'The Book of O'Conor Don'. This manuscript was written at Ostend in 1631 by a scribe named Aodh Ó Dochartaigh for Somhairle MacDonnell. The latter fled Ulster in 1615 when implicated in a plot to organise a rising in the province and he subsequently served as an officer in the Irish regiment in the Spanish service in Flanders. This collection contains a diverse selection of religious and didactic material as well as historical and political work.[4] The third and latest in date of the manuscript anthologies is that compiled by Fearghal Dubh Ó Gadhra, O.S.A., who worked on the manuscript in various cities in the Low Countries ('san Tír Iachtair') between 1655 and 1659. The latter collection is varied in composition and encompasses historical, religious and political material.[5]

The considerations which encouraged the exiled Gaelic élite to record such literary and historical matter may be traced to two related factors. Firstly, the diverse range of material copied indicates that the motive was to some extent cultural in focus. By the time of King James's death in 1625 it must have been evident that however likely the restoration of Gaelic political autonomy, the replication of the traditional system of bardic privilege and patronage was no longer tenable. An era in the history of Gaelic scholarship had ended. In a civilisation which set a high premium on its traditional lore and history, it is no surprise to find the scholarly and political élites attempting to ensure the survival of a threatened cultural patrimony which now seemed increasingly fragile in the context of adverse socio-political conditions. Importantly, the move to collate a permanent record of Gaelic civilisation was not just an act of homage to a rich cultural history, it was also concerned with the affirmation of contemporary political and cultural aspirations in the face of foreign disruption of traditional Gaelic social and discursive modes. If the historicity of the Gaelic presence in Ireland were ever to be questioned or contested in an uncertain historiographical future, such manuscript collections would effectively document the Gaelic contribution to and dominance in the shaping of Ireland's social and cultural geography. Evidently, the conservation of the Gaelic cultural patrimony was motivated by practical political considerations as much as disinterested antiquarianism. The fact that the poems relevant to the present study were considered worthy of scribal preservation so soon after the events which they reflect or chronicle is significant. Inclusion in manuscript anthologies indicates their historical or contemporary relevance for the scribes and commissioning patrons of these collections in the immediate aftermath of political upheaval.

The Accession of James Stuart and Bardic Optimism

James Stuart's elevation to the throne of the English kingdom in 1603 provides the subject matter for two celebrated and much discussed bardic compositions. Eochaidh Ó hEódhusa in a poem entitled 'Mór theasda dh'obair Óivid' and Fearghal Óg Mac an Bhaird in 'Trí coróna i gcairt Shéamais' read the inauguration of James's reign as a new and hopeful beginning in the history of the *Gaoidhil*. The fundamental basis for their recognition and support of James lay in the purported Gaelic ancestry of his Scottish forebears. The elaborate Gaelic pedigree of the Stuart monarchs and the belief that the *Gaoidhil* had a foremost place in their affections was to become an increasingly desperate leitmotif of Gaelic political thought and literature in the seventeenth and eighteenth centuries.[6] The positive tone of Mac an Bhaird's approach is apparent in the opening couplet where he suggests that the sight of the three crowns in James's royal charter was in itself a reason for celebration ('cia dhíobh nachar dheighfhéaghais?').[7] The three crowns in the monarch's possession ('trí coróna um cheann Shéamais'), those of England ('coróin Sagsan'), Ireland ('coróin iongantach Éireann') and that of Scotland ('coróin Alban iathghuirme'), prompt a detailed genealogical audit of James's right to rule the three kingdoms, especially Ireland. To complement his expert genealogical focus, the author also touches on some other manifestations of his subject's dynastic credentials. Drawing on the traditions of Gaelic pseudo-history and of Christian kingship, he notes that the Stuart sovereign's accession had been prophesied ('ní sgéal rúin rádh na leabhar') and that Scotland's crown had been bestowed on him by divine ordinance ('ó Dhia dhó do deonoigheadh'). Of course, such conceits would not have been out of place in a poem of validation for a less grand Gaelic magnate.[8] By quatrain six he moves away from prefatory generalities to offer a specific statement of James's ancestral dues ('ós am cóir dá chraobhsgaoileadh'). Dealing with Scotland first, he recounts how the country was held by nine of James's forebears ('ag naonbhar roimhe dá fhréimh'), whose names Mac an Bhaird enumerates consecutively and the list culminates with Mary, queen of Scots ('Badh lé Alba ó mhuir go muir máthair an airdríogh uasail'). By virtue of his place in this line of regal succession, James exercises lawful mastery over the Scottish kingdom ('ag sin ceart do chairteise ar caomhAlbain bhfinn bhfleadhaigh').[9] Mac an Bhaird proceeds to devote five quatrains to James's case for the English throne by emphasising the fact that his great-grandmother, Margaret, was the daughter of the English king, Henry VII. Thus, by reason of his descent from Margaret Tudor (1489–1541), James's 'charter' entitled him to assume the designation 'lord of royal London' ('triath ríoLunndan do rádh ruibh').[10] Closer to home, the author was evidently anxious to touch on the implications for Ireland of James's advancement and he devotes the remainder of the poem to this issue. Hitherto, the piece had effectively been a traditional bardic inaugural ode, intent on underpinning a lord's territorial claims by means of a conventional genealogical presentation. It is in his brief, but highly original, comments on Ireland that the poet raises the intellectual quality of his commentary to a level far more sophisticated and discerning than that of the often repetitive bardic eulogistic mode.

Having contextualised the Scottish and English inheritances, Mac an Bhaird takes it on himself to address political advice to James: given that he enjoyed a dynastic right to the kingdom of Ireland, the king should never contemplate the idea of annexing the island by force. Since James is already the island's legitimate sovereign, he implies that such strategic reasoning would be specious:

> A lámh as díorgha dligheadh
> – a-nois i gcéill cuirfidhear –
> ná [bí ag] teacht ar éineing d'uaim
> 's do cheart ar Éirinn armruaidh.

> O prince whose hand gives straight judgments,
> I will now say this to you: talk not of
> 'taking in new territory' [adding Ireland to your kingdom]
> seeing that you already have a right to red-sworded Ireland.

A manipulative element in Mac an Bhaird's political narrative becomes apparent in the ensuing quatrain. He alludes to an obvious source of disquiet: English claims to legislative and administrative suzerainty in Ireland. In fact, the author's choice of terminology here appears to suggest that while English jurisdictional authority definitely troubled him, he fully recognised the actuality of the English presence. His use of the present tense of the substantive verb appears to leave little doubt that Mac an Bhaird acknowledged the extent of crown hegemony in Ireland c. 1603:[11]

> I gcúirt Shagsan na sreabh seang
> a-tá ardchoróin Éireann;
> tuar maothchroidhe a bheith san mbrugh
> fa bhreith laochroidhe Lonndon.

> In the court of fair-streamed England is
> placed Ireland's noble crown; it means misery
> of heart to see it in that land in the
> power of the warriors of London.

The accession of a Scottish sovereign with Gaelic ancestry to the English throne offers a means of circumventing unfettered English dominance in Ireland. The poet's joy at James's good fortune is not quite as disinterested as it may seem, for he discerns in his most recent elevation a means of diffusing English influence in post-Kinsale Ireland. Mac an Bhaird supports his depiction of James's automatic assumption of Ireland's crown, not that the latter for a moment needed to be reminded of what he had inherited, by means of a venerable conceit, that of the espousal of the lord to the female embodiment of his territory ('is tú a céile ar chomhardhaibh'). In 'Trí coróna i gcairt Shéamais', the poet displays a remarkable shrewdness of political analysis, rendered all the more exceptional by his latent exploitation of conventional imagery for the purposes of an innovative discursive initiative. Conscious of the political impasse which confronted the Gaelic polity, Mac an Bhaird invokes the origin myth of the Stuart dynasty as an ideological base from which to posit the curtailment of Anglo-Saxon ambitions.[12]

In 'Mór theasda dh'obair Óivid', Eochaidh Ó hEódhusa likewise celebrates the accession of James Stuart to the English throne suggesting that such a great event would have merited Ovid's literary attentions, presumably in his verse chronicle of great transformations, *Metamorphoses*. In his view this dynastic windfall marks the inauguration of an era of illustrious good fortune and prosperity ('gach ní d'fhilleadh ar fheabhas'). Liberty of speech has been restored to the weak ('Atá libeirte a labhra 'gun anbhfainne agallmha') and concomitantly the voice of injustice now lies subdued ('guth na héagcára as íseal'). The three kingdoms have attained a degree of harmony ('Suaimh-nighthear gan ghoimh gan ghliaidh díosgoir dian 'sa dá dheirbhshiair'), while the fruits of this new epoch of good fortune are, of course, to be attributed to James's earthly apotheosis:[13]

> An ghrian loinneardha do las;
> sgaoileadh gach ceó Cing Séamas;
> tug 'na glóir comhorchra cháigh:
> móir na comhortha claochláidh.

> The brilliant sun lit up:
> King James is the dispersal of all mist:
> the joint mourning of all he changed to glory;
> great the signs of change.

People in Ireland had particular reason to be thankful for this political transformation. Indeed, Ó hEódhusa claims that they had supposedly forgotten their woes ('gur dhearmaid gach duine dhíon treabhlaid na n-uile imsh-níomh') and he suggests that an appropriate juncture was at hand for his compatriots to bid farewell to a 'yoke of anxiety' ('ceiliobhradh dár ccuing imnidh'). In speaking of the past distress of the Irish, who are defined in eth-nically-inclusive terms as 'the troubled people of Ireland' ('popal imsh-níomhach Éirionn'), he must surely be referring to the latter part of Elizabeth's reign when the consolidation of the crown's writ was effected.[14]

Ó hEódhusa intimates obliquely that accelerated English expansionism has hardly been propitious from an Irish viewpoint, regardless of indigenous ethnic provenance. Like Mac an Bhaird in 'Trí coróna i gcairt Shéamais', he discerns in the arrival of the Scottish monarch in Whitehall some portents of optimism for the Irish. Again reflecting Mac an Bhaird's interpretation, it is implied that the presence of a Stuart sovereign in London will possibly dilute the otherwise uncushioned impact of Anglo-Saxon dominion in Ireland. His treatment of what is envisaged as the curtailment of the expansionist thrust in crown policy is obscure. Possibly anxious to placate the Dublin regime on the demise of the Tudor Queen, he speaks of a 'fallen brightness' (namely, the Elizabethan era) overtaken by the great splendour which embodies the reign of James ('deallradh éagcoimse as ann tig an chéadshoillse an tann tairnig'). Curiously, this observation appears intended as a reason why London should acquiesce with confidence in the overlordship of James. Paradoxically, but perhaps more candidly, Ó hEódhusa in the following quatrain proposes to interpret the accession of the new king as a diminution of London's sovereignty ('Bearrradh flaithis bhfear Lunndan'). Though her subjects grieved the day Elizabeth died, their sorrow rapidly acceded to joy ('lá a rathuirse bás a mbróin') and by evening there was promise of greater glory ('dob fhás athshoilse um iarnóin').[15] Somewhat disingenuously, Ó hEódhusa advocates the notion of a Jacobean era of glorious success while concurrently implying that English hegemony in Ireland might be diminished along the way.

Not content with hailing James as a messianic defender of Britain and Ireland, Ó hEódhusa declares, rather implausibly, that his reign will result in the propagation of universal good and that, accordingly, James Stuart's elevation should be welcomed all over the world ('Ionann san uile dhomhan as oircheas a fhiadhoghadh'). The viewpoints formulated in both 'Trí coróna i gcairt Shéamais' and 'Mór theasda dh'obair Óivid' are affirmations of renewed bardic confidence in the aftermath of a traumatic process of professional retrenchment and government persecution. Ó hEódhusa's confidence in the Stuart dynasty contrasts dramatically with the earlier dispirited complaints of an anonymous Munster poet composing sometime in the initial decades of Elizabeth's reign. Despairing at the apparent attrition of the Gaelic polity, this poet feared for its imminent disintegration unless the assistance of overseas allies was forthcoming:[16]

> Crúaidh an cás a ttarlamair
> ar tteacht deiridh an domhain,
> acht gurab iad allmhuraigh
> is dócha dhúinn dár ccobhair.
>
> With the end of the world upon us, our
> plight is harsh indeed, but that the
> foreigners are the most likely prospect
> for us of help.

By 1603 the foreign allies of the *Gaoidhil* had come and gone: one immediate source of potential accommodation, in an otherwise inauspicious political climate, lay in the exploitation of James's tenuous Gaelic links. Unfortunately for Ó hEódhusa and Mac an Bhaird and the seigneurial élite whose thinking they may well have reflected, James had neither desire nor reason to emphasise his Gaelic connexions on arrival in the English capital.

Ironically, the *Gaoidhil* were once again making their case to a foreign dynast.

The acccession of the Stuart king to the English throne may be said to have temporarily boosted the morale of bardic poets, particularly in the early years of his reign. There is some evidence of a reinstatement of former bardic poise, even arrogance, in several poems composed between 1603 and 1607. Eoghan Ruadh Mac an Bhaird's composition, 'Dána an turas tríalltar sonn', testifies to a renewal of vibrant Gaelic self-assurance. In December, 1602, Rory O'Donnell, brother of Hugh Roe (ob. 1602), submitted to lord deputy Mountjoy. Earlier in the same year, Mountjoy had crossed the Blackwater with a force of three thousand men and had begun to lay waste the Gaelic heartlands of Ulster. Subsequent to his initial surrender, Rory repaired to Dublin and London to secure his peace with the government. The culmination of O'Donnell's submission was his ennoblement as the earl of Tyrconnell in September, 1603. 'Dána an turas tríalltar sonn' was composed on his departure for Dublin. It is characterised by two contrasting emotional strands: one of apprehension for the fate of O'Donnell at the hands of his erstwhile enemies and another of quiet confidence in his ability to circumvent the difficulties ahead. Like Ó hEódhusa and Fearghal Óg Mac an Bhaird, Eoghan Ruadh harboured no illusions about a return to unconditional Gaelic autonomy. He too suggests that strategic political accommodation was henceforth essential if the *Gaoidhil* were to retain a measure of political autonomy. The poet's outlook is evident in the opening quatrain where he equates O'Donnell's journey to Dublin with the end of untrammelled Gaelic suzerainty ('geall re hoighidh an eachtra, doiligh earr na huaisleachta'). Yet Rory had no choice, his fate had already been decided by the callous and incontrovertible fortunes of war ('Le leathtrom cogaidh Chraoi Fhloinn do mealladh mac Uí Dhomhnoill'). The leader of the O'Donnells must meet the men responsible for his submission ('aighidh ar an lucht ros ling'). Ominously, where O'Donnell formerly went to wreak havoc, he now sued for peace ('Na róid ina roicheadh soin go ttrásda a ttreallmhaibh cogaidh, taidlidh go síothchánna sonn').[17]

Although mindful of O'Donnell's less than encouraging bargaining position, the poet manages to maintain a degree of confidence in Rory's ability to manipulate English fears to his own ends. Indeed, O'Donnell's coevals considered his mission to Dublin a task well suited to his skills ('Gidh eadh, measaid óig Eamhna . . . an turussa . . . 'na chéim urusa aige'). In spite of his controversial career, the crown administration was prepared to overlook his transgressions, so keen was the desire to secure peace ('Foghla gráineamhla an ghille ní chuimhnigh cath Duibhlinne'). For not withstanding past actions against them, the English were certain to pardon him ('A ndearna orra, as é a shuim, maithtear do mhac Uí Dhomhnaill').[18] This positive tone is continued in the remaining stanzas of the poem. Mac an Bhaird highlights the importance of the O'Donnell dynasty in Ireland and suggests that once the lord deputy had secured peace he would be little concerned with outstanding malcontents, since their subsequent surrender was merely a formality:

Ón tráth fa ttáinig 'na cceann
fear ionaidh airdríogh Éireann,
brígh 'na ccéimiondaibh ní chuir,
sídh Éirionnaigh ní híarthuir.

Since the deputy of Ireland's high king
came to them, he sets no store by
their doings, peace is sought with
no Irishman.

The poet's attribution of the description 'Ireland's high king' to James ('airdríogh Éireann') and the inclusive categorisation of his compatriots as 'Irishmen' (*Éirionnaigh*) rather than *Gaoidhil* is reminiscent of Ó hEódhusa's conceptual approach in 'Mór theasda dh'obair Óivid'. Once it becomes known to the Irish that the leader of the O'Donnells had proceeded to a peace convention in Dublin, the English can then rest assured of their security ('Faigsin codhnaigh Chlann Dálaigh i nÁth Cliath a ccomhdhálaibh dáil cháomhanta do chrích Ghall').[19] While Mac an Bhaird's confidence in the strength of Rory's position may seem overly optimistic in the context of the *status quo* in 1603, it is worth remembering that O'Donnell secured preferential government favour in the face of similar demands from his cousin, Niall Garbh O'Donnell, a sometime ally of the administration.

Two other poems attributed to Eoghan Ruadh Mac an Bhaird are also indicative of a phase of bardic ideological renewal characterised by a resourceful consciousness of prevailing realities. Poems such as 'Cia re bhfáiltigh fian Éirne' and 'Rob soraidh an séadsa soir' present the view of an author cognisant of the limitations in the Gaelic position in the post-Kinsale period, but who, nonetheless, is ready to adapt to circumstances to ensure a continued measure of bardic influence.[20] 'Cia re bhfáiltigh fian Éirne' was composed to celebrate the birth of a son, Hugh, to Rory O'Donnell and his wife Bridget (née Fitzgerald), in 1606.[21] As might be expected, the poet invokes the conventions customary to a composition of this type. The birth of an heir and son to the earl of Tyrconnell is welcomed and acclaimed by the people of his lordship ('Ní hiongnad fáilti dá bhfuil roimhe ag crích chloinne Dáluigh').[22] The poem's main interest, however, lies in the frank references made to the recent troubled history of the O'Donnells. Mac an Bhaird regards Hugh's birth as an omen propitious to a brighter future for the O'Donnells and as a promise of the alleviation of communal misfortune ('d'éis choimhfhillti ar a séan soin'). He points to the death of Hugh Roe in 1602 as a deciding factor in the failure of O'Donnell fortunes:[23]

Ó ló éaga Aodha Ruaidh
atá an laochruidh lán d'anbhuain,
i gceas naoidhion gus anocht
bheas ag caoineadh a gcumhacht.

> From the day of Hugh Roe's death the heroes
> have been full of dismay, in weakness of
> travail until tonight, perchance bewailing
> [the loss of] their power.

The newly-born Hugh epitomised the renewal of the O'Donnell family ('dia a n-aithbheodhuigh as sé sin'), constituting as they did a bulwark against English machination ('cosg iarghná na taoibhe tall') and in this respect representing the hope of the nobility ('grian-lá saoire na saorchlann').[24] In other words, Mac an Bhaird envisaged a consolidation of Gaelic prospects and a diminution of English influence. Nonetheless, he appears to acknowledge the contemporary political situation, though positing a more secure foundation for traditional seigneurial autonomy. Critically, there is no evidence in the poem to suggest that he envisaged a campaign of armed resistance to the crown administration.

A corresponding sense of pragmatism is apparent in Mac an Bhaird's attributed 'Rob soraidh an séadsa soir', which he composed *c.* 1607(?) in the form of a verse adieu for Turlough Mc Art O'Neill. The latter visited England at that time in an attempt to obtain official support for his bid to hold the family lands directly from the crown rather than from the earl of Tyrone.[25] This piece could well be interpreted as an example of bardic hyperbole because of the overly grandiose aspirations ascribed to Turlough. At the time of its composition, however, it was no doubt intended to serve as nothing more than a morale booster for a junior scion of the O'Neill family. The poet is simply performing the customary duties required of a *fileadh* in a situation where his patron proposes to secure the family's lands ('Do chuaidh go Lundain tar lear, d'fhaghail oighreachta a shinnsear').[26] Much time and effort is devoted to appropriate comments on Turlough's aristocratic pedigree in order to endorse his suitability for the mission in hand ('Dósan go madh réim ratha mac Airt ua gach ardfhlatha'). Yet when the conventional verbiage is pared away, the nub of the poet's argument centres on two deceptively simple quatrains towards the beginning of the poem. Here he emphasises a factor essential to the success of Turlough's plan. Unless he secures the favour of King James the journey will have been in vain:[27]

> Re headh iomagallmu an ríogh
> go madh ionann d'ua na n-áirdríogh,
> slat na bhfírfregra ngeal glan
> fofhear na sír-eagna Solamh.

> Go ngabha rí Sagsan soin
> briathra millsi ua Eoghain,
> cisde chliar fíorghlan na bhfionn
> da riar fa ríoghmhagh Raoilionn.

During the time of [his] interview with the
king may this descendant of the high kings –
the scion of true answers (?) bright, pure –
be an equal to Solomon of perpetual wisdom.

May the Saxon king accept the sweet
words of the descendant of Eoghan,
treasury of true poets of the Fair,
being served throughout the royal plain of *Raoilionn*.

In fact, James Stuart did determine Turlough's fate in London. Despite the poem's traditional presentation, the author admits that executive authority lay within the purvey of the crown. As it happened, Turlough was unsuccessful in realising his objectives and he returned home with permission to continue residence in the family lands, which were to be held from the earl of Tyrone.[28]

James's accession in 1603 thus provided a brief moment of ideological respite for the bardic élite. The Gaelic origin myth of the Stuart dynasty encouraged a perception that a benignly disposed James might ameliorate the most intrusive features of the Elizabethan conquest. The weakening of the bardic institution during Elizabeth's reign suggests that expectation of royal favour was both professional and political in focus. At this juncture, bardic aspirations coincided neatly with those of the Gaelic seigneurial élite as a whole. In advocating flexible accommodation to the new dispensation, some poets sought to present an ideological case for the conservation of the remaining vestiges of Gaelic autonomy. A high degree of continuity in Gaelic social and political custom was essential to the viability of the bardic apparatus and it was with this imperative in mind that poets attempted to mediate change in the context of selective adaptation as opposed to outright socio-political transformation.[29]

Bardic Socio-political Narrative, 1607–1612

The expectation or illusion that Gaelic sovereignty might be guaranteed under the supposedly benign auspices of James was severely strained when the earls of Tyrconnell and Tyrone sailed for the continent on 4 September 1607. Their flight and the subsequent failure of Sir Cahir O'Doherty's revolt in 1608 cleared the way for the wholesale plantation of six counties in Ulster with English and lowland Scots settlers.[30] If a watershed may be identified over the protracted course of bardic decline, it is the year 1607 which must be highlighted rather than Edmund Curtis's 1603. The brief flourish of optimism evident in the work of some poets on James's ascent to the throne was now all but submerged by a wave of embittered anguish. This section examines bardic reactions to accelerated political and social change as they relate to four particular themes: bardic corporate paralysis, the eclipse of the seigneurial élite, the ongoing merger of Gaelic and Anglo-Norman interests and bardic perceptions of the established church.

In 1603, Eochaidh Ó hEódhusa facetiously professed a wish to exchange the convoluted rules of syllabic poetry for the easy rewards of popular and unsophisticated doggerel ('ár shórt gnáthach grés robhog, is mó as a moltar sinde'). Declaring that his banality of expression would not be matched even by inveterate simpletons ('Mo gheallsa ar bhuga ar mhaoile ní bhérdaois daoithe an bheatha'), he claims that the composition of popular verse is more rewarding than bardic poetry. At this stage, Ó hEódhusa's tone in 'Ionmholta malairt bhisigh' is assuredly one of ironic banter.[31] By 1607 other poets had begun to echo, altogether less whimsically, the mock sentiments expressed just a few years earlier by the distinguished Fermanagh poet. If Ó hEódhusa could allow himself the luxury of sceptical condescension with regard to new developments, his fellow poets in the years after 1607 were to confront a scenario where no such option was feasible. The complaint that poets no longer enjoyed the profits to which their profession had historically entitled them becomes much more common after 1607. For instance, Mathghamhain Ó hIfearnáin in 'A mhic ná meabhraigh éigse' counselled his son against taking up the family profession of poetry ('ceard do shean rót róthréigse'). While composition of poetry merited the highest respect ('tús anóra gér dhual di'), now the bardic profession was without profit ('gá tarbha dán do dhéanamh').[32] Fear Flatha Ó Gnímh addressed the same question in 'Mairg do-chuaidh re ceird ndúthchais'. Like Ó hIfearnáin, he argues that it was wiser in current circumstances not to follow the hereditary bardic vocation ('rug ar Bhanbha mbarrúrthais nach dualghas athar is fhearr'), and that the offspring of bardic families should instead seek alternative work ('malairt oibre ionnsaighthear'). He laments that bardic poets were not trained in a practical trade before taking up their apprenticeship in versification and traditional scholarship ('Mairg d'ollamh dá nárbh aithnidh ceard nábudh cúis iomaithbhir'). Ó Gnímh traces the decline of the bardic ethos to the diminishment of the Gaelic élite ('Do mhionughadh na mac ríogh, cuirthear na duana i ndimbríogh'), in present conditions poets are better off as ploughmen (''na gcriadhairibh oir gurbh fhearr do sgoil fhiadhoirir Éireann').[33]

Increasingly isolated as a result of the reversal of fortune endured by formerly affluent patrons, bardic poets were obliged to acknowledge a professional impasse. The attrition of the superior echelons of the Gaelic polity had been proceeding at a gradual pace since the failure of the Desmond rebellion in 1583 – indeed, this process had begun even earlier in areas adjacent to the Pale. The drop in the number of patrons willing to support poets must have reached an unprecedented low with the departure of O'Neill, O'Donnell and Maguire from Ulster. In future, patronage might be had only from a much depleted cohort of minor families such as the O'Haras in Leyney and the Clandeboye O'Neills. Moreover, with the progression of time and through force of political pressure, many élite families tended to become anglicised. Of course, shrinking patronage was a symptom rather than a cause of the disintegration of the bardic institution. In a jurisdiction where common law increasingly prevailed, the sanctioning role of poets rapidly became redundant. The elaborate ideological stock-in-trade of the bardic apparatus had no meaningful role in a society ordered in accordance with the norms of English governance and primogeniture in particular. Furthermore, a process of profound trauma and self-assessment for the poets was coloured by exposure to continental humanism while the deep-seated anguish reflected in the poetry is an indication of a professional élite reacting to self-metamorphosis in the face of both social disruption and cultural challenge.

The fall off in seigneurial engagement is reflected in vehement bardic complaints that members of the élite had turned away from poetry and in the aspersions cast by *fileadha* on the work of popular folk poets. When Fear Feasa Ó an Cháinte addressed a poem outlining his straitened circumstances to the Munster nobleman, Florence MacCarthy, he lamented that no one among the *Clann Charrthaigh* saw fit to extend him support. In his opinion, the MacCarthys resembled all other men, with no particular distinguishing trait, for if they were still loyal to Gaelic mores it had eluded his notice ('siad na ndaoinibh mar gach ndreim, más Gaoidhil iad ní aithnim').[34] Equally repugnant to the bardic sensibility was the idea that the stressed verse of popular poets should merit wider recognition than their work. While bardic poets suffered the loss of their most influential patrons and witnessed the progressive enfeeblement or anglicisation of the lesser rungs of aristocratic Gaeldom, the popular culture of the lower reaches of Gaelic society must have remained relatively undisturbed. The expression of bardic contempt for the calibre and popularity of demotic poetry is a common enough theme in bardic work of the period.

Articulated from a bardic viewpoint, Fear Feasa Ó an Cháinte's 'Mór do-ghníd daoine dhíobh féin' is a biting indictment of popular pretensions to learning. He inveighs against those elements who disregard traditional scholarship and yet vaunt their supposed erudition ('Maoidhid do bhriathraib baotha, go mbíd fesach fíorshaotha; gan d'eladain ann acht sen'). Ó an Cháinte presents one of those he so despises, declaring the composition of bardic poetry a futile activity ('ní maith an dán re déiniom'), while even the most intricate of syllabic compositions elicits a dismissive comment from such characters ('Is dona an dán an dán soin'). He is emphatic in his attribution of plebeian origins to bardic detractors, for instance one such sceptic is termed a 'bastard':[35]

> D'egla go lenfaide a lorg,
> adeir trú bhíos na bhastord;
> ní chongbann a chuma anos,
> ní fhognann sunna an senchos.

> For fear lest his own derivation be
> investigated your scamp that is a bastard cries:
> 'antiquarian lore no longer keeps its shape (is out of fashion now);
> among us here it will not do at all!'

It is significant that Ó an Cháinte should borrow from English to denigrate a supposed social inferior. The choice of 'bastard' was probably aimed at an emergent cadre of native society who sought to master English as a means of improving their social and financial lot. A knowledge of that language would, no doubt, have been vital for those eager to prosper under the new order. For instance, the anonymous author of *Pairlement Chloinne Tomáis* (composed 1608–15), lampoons arriviste elements for their ineffectual and often ludicrous attempts to speak English.[36] Internally-focused Gaelic social tension informs many of the complaints made by *fileadha* about reduced circumstances. Given that the emphasis and operation of the bardic institution was anchored to a viable aristocratic network, it was inevitable once it began to dissolve that many aspects of the bardic code of practice should become obsolete. This process of dislocation is vividly delineated, for instance, in Fear Feasa Ó an Cháinte's indignation at popular indifference to learned pronunciation of Irish ('In áit na soibhés sennda, is na nguithedh ngaoidelta; a gcerda naoide is mairg mhór').[37]

Bardic participation in an élite nexus is implicit in Fear Flatha Ó Gnímh's celebrated elegy entitled 'Táirnig éigse fhuinn Ghaoidheal'. A reference in the poem to the death of Eochaidh Ó hEódhusa suggests that it should be dated to approximately 1612.[38] By means of a roll-call of illustrious bardic families, the poet creates a simple but effective memorial to an eclipsed caste ('ár gan fhuighleach a n-ársoin'). Although this enumeration of the leading bardic families is primarily of antiquarian interest, it is the articulation of the root cause of bardic decline which is particularly enlightening. In Ó Gnímh's view, the inversion of the previously ascendant social order had precipitated bardic dissolution. He claims that the privileging of the lower orders at the expense of the élite had engendered contempt for bardic poetry:[39]

> Tug fógra dhámh an domhain
> is col d'fhagháil d'ealadhain
> fuil chrannda dá cora i gcion
> 's na fola arda íseal.

> The proscription of the entire bardic class,
> and the contemptuous attitude to poetry,
> have resulted from the debasement of noble stock
> and the elevation of base blood.

Obviously exercised by this perception of social anarchy, Ó Gnímh broods on the same point in 'Mairg do-chuaidh re ceird ndúthchais'.

Mathghamhain Ó hIfearnáin provides an appropriate concluding testimony in the present review of bardic self-perception in the years 1607–1612. In a previous reference to 'A mhic ná meabhraigh éigse', it was seen that Ó hIfearnáin advised his son against following a career in poetry. However, he did append a codicil to this warning stating that if determined to become a poet his son should not deal with the *Gaoidhil*, but rather focus his attentions on English clients ('dá molair ná mol Gaoidheal'). Unfortunately, those who undertook to laud the *Gaoidhil* could expect to be reviled on this account ('tuar faladh d'aoinfhear lér bh'áil maladh Gaoidheal do ghabháil'). Rather, an aspiring poet is best advised to praise the English, who, in any case, were now the most likely source of support ('mol-sa crú gasraidhe Gall ós rú is casmhaile cumann').[40] Actually, Ó hIfearnáin's suggestion is not quite as far-fetched as it may seem in retrospect. The evidence does indeed reveal that poets were ready to compose for English newcomers, primarily in order to posit a process of inculturation, and that in turn some newcomers were willing to extend a certain level of patronage to poets.[41] Generally, while poets bemoaned disappearing bardic privilege, it needs to be stressed that these plaintive dirges are too easily overemphasised by contemporary scholars and as such are assigned an unwarranted significance in the overall interpretative context. If the testimony of professional trauma is to be read accurately, it must also be remembered that despite great upheaval, or perhaps more accurately because of it, James's reign witnessed impressive bardic ideological reassessment. No doubt, *fileadha* were dismayed by bardic corporate stasis and troubled by a relatively fluid social interchange resulting from the emasculation of the Gaelic élite, but their surviving work demonstrates how subtly they coped with contemporary events. If not overwhelmed, how did poets respond to the dissolution of Gaelic autonomy and how did they interpret the consequences of the flight of the northern earls? In the following paragraphs, a selection of poems is examined which bring these questions into clearer focus.

'Cáit ar ghabhadar Gaoidhil?', attributed to Lochlainn Ó Dálaigh, laments the destruction of an élite Gaelic milieu. Moreover, references in the poem to the Ulster plantation suggest that it was composed *c.* 1610. The poet presents a symbolic outline of a world where youths hunted, wined and dined, and relaxed at their leisure to the strains of poetic declamations in noble households. Now that life-style was imperilled and the old haunts of the aristocracy lay deserted or occupied by foreign settlers ('fuaras bruidhne Banbha Cuinn, buidhne a h-adhbha 's ní fhaghuim').[42] He notes ironically that the disappearance of leading noblemen had not resulted from magical incantation ('Ní briochd síodhuidhe seanta . . . do léircheil oirne ré h-eadh na roighne ó ghléithreibh Ghaoidheal'). In reality, they had been obliged to follow the path of exile ('meic ríogh ó bhionnardthoigh Bhreagh, ionnarbthoigh dhíobh do dhéineamh') and in their place had come a motley crew of English and Scots settlers:[43]

Atá againn 'na n-ionadh
dírim uaibhreach eisiodhan
d'fhuil Ghall, do ghasraidh Mhonaidh,
Saxoin ann is Albonaigh.

We have in their stead an arrogant impure
crowd of foreigners' blood,
of the race of *Monadh*
– there are Saxons there, and Scots.

More specifically, the anonymous poem 'Mo-chean don loingse tar lear' and Fearghal Óg Mac an Bhaird's 'Mór an lucht arthraigh Éire' both lament the flight of the earls of Tyrone and Tyrconnell and Cú Chonnacht Maguire in 1607. Mac an Bhaird emphasises how the departure of the earls devastated Ireland ('Do ghad a hanam aisde, Éire na gcuan gciomhaiste'), for in their wake they left behind an exhausted country ('cuire san luing-sin tar linn do thuirrsigh uile Éirinn') and their departure engendered universal lamentation in Ireland ('s tug a ndul tar fairrge bhfinn gul gacha hairde i nÉirinn').[44] In a strikingly fresh deployment of a stock theme in Gaelic literature, the author represents their loss to the island as the equivalent of an unprecedented raid for booty inflicted on the country ('ar Mhúr Dá Thí Teach Lughaidh; creach mar í ní hionnshamhail').[45] Their removal is unambiguously construed as a profound tragedy affecting the entire island of Ireland. Mac an Bhaird and the author of 'Mo-chean don loingse tar lear' agree in their assessment of the political prospects facing post-1607 Gaelic society and crucially both view the loss of O'Donnell and Tyrone as an inestimable blow to the preservation of Gaelic autonomy. The sundering of dynamic leadership from the polity had, in their opinion, left it bereft of focus. Mac an Bhaird argues that Ireland's glory is aboard the vessel taking the earls to the continent ('glóir Banbha i mbáirc na deise') and he declares that prospects of future prosperity for the island have figuratively embarked with O'Neill and O'Donnell ('ana Gaoidheal Ghuirt Fhionntain is toirthe craobh Fhuinn Uisnigh ar-aon san luing luchtmhair-sin').[46] The author of 'Mo-chean don loingse tar lear' is also specific in his delineation of the impact which the exile of O'Neill and O'Donnell had registered on Ireland.[47] He considers the flight to have drained the vigour and potency of the Gaelic Irish ('na Gaoidhil aniú sa neart go fiú an aoinfhir ar n-imtheacht') and now Ireland lay deprived of every last trace of vitality ('Ní mhaireann déis an eathair . . . dé don Bhanbha ar beathughadh'). The vessel which sailed from Lough Swilly in September 1607 bore with it across the seas the authentic political sovereignty of Ireland:

Do chuaidh oireachus bhfear bhFáil
anonn uainne don Easbáin
tar sál re lucht na luinge
tár as a ucht oruinne.

> The sovereignty of the men of *Fál* has gone
> from us to Spain, across the sea with the
> ship's company; we are in disgrace
> because of it.

The poet wishes that the departure had never occurred ('Dá mbeith nach beidis san luing'), but now that the earls had sailed for the continent it was truly a cause of bitter regret ('cúis doilghe a síneadh tar sál').[48]

Bardic apprehension that the removal of Gaelic grandees from Ireland would herald the truncation of an autonomous Gaelic polity was further exacerbated by the deaths in Italy of Rory O'Donnell and Cú Chonnacht Maguire in 1608.[49] Eoghan Ruadh Mac an Bhaird composed 'Truagh do chor a chroidhe tim' on hearing of the illness which ultimately led to Rory's death. While Mac an Bhaird conveys a sense of heartfelt sadness on hearing of O'Donnell's condition, he makes it clear that his deepest fear stemmed from the thought of O'Donnell's possible loss to Ireland ('achd don triall tarla roimhe, 's d'iath Bhanbha go mbeanfoidhe'). Addressing O'Donnell directly, he relates metaphorically that were Ireland to hear what he had learned about the earl's predicament, the country would presume its ruin imminent ('do mheasfadh a míobhuadh féin'). If the Irish learned of his misfortune, they would unanimously ask who would become their guarantor, if Rory were to pass away ('cía linn do laoidhfidhe anocht, ó saoilfidhe inn d'fhurtocht?'). He concludes with a fervent prayer for O'Donnell's recovery and he observes that only his enemies are left unmoved by Rory's plight ('ní bhí achd námha léan neamhthruagh').[50]

A corresponding theme of personal and pan-insular bereavement is replicated in a poem composed by Fearghal Óg Mac an Bhaird entitled 'Truagh liom Máire agus Mairgrég'. A lament for the deceased and exiled members of the O'Donnell family, which, at the time of the poem's composition, was represented in Ireland by two remaining sisters, Mary (Máire) and Margaret (Mairgréag). The third O'Donnell sister, Nuala, had joined her brother in his flight from Ireland. The poet refers to the deaths of the brothers Hugh Roe (ob. 1602), Cathbharr (ob. 1608) and Rory (ob. 1608). Another brother, Manus, had died of battle wounds in Ireland in 1600.[51] As in 'Truagh do chor a chroidhe tim' the poet expresses personal sorrow but concludes that communal grief for Ireland's loss of her patrician defenders must be greater:[52]

> Ní hí Mairgrég ná Máire
> chaoinim, is cúis diombáighe,
> acht an cor-sa ar cró na bhFionn,
> mó sa mhó osna Éiriond.

> I mourn not for Margaret nor Mary
> – that is ground for sorrow – but for this fate
> that has fallen upon the land of the Fair,
> greater and ever greater is the sighing of Ireland.

The same sense of communal bereavement is explored by Eochaidh Ó hEódhusa in his 'Beag mhaireas do mhacraidh Ghaoidheal' composed for Sir Brian MacMahon (ob. 1622) of Oriel sometime between 1607 and 1612.[53] While he eulogises MacMahon as expected, this piece is just as much concerned with the depressed condition of the Gaelic polity as with the fortunes of the lord of Oriel. He dwells on the dispirited and abject state of the Gaelic Irish, claiming that so miserable was their daily existence, that it must be equated with living death ('geall re bás a mbeatha ghnáth') and he generally discerns reason for lament everywhere ('gach ní ad-chiu ní fátha faoilte'). The Gaelic Irish had exchanged their pride for passivity ('Tugsad ulcha ar inntinn chúthail') and their vivacity for sadness ('s céadfadh ar múith'). Reaching the end of a period of good fortune ('téarma a gconáigh do chaith siad'), they had in effect been overwhelmed by an eclipsing deluge ('gur mhúch tuile orchra iad').[54] This poem and those examined above offer a vivid account of how bardic poets perceived élite Gaelic society and culture in the post-1607 period. Acknowledging that aristocratic Gaeldom confronted decisive political and social challenge, they enunciate this realisation with forceful clarity and cogency.

As will be clear from earlier discussion of 'Fearann cloidhimh críoch Bhanbha', Tadhg Dall Ó hUiginn sought to legitimate the Anglo-Norman presence in Ireland within the contextual parameters of Gaelic historical orthodoxy by proposing to unite the Gaelic Irish and gaelicised descendants of medieval colonists within a shared identity of common cultural sensibility and reference. Aspects of Ó hUiginn's inclusive ethnic outlook are mirrored in other poems composed after 1607. Historically, bardic poets were prepared to benefit fully from the patronage provided by families of Anglo-Norman pedigree, yet the medieval settlers were never systematically stitched into the seam of conventional Gaelic ideology.[55] References in poems composed after 1607 evidence a sophisticated bardic recognition of the feasibility of the formal coalescence of Gaelic and gaelicised Anglo-Norman identities in the face of New English distrust. A coherent presentation of inclusive ethnic consciousness is made in a poem, 'A leabhráin ainmnighther d'Aodh', which was composed by Eoghan Ruadh Mac an Bhaird for Hugh, son of Rory O'Donnell. While its date of origin is unclear, it was obviously composed on the continent. Moreover, the absence of reference to Rory and the portrayal of Hugh as the people's guarantor ('Aodh Ó Domhnaill, dóthchus cáigh') may be taken to suggest that it was composed after Rory's death in 1608.[56] The poem was intended to accompany a manuscript translation Mac an Bhaird had made of a treatise on warfare ('leabhar ar riaghlachaibh et ar inneall an chogaidh') and which apparently was for presentation to Hugh.[57] No trace now remains of the manuscript, although its loss in no way detracts from the poem's main historical interest, namely its articulation of a revamped ethnic consciousness. While Mac an Bhaird directed his translation at Hugh O'Donnell in particular, he is equally specific in his stated objective to have this volume circulate among the grandees of Ireland:[58]

Ar son go sealbhuighim sibh
d'Ú Dhomhnaill tar fonn bFionntain,
an fonn ar gach taobh tiomchuil,
ronn ris gach n-aon d'Éirionnchaibh.

Though I present you to O'Donnell
above all in Fintan's land, go around
the land on every side, share with
every Irishman.

He envisaged all Irishmen, of both Gaelic and Anglo-Norman stock, avail-
ing of the military manual's guidance and the descendants of the Gaelic *Síol
Eoghain, Cinéal gConaill, Ír Éireamhóin, Éibhear* and *Lughaidh* are enumerated
in this regard along with families of Anglo-Norman descent such as the Butlers, Burkes and Geraldine Fitzgeralds ('na Búrcaigh, na Builtéaruigh, na
Gearoltuigh'). In the following stanza, Mac an Bhaird again reiterates his
desire to see the manual used with profit by *Gaoidhil* and *Gaill* alike:

Ar neach do shliocht Gaoidhil Ghlais
ná ceil gach iúl dá n-úarais,
ná ar Sheanghallaibh fóid na bhFionn,
lér cheanglamair óig Éirionn.

Conceal from the race of *Gaoidheal Glas* no
knowledge that you have found, nor from the
Anglo-Normans of the land of the Fair, with
whom we, the warriors of Ireland, have united.

The poem concludes with a valedictory allusion to the theme of ethnic
coalescence by extending a blessing to both historic communities who are
collectively described as 'our own *Gaoidhil* and Anglo-Normans' ('Ar nGaoidh-
il ar bFionnghoill féin').[59] Of course, this mutuality of interests is predicated
on the factor of common participation in the rituals of élite Gaelic culture. In
fact, the privileging of a Gaelic cultural vision is an essential component in
bardic facilitation of inter-ethnic coalescence and underlines the extent to
which the majority host culture dominated this unequal ideological merger.

Elements of the same sympathetic attitude to historic ethnic diversity are
also evident in two other poems composed around the same time as 'A
leabhráin ainmnighther d'Aodh'. In 'Fogus furtacht don tír thuaidh', Fearghal
Óg Mac an Bhaird hails Hugh, son of Rory O'Donnell, as the guarantor of his
kindred and Ireland, while towards the close of this poem of fifty-two stanzas, it is noted that Hugh could rely not only on the backing of the *Gaoidhil*
but also on that of the Anglo-Normans, 'the English longest settled in Ireland'
('s na Goill as sine i gClár Chuinn').[60] In 'Beannacht ar anmain Éireann', Fear
Flatha Ó Gnímh speaks of an onslaught against Gaelic culture and society,

dwelling especially on the straitened circumstances of prominent septs such as the O'Donnells, O'Neills, and Maguires. Significantly, he includes the Munster Fitzgeralds in a representative list of Irish grandees ('mo thruaighe gléire Gearailt').[61] There was, then, a formally-mediated acknowledgment among these poets that the gaelicised descendants of Anglo-Norman colonists should no longer be excluded from Gaelic historical orthodoxy simply on account of non-Gaelic antecedents. The catalyst powering a re-evaluation of conventional attitudes to ethnicity derived from early modern New English expansionism. The manifestation and cultivation of an inclusive notion of politicised nationality typifies bardic capacity for conceptual innovation in the midst of structural dissolution. The reconfiguration of ethnic identities was a critical step in the creation of an Irish nationality defined by the ideological constants of religion, culture and territorial sovereignty.

It has been argued in the foregoing chapter that the surviving evidence illustrates no theological engagement on the part of the bardic caste with sectarian polemics during Elizabeth's reign. In fact, the most detailed and informed extant response to the Protestant reformation comes not from classical poets, but from two Gaelic churchmen and littérateurs, Eoghan Ó Dubhthaigh and Maolmhuire Ó hUiginn. The muted reaction of the bardic caste to questions of religious controversy seems to have remained fairly constant during James's reign. While a handful of poems dating to the early years of the seventeenth century manifest concern at the negative social implications posed by anti-Catholic measures, these declarations of apprehension are neither developed nor systematic. It is not altogether surprising, in light of similar evidence from the Elizabethan period, to find the most sustained response to ecclesiastical issues, in Gaelic verse in the early years of James's reign, emanating from a cleric immersed in a continental counter-reformation milieu, Giolla Brighde Ó hEódhusa. Among bardic poets, Eoghan Ruadh Mac an Bhaird reflects a measure of social concern with the localised impact of Protestant reformers. In the poem, 'Maith an sealad fuair Éire', he dedicates a monumental tribute of ninety-one stanzas to the memory of Rory, earl of Tyrconnell (ob. 1608). Combining two thematic strands, the poem is concerned with O'Donnell while concurrently presenting an elegiac celebration of Gaelic history over three thousand years, culminating contemporaneously in the depredations of the most recent influx of newcomers.[62] The author highlights and lauds the stout resistance mounted by the O'Donnell sept against the extension of the crown's writ. Significantly, Mac an Bhaird also emphasises what he perceived as O'Donnell hostility to the established church. For instance, the O'Donnells refused to countenance in their territory what are disparagingly described as Luther's sect ('sect Lúitéir'), Calvin's teaching ('léighionn Cailbhín') and heretical bishops ('ná maor easbog eithrigigh'). Apparently, while churches throughout Ireland were profaned ('ar dtruailleadh Eaglas Éirionn'), those at Derry and Raphoe remained inviolate ('nír coilleadh a gcádhas sin'). He juxtaposes O'Donnell opposition to the established church with their implacable political hostility to the crown administration, which, it is implied, feared that its objectives would remain unrealised in the northern province:[63]

> Nách báidhfead an creideamh cóir,
> nach bíadh cumhacht gun choróin,
> roiriaghladh do réir a tol,
> ná coimhíarnadh d'fhéin Ulodh.

> That the true religion would not be suppressed,
> that the crown would not have power nor ruling
> according to its will,
> nor grief and vexation for the heroes of Ulster.

Mac an Bhaird reverts to the theme of sectarian tension towards the poem's conclusion, possibly in deference to a personal commitment to the Catholic faith. At this point, he expresses regret at the present condition of church organisation, the neglect of worship and the intrusion of ministers of the reformed church into the Raphoe and Derry benefices. Nonetheless, his distress at recent ecclesiastical developments seems to be motivated more by social concern than by theological preference. The clear impression is given that the old ecclesiastical regimen is esteemed more for its useful communal role and not because of any particular allegiance to church dogma:[64]

> Gan oirchinneach na fhorba,
> gan chléireach, gan chomhorba,
> gan fhear gcoirne, gan mhaor minn,
> gan oighre ar naomh ná noimhchill.

> (They have, namely, Derry and Raphoe) no steward of church lands, no glebe lands, no clergyman, no successor to ecclesiastical benefice, no tonsured man, no gentle steward, no heir to a saint, no heir to holy churches.

When he laments the demise of so idiosyncratically Gaelic an office as that of *airchinneach* or hereditary occupant of ecclesiastical lands, it must be assumed that he valued the medieval church especially for its temporal functions in society.[65] It is highly probable that he interpreted the suppression of the Gaelic church as yet another assault in a campaign aimed at the attrition of an élite social nexus. This emphasis on the essentially secular focus of Mac an Bhaird's assessment of reform is confirmed by his earlier overt association of opposition to the established church with resistance to political challenges posed by the crown administration.

While there are fleeting and undeveloped allusions to religious persecution in poems such as 'Beannacht ar anmain Éireann' and 'Cáit ar ghabhadar Gaoidhil?', the most extensive engagement with the topic at this period comes from Giolla Brighde (alias Bonaventura) Ó hEódhusa. 'Truagh liomsa, a chompáin, do chor' is an important example of Gaelic counter-reformation polemic. Considering that Ó hEódhusa was well versed in bardic scholarship and that he may have worked as a poet prior to taking holy orders, this composition should be read as a product of a bardic training subsequently complemented and intellectually enriched through contact with a militant counter-reformation philosophy. Ordained a Franciscan priest in 1609, Ó hEódhusa was sometime lecturer in philosophy and theology at the Irish Franciscan college of Saint Anthony in Louvain. His most enduring and influential work must have been his catechism in Irish, published as *An Teagasg Críosdaidhe* at Antwerp in 1611. This devotional aid enjoys the distinction of being the first Roman Catholic manual published in the Irish language. Ó hEódhusa owed much, by way of inspiration and example, in the production of his primer of religion to earlier work by Peter Canisius and Cardinal Bellarmine.[66] Its popularity was such that it was reprinted posthumously by the Franciscans at Louvain sometime in 1614–15. Ó hEódhusa died in November 1614 and it is unlikely that he himself was able to supervise the printing of the second edition. 'Truagh liomsa, a chompáin, do chor' was one of three poems printed on the press at Saint Anthony's College and inserted into the Louvain edition of *An Teagasg Críosdaidhe*. The poems were probably published from manuscript copies left behind by the author.[67] No information survives to indicate when Ó hEódhusa composed 'Truagh liomsa, a chompáin, do chor'. However, the fact that there are some thematic parallels between the poem and his catechism suggests a likely date of *c.* 1610–11.

In a preamble to the Louvain edition of 'Truagh liomsa, a chompáin, do chor' it is stated that Ó hEódhusa composed the poem for a friend who had fallen prey to heresy ('d'fhíorcharaid áiridhe dhó, do thuit i n-eiriceacht').[68] No record of this person's identity is extant and, in fact, it is quite possible that the poet addressed an imaginary subject to allow himself free rein to present his case. Essentially a strenuous defence of Roman Catholic doctrine, he mounts a blistering attack on Lutheranism and Calvinism. Roman Catholicism is held to constitute the one true faith and its theological supremacy and authority may be traced in a direct line of continuity to the present from the time of Saint Peter ('ó ló Pheadair gus an lá a-niú'). In the case of Ireland, Saint Patrick had planted the seeds of this supposedly authentic and incontrovertible faith on the island, thus establishing a link with the early Christian faith as represented by Rome. This assertion aimed to highlight his assessment of the supposedly interloping position of the reformed church. If Rome was linked by a common line of descent with the church of Peter, it followed that the intellectual and theological validity of the reformers must be defective. Moreover, the theological credentials of the Catholic church were further guaranteed by its universal homogeneity. Crucially, Rome's validity centred on its allegiance to both scripture and received tradition:[69]

Atáid briathra Dé ar dhá mhodh
– creidthe ón Eaglais gach modh dhíobh:
cuid dhíobh san sgrioptúir atá,
cuid ar cuimhne ag cách do shíor.

The words of God are preserved in two forms –
each form must be believed from the church:
some are in scripture, others have always
been in the memory of all.

This line of argument finds a counterpoint in the work of James Ussher (ob. 1656), the Church of Ireland's most outstanding native scholar and theologian in the seventeenth century. Acutely conscious of Roman claims to unique historical integrity because of adherence to an ancient ecclesiastical tradition, Ussher, by way of rebuttal of criticisms of Anglicanism's pedigree in Ireland, devoted considerable scholarly labour to establishing the Church of Ireland as the authentic historical and theological heir to the early Celtic church.

In character and form, Ó hEódhusa's polemic is fairly typical of counter-reformation attitudes. In addition to his advocacy of the Roman Catholic case, he expends considerable effort on ridiculing the personal and theological qualifications of Luther and Calvin. He paints a sordid and distinctly unflattering picture of both. Luther, for example, is portrayed as a lecherous charlatan ('cailleach dhubh aige 'na mnaoi,'na mhanach gé dho bhí sé'), while a penchant for sodomy is attributed to Calvin. These accusations were echoed shortly afterwards by Flaithrí Ó Maolchonaire in his devotional work, *Sgáthán an Chrábhaidh*, published in Louvain in 1616.[70] Ó hEódhusa rails against the Protestant assignation of primacy to scripture and also faults what he claims as the reformers' indifference to received tradition ('nách lór an sgrioptúir a-mháin, gan chuimhne ngnáith bhréithre Dé').[71] This poem is more strictly a reflection of counter-reformation ideology than a peculiarly bardic response to religious flux. Yet it represents a wider reflection of contemporaneous Gaelic attitudes in so far as Ó hEódhusa combines the bardic mindset with counter-reformation attitudes to present a coherent critique of the reformed church. While his argument may not be particularly original by contemporary continental standards, it is important in an Irish context. The cultural assumptions implicit in his use of the Irish language and the claim that Catholicism is the religion of Gaelic tradition are key constituent elements in the evolving collocation of faith and fatherland. The larger extant bardic corpus, however, reveals that bardic poets undertook no extended critical engagement with issues of contemporary religious controversy in either the reign of Elizabeth or that of James. It is not without significance, therefore, that the most considered criticisms of the Protestant reformation have come from Gaelic poets in holy orders and not from professional poets. The limited number of bardic authors who did attempt to grapple with the implications of the reformation were evidently motivated more by individual loyalty to a pre-reformation communal Catholicism than by a sense of counter-reformation polemicism. Generally, it seems that counter-reformation Catholicism was not a fundamental constitutive consideration in their communal and cultural self-perception. Yet, a concurrent movement directed mainly by Gaelic clerics, especially Franciscans, and some gaelicised Anglo-Norman intellectuals, powered the cultivation of a potent and symbolic interlinking of Gaelic culture with Roman Catholicism. It was imperative to the success of the counter-reformation in the context of the prevailing English/Irish binary ethnic opposition that Catholicism be automatically credited as both integral and complementary to Irish Gaelic identity. The perception of Gaelic as synonymous with Catholic was inherently politicised because its obvious corollary was to locate Anglicanism firmly within the camp of the English newcomer and to classify it as an essentially alien phenomenon.

Bardic responses to political and social change during the years from 1607 to 1612 are characterised by an overall realisation that the polity which had nurtured the bardic system was seriously imperilled. Given the communal focus of the bardic structure, the dissolution of a relatively autonomous decentralised political framework could only spell disaster for a bardic élite attempting to weather the crisis unchanged in outlook or practice. The challenge facing bardic poets after 1607 was not whether they could sustain the bardic apparatus, for that was impractical in the radically altered political conditions, but rather if they could manipulate the existing poetic mould to provide relevant and coherent responses to new social and political combinations. The evidence available for the period 1607–12 demonstrates that poets interpreted the conflict between the Gaelic Irish and the New English as a struggle embracing distinct ethno-cultural identities for the control of land and power in Ireland. Fear Flatha Ó Gnímh composed 'Mo thruaighe mar táid Gaoidhil!' shortly after the launch of the Ulster plantation in 1609–10. Acutely conscious of the weakness of the Gaelic position, he relates how the English had now taken possession of Irish land ('Treóid Ghall i gcluaintibh a gcean') and how the Irish were subject to foreign diktat ('Éireannaigh fá fhéin eachtrann'). In his opinion, the Gaelic Irish had lost the vital battle for control of the land and thus had relinquished the opportunity to re-establish their autonomy. Without such a restoration, the poet is aware that the immediate viability of Gaelic society appears uncertain, its disintegration entailing the replacement of the former élite by an Anglo-Saxon ascendancy ('biaidh saoirÉire 'na Saxain'). Under the new dispensation, there would be no privileged role for the bardic caste.[72] Henceforth, the armies of Europe provided employment for their erstwhile patrons, while the poets adapted to prevailing circumstances as best they could.[73]

Realistic acknowledgment of English suzerainty in Ireland is easily discernible in bardic poetry of the period 1607–12. In the early years of James's

reign, as noted above, it is possible to discern qualified optimism in the outlook of the Gaelic literati, however, there is no doubt that from 1607 onwards
this sentiment rapidly dissipates. Bardic poets certainly diagnosed the precise
implications of the flight of the earls and the poetry reflects their concern for
the viability of a Gaelic autonomy essential to the survival of bardic culture.
Their engagement with an unfavourable socio-political environment was at all
times underpinned by a providentialist account of Ireland's plight. Bardic
analysis, however, was not innately negative and did allow for a positive reactive dynamism. The intellectual capacity to envisage positive transformation
stemmed largely from the belief that divine disfavour with the Gaelic Irish
would, sooner rather than later, be replaced by more benign circumstances.
Indeed, some still hoped that Gaelic autonomy might yet be reinstated. In
'Fogus furtacht don tír thuaidh', Fearghal Óg Mac an Bhaird depicts Hugh,
son of Rory O'Donnell, as the potential liberator of Ireland, coming across the
seas to free his people from bondage ('triallfaidh le chabhlach tar cuan').[74]
This image of the imminent arrival of the messianic figure of liberation
becomes an important topos in popular Irish and Scottish Gaelic poetry in the
late seventeenth and early eighteenth centuries. Even Ó Gnímh qualifies the
gloomy outlook of 'Mo thruaighe mar táid Gaoidhil!' by allowing for the possibility that the Gaelic Irish would possibly yet achieve contentment ('nó an
mbia an t-athaoibhneas againn?').[75]

Bardic Readings of Gaelic Retrenchment, 1607–12

Although bardic responses to unfolding socio-political developments are
informed by an unsentimental realism, the broader analysis of Gaelic
misfortune is unremarkable in so far as it conformed to the common contemporary European providentialist explicative mode. Breandán Ó Buachalla has
demonstrated in detail how bardic poets invoked a providentialist theory of
causation to account for Gaelic difficulties. This overarching explanation was,
in turn, further complemented by reference to traditional prophecies. In summary, therefore, the currently prevalent interpretation of the Gaelic predicament was that it had resulted from God's anger with the *Gaoidhil*, who it was
claimed had fallen from divine favour because of overweening pride and moral
turpitude. Some bardic authors adduced a biblical precedent in further refinement of this scenario by positing a comparison between the enslaved Gaelic
Irish and the dispossessed Old Testament Hebrews.

Towards the close of the sixteenth century an anonymous poet addressed
the composition, 'Bí ad mhosgaladh, a mheic Aonghais', to a Scots Gaelic
nobleman, Sir James MacDonnell. The latter is encouraged to quit his native
Islay to come to the assistance of a beleaguered Ireland. To contextualise his
request, the author alludes to a prophecy attributed to the legendary Fionn
Mac Cumhaill, which foretold that Ireland would one day be subject to foreign domination ('"Beid Gaoidhil a nglasaibh Danar", adubhairt Fionn'). Con-

veniently enough for present purposes, Fionn had also predicted that Ireland would in due course be liberated ('fortacht a ndán d'Inis Eachaidh') by a great hero ('bile sháorfas Éirinn óigh'), in this specific instance, MacDonnell.[76] This was not the first time that such a prediction was ascribed to Fionn. In a Fenian lay, 'A bhean labhrus rinn an laoídh', composed about the middle of the thirteenth century, Fionn also warned of a foreign invasion of the island.[77] Predictions of this sort were not the sole preserve of the Fenian tradition; saints such as Colm Cille, Caillín and Ciarán of Saighir, for instance, were also credited with prophetic knowledge of alien suzerainty in Ireland.[78]

The assumption that Ireland faced predetermined disaster also figures in poetry composed after 1607, but generally in a form qualified to accommodate the concept of divine retribution. Eoghan Ruadh Mac an Bhaird composed 'Anocht is uaigneach Éire' soon after O'Neill and O'Donnell departed from Ireland and as such it is effectively a lament for a disappearing patrician Gaelic world. Mac an Bhaird introduces the notion of a venerable prophecy which predicts catastrophe for the Irish and their island. In this instance, however, the poet refers to an unidentified seer who had alluded to God's anger with Ireland's élite ('Do thairrngir fáidh fada liom, a fhearg ré huaislibh Éirionn').[79] In the post-1607 'Fríth an uainsi ar Inis Fáil', in which he hails the earl of Tyrconnell as an Irish liberator, Mac an Bhaird again invokes the same notion of divine wrath almost word for word ('Do gheall fáidh – fada leam a fhearg re huaislibh Éireann, nach maithfidhe le Dia dháibh').[80] In 'Mo thruaighe mar táid Gaoidhil!', Ó Gnímh speculates that Colm Cille's prophecy concerning the arrival of a foreign host was now being realised ('Nó an dtiocfa is-teach ar thairngir do shluagh Danar ndúraingidh . . . an prímhéarlamh cáidh Coluim?').[81]

A dominant thread in bardic exegesis of the eclipse of Gaelic autonomy is evident in the common invocation of a providentialist causation to contextualise communal misfortune. Mac an Bhaird, in 'Anocht is uaigneach Éire', argues that it was not intrusive foreigners who had effected the banishment of the Gaoidhil, rather divine wrath had resulted in their exile ('fearg Dé re chách dá gcolgadh is hé is fáth dá n-ionnarbadh').[82] He adopts the same rationale, albeit in a more nuanced presentation, in 'Fríth an uainsi ar Inis Fáil'. 'Misbehaviour in former times' ('a n-aindligheadh eacht eili') is mentioned and the question is posed as to whom among the Irish could deny that they had merited divine censure. Combined Gaelic and Anglo-Norman pride enabled evil to prevail in Ireland:[83]

> Fine Gaoidheal, sean-Ghoill féin,
> tearc dhíobh, dá gcluintí a gcaithréim,
> nachar tairngeadh tocht re a dteann,
> gur maidhmeadh olc na hÉireann.

> Stock of the Gaoidhil, the Anglo-Normans themselves could their
> battle-roll be heard, there would be but few of them, for whom

the curbing of their strength had not been prophesied, such that
Ireland's evil climaxed.

Fear Flatha Ó Gnímh's poem, 'Gearr bhur ccuairt, a chlanna Néill', which
he composed *c.* 1607, reflects Mac an Bhaird's emphasis on communal pride
in the provocation of the manifestation of divine wrath. Ó Gnímh deals exclusively with the downfall of the seigneurial house of O'Neill, whose demise he
attributes to pride ('gurb é an easumhla is fochainn . . . 's do bhoing Ua Néill
Naoighiallaigh') and failure to submit to divine ordinance ('do Dhia dá madh
ísiol sibh cia lé ttíseadh bhur ttoirnimh?').[84]

Lochlainn Ó Dálaigh in 'Cáit ar ghabhadar Gaoidhil?' is also quite specific
as to why the Gaelic Irish had entered a calamitous phase in their history. On
foot of divine retribution, they had been dispossessed of land and replaced in
its possession by Scots and Englishmen ('Díoghaltas Dé as adhbhar ann – fir
Albon, ógbhaidh Lunnand do anadar 'na n-áit sin –').[85] A variant of the idea
that God had avenged himself on the Irish occurs in Eoghan Ruadh Mac an
Bhaird's famous poem, 'A bhean fuair faill ar an bhfeart'. Depicting a bereaved
Nuala O'Donnell mourning in solitude before the tomb of her kinsmen in
Rome, the author suggests that had her relatives been buried at home, Nuala
would not have been left to bear her grief alone. The image of the melancholic
Nuala before the lonely tomb is one of powerful poignancy. Mac an Bhaird
advises his subject to accept her lot as an expression of God's purpose ('do réir
thagha an Tí ó bhfuil go ragha gach ní, a Nualuidh'). Indeed, given that she
has managed to survive the wave which had metaphorically overwhelmed her
family, she ought now to intercede with God to lay aside his anger with the
O'Donnells:[86]

> A ríoghan fhréimhe Dáluigh,
> tánuig ón tuinn iombádhuigh,
> nach rabh ní as sia a fherg ret' fhuil
> fagh ó Dhia, an Ceard rod chruthuigh.

> O queen of *Dálach's* line, that has escaped
> from the whelming wave, that his wrath against
> your kindred continue no longer, obtain from
> God, the Artificer who fashioned you.

In their provision of historical parallels to substantiate and validate their
analysis, bardic poets certainly worked from examples of divine punishment
of overweening pride in the Bible or in the relatively widely-circulating apocryphal texts in Irish, in an effort to explicate the Gaelic predicament. The
Bible makes it clear that the very root of sin is pride and it is likely that poets
adopted this convenient paradigm to locate the background to communal
misfortune. Of course, they were not unique in their contemporary espousal
of the providentialist theory. In fact, providentialism was generally recognised

by contemporary European intellectuals and theologians. In the seventeenth century it was commonly believed that God intervened continuously in the world he had created. Unpleasant manifestations of providence were invariably a punishment for either individual or communal wrongdoing. In this respect, when bardic poets undertook to account for the eclipse of Gaelic autonomy, they availed of a common European schema of explication to illuminate communal misfortune.[87]

Eoghan Ruadh Mac an Bhaird in 'Anocht is uaigneach Éire' posits the comparison of the Gaelic Irish with other peoples severely censured by God for their pride. For instance, the plight of the *Gaoidhil* is compared with that of the Hebrews in Egypt ('Rug ortha – ní cóir a cheilt – an bhruid do bhí san Eigheipt') and it is maintained that God had on several occasions punished the sinful with due retribution:[88]

> Ní hé an éanuair amhlaidh sin
> do chuir Dia a ndiaidh an pheacuidh
> iomad cráidh bochta agus broid
> gorta pláigh agus peannoid.

> This is not the only time that after sin
> God has so sent torture great, and poverty,
> and slavery, famine, plague, and retribution.

Adam and Eve, the architects of the Tower of Nimrod and the tribe of Judah were all punished by God for their pride, moral degeneracy and disobedience.[89] The imagery of the Hebrews was also invoked by Lochlainn Ó Dálaigh in 'Cáit ar ghabhadar Gaoidhil?' when he mentions God's anger with the *Gaoidhil*, although he stresses they were not the only people to have suffered in this fashion. Like the Gaelic Irish, the men of ancient Israel ('Meic Israhel na n-arm nglan') and the Jews led by Judas Maccabaeus ('sliocht mhór Macabéos') provoked divine chastisement.[90] Fear Flatha Ó Gnímh's 'Mo thruaighe mar táid Gaoidhill' also presents the Gaelic/Hebrew model in a direct comparison of the two peoples ('Cosmhail re Cloinn Isra-hél thoir san Éighipt ar éidréan').[91] The proactive political implication of Gaelic parallels with the Jews must be stressed in the context of early modern crown aggrandisement. The belief that the Gaelic Irish might yet be liberated by a messianic hero, as Moses had done in the case of the Hebrews, illustrates how poets imparted an unquestionably forward-looking codicil to a potentially passive and acquiescent interpretative framework.

The possibility that the Gaelic Irish might assuage the anger of God by their timely repentance also represents a further positive extension of the providentialist scheme. Eoghan Ruadh Mac an Bhaird in both 'Fríth an uainsi ar Inis Fáil' and 'Anocht is uaigneach Éire' argues that the Gaelic Irish should collectively expiate their transgressions before God:[92]

Fada an tréimhsi atáithí i mbroid,
freagraidh so, a phobul Pádraig,
th'aire ribh, a chlann chroidhe,
ag sin am na haithrighe.

Long have you been in captivity, respond
to this, O flock of Patrick, give heed to
yourselves, darling children: the time of
repentance is at hand.

To emphasise his point, Mac an Bhaird concludes 'Anocht is uaigneach Éire' with a prayer that the *Gaoidhil* should atone for communal wrongdoing and thus mollify God ('s fearg an Choimdhe do chlaochlúdh').[93] While the Hebrews had the good fortune to have had Moses to direct them, with the departure of the northern earls the Gaelic Irish had no such figure of authority ('sgan Maoisi a nÉirinn againn').[94] Similarly, Fear Flatha Ó Gnímh in 'Mo thruaighe mar táid Gaoidhil!' laments the fact that no Moses-like figure had emerged to alleviate the Irish plight ('an t-athMhaoise nár fhéag ruinn').[95] By encouraging their coevals to make amends before God, poets indisputably located human action within a Christian directive schema which contrasts markedly with the religious ambiguity of the classical bardic validatory ethos. For centuries, poets had readily accessed the Judaeo-Christian tradition, nonetheless bardic ideology was reticent in its formal acknowledgement of overt Christian influence. Early modern upheaval divested poetry of the strictures and archaisms of the medieval Gaelic tradition. Cultural and social flux forcibly propelled the poets into the mainstream of European political debate. In proposing an essentially Christian analysis of Gaelic misfortune, the bardic response was neither archaic nor unique, but one which was wholly recognisable in the context of early seventeenth-century European cultural and political debate.

The emasculation of the élite and the concurrent atrophy of the corporate bardic apparatus are fundamental constants in bardic political reflection at this stage. Reality is not eschewed in favour of nebulous antiquarianism, bardic poets chronicle with acuity the attrition of the Gaelic polity and culture and their diminished professional prospects. What is striking about bardic activity in the period covered by this chapter is the intellectual agility manifested. Evidently, the defeat of the Irish forces and their Spanish allies at Kinsale was not recognised by poets as a final historical watershed. In contrast, the Jacobean accession was interpreted within an ideologically positive framework. The literati imply that the elevation of a dynast with Gaelic forebears to the English crown may possibly ameliorate the aggressively Anglo-Saxon ethos of the conquest. The flight of the northern earls, however, is a seminal event in the shaping of the final phase of bardic attitudes to the English presence. In the aftermath of 1607, the providentialist reading of contemporary upheaval served to underline a fundamental ideological shift among bardic poets. The ferment discernible in the poetry, coloured by various strands of humanist and counter-reformation influence, was not simply a case of academic interchange. As poets renewed and invigorated their *oeuvre* with the inclusion and development of new themes, it is argued in this study that their corporate response to change was marked by coherence and verve. Certainly, the evidence cited contradicts Michelle O Riordan's argument that the bardic response is typified by acceptance of a *fait accompli*. For instance, the militant implication of the Gaelic/Hebrew comparison is perhaps the most explicit rebuttal of O Riordan's antiquarian reading.

Something of the mental resilience of the bardic élite and other native scholars is clear from what the meagre historical record reveals of the literati's circumstances at this time. Evidently, to ensure their material survival the native literati were quite prepared to accept pardons from the crown authorities and even land grants where possible.[96] It is known that Eoghan Ruadh Mac an Bhaird, author of several poems reflective of a pan-Hibernian outlook, was granted an official pardon and performed jury service in 1603. Likewise, Fear Flatha Ó Gnímh was granted a pardon in 1602.[97] Indeed, the fiants reveal many other examples of bardic poets in receipt of crown pardons. It is instructive to look at the position of the Gaelic literati within a particular geographical area. Firstly, it is necessary to understood how the learned élite generally managed to retain a short-term measure of financial well-being. In 1606 Sir John Davies, solicitor-general for Ireland, wrote to Sir Robert Cecil, earl of Salisbury, concerning a reconnaissance tour he and lord deputy Chichester had made of the northern counties of Cavan, Monaghan and Fermanagh. Davies provides an interesting report of an examination made by his party into the land tenure system of the Fermanagh area. Throughout his letter it is evident that the English authorities, when confronted with the labyrinthine Gaelic system of land allocation, were very much reliant on the native learned orders for guidance. Mystified by the precise significance of the peculiarly Gaelic hereditary ecclesiastical offices of *airchinneach* and *comharba*, Davies records that he had 'an Irish scholar' write an account in Latin about their functions.[98] In an attempt to define the nature of Maguire's mensal lands, the English found it necessary to have a translation made of a relevant Irish manuscript in the possession 'of one O'Brislan, a chronicler and principal brehon of that country'.[99] In 1609, Davies wrote to Salisbury about an inquisition with which he was associated in the O'Cahan lordship. In order to define the extent of church lands, a jury of fifteen was appointed, thirteen of whom had a ready knowledge of Latin. Davies remarks that they 'gave us more light than ever wee had before touching the originall and estate of Herenaghes and Termon Lands'.[100] Paradoxically, despite the disintegration of their traditional milieu, the poets and other members of the learned élite were not without their own value in the new dispensation. The authorities in Dublin needed the assistance of at least some of the educated native populace in order to implement the logistics of their plans for plantation and reformation.[101] For example, the consolidation of the new regime did not result in immediate material dispossession for the learned families of Fermanagh. Three members of the Ó Breisleáin family, hereditary jurists to the Maguires, were pardoned in 1603. The 'O'Brislan' encountered by Davies was a member of this sept.[102] The Fermanagh poet Brian Ó Corcráin, to whom seven poems are ascribed in the 'Book of O'Conor Don', rendered jury service in 1603. In 1609 he served as a juror for the plantation commissioners in Enniskillen. Subsequently, in 1610–11, he secured a grant of land in the barony of Clanawley.[103] Eochaidh Ó hEódhusa was pardoned in 1607 and, in 1610–11, he received land grants in the baronies of Clanawley and Coole/Tirkennedy.[104] Clearly, it was possible for some of the literati to maintain a degree of financial liquidity under the new regime.

Although the extant evidence demonstrates the intellectual versatility of bardic poets, it also poses tantalising questions regarding the implicit conditions by which the Gaelic literati came to terms on a daily basis with the ascendant order. Unfortunately, a paucity of evidence allows no firm conclusions to be drawn. It may plausibly be argued that the aura of genealogical prestige underwriting James Stuart's status in the Gaelic world view retained its currency. It is likely that the literati distinguished the elevated persona of the monarch from the less congenial aspects of the crown's programme in Ireland. Gaelic scholars may have regarded interchange with the new order as implying nothing more than inevitable administrative or financial engagement with the no doubt misguided representatives of an ethnically-Gaelic sovereign. Furthermore, in the absence of bardic compositions actually endorsing the departure of the earls or supporting the northern plantation, it is reasonable to conclude that whatever factors guided bardic poets in their encounters with the crown administration, they were not motivated by a desire to impart ideological endorsement to the actuality of Anglo-Saxon hegemony.

FAITH AND FATHERLAND
1612–1625

'But since the crown of this kingdom, with the undoubted right and title thereof, descended upon his majesty; the whole island from sea to sea, hath been brought into his highness's peaceable possession; and all the inhabitants, in every corner thereof, have been absolutely reduced under his immediate subjection'. Sir John Davies

In 1612 Sir John Davies published his famous study of why the English crown had never managed to subjugate Ireland completely until the beginning of James's reign.[1] Explicit in Davies's analysis is the axiom of crown supremacy in Ireland and his commentary is informed by the security of a conquest accomplished. This self-congratulatory confidence was, of course, not without foundation. The departure of the earls of Tyrone and Tyrconnell, who were arguably the last remaining factional bulwark against absolute English dominance in Ireland, paved the way for the final phase in the extended Elizabethan and Jacobean conquest. The process of the plantation of six Ulster counties with English and Scots settlers was soon set in motion. The plantation concept was underpinned by the crown's objectives of economic and social anglicisation of these areas. The two east-Ulster counties of Antrim and Down, where the two earls had no remit, remained unescheated, and as such were not subject to the official scheme for plantation. The increasingly dismal financial position of native landowners, however, facilitated what was, in effect, an informal plantation of these counties by English and Scots investors. It must be emphasised, therefore, that this chapter's thematic discussion begins at a point when Ireland experienced political and legislative transformation within a telescoped time-scale. The eclipse of formerly powerful Gaelic and gaelicised Anglo-Norman landed families was a central factor in the overall process of change and realignment. Hitherto, despite the ongoing attrition of customary sources of patronage, poets continued to operate within a recognisably Gaelic milieu. While the impact of English social and administrative encroachment was in many areas realised piecemeal, bardic poets could in the short term sustain the illusion of working within ideological parameters similar to those of their precursors. Admittedly, the base structure of an untrammelled élite Gaelic polity had been progressively whittled away since the shiring of Leix and Offaly as far back as 1557. Ultimately, such varying degrees of local or regional autonomy as remained were severely truncated or obliterated entirely following the enactment of common law in Ireland,

Tyrone's departure and the plantation in Ulster. It is necessary to differentiate bardic poetry composed before the flight of the earls and the Ulster plantation from work originating after these seminal events. The compositional context of post-plantation bardic poetry, most obviously in Ulster, must be highlighted in so far as bardic poets moved in a significantly altered ideological and material environment.

This chapter focuses on two themes broadly emblematic of the final phase of classical bardic activity. First, the professional bardic outlook is assessed in the context of a social environment no longer subject to the factional or dynastic imperatives of an Irish-speaking élite. Second, bardic perceptions of the indigenous social and political dilemma in the period 1612–25 are explored. It is always necessary in the interpretation of bardic poetry to recognise the subtle implications posed by the contractual obligations of many of the poems. While poets were, in terms of patronage at any rate, generally constrained to manoeuvre in line with the criteria laid down by canonical practice, this did not mean that they were unable to subvert the conventional bardic form for what may be termed extramural considerations. In the chapter entitled 'Continuity and Reaction in Two Poem-Books', it is argued that once the ostensible objective of such poetry is recognised, its value as historical source material for Gaelic *mentalités* can be more accurately gauged. This proviso regarding the manifest legitimatory function of much if not the greater part of the bardic corpus continues to be valid in the time span covered by the present chapter. A certain amount of patronage was still available to poets notwithstanding the dispersal abroad of leading Gaelic families and the incipient anglicisation of their coevals remaining in the country. If bardic poets in the period 1612–25 served patrons of diverse and often non-Gaelic origin, it is important to remember that they were still required to accommodate their art to the demands of continued patronage. Professional dependence on sponsorship certainly curtailed their already limited scope for ideological manoeuvre and this predicament was further complicated by reason of the land grants allocated to poets in the first decade of James's reign. Indeed, the limits and obligations, whether perceived or actual, consequent on such grants may have quite possibly detracted from the wider presentation of a dissenting political perspective. It is proposed that the work of the poets in this final bardic phase was marked by a continuity liberally leavened with ideological innovation. This sense of regeneration stemmed in part from the need of poets to adapt their work to an ever-decreasing and heterogeneous cohort of actual or potential patrons. It will also be demonstrated that a consciousness of the calamity which beset the Gaelic polity constitutes a distinctive strand in bardic discourse. The acute political sensibility evident in poetry composed in the early years of Stuart rule continues to feature in the latter half of James's reign. A critical mediation of English suzerainty is a key characteristic of bardic assessment of contemporary political and social conditions. The following analysis is structured around two sections: the first centres on a discussion of continued ideological innovation while the second proposes to elucidate aspects of bardic responses to crown hegemony.

Continuity and Innovation in Bardic Poetry, 1612–25

Sometime around 1610 Eochaidh Ó hEódhusa composed a piece entitled 'Dá ghrádh tréigfead Máol Mórdha' for Maolmórdha O'Reilly (ob. 1618) of east *Bréifne*. In this poem, possibly among his last, Ó hEódhusa speaks regretfully of the misfortune which he felt he had brought on his former patrons ('an té is carthanach fám cheann nach marthanach é acht aithghearr').[2] Having witnessed the fall of the O'Donnells, O'Neills and Maguires, Ó hEódhusa vows to suppress his devotion to O'Reilly to spare him the indignity endured by his other benefactors ('an té charuim 's é a olc, ní thaghuim é re hannsocht'). This decision is emphasised when he recounts an exemplum of classical provenance about Cornelia, who felt that her ill-fated love had proved calamitous for both her husbands, Marcus Crassus and Pompey. The defeat of the latter caused Cornelia to voice aloud her regret at not marrying Caesar, who would have then borne the brunt of her attendant bad luck rather than Pompey ('ós dom bhéasaibh ar bhean rum/gan Césair mur fhear agam'). Comparing himself to Cornelia ('Ar a haisde is aghtha dhamh'), Ó hEódhusa maintains that he will forsake O'Reilly and concentrate his attentions on the English and thereby attach his misfortune to them ('mo rún carthuin comhoidhigh').[3] The response to the crisis which had enveloped the great Ulster families is characteristically forceful and Ó hEódhusa's sentiments form an appropriate introduction to this section. Given that he died soon after the composition of the O'Reilly piece, and since there is no evidence to suggest that he sought the patronage of crown officials or colonial settlers, it seems reasonable to assume that Ó hEódhusa was denied the opportunity to act on his dramatic vow. If Ó hEódhusa was spared the clearly disconcerting challenge of adapting his professional routine to unprecedented circumstances, how then did his surviving colleagues negotiate the quandary of operating within a jurisdiction in which the bardic institution was rapidly deprived of either a meaningful or effective legitimatory role? It will be argued that bardic poets manipulated politically-malleable aspects of their canon to enable them to praise individuals instrumental in the emasculation of the Gaelic polity, while simultaneously avoiding overt validation of actions particularly repellent to the bardic sensibilty. Such thematic duality is hardly surprising in a situation where poets sought to maximise the amount of material benefit accruing to them from a diminishing store of patronage and bardic connoisseurship.

Something of the complexity of bardic *mentalités* in their reaction to conflicting challenges is evident in two poems composed by Flann Mac Craith. The death in November 1614 of Thomas Dubh Butler, the tenth earl of Ormond, ended the extraordinary career of a veteran ally of the crown in Ireland. Educated at the court of Edward VI, Ormond enjoyed access to the English élite which few, if any, of his Irish rivals could hope to emulate. From his return to Ireland in 1555, he had worked to restore the ailing fortunes of his family, while at the same time scheming assiduously to present himself as an honest broker to the government. Over the next thirty years or so Ormond was to emerge supreme from the extended internecine rivalry which had long prevailed between the seigneurial houses of Ormond and Desmond. Simultaneously, he deftly outmanoeuvred his critics in the English administration.[4] Flann Mac Craith composed 'Eólach mé ar mheirge an iarla' sometime after Ormond's death in 1614. A traditional elegy commemorating the life of a pre-eminent Irish grandee, it employs the *caithréim* or battle-roll device to present an extensive list of successful military encounters undertaken by Thomas Dubh during his lengthy career.[5] Beginning with the young Ormond's role in the suppression of Sir Thomas Wyatt's rebellion in 1554 ('Gabháil Bhoëit – beag dá shéan – táinig le Tomás Buitléar'), the author presents a detailed account of services rendered the crown by Ormond. Among the campaigns itemised, he mentions Ormond's part in the crown offensives against Shane O'Neill in the period 1556–63 ('Ar Seaán neartmhar Ó Néill/tug maidhm gér dheacar dhoi-séin'), against Domhnall O'Brien of Thomond in 1558 and against his nephew Conor O'Brien in 1570, against the MacDonnells in 1584, and he also takes care to highlight Ormond's prominent part in the suppression of the Desmond rebellion of 1579–83 ('s do chuir gach aoinneach umhal, a Muigh dhaoineach Dheasmhumhan'). In sum, no part of Ireland had escaped Butler's attentions ('Ní fhuil éineang d'Inis Fáil/gan lorg each Iarla Gabhráin').[6] Mac Craith concludes this account of Ormond's significant and surely premeditated role in the neutralisation of the Gaelic élite by portraying him, in somewhat ironically contradictory terms, as the guarantor of law and order ('Nír fháguibh ar aoi a oirbheirt . . . foghluidhe ná creachthóir cruidh/seachnóin collMhuighe Cobhthuigh') and as a traditional reiver in turn ('creachthóir beann mbruachdhubh mBanbha'). Indeed, he suggests that he had not done full justice to Ormond's plundering exploits ('Iomdha críoch do creachadh lais/nach maoidhim ar mac Séamais') and he goes so far as to claim that Butler was master of Ireland in his day ('gur chuir triath na ngéir-reann nglan/iath Éireann ar a fhocal').[7] On this occasion, Mac Craith was evidently neither prepared nor in a position to evaluate the wider implications of Ormond's career and instead resorts to open-ended and formulaic bardic reportage. The depiction of Ormond as an ultra-efficient cattle-rustler hardly serves to encapsulate the full impact of his influence and action in Elizabethan Ireland.

In composing his elegy for Ormond, Mac Craith was confronted by a crux commonly faced by bardic poets at this stage. He had the choice of adhering to the bardic canon to produce a conventionally flattering elegy or he could adopt a more radical alternative by composing a measured analysis of his subject's career. Unfortunately, the earliest extant copy of 'Eólach mé ar mheirge an iarla' is recorded in a late eighteenth-century manuscript and thereby precludes an investigation of possible contractual obligations, if any, by which the author was bound.[8] An alternative light on Flann Mac Craith's political outlook is discernible in a poem preserved in the O'Gara manuscript. In the undated 'Iomdha éagnach ag Éirinn', which was certainly composed after 1607, Mac Craith laments the enslavement of Gaelic Ireland. The country is presented as a tragic widow who instead of mating with a partner of appropriate native stock had consorted unwisely with foreigners. Significantly, the pioneering Victorian Gaelic scholar, Standish Hayes O'Grady, regarded the poem as an attempt to summon forth new national leaders.[9] The contrast in outlook and perception between 'Eólach mé ar mheirge an iarla' and 'Iomdha éagnach ag Éirinn' underlines the need for contextualised interpretation of the constraints imposed by the contractual requirements of bardic discourse. Unfortunately, although there is no extant evidence regarding the background to the composition of 'Iomdha éagnach ag Éirinn', it is tempting to read this poem as a candid expression of the author's political outlook.

In spite of an apparently rigidly-codified system of bardic validation, some poets adapted and manipulated the criteria of lordship by citing new standards as an alternative to quasi-medieval modes of characterisation. Fear Flatha Ó Gnímh composed 'Ní haineamh óige i bhflaithibh' to mark the succession of Henry O'Neill to his father, Sir John (Seaán), in Lower Clandeboye in north-east Ulster in 1617. Traditionally in these circumstances a poet would have strengthened the hand of a young and inexperienced heir by alluding to his requisite valour and martial qualities. Of course, by 1617 such heroic traits were effectively redundant in a province transformed by plantation and by the imposition of the crown's writ. Instead, Ó Gnímh emphasises the more appropriate virtues of learning and education embodied by Sir Henry (ob. 1638) and he also makes a point of commenting on his knowledge of law.[10] It is observed that Sir Henry harbours no desire for plunder or military exploit ('Ní rún cean ní hintinn áigh/a tá i meanmain mhic Seaáin'), on the contrary, such forms of behaviour are no longer admissible in élite circles ('malairt tar an uairsin ann/ag uaislibh raghuirt Fhreumhann').[11] Bardic poets often appended several quatrains in honour of their patron's wife to the main body of a poem. In this case, the verses composed by Ó Gnímh for O'Neill's wife are interesting in so far as they propose to accommodate an Englishwoman to conventional bardic images of a lord's spouse. Sir Henry had married Martha, the daughter of Sir Francis Stafford, a New English government official and latterly a settler in east Ulster. In this instance, Ó Gnímh's use of a traditional device is particularly innovative. The poets generally employed such appendages to emphasise the nobility and beauty of their patron's choice in marriage. Undaunted by her non-Gaelic background ('Bean nach do bhantracht Banbha'), the poet immediately touches on her foreignness by describing Martha as a modest and gentle lady of noble English stock ('gnúis náir as maothbhanda modh do mhnáibh saorchlannda Saxon'). Similarly, Ó Gnímh highlights her patrician rank by observing that Sir Francis Stafford had been ennobled by Elizabeth ('ón phrionnsa, inghen Énrí . . . ainm do uaisligh a hathair'). Ultimately, however, the poet is determined to assimilate Martha to Gaelic norms and to divorce her from English custom. In a telling statement, he claims that since Martha had adopted the life-style of a Gaelic woman ('Marta ó chuireas a cearda re béusoibh ban gaoidhiolda') she should henceforth be considered an Irishwoman ('meastur í re haindribh Breagh').[12] Martha's status in this poem is predicated on her inculturation to Gaelic modes of civility and it presumes the occultation of her English identity.

The survival of poems addressed to her indicates that Martha Stafford was popular among bardic poets, though curiously on the death of her husband Sir Henry in 1638, she apparently no longer figured in classical verse. This might be taken to indicate that as far as the poets were concerned, Martha's main significance lay in the fact that she was the wife of the head of a noble Gaelic household.[13] Certainly, Fear Flatha Ó Gnímh composed 'Mná tar muir maith re Gaoidhil' with the intention of accommodating Martha to a Gaelic mould and of assuring Sir Henry of the propriety of marriage to a foreigner ('techt na mban gcéibhfhionn gcnistiogh go magh nÉirionn innistior'). By way of affirmation of O'Neill's choice, the poet draws not unexpected comparisons with figures from an heroic Gaelic past. In pursuit of exemplary parallels, characters such as Úna, Earc, Eithne and Caireann are invoked as evidence of foreign women who had partnered Gaoidhil and in turn given birth to heroes in the Gaelic tradition ('Ní do mhnáibh Insi Ealga').[14] Martha is depicted as another in a long list of women who had settled among the Gaelic Irish ('Bean dona mnáibhsin Martha'). An unusual parallel is adduced to encapsulate his view of Martha's arrival in Clandeboye when he observes that several types of precious stone, as well as oil and wine, are imported to Ireland. Of course, such valuable commodities are externally-sourced because these items are not naturally available on the island itself ('ní gnáth pór bona i mBreghoibh d'ola, d'ór nó d'fhíneamhoin'). In this particular case, a woman had come from overseas to become O'Neill's spouse ('ben tar tuinn go triath Conghuil') in the same fashion as a splendid treasure or jewel might be shipped in from abroad ('Mur shéd mbuaidhe do soich sonn, nó mur chloich nuaidhe neumhonn').[15] It is obvious, however, that Ó Gnímh assumed the gaelicisation of this particular newcomer. Although, gold might be mined abroad, it could be smelted and thus take its final shape in Ireland ('Meinic do bruinneadh abhus ór nach i nÉirinn fhásus') and a similar evolution is postulated in the case of Martha ('caor as an mianach Marta').[16] Ultimately, in order to protect the integrity of the Gaelic and gaelicised élite, only the select few could be incorporated within its ranks ('uathadh aicme is ionchora i gcló an tsílsi Gaoidhil Ghlais'). Even though the Gaoidhil were themselves once newcomers in Ireland, their ethnic supremacy is explicit in the poet's reasoning ('Gaoidhil Fhódla gidh íad sin cuirmíd ós cionn gach cinidh').[17] The evidence of 'Mná tar muir maith re Gaoidhil' sheds interesting light on what has been noted in the foregoing chapters as a bardic expansion of the horizons of Gaelic cultural identity. Ó Gnímh's approach to Stafford is underpinned by the premise of inculturation: in return for her formal incorporation within the bardic paradigm, Stafford is expected to accommodate herself to Gaelic modes of civility. If the poets were prepared to recast the criteria for inclusion within the Gaelic ethnic schema, they only did so while consciously privileging Gaelic culture in the process. The dynamic of putative, albeit culturally conditional, inculturation evidences evolving Gaelic notions of politicised communal identity.

A poem composed by Domhnall Ó hEachaidhéin also supports the assumption that Martha Stafford was expected to assimilate to Gaelic norms. In the composition, 'A Mharta ceanglum connradh', Ó hEachaidhéin sought Stafford's patronage employing standard bardic terms of reference: he offers to detail Martha's virtues ('do shíor dod reic ó rathoil') in exchange for her material support ('s bí linn ag seilg ar sochair'). To heighten the discursive impact, Ó hEachaidhéin introduces the time-honoured theme of the transience of fame accorded by material wealth in comparison with the enduring reputation which bardic eulogy bestowed ('ní mhair maoin acht eadh uaire; buaine a sheal daoibh ar ndáinne').[18] Obviously, Stafford was not of Gaelic origin, yet this genealogical fact does not seem to have perturbed the poets overly. So long as it could be asserted that patrician blood coursed in her veins, even if English blood, Martha could be succinctly located within an appropriate social niche. Evidently, the vital litmus test of acceptance was not immediately that of ethnic origin but rather that of beneficent disposition to Gaelic mores. It appears from what Ó Gnímh and Ó hEachaidhéin say, that notwithstanding her English birth, it was presumed that she would conform to the stereotype of a Gaelic chatelaine.[19]

The fact that poets were prepared to incorporate newcomers or foreigners within a Gaelic discursive framework is exemplified by the evidence in a poem composed by Tadhg Ó Dálaigh c. 1618.[20] Judging from references made in the poem, 'Gabh mo gherán, a Sheóirse', it seems that Ó Dálaigh's status as chief poet and Ó Dálaigh Cairbreach were challenged by an unidentified rival. To exacerbate matters, the Ó Dálaigh ancestral lands at Muntervary in west Cork were now apparently subject to an unspecified tax or cess. In a resourceful bid to secure the ending of what he considered patent injustices, Ó Dálaigh addressed this poem to Sir George Carew (ob. 1629), who on his appointment as president of Munster in 1600 had proved a highly effective servant of the crown. On arrival in the province, the new president had immediately set about neutralising the supporters of the earl of Tyrone and his southern puppet, James Fitzthomas Fitzgerald. The latter had set himself up as the legitimate heir of his late uncle, the earl of Desmond (ob. 1583), with O'Neill's encouragement. Fitzgerald's ambitions were short-lived and within a year Carew had succeeded in imprisoning him and smashing Tyrone's control of the province.[21] No doubt fully aware of Carew's earlier dramatic Irish career, Ó Dálaigh was nonetheless encouraged to address Sir George by reason of a tenuous Carew link with the lands occupied by the Ó Dálaigh sept at Muntervary. The Carews were first granted lands in Cork as early as the twelfth century. Robert Carew may have made a grant of land at Muntervary to the Uí Dhálaigh sometime between 1215 and 1245. Towards the close of the fourteenth century, however, the fortunes of the Carew family declined and they subsequently lost their holdings in west Cork. In 1568 the Carew claim to these lands was reactivated by Sir Peter Carew of Devon and on the death of Sir Peter's heir in 1580, their cousin, Sir George Carew, unsuccessfully championed the family case.[22]

Ó Dálaigh addresses Carew on the basis that he was his rightful chief poet by virtue of the two families' supposedly continuous record of mutual links ('Seanbháidh do réime romhuibh rem chinedh do chualabhair'). The Carews in particular among the English had been the object of Ó Dálaigh allegiance ('d'fhuil Gall a-nú ná a-nalluin rann ach tú nír thógamair') and he centres the case for his family's devotion to the house of Carew on the latter's original land grant to them in Muntervary ('Rinn cheana do chinn fhine mar fuair cenn ar gceirdi-ne'). Accordingly, Ó Dálaigh hails Carew as his overlord ('fa Dhia is tú mo thighearna') and in consideration of the fact that the Uí Dhálaigh were hereditary bardic poets to the Carews, he declares himself Sir George's rightful chief poet ('Mise th'ollamh fíre féin'):[23]

> An té ó dtáinig tusa
> 's a' t-ollamh ór fhásus-sa,
> sinn araon a ndá n-oigher;
> a raon linn an leanfaider?

> The progenitor from whom you are
> descended and the *ollamh* from
> whom I grew, you and I are their
> heirs; shall we follow their course?

Of course, Ó Dálaigh's overriding concern in the composition of this piece stems from grievances outlined in the course of the poem and which he obviously hopes may be addressed by Carew's influential intervention ('Deacair nach bhfuil d'fhíachuibh ort cuid dom' anforlann d'fhurtacht'). It appears that the validity of the poet's right to style himself Ó Dálaigh Cairbreach had been challenged by elements within his family ('Don chuid eile dom fhine anois a n-eirr mh'aimseire . . . ná fuilngidh mé du mhuchadh') while he also bemoans the taxation of the family holding ('má tá sin daor 'na dheghuidh do bhí saor 'gár sinnseruibh').[24] Although addressed to an Englishman, 'Gabh mo gherán, a Sheóirse' is a reaffirmation of the traditional bardic concept of the patron/poet nexus. In return for his services, the bardic poet was entitled to expect material reward and protection from his patron. Having asserted his claim to recognition as Carew's chief poet, Ó Dálaigh rounds off his argument with a conventional allusion to the fame which eulogy was held to confer. In return for their grant of land to the Uí Dhálaigh, the Carews had obtained an enduring reputation because they had been lauded by Ó Dálaigh poets ('bladh as buaine iná an aidhbhsi do an uaine oruibh-si'). Predictably enough,

Ó Dálaigh declares that he too will perpetuate the fame of Sir George by composing a battle roll enshrining his deeds ('Damh-sa as cóir a chur i gcéill, atá re cur id chaithréim').[25]

The picture presented of Carew's Irish exploits is couched in positive and uncritical terms. According to Ó Dálaigh, Sir George's arrival in Ireland signalled the beginning of a new era of respect for law and peace ('gan fher faghla 'ghá foghuil Banbha as-teagh go ttugobhair') and it is claimed that he was especially attentive to the interests of the Gaelic Irish ('tú ad bharánta ar theacht as-tteagh a neart gabhála Gaedheal'). In short, Carew had rid Ireland of multifarious evils:[26]

> D'fhortacht Éireann, go dul duibh
> le dírmuibh láech ó Londuin,
> do-chuaidh ort an ardbhladh,
> ní fhuair a holc d'ionarbadh.

> Until you left London with a large body of
> troops to help Ireland she had not succeeded
> in banishing her evils;
> the fame of doing it fell to you.

The depiction of Carew's service in Ireland deliberately borders on the apolitical while it is implied that his guiding objective was simply to banish anarchy and lawlessness from the country. Carew had succeeded in his mission, in so far as the full realisation of his programme was feasible:[27]

> Do fhágbhuis, ó chenn go cenn
> an fonn aoibhinn-se Éireann
> gan ghuid, gan éginn, gan olc
> gan bhruid, dárbh fhéitir fhortacht.

> You left this beautiful land of Ireland free,
> from end to end, from thieving, violence, evil
> and rapine in so far as it could be done.

Importantly, by approaching Carew as if he were an ersatz *Gaedheal*, Ó Dálaigh proposes to inculturate him within a Gaelic mould in the same way as Ó Gnímh and Ó hEachaidhéin aimed to inculturate Martha Stafford. Although the ideological momentum predicating an alliance of Gaelic and gaelicised Anglo-Norman interests was firmly established by this period, efforts to inculturate New English personalities must be seen to be in tension to some extent with the enterprise of developing an inclusive notion of Irish nationality embracing the Gaelic and Anglo-Norman communities alike. Yet despite the difficulties of accommodating the New English presence in the context of the concept of an emergent politicised Irish nationality, it must be acknowledged that efforts to inculturate settlers or newcomers again testify to a resourceful bardic outlook.

At the immediate level of personal self-interest, Ó Dálaigh had nothing to gain from an unsympathetic or penetrating review of Carew's earlier actions in Munster. Instead, he resorts to vague generalities which could be linked conveniently to what he disingenuously portrays as Carew's peace-keeping role in Ireland. It is implied in the poem that its author travelled to England in person to present his composition to Carew ('tar muir fad thúairim thánag'). Accordingly, it is understandable that he should have circumvented critical engagement with Carew's distant campaigns in Ireland.[28] Given the supplicatory premise to the poem's composition, it follows that Ó Dálaigh was in no position to adopt a negative or controversial stance. Furthermore, there is some evidence to suggest that Carew possessed a working knowledge of Irish and this consideration further explains Ó Dálaigh's likely journey across the Irish Sea together with the deliberately understated political representation in the poem.[29] Notwithstanding his initiative in seeking out and directly addressing this sometime crown functionary, Ó Dálaigh continues to envisage the possibility of a traditional poet/patron relationship. References to the distinction bestowed by eulogy make it clear that the poet basically planned to locate Carew within an orthodox Gaelic framework. It is ironic that this poem should owe its preservation to Carew's own self-interest in having his family's claim to the Muntervary and other lands in west Cork officially sanctioned. In the work entitled *Pacata Hibernia*, published posthumously in 1633, Carew provided an outline of his ancestors's early presence in west Cork which was similar to that sketched by Ó Dálaigh.[30] If Carew used the poem in his attempts to validate a family land claim, he had, unwittingly perhaps, exploited bardic poetry in a very traditional way. With regard to Ó Dálaigh, it may be concluded that he was simply undertaking the legitimatory function inherent to bardic practice, but on this occasion in a manner implicitly adapted to significantly different power structures.

It has already been noted that the eclipse of several prominent aristocratic households, particularly in Ulster, resulted in the reduction of the level of lucrative patronage available to poets. Concomitantly, it must be remembered that many noble Gaelic families managed to negotiate the difficulties imposed by both the Nine Years War and the subsequent Jacobean settlement. Those families who succeeded in retaining control of part or all of their lands did so at the cost of acquiescence in the crown's political writ and more often than not of recognition of the established church's authority. If, as will be evident from the material discussed above, poets were prepared to incorporate newcomers within the bardic evaluative schema, attitudes to surviving patrons of the old order, who conformed to new political dictates, are of corresponding interest. In fact, the poets' co-operative attitude to some apparently well-disposed newcomers might suggest that in the case of active Gaelic patrons a similar political reticence was adopted.

The O'Briens of Thomond were a leading Munster family who succeeded in averting, mainly by strategic accommodation to crown policies, the attrition of the Gaelic élite. Conor O'Brien (ob. 1581), the third earl of Thomond, had managed to win the lordship of Thomond in 1558 by throwing in his lot with the English authorities against the ruling lord, his uncle Domhnall (ob. 1579). With the exception of a brief period of exile in France in 1570, Conor remained loyal to Elizabeth until his death in 1581.[31] His son and successor, Donnchadh (ob. 1624), proved a steadfastly dutiful subject of the crown. Indeed, Donnchadh spent some time at Elizabeth's court in the late 1570s where it appears that the earl of Ormond (ob. 1614) persuaded O'Brien to conform to the established church to ingratiate himself with the monarchy.[32] Despite the anglicising influences which were brought to bear on Donnchadh, he actively cultivated an interest in Gaelic culture. For instance, he seems to have long enjoyed the friendship of the poet Tadhg Mac Bruaideadha. The latter composed the poetic *speculum principum* entitled 'Mór atá ar theagasg flatha' for O'Brien, probably on his accession as fourth earl of Thomond in 1581. Four other poems which this author composed in honour of O'Brien are also extant.[33] In 'Eascar Gaoidheal éag aoinfhir', Mac Bruaideadha laments the death of Donnchadh in 1624.[34] He delineates a composite picture of Thomond's character portraying him both as an old-style Gaelic grandee and as an unwavering servant of the crown in Ireland. Although the service undertaken by O'Brien on behalf of the English administration is chronicled, the poet draws no immediately obvious political inferences. In the introductory stanzas it is claimed that the death of Thomond constitutes a grievous blow to the Gaelic Irish and his passing has left them very vulnerable ('cneadh léar teascadh a dtreise'). It is stated that with the support of Thomond, the Gaelic Irish had been supreme in their own land and because of his demise their suzerainty has been severely eroded:[35]

> A-né ria n-éag don Iarla
> i gCrích Éireann airmniamhdha,
> gé tá a dteann ar neimhthní a-niodh
> do-bheirthí geall na nGaoidheal.

> Although their strength is as nought today,
> yesterday, before the death of the earl,
> the supremacy of the Irish obtained in the land
> of bright-weaponed Ireland.

Mac Bruaideadha introduces a topical illusion in the next stanza which is easily overlooked in a poem of sixty-one quatrains. In this particular instance, it is argued that the threat of retribution from Thomond had imposed a limit on the number of foreigners proposing to occupy Gaelic lands ('Lughaide dánacht Danar ar a n-áitibh d'átaghadh').[36] Before attempting to determine the significance of this reference, it is necessary to look at the poet's treatment of Thomond in the rest of the poem.

For the most part, this composition is concerned with recounting the martial exploits of O'Brien and services rendered to the crown. The poet's approach to Thomond's career is reminiscent of the battle-roll device with a central narrative emphasis on the late earl's utility to the crown or more particularly to James Stuart. If the death of Thomond represented a tragic loss for the Gaelic Irish and Ireland, it was no less a blow to the monarchy ('Mairg rí bhós dár beanadh sin'). As long as O'Brien lived, James could always rely on his military backing in Ireland ('Námhaid do thuinn ná do thír ní budh eagail dá airdrígh'), proof of his allegiance to the crown being most vividly reflected in forty-four years of devoted service to both Elizabeth and James ('Ceathracha is ceithre bliadhna . . . atá ag cungnamh don Choróin').[37] Mac Bruaideadha's emphasis on O'Brien's loyalty to James is another manifestation of the Stuartist sympathies evident in the work of the poets. Mac Bruaideadha likewise invoked James Stuart's Munster lineage in a poem he contributed to the bardic debate known as *Iomarbhágh na bhfileadh*.[38] In addition to highlighting Thomond's royalist stance and his various military adventures, the poet pays the expected stock compliments to his subject. Not simply mourned by Munster and Ireland alone, O'Brien's passing is lamented by both the Gaelic and English élites ('Ardfhola Gaoidheal is Gall'), while Mac Bruaideadha professes personal sadness at the death of the earl ('na déara ag snighe fár snaidhm') and dramatically implores God to be soon permitted to join O'Brien in eternity ('A Dhé, dá dtagradh tusa . . . m'éag ina ghoire go grod').[39] Fortunately, bardic praise ensures lasting fame for O'Brien ('Mairid fionnlaoidhe fileadh . . . ó mbudh beó choidhche ar cuimhne gan reó ndoirche ar nDonnchaidh-ne').[40] The poem may be said to be characterised by two narrative currents which are mutually complementary. Mac Bruaideadha makes the argument that Thomond was a vigilant defender of the *Gaoidhil* who had managed to deflect the excesses of English expansionism in Ireland ('Lughaide dánacht Danar ar a n-áitibh d'átaghadh'); in tandem with this approach he also highlights O'Brien's personal allegiance to James ('Méad a rodhúthracht dá rígh').[41] The picture presented of Thomond is essentially that of an orthodox Gaelic magnate, although this assessment is qualified by the recurrent emphasis on O'Brien's devotion to James. Of course, Mac Bruaideadha is ready to sanction Thomond's support for a monarch who could boast of a regal Gaelic pedigree. Yet it must be remembered also that this poem dates to around 1624, by which time the hope placed in James Stuart by the Gaelic literati must well have appeared overly optimistic. A certain disenchantment is hinted at in the poet's claim that Thomond had been a countercheck to English appropriation of Irish land. While in no way questioning the impeccable credentials of James Stuart's entitlement to the kingdom of Ireland, Mac Bruaideadha concurrently aims to contain the decline of the Gaelic ethos. The poet's rationale suggests that while a Gaelic lord like Thomond held sway, he guaranteed a measure of Gaelic cultural and social integrity. The demise of a celebrated patron was naturally a portentous occasion and partly explains why the poet interprets his passing as a calamity for the *Gaoidhil*. On the other hand, bardic manipulation and accommodation of the new order was undoubtedly facilitated as long as men like O'Brien continued to provide a degree of bardic patronage essential to the viability of élite Gaelic culture in the face of radical change.

Sir Raghnall MacDonnell (ob. 1634) is another example of a Gaelic grandee who succeeded in maintaining, if not consolidating, his position during James's reign. MacDonnell laid a dubious claim to the lands of his deceased brother at the Route in Antrim, notwithstanding the fact that according to common law they were due to pass to the dead man's son. Sir Raghnall made a no less tenuous case for his possession of the Glens of Antrim. As north-east Ulster had been notoriously unsettled in the last decades of the sixteenth century, James was anxious to introduce an effective measure of stability to the area. By 1605 MacDonnell's claims had been countenanced by a sovereign eager to encourage a swift settlement.[42] Like Donnchadh O'Brien in Thomond, MacDonnell also extended a certain amount of patronage to bardic culture. The Ó Gnímh family probably supplied hereditary poets to the MacDonnells and it is evident that Sir Raghnall was entitled to call on the poetic services of Fear Flatha Ó Gnímh. The latter composed 'Éireannaigh féin fionnLochlannaigh' in honour of MacDonnell sometime between his creation as earl of Antrim in 1620 and his death in 1634.[43] In this work, Ó Gnímh lauds the *Gaoidhil* of Scotland, the MacDonnells and Sir Raghnall. Although the MacDonnells had migrated to Antrim from the Western Isles as early as the fifteenth century, the poet dwells in detail on what is presented as their original Irish Gaelic ancestry. He highlights the MacDonnell descent from the legendary Colla Uais, who alone of the three Collas was said to have left Ireland, settling instead in Scotland.[44] Ó Gnímh argues that it is for the best that the MacDonnells returned to Ireland ('maith deireadh na deoraidheachta') given that Scotland was not their mother country ('Tír dúthaigh chláir chríchfhionn Mhonaidh dháibh níor dhúthaigh mhátharbhunaidh'). Sir Raghnall is praised in the customary bardic mode and among other outstanding virtues his beneficial influence on the natural world is mentioned ('Lán arbha i ngach iothlannchuilidh').[45] This is a traditional poem in that Ó Gnímh aims to validate Sir Raghnall's position in north-east Ulster by invoking the ideological sanction of Gaelic orthodoxy. The poet employs a venerable origin legend to locate the MacDonnells within an illustrious pseudo-historical tradition with the objective, in this case, of accounting for their relatively recent presence in Antrim. The poem validates Sir Raghnall within a Gaelic context and basically represents an exercise in the justification of his activities in north-east Ulster. The historical record shows, however, that from 1605 onwards Sir Raghnall's position in Antrim owed more to the support he secured from the crown than to his espousal of the Gaelic seigneurial code. Although MacDonnell's legal standing within east Ulster was safeguarded as a result of the royal patent he obtained in 1605, even in the years following 1620 he felt it appropriate to have a poem such as this composed in his honour. This fact implies that he felt obliged to justify himself to a largely Gaelic audience.

Indeed, other material of bardic provenance illustrates that MacDonnell was not adverse either to exploiting Gaelic scholarship to justify himself to the English administration. In 1604 MacDonnell had been granted the island of Rathlin by James. In 1617, however, the crown's legal right to grant Rathlin was challenged by a Scottish landowner, George Crawford. After a long and labyrinthine legal battle, Sir Raghnall succeeded in retaining possession of the island. Among the documents which MacDonnell had drawn up in 1618 to support his case was his genealogy in Irish compiled by Fear Flatha Ó Gnímh. This document was subsequently transmitted to Sir George Carew, as part of a brief submitted to him by both litigants.[46] Certainly, Ó Gnímh was prepared to accommodate to prevailing administrative and legal circumstances. Yet the means which he used in this instance to cater for his patron's requirements in the context of a non-Gaelic jurisdictional arrangement was the conventional bardic device of dynastic and genealogical validation.

Bardic poets were forced to respond to new social and political challenges throughout the Jacobean period. It has been demonstrated that this reactive impulse extended to the composition of poetry for English-speaking newcomers in an effort to incorporate these subjects within the compass of bardic ideological parameters. Not unexpectedly, bardic poets still depended largely on the patronage of the surviving Gaelic seigneurial houses and adopted a strategic approach to patrons' political preferences or religious predilections. Bardic flexibility in this regard finds a correlation in the ambiguous attitudes displayed towards Gaelic culture by the English-speaking establishment. While officials like Fynes Moryson argued for the extirpation of the Irish language, influential figures such as the scholarly Palesman James Ussher and George Carew were increasingly conscious of the language's historiographical importance if the history of Ireland were to be comprehensively researched.[47] Some settlers were also positively inclined towards Gaelic culture, if only for practical utilitarian purposes. For example, Richard Boyle (1566–1643), first earl of Cork, engaged a teacher with a knowledge of the language to tutor his two sons while they attended Eton. Aware of its communicative advantages in the advancement of Protestant evangelisation, Boyle was also keen that Irish-speaking clergymen be appointed to vacant benefices and he warmly welcomed Uilliam Ó Domhnuill's translation of the New Testament (1602–3).[48] Depositions taken after the 1641 rebellion suggest a fairly common acquaintance with the Irish language in settler households.[49] Likewise, the Church of Ireland promoted fitful and largely ineffectual attempts to provide for the religious instruction of the Gaelic Irish through the medium of their language. The most notable and lasting results of occasionally benign Anglican attitudes to the language were the translations of the New Testament and the *Book of Common Prayer* (1608) under the direction of Uilliam Ó Domhnuill. Unfortunately, it was not until 1685 that the Irish Old Testament was published. Further-

more, a general Protestant linguistic deficiency was compounded by the failure of the recently founded Trinity College in Dublin to provide an Irish-speaking ministry. This shortage in appropriately-qualified personnel severely
impeded the prospect of effective Protestant evangelisation.[50]

The uncertain ambivalence of the incoming colonial élite to Gaelic culture
is graphically documented in the case of Mathew De Renzy (1577–1634). Of
German birth, De Renzy lived the life of a settler in the midlands locality
known as Delvin Mac Coghlan, in King's County, from 1613 to 1618–19.
Thanks to the survival of De Renzy's letters from the years 1613 to 1620, it is
possible to obtain a fascinating insight into the outlook of one, admittedly
uncommon, settler.[51] De Renzy was unusual both in that he set himself to
learn Irish and in the extent to which he mastered his chosen subject. Especially interested in the classical bardic culture, he took instruction in that
branch of Gaelic scholarship from Conchobhar and Tadhg Mac Bruaideadha
in Thomond. Tadhg Óg Ó hUiginn of Leyney also tutored De Renzy in the
intricacies of the learned medium.[52] Such was the level of his proficiency that
between c. 1608–11 he is reputed to have compiled a grammar and dictionary of Irish.[53] Later, when De Renzy lived in Delvin Mac Coghlan as a settler, his knowledge of the language was to be of much practical benefit.[54]
Although cognisant of the communicative advantages of speaking the language and possessed of an antiquarian interest in Gaelic scholarship, De
Renzy was adamant that if English suzerainty were to be securely established
in Ireland, Gaelic culture would have to be neutralised and preferably elimi-
nated. Essentially, he argued that there was no room for two contrasting and
conflicting cultures on the island and he believed that continued Gaelic cultural vitality would serve as a constant reminder to the *Gaoidhil* of their ethnic and cultural distinctiveness *vis-à-vis* the colonial settlers. The emphasis on
genealogy in Gaelic culture, he maintained, could only be a perennial irritant
in the conversion of the Irish to Anglo-Saxon mores. Moreover, De Renzy
claimed he had detected a significant pattern in the native tradition, believing
that an overriding drive to inculturate newcomers within an indigenous cultural paradigm represented a fundamental Gaelic ideological premise. He
feared that the New English settlers would be culturally swamped, as the
Danes and Anglo-Normans had been in the past, by the Gaelic Irish or what
he called 'Clan na Milegh'.[55] An acute observer of developments on the island,
he realised correctly that the Gaelic literati were vital to the transmission of
ideological orthodoxy and on this basis advocated a campaign of unyielding
hostility to the native intellectual élite. De Renzy envisaged the necessary
eradication of the Irish language, arguing that 'languages doe maintaine a
record of antiquitie'.[56] Curiously and not a little ambiguously, the austere
colonialist policies propounded by De Renzy were belied on the ground by
his active engagement with bardic culture. This interest in the Gaelic tradition
was underpinned to a certain extent by his desire to contextualise the historical and contemporaneous circumstances of the English presence in Ireland.

In addition, his cosmopolitan background and relative linguistic sophistication must have contributed to a predisposition to engagement with the dominant culture of the country in which he had settled.

The De Renzy correspondence underscores two considerations relevant to this study. First, De Renzy was ambivalent in his approach to Gaelic culture, embracing its expression in practice while, at a theoretical level, decrying its influence. As already noted above, this form of dichotomised cultural ambivalence was not unique to the German planter. Bardic evidence illustrates readily how the Gaelic literati succeeded in exploiting this duality with the intention of inculturating newcomers. Second, De Renzy feared the influence wielded by the literati as a powerful élite. If their remit had been exclusively antiquarian and apolitical, De Renzy would certainly not have targeted them as a serious threat to the long-term aspirations of the new order. A clear-sighted political analyst, he realised that the literati were well-qualified to question and undermine colonial ideological assumptions, while he also identified the dynamic of inculturation as an effective means of passively augmenting Gaelic cultural dominance.

The evidence documented here illustrates that poets were ready to engage with newcomers while concurrently manipulating the conventional bardic canon to mediate contemporary challenges and influences within a familiar framework. Of course, De Renzy was wholly accurate in his identification of a drive towards ethnic inculturation on the part of the literati. Poets were prepared to adapt to the exigencies of securing new patrons, but they did so as far as possible along the lines of a formulaic paradigm. They recognised an essential strand of continuity in the Gaelic noble families who had withstood the consolidation of the Jacobean administration and, regardless of the means these families had invoked to negotiate their survival, poets remained available to serve them professionally.[57] With the progressive anglicisation of the Gaelic upper echelons, the bardic legitimating function faced obsolescence and the conventional articulation of the bardic ethos was strategically reworked in a process of re-evaluation which extended back to Elizabeth's reign. As opportunities to acquire patronage declined, so too did the composition of purely functional poetry. The innovative themes developed in the Elizabethan and Jacobean periods were to outlive the actual atrophy of the corporate bardic structure when subsequently they figured also in the work of a pioneering group of gentlemen poets. It is incorrect to speak of the final termination of the bardic tradition in the years after 1607, when in fact, this period witnesses a coherent bardic realignment within an overarching context of Gaelic cultural renewal.

Bardic Ideological and Corporate Evaluation, 1612–25

Focusing initially on the ideological concerns of the poets, it will be argued that a politicised national consciousness constituted a fundamental feature of the contemporary bardic outlook. Critically, this burgeoning sense of Irish nationality was complemented by concurrent and deliberate efforts to interlink Gaelic culture with Roman Catholicism. This apparently symbiotic union was greatly facilitated by the failure of the Church of Ireland to utilise Irish as an evangelical medium in any meaningful way thereby confirming popular perception of Anglicanism as merely the religious ancillary of the colonial administration. In stark contrast, the Irish Franciscans at Louvain had, from 1611 onwards, begun to publish devotional works in the vernacular. Over the coming decades this university city in the Spanish Netherlands was to serve as the continental focal point for combined Gaelic counter-reformation and cultural activity. This section's other focus centres on bardic responses to an increasingly dismal corporate predicament. Perceptions of the social and political ramifications resultant on the paralysis of the institutional bardic apparatus are examined.

On 11 January 1615 a patrician Catholic priest called Brian Mac Giolla Phádraig copied a poem of his own composition into the poem-book of Aodh Buidhe MacDonnell (ob. 1619) of Tinnakill, Co. Leix. The author, a scion of the Fitzpatrick family of Upper Ossory, was about to leave for the continent to further his training and he composed 'Truagh t'fhágbháil, a Inis Chuind' as a verse farewell to Ireland and her people.[58] Mac Giolla Phádraig appears to have been well-acquainted with bardic scholarship. In 1622, for instance, he copied some material into the O'Byrne poem-book.[59] While obviously conversant with bardic precepts, he was also very much the product of a counter-reformation formation. Clearly not a professional poet in the conventional Gaelic sense, he was representative of an emergent cohort of amateur poets familiar with the bardic ethos. This poem is interesting in terms of what it reveals of the outlook of an Irish-speaking counter-reformation priest. It complements Giolla Brighde Ó hEódhusa's 'Truagh an t-amharc-sa, a Éire', which was also composed on its author's decision to leave Ireland to study on the continent.[60] The origins of the exile poem genre may be partly traced to the renaissance notion of patria and to the fact that for many élite Irishmen exile was to become an inevitable career necessity.[61] Mac Giolla Phádraig presents a utopian vision of Ireland and early in the composition declares that he was leaving simply because he wished to undertake higher studies ('Ní fhúigfinn tú, a threabh na Niall . . . acht d'ardughadh mh'ealadhna'). A subtle association of Roman Catholicism with Ireland is apparent in stanza three when he protests that his leave-taking is occasioned not by hatred but rather out of love for his country ('ní d'fhuath ort acht d'ionmhoine, tug ar mh'óidh triall ód tuinn-si').[62] Since the poet is going abroad to study theology, this seems to imply, to some extent, a patriotic motivation. Crucially, love of homeland and allegiance to Roman Catholicism are implicitly linked. Mac Giolla Phádraig's patriotism is not simply a question of adherence to an abstract concept or geographical entity. It is as much inclusive of people and culture as territory. Emphasis is placed on his regard for the island's inhabitants ('mo ghrádh dhod dhroing dhílis-[s]i . . . mo shearc d'fholach [ní fhéadaim]') and he highlights his sadness at the prospect of leaving not only out of love of Ireland but also because of attachment to her inhabitants ('Ní tú, a chríoch, chaoinim uile acht do mhná 's do mhacraidhe').[63] He salutes members of his own family and the prominent patrician families of his home province of Leinster, including Anglo-Norman households such as the Graces, Fitzgeralds and Butlers in his list, as well as the Gaelic Kavanaghs, O'Dempseys, O'Ferralls, O'Mores, O'Conors Faly, O'Melaghlins and the McGeoghegans.[64] Importantly, Mac Giolla Phádraig's loyalties are not exclusively regional and the tribute concludes with the inclusion of all Irish people within the scope of his sentiments ('beannacht uaim ag gach aoinneach . . . dá bhfuil i nÉirinn armruaidh').[65] He rounds off the poem by invoking a third constituent element to substantiate his vision of the Irish *patria*. The concepts of territory and people are complemented by a cultural factor combining to produce a three-tiered articulation of national identity. Significantly, this sense of communal consciousness is both Gaelic and Roman Catholic in timbre. After land and people, he turns to the religious and the literati and an unidentified order of priests is saluted ('An t-ord cárbhaidh do char sinn'), possibly the Franciscans since their influence is evident in Mac Giolla Phádraig's 'Do-ghén dán do naomhuibh Dé'.[66] Poets, historians, doctors and musicians are ranked after the clergy as worthy of farewell ('leagha is ollamhain Éireann'; 'Aos dána na ngréas ngreanta 's a[n] lucht seanchadh suaitheanta'). Given the author's own clerical credentials, it is not altogether surprising that he should accord primacy of place to fellow priests in his enumeration of Irish scholars ('slán ar dtús dóibh do dhlighfinn').[67] This seemingly insignificant emphasis is another reminder of the highly-influential collocation of Gaelic culture and Roman Catholic faith which emerged over the course of this period.

It has already been documented in 'A Pattern Established 1558–1603' how the emergence of a *patria*-focused exile genre can be traced to Uilliam Nuinseann, who, when a student at Oxford in the early 1570s, composed a poem articulating a viewpoint quite similar to that delineated by Mac Giolla Phádraig.[68] In 'Fada i n-éagmais inse Fáil', Nuinseann also consciously interlinked Gaelic culture with Catholicism, while concurrently presenting Ireland's inhabitants in terms of an ethnic amalgam of Gaelic and Anglo-Norman drawn together by a common cultural and religious experience. Séathrún Céitinn's (*anglice* Geoffrey Keating) 'Mo bheannacht leat, a scríbhinn', composed in France *c.* 1606, is another work in the mould of the exile genre celebrating faith and fatherland. For instance, Céitinn laments his separation from both clerical colleagues and the literati in much the same vein as Nuinseann and Mac Giolla Phádraig. While Céitinn does not advert directly to a coalescence of Anglo-Norman and Gaelic interests, this assumption is surely implicit in his conscious decision to opt for Irish as a primary means of social and intellectual expression.[69] The sentiments articulated in 'Truagh t'fhágbháil, a Inis Chuind' are not especially original, but they are of some historiographical value in so far as they attest to the cultivation of an ideological symbiosis of Gaelic culture with the Roman faith. Similarly, in another later poem attributed to Mac Giolla Phádraig, his identification of the political potential of cultural allegiance is apparent when he castigates the adoption of English habits by unidentified elements in Ireland. Composed, as was his 1615 exile poem, in the popular *amhrán* or stressed metre, 'Och! mo chreach-sa fasion Chláir Éibhir!' is reflective of social dislocation in Cromwellian times.[70] Mac Giolla Phádraig, who had returned to Ireland by 1617, ministered in the diocese of Ossory, where he was appointed vicar apostolic around the year 1652. Shortly afterwards, he was reputedly beheaded by a band of marauding Cromwellians.[71]

Mathghamhain Ó hIfearnáin contributed one poem to the extended collective bardic debate between poets from the northern and southern halves of Ireland or *Leath Chuinn* and *Leath Mhogha* respectively known as *Iomarbhágh na bhfileadh* ('Contention of the Bards' 1616–24). The composition, 'Créad fá dtá Tadhg is Lughaidh', is remarkable for the clarity of perception it presents in a bardic *tour de force* frequently characterised by quasi-baroque verbiage. This extended battle of scholarly wits is a Gaelic manifestation of the contemporary European fashion for antiquarian investigation, although it was later dismissed by Anthony Brody (*fl.* 1672) as a 'magna sed inutilis controversia'.[72] In this poem, the author relates the fable of a cat and fox who fought about the distribution between them of a pig they had trapped. While they bickered among themselves, a wolf chanced on them and taking advantage of their distraction, he immediately devoured the pig ('Tig onchú uaibhreach allaidh chuca mar do chualamair'). Ó hIfearnáin explains the implications of the tale he had related as follows ('Baramhail do bheirim dí'): the fox and the cat represent the quarrelsome poets Tadhg Mac Bruaideadha and Lughaidh Ó Cléirigh, while the pig's fat symbolises the land of Ireland ('iath Éireann íoth na muice'). Equally emblematic, the predatory wolf represents a foreign mercenary ('an Gall-óg onchú an áithis').[73] A similar frankness is also manifest in two poems in which Ó hIfearnáin laments the downward trend in bardic fortunes.[74] Evidently, Ó hIfearnáin was conscious of the failure of poets engaged in the 'Contention' to contextualise or even acknowledge the potential or actual implications of the sea change which had unfolded in Ireland. His disquiet in this particular instance is paralleled by other bardic poets more generally and it is with these various and complementary readings that the remainder of the present chapter is concerned.

Only one composition, an elegy on Donal O'Sullivan Beare (ob. 1618), appears to have survived from the corpus of an elusive poet called Domhnall Ó Dálaigh. O'Sullivan Beare, best known to posterity for his audacious march from Glengarriff to Leitrim in 1602, was assassinated in Madrid in July 1618 by an Anglo-Irishman named John Bath. The work beginning 'San Sbáinn do toirneadh Teamhair' was presumably composed in or shortly after 1618.[75] Like Tadhg Mac Bruaideadha in his elegy for the fourth earl of Thomond (ob. 1624), Ó Dálaigh equates the passing of his subject with the general eclipse of Ireland ('gan chéile fá chiaigh dtoirse Éire a ndiaidh an Domhnoill-se'). Concomitantly, the Gaelic Irish had now embarked on a period of distress and were destined to lose their former glory ('glóir a tromshlóigh dá thurnamh'). The conceits characteristic of elegy are invoked, for instance O'Sullivan Beare is reported to have been mourned by his family and the nobility in general while concurrently nature supposedly manifested its sorrow at his demise ('An uile dhúil 'na dheaghuidh . . . d'aonbháidh orchra ceann a gceann').[76] There is an apparent contradiction in Ó Dálaigh's treatment of O'Sullivan Beare's relationship with the English. To heighten the dramatic impact of his murder, the poet maintains that not only had Ireland been bereaved by his passing but so too had Spain and England. A reference to grieving English military commanders probably alludes to the support which O'Sullivan Beare received from the crown to enable him to become lord of his sept in 1593 against the opposition of his uncle ('Riú bheanus an teidhm tinn-si cinn ghaisgidh na Gaillinnsi'). Moreover, the implication of the ensuing quatrain suggests that O'Sullivan Beare had been a staunch advocate of the crown's strategic interests ('Na mbearnaidh bhaoghuil do bhaoi Domhnall gan fhosadh aonlaoi').[77] Nevertheless, the poet quickly switches to the diametrical opposite of this approach when, in quatrain thirty-one, O'Sullivan Beare is deftly metamorphosed from sometime English ally to Gaelic liberator:[78]

> Re Gallaibh go nuaidhe a-niogh
> aoinfhear do ghasruidh Ghaoidhiol,
> a gcaoi imreasuin ní fhuil
> fá fhinnleasuibh Chraoi Cobhthuigh.

> In all the fair dwellings of Ireland there is
> to-day no man of the Gaelic company capable
> of resuming the struggle against the foreigners.

In a manner remarkably similar to Tadhg Mac Bruaideadha's assertion that the death of the fourth earl of Thomond (ob. 1624) cleared the way for Anglo-Saxon designs on Irish land, Ó Dálaigh argues likewise in the case of the late O'Sullivan Beare. With the latter's demise, the English are enabled to assume unchallenged control of Ireland ('Éire mar budh dúthuigh dháibh fúthuibh féin ar n-a fágbháil'). Evidently, he foresees the negative consequences of English annexation of lands formerly in Irish Gaelic possession:[79]

> Beanfaid a n-áit do Chloinn Chuirc,
> don chloinn ní maith an mhaluirt:
> a bhfionnbhruidhne, a gcúirte cloch,
> dúinte ar mbiodhbhuidh-ne, bearnoch.

> They will take their places from the descendants of *Corc* –
> it is not a good exchange for that race:
> their fair castles, their stone courts,
> are [now] breached and [have become] the fortresses of our enemies.

In fact, Ó Dálaigh harbours no illusions about the likelihood of reversing recent developments: the death of O'Sullivan Beare has impacted adversely on the prospect of Ireland's recovery from catastrophe ('Acht lá díoghla druim ar dhruim ní bhia ag Éirinn d'éis Domhnuill'). Yet Ó Dálaigh was not prepared to rest his case on the basis of O'Sullivan Beare's death alone, for at one point in the poem he touches on the general absence of leadership among the Gaelic Irish and the pessimistic prognosis this entailed for the relief of communal misfortune ('sgaoileadh ní chlaisdir 'na gcionn, gaisgidh Ghaoidheal a ngéibhionn').[80]

Aspects of the argument already advanced to account for Mac Bruaideadha's emphasis on O'Brien's allegiance to the crown also help explain why Ó Dálaigh, in a poem characterised by a sense of politicised national identity, chose to allude to his subject's distant engagement with the English administration ('seal caoine ar mhnáibh san Mhumhain dáibh ní saoire a Saghsanaibh').[81] Literary evidence suggests that bardic poets in particular, and the Gaelic literati in general, made no *a priori* theoretical objection to the English monarchy claiming the overlordship of Ireland given appropriate satisfaction of certain inalienable dynastic and cultural desiderata. What concerned *fileadha* fundamentally, however, was the affirmation and cultivation of Gaelic cultural integrity, which was in itself dependent on a degree of Gaelic social and financial autonomy. The characteristic which poets prized most in a patron, regardless of ethnic provenance, was support of the Gaelic cultural ethos. 'San Sbáinn do toirneadh Teamhair' testifies to Ó Dálaigh's acute political judgement. Despite a fleeting reference to its subject's former and admittedly opportunistic pro-crown stance, the overall tone of the poem is one of empathy for the beleaguered position of the Gaelic Irish. The interlinking of Catholicism with a politicised national consciousness is another aspect of the poem which merits attention. Quatrain thirty articulates an unambiguous identification of government hostility to Catholicism with the political emasculation of the Gaelic Irish:[82]

> Gan lá cádhais ar chealluibh
> neamhthoil d'ord is d'Aifreannaibh,
> móid re laoidhibh a leabhar,
> na Gaoidhil dá ngeimhleaghadh.

> There is never a day when churches are venerated,
> there is no affection for orders or for Masses,
> there is anger towards the verses of their books,
> the *Gaoidhil* are being put in fetters.

The image of the Gaelic Irish persecuted for their allegiance to the Catholic faith is highly potent and underlines the extent to which issues of political autonomy and religious freedom rapidly became enmeshed at this stage. In explanation of O'Sullivan Beare's death, Ó Dálaigh utilises a motif common in the bardic corpus when he claims that God's anger with the Irish had resulted in the premature death of the west Cork nobleman ('cré ar ar gcoill-bhile do-bhir oirbhire Dé ar na daoinibh').[83] Although the providentialist concept of divine retribution and the casting of the Irish for comparative historical reasons in the role of the dispossessed Israelites were frequently invoked in the work of bardic poets, it is significant that these themes continue to figure prominently in the poetry of the new generation of gentlemen authors such as Pádraigín Haicéad, Fear Dorcha Ó Mealláin and Dáibhí Cúndún.[84] Certainly, Ó Dálaigh's emphasis on faith and fatherland was not inappropriate in a poem for O'Sullivan Beare. As early as 1602, in a letter to King Philip III of Spain, O'Sullivan Beare depicted the conflict between the Irish and the New English as possessing an ethno-sectarian dimension. In his opinion the English were 'cruel, malignant and heretical enemies' ('ar n-eascarad gcruadhálach mallaighthe mí-chreidmheach') while resistance to their expansionism is described in terms of a 'Catholic war' ('sa chogadh chatholica-sa').[85]

In the poem beginning 'Soraidh slán ler saoithibh saoidheachta' Eoghan Mág Craith bemoans both the ailing bardic institution and what is presented as the pitiful degradation of facilities for Roman Catholic worship. No evidence survives to enable the precise dating of this piece, however, Mág Craith's poem, 'Tugadh an t-ársa ar Éirinn', in which he laments the disturbed condition of Ireland, was composed in 1620 according to a seventeenth-century manuscript and this reference, at least, establishes the author's floruit.[86] Mág Craith complains that churches have been reduced to hovels ('Mo thruagh toighe Dé 'na ndúrbhoithibh'), inhabited by churls and no longer hosting divine worship within their precincts ('fa mhúchdhoighir choire 's gan É dá íoccabhair'). Indeed, Mass was celebrated outdoors in woods ('Iodhbairt Chuirp Dhé fa dhíon fhiodhbhaidhe') while foreigners controlled traditional ecclesiastical sites ('s ainbhfine i ngach cill aolta oirnidhe'). To exacerbate matters further, he claims that God was no longer prayed to for remission of sins ('s gan É dá bhionnghuidhe i ndíol ar n-uilc 'ná ar n-oirbhire').[87] Although Mág Craith provides a graphic reflection of contemporary pressures on the institutional Catholic church, his juxtaposition of bardic and church difficulties serves to link élite Gaelic culture with the plight of Catholicism in support once more of a powerful ideological alignment.

The first concerted institutional drive to equate Roman Catholicism with Gaelic culture was undertaken not in Ireland but in continental Europe. Giolla Brighde Ó hEódhusa's catechism, *An teagasg críosdaidhe*, published in Antwerp in 1611, marked the launch of a coherent strategy on the part of the Irish Franciscans in Louvain to supply devotional material in the vernacular with a militant counter-reformation message.[88] As early as 1593 Flaithrí Ó Maolchonaire (ob. 1629) had translated a Spanish catechism into Irish, the unpublished manuscript of which he forwarded to Ireland in 1598. In 1616 *Sgáthán an chrábhaidh*, his translation of the Spanish devotional text entitled *El Desseoso*, was published. Significantly, Ó Maolchonaire was relentless in his opposition to the New English presence in Ireland. He had accompanied the Spanish force to Kinsale in 1601, subsequently leaving the country with Hugh Roe O'Donnell. Both were destined never to return home. In 1607 Ó Maolchonaire was on hand at Douai to meet the earls of Tyrone and Tyrconnell, from where he escorted them to Louvain. Nominated to the archbishopric of Tuam in 1609, Ó Maolchonaire was involved as late as 1627 in a proposed invasion of Ireland to overthrow the crown administration.[89] The renowned theologian Aodh Mac Aingil published his original work, *Scáthán shacramuinte na haithridhe,* in 1618. Before entering the Franciscan order sometime around 1603, Mac Aingil had served as the tutor to Hugh O'Neill's two sons and was nominated archbishop of Armagh in 1626, the year of his death.[90]

The devotional manuals published by Ó hEódhusa, Ó Maolchonaire and Mac Aingil represent a watershed in the development of early modern Gaelic culture. Both Ó hEódhusa and Ó Maolchonaire came from learned families, the former from a celebrated Fermanagh bardic family, while the latter's forefathers had served as historians to the O'Connors and MacDermots of Connacht. Both had spent time in bardic schools, subsequently reading theology and philosophy, Ó hEódhusa at Douai and Ó Maolchonaire at Salamanca. Mac Aingil was educated at a grammar school on the Isle of Man and later studied at Salamanca. Although not reared in a bardic milieu, he was, nonetheless, an accomplished poet in Irish.[91] As well as being the most respected Irish theologian of his generation, Mac Aingil was recognised as a leading authority on the writings of John Duns Scotus. It is symptomatic of the profound diversification taking place within Gaelic culture that scholars who would formerly have followed the hereditary family profession now chose to utilise native scholarship to promote distinctly non-traditional objectives. Imbued with a counter-reformation ethos, they manipulated conventional literary forms to suit the needs of their ideology. If bardic themes were adapted by a new breed of poets, the Louvain school was just as far-reaching and radical in redirecting the focus of a venerable cultural patrimony. For the Louvain authors, the important question was not so much a reworking of existing themes but the creation and evolution of a new mindset encompassing polemical propaganda and print, a medium all but untested in Irish. Nicholas Canny has rightly stressed the importance of the Louvain school and its publications programme in the modernisation of Gaelic *mentalités*. However, his argument that this transformation began only with the first sustained Gaelic Irish contact with counter-reformation Europe after 1607 is inaccurate. The evidence assembled here suggests that general re-evaluation and modernisation of traditional conventions and themes had already begun in the middle years of Elizabeth's reign.[92]

Obviously, the course of the Protestant reformation in Ireland was of particular concern to committed counter-reformation agents such as Ó hEódhusa,

Ó Maolchonaire and Mac Aingil and this factor accounts for their determination to provide devotional material in the vernacular to counteract earlier Anglican achievements in the area of Gaelic religious publications. Mac Aingil, for instance, in his preface to *Scáthán shacramuinte na haithridhe* readily admitted that his labours had been motivated in part by a wish to redress the possibly baneful influence of the Protestant translations of the New Testament and he dismissed the *Book of Common Prayer* as the 'book of heretical hell' ('Leabhar Iffrinn Eiriceachda'). More personally, Mac Aingil was also conscious of a deficiency in the Irish contribution to the counter-reformation movement and it obviously pained his sense of patriotism to admit that other Catholic 'nations' already had similar manuals in the appropriate vernacular ('Bíd leabhráin mar so ag gach náision Chatoilic eili'). The persecution of Catholicism in Ireland, held Mac Aingil, meant that there was an especially acute demand for such works in his own 'nation' ('atáid do riachdanas ar an náision dá bhfuilmidne go spesialta'). Although there is no overtly anti-English sentiment in *Scáthán shacramuinte na haithridhe* – indeed the author is careful to proclaim his loyalty to James ('don mhúintir atá fá mhórdhachd an ríogh scríobhuim so') – the advocacy of the notion of an Irish-speaking Catholic nation was clearly implicit in Mac Aingil's outlook.[93] While the Louvain movement to publish religious tracts in the vernacular was formally inspired by the example of contemporary continental Catholicism and supposedly exclusively devotional in focus, the end results were to prove to be as much political in character as confessional.

The programme of the Louvain school also contributed to the adoption of innovative attitudes to prose writing in Irish. Importantly, all three authors eschewed the often recondite literary style of the Gaelic literati in favour of one which was limpid in idiom. This development is another reflection of an ongoing modification of classical bardic scholarship. However, such was the enduring shadow cast by conventional usage that all three authors felt obliged to justify their departure from previous norms. Ó Maolchonaire excuses what he considered the simplicity of his style by stating that he wrote for the benefit of an unlearned audience with no special knowledge of the scholarly complexities of the language ('chum leasa na ndaoine simplidhe, nách foil géarchúiseach a nduibheagán na Gaoidhilge').[94] Mac Aingil pre-empted any criticism of his decision to write in an accessible style when he states that he had undertaken the work to inculcate repentance rather than to teach Irish ('nách do mhúnadh Gaoidhilgi sgríobhmaoid achd do mhúnadh na haithrídhe').[95] As far as Ó hEódhusa was concerned, his choice of an uncomplicated style was simply a matter of opting for clarity and intelligibility to facilitate a wide audience ('Lé hóradh briathar dá mbeinn, mór dhíobh fá chiaigh dho chuirfinn').[96] The primary purpose of Franciscan efforts to publish these Irish-language tracts was to impede the progress of the reformation in Ireland. The fact that these authors felt confident enough to exchange the archaisms of the learned medium for a more accessible and therefore more effective style indicates the degree to which they redefined the operational parameters of conventional Gaelic scholarship. The precise influence of these publications at home in Ireland is not easy to quantify because of a dearth of detailed evidence for reading habits in early modern Ireland. Nonetheless, their unquestionable popularity in manuscript form, especially Ó hEódhusa's catechism, attests to considerable oral circulation.[97] Moreover, the Louvain tracts were complemented by the work in Ireland of the Bordeaux-trained priest Séathrún Céitinn (ob. c. 1644). Well-versed in counter-reformation and English recusant literature, he compiled his unpublished defence of the Mass sometime around 1615.[98] Like Ó hEódhusa's catechism, *Eochair sgiath an aifrinn* secured an extensive readership and oral audience in manuscript form. The use of Irish by the Louvain school and by Céitinn as a medium for the dissemination of counter-reformation propaganda exemplifies a systematic association of Catholicism with Gaelic culture. Of course, this ideological combination was not original in itself. Eoghan Ó Dubhthaigh (ob. 1590) had stressed the apparent 'Englishness' of the Elizabethan reform movement in Ireland and he evidently sought to equate Gaelic cultural integrity with an unfettered Roman church. Indeed, the move to present Catholicism as the integral confessional expression of Gaelic civility is already apparent among the first generation of counter-reformation reformers. For instance, Richard Creagh (1525?-85), Catholic archbishop of Armagh, produced a catechism in Irish, in addition to compiling a grammar of the language.[99] First-hand exposure to contemporary European politics, the philosophy of the counter-reformation and the prestige of the printing press all combined to inform Franciscan efforts to initiate a comprehensive and potent articulation of the concept of an Irish-speaking Catholic Ireland.

This chapter's last focus is on the reaction of the poets to their corporate predicament. A comprehensive analysis of bardic self-perception in the period 1603–12 forms part of the preceding chapter and given that the vocational concerns of the *fileadha* appear to remain fairly constant throughout James's reign, it is instructive to look at two select aspects of this question in detail. Fearghal Óg Mac an Bhaird's distinctive voice has regularly been invoked in this book and it is appropriate, therefore, to discuss some of his final poems composed while an exile in Louvain. In addition, evidence for the deterioration of professional modalities within the bardic institution is reviewed. Many poems examined in this chapter reflect diminished levels of patronage after 1603. In Ulster alone, for instance, the main branches of three major Gaelic families, the O'Neills, O'Donnells and Maguires, all generous benefactors of Gaelic scholarship, ceased to play any such role in the region after 1607. The curtailment of opportunity in Ireland was such that several *fileadha* migrated to Gaelic Scotland in search of employment.[100] An already unfavourable situation was made worse by the progressive anglicisation of elements of the remaining Gaelic élite.[101] It has been noted in the previous chapter that in Ulster some of the Gaelic literati managed to obtain grants of land under the terms of the plantation. However, the indifferent financial performance of the native landholders in the six planted counties must also have affected them adversely.[102] The disintegration of the social and economic basis underpinning élite Gaelic culture, as Eoghan Mág Craith noted at the time, deprived bardic poetry of its functional milieu ('Fáth ar ndána do dhola i ndísbheagadh, sgísleagadh ó Mogha 's a gcána ag cách dá gcraosslogadh').[103]

Brian Ó Gnímh's poem beginning 'Cuimseach sin, a Fhearghail Óig' suggests that the bardic institution's vocational momentum had begun to falter by the late sixteenth century. Reflecting the appearance of fissures in the hitherto monolithic corporate facade, Ó Gnímh criticises Fearghal Óg Mac an Bhaird for breaching bardic convention by apparently composing on horseback ('ag deilbh ghlanoige ar ghearrán'), and not in the prescribed darkened chamber ('Gan boith ndiamhoir').[104] Ironically, Fear Flatha Ó Gnímh, probably Brian's son, was subjected to similar criticism in a poem composed sometime between 1617 and 1638. In 'Cia meisi nó an macsa Seaáin', Lughaidh Ó hEachuidhéin calls on Sir Henry O'Neill (ob. 1638) of Lower Clandeboye to grant him the post of chief poet. Emphasising how his ancestors had been retained as poets by the O'Neills, Ó hEachuidhéin claims that other noblemen had their own personal poets and, because of this, O'Neill should not break with custom. To highlight his plight, he draws O'Neill's attention to Fear Flatha Ó Gnímh, disparagingly described as 'poet of the masses' ('file an tslúaigh'), observing that Ó Gnímh, despite his popularisation of poetry, enjoyed the esteem of well-placed Ulster families, in contrast to Ó hEachuidhéin's own situation.[105] The aspersions cast on Ó Gnímh may well be ascribed to frustration or jealousy on the part of his detractor. However, the pejorative label 'file an tslúaigh' is fairly concise in this particular context. It implies that Ó Gnímh had reworked his style to broaden his audience range to include those not particularly acquainted with élite culture. This suggests that Ó Gnímh experimented with stressed metres and a demotic vocabulary. In fact, this reference offers a precious glimpse of poets seeking a wider forum of social engagement and of diversification from the formal social ambit of bardic composition. Furthermore, Ó hEachuidhéin's comments expose the tension inevitable in a situation where a venerable and authoritative literary canon was, of necessity, in the process of radical recasting.

The diversification in bardic custom and discourse which ultimately privileged the work of a new non-professional poetic cohort is reflected in the poem beginning 'Sona do cheird, a Chalbhaigh'. Composed by a Scottish Gaelic *fileadh*, Cathal MacMhuirich (*fl.* 1625), it is addressed to a poet called Calbhach, probably an Irishman with Antrim connections.[106] MacMhuirich faults Calbhach's behaviour in two particular areas: his unfortunate sense of etiquette and his relaxed attitude to the nuances of syllabic composition. Bardic social protocol was apparently infringed by the Irishman's loutish conduct and his unsuitability to move in patrician circles is stressed. Tellingly, MacMhuirich is dismayed that Calbhach should be so successful notwithstanding his manifest indifference to bardic scholarship. In fact, Calbhach enjoyed prestige and success without undergoing an overly rigorous training ('tarrla d'onáir is d'ágh ort gabháil re dán gan docracht'). Accordingly, his poetry is supposedly characterised by inexactitude and verbal infelicity:[107]

> Maith an ceird do thogh tusa
> d'fagháil muirne is macnusa,
> dénamh rann gan chóir ccertuis
> a n-am óil is oireachtais.

> Good is the trade you have chosen to win
> affection and luxury – the making of
> incorrect verses at the time of drinking
> and assembly.

MacMhuirich, for his part, intimates personal regret at having followed bardic convention with so little profit: contemporary upheaval had contributed to the eclipse of bardic poetry (''s gan sbéis ag duine dar ndán d'éis na cruinne do chaochládh'). The poem finishes on a note redolent of classical bardic conceit with MacMhuirich suggesting, with more than a touch of intellectual hauteur, that it would have been lamentable had he compromised his professional integrity in the manner of Calbhach's behaviour ('Ceird an Chalbhaigh acht gidh cóir dul 'na seilbh budh dál dobróin').[108] This evidence indicates that by the 1620s the composition of poetry in strict syllabic metres constituted the preserve of a diminishing and no doubt ageing clerisy. It was not solely a question of decline, however, because this period also witnessed a simultaneous surge in the composition by gentlemen or amateur authors of poetry in stressed metres which bears a bardic impress.

The date of Fearghal Óg Mac an Bhaird's departure from Ireland is unclear and no evidence regarding his continental exile appears to be extant, apart from three poems he composed while living in Louvain c. 1616–18.[109] Excepting passing references to the consolidation of English suzerainty in Ireland in the compositions entitled 'Ní maith altuighim m'anáir' and 'Éisd rem égnach, a fhir ghráidh', Mac an Bhaird in this trilogy is primarily concerned with his material and social degradation. In 'Éisd rem égnach, a fhir ghráidh', he explains to Flaithrí Ó Maolchonaire that English persecution caused him to journey to Louvain ('Goill dom athchur 's dom arguin rom tug go Labháin tar linn'). Given that both 'Fuarus iongnadh, a fhir chumainn' and 'Éisd rem égnach, a fhir ghráidh' are addressed to Ó Maolchonaire with the intention of soliciting financial aid, the author concentrates on his current reduced circumstances. It is related that he had lost his wealth and status in Ireland ('Do choilleas onóir m'anma 's mo bhuar 's mo lucht leanamhna') and how he had left behind what remained of his former prosperity ('Thiar do fhágbhus earr mo chonáigh'). In 'Ní maith altuighim m'anáir', it is observed that he possessed neither land nor seigneurial patronage (''s bheith gan tír gan tighearna') and because of the atrophied condition of the bardic institution, he can no longer count on the presence of a minor grade of poet to accompany him on his travels ('mé gan fiú an bhaird do bhuidhin . . . ní beo anáir m'ealadhan').[110]

Mac an Bhaird's other major theme in the Louvain poems is what he portrays as destructive social upheaval in Ireland. In 'Fuarus iongnadh, a fhir chumainn', he emphasises his social denigration, which was rendered all the more unpalatable by what he perceived as the unprecedented prosperity of his formerly servile inferiors. Those who were obliged to defer to him in the past now slight him ('cádhus uatha ní fhuair mé – na daoine dar dhual ar n-ion[n]ramh'). While *arrivistes* thrived, Mac an Bhaird's situation deteriorated ('gan m'ana ag fás – foirfe an coll – is toice ag fás ag mac moghadh'). He implores Ó Maolchonaire to help him restore his status, so sparing him the indignity of moving in plebeian company ('tuig, cheana, nach cubhaidh rinn gan bheith i ngoire d'fhuil uasail').[111] The viewpoint articulated in the poems addressed to Ó Maolchonaire is undeniably élitist and reflects the severely degraded outline of the formerly ascendant poet/patron nexus. Evidently, Mac an Bhaird does not attempt to evaluate the political or social circumstances of the upheaval contributing to his exile. Yet, in two of these poems he is addressing a figure who had spent his youth in a bardic milieu and it is logical that Mac an Bhaird should have opted to frame his case in terms of reference immediately and mutually cogent to both parties. Mac an Bhaird, exiled and near destitute, seeks to enlist Ó Maolchonaire's sympathy by stressing a shared cultural inheritance and history. If these poems are read in the form of *cris de coeur* from one Gaelic scholar to another, it follows that deep emotion rather than critical awareness should predominate. The personal histories of Mac an Bhaird and Ó Maolchonaire present a diptych of the transformation of the Gaelic intelligentsia: the purveyors of a venerable corporate ethos face extinction while concurrently a new breed of innovators meets with tremendous success. If Ó Maolchonaire successfully refocused and regenerated a communal patrimony, he did so in the context of becoming an important European scholar, an expert on Saint Augustine and friend of Philip III and Jansen. Ironically, while Mac an Bhaird can himself claim credit for his dynamic engagement with unprecedented challenges, it was his personal tragedy, like all *fileadha* of this generation, to number among the last custodians of a magisterial tradition which stretched back centuries.

This chapter's objective has been to highlight two particular themes common in the contemporary bardic corpus, namely the assimilatory premise articulated in the poetry and the politicised sense of national identity developed by poets. Of course, poets continued to seek and accept patronage from Gaelic patrons who had acquiesced in, or in some cases, actually facilitated the crown's expansionism. Participation in the modes of high Gaelic culture was frequently the decisive criterion in bardic evaluation of a patron's social credentials. Undoubtedly, poets often consciously refrained from overt political commentary so long as they could assume a benevolent approach on the part of patrons to bardic culture and their complementary appreciation of the social mores and outlook it mirrored. Yet allegiance to a Gaelic cultural paradigm, even if mediated through apparent political conformity, was in itself an inevitable form of dissidence in the face of the dominant Anglo-Saxon political and social model. The very real dangers attendant on a perceived conflict of loyalties induced many surviving Gaelic and gaelicised noble families to shed over time the apparent burden of their cultural inheritance. Several poems evidence the currency of a coherent sense of politicised nationality in the outlook of bardic and non-professional poets. Certainly, these poets recognised the implications posed by the dismantlement of aristocratic Gaelic society consequent to a process of political and economic emasculation. Bardic responses were to some extent gloomy in so far as poets inevitably registered the disturbing reverberations of the chaos unleashed on the élite. On the other hand, however, bardic analyses of dislocation acquired a proactive resonance thanks to the invocation of the providentialist concept and the obvious utility of the Gaelic/Hebrew comparison with its redemptive promise. The years after 1612 witnessed the ongoing currency of reactive strategies and themes which date back to Elizabeth's reign, namely, the predication of the coalescence of interests between the historic Gaelic Irish and gaelicised Anglo-Norman communities and the momentous ideological interlinking of Roman Catholicism and Gaelic culture. A highly innovative aspect of the bardic corpus reflecting the influx of newcomers during the Jacobean period is that of the premise of inculturation. As demand for the bardic validating role had been largely obviated by new socio-political circumstances, it is not surprising that the poetry documents the corporate anguish of a traumatised caste. Yet such declarations of despair are all too easily overemphasised, especially at the cost of obscuring a more accurate picture of a remarkably vibrant and resourceful Gaelic cultural ambience.

After the last generation of hereditary *fileadha* had passed away, their offspring were generally subsumed into the amorphous mass of dispossessed Irish-speakers. For Dáibhí Ó Bruadair (*c.* 1625–98) the ignorance of those descended from old bardic families was a poignant reminder of former glories:[112]

> D'aithle na bhfileadh n-uasal,
> truaghsan timheal an tsaoghail;
> clann na n-ollamh go n-eagna
> folamh gan freagra faobhair.

> Gone are all the noble poets,
> Sad the darkness of the world;
> The children of those learned *ollamhs*
> Now are void of keen retorts.

By the close of the seventeenth century, bardic poetry had already become the focus of antiquarian enquiry. In 1699 the Oxford savant and philologist Edward Lhuyd, while on a tour of Ireland, met with 'one Eoin Agniw' (namely, Ó Gnímh) in Co. Antrim. Lhuyd recorded that Ó Gnímh was a descendant of the family who had been hereditary poets to the O'Neills of Clandeboye. This character, however, was no privileged scholar, for 'he had forsaken the Muses and betaken himself to the plow' because the family lands had been 'taken away from his father'. Ó Gnímh was readily induced by the prospect of cash to part with family manuscripts and Lhuyd noted with unconcealed satisfaction that he had 'made an easy purchase of about a dozen ancient manuscripts on parchment'.[113] Such was the haphazard fashion by which a small fraction of the bardic legacy was preserved for future generations. Certainly, the demise of classical bardic culture deserves to be nostalgically lamented. Nonetheless, it must not be supposed, as the *fileadha* did, that their fate was synonymous with the disappearance of an autonomous native cultural tradition. In fact, the early seventeenth century witnesses a general Gaelic cultural renewal, which is the appropriate context in which to see the modernisation and transformation of the old order.

THE BARDIC CORPUS AND
NATIONAL IDENTITY

Cultural historians and literary scholars alike are indebted to Mícheál Mac Craith for his valuable survey of the impact of the renaissance on the Gaelic literary tradition. Developing an insight first advanced by Edmund Curtis, he has demonstrated the significant extent to which Gaelic literature bears the imprint of the renaissance. Unfortunately, when he comes to assess the potential of bardic poetry as a source reflective of new trends and influences in the literature, Mac Craith all but excludes classical bardic verse from his proposed Gaelic renaissance canon:[1]

> When one turns to consider the corpus of Gaelic literature in the sixteenth century or of any other century, one immediately thinks of bardic poetry. The student of bardic poetry is apt to be disappointed, however, if he hopes to find evidence of a new world view readily present in the lines of eulogistic verse.

Mac Craith also suggests that the functional nature of the poetry obviated the evolution of a modernising bardic outlook. At first glance, this assumption of innate bardic conservatism seems convincing and, indeed, the preceding analysis of the Maguire and O'Hara poems tends to support Mac Craith's interpretative caveat to some extent. Nevertheless, the initially unpromising Maguire and O'Hara material has also revealed the extent to which innovative attitudes permeate a selection of determinedly 'professional' poems. In fact, this book's overriding objective has been to argue for a fundamental reconsideration of what has largely been portrayed as an insistent and dogmatic bardic adherence to an antiquated and inflexible world view. In view of the evidence presented in successive chapters in this study, it is obvious that Mícheál Mac Craith's proviso regarding the early modern bardic corpus is in need of considerably more nuanced qualification. In fact, the student of early modern bardic poetry must disentangle two apparently contradictory sets of dichotomies. First, it is possible to propose an interpretative resolution of the primary dichotomy of simultaneous ideological renewal and corporate paralysis. Second, the dichotomy emanating from an intellectual experience coloured by concurrent and contrasting strands of conservatism and innovation can be contextualised within a credible interpretative framework. It is feasible on the basis of the evidence presented in this book to argue that the transformation of bardic culture at the end of the sixteenth and beginning of the seventeenth centuries evolved into a double helix form which encom-

passed mutually-complementary ideological renewal and corporate contrac-
tion. Conventional bardic scholarship could only incorporate the influence of
humanist and counter-reformation trends by means of the strategic adaptation and rationalisation of medieval codes of practice. Furthermore, the configuration of this inevitable and essential cultural interface, which combined
both growth and facilitative decay, was further determined by the imperatives
dictated by conquest and colonisation. Ironically, the extension of English
hegemony in Ireland which did so much to disrupt Gaelic sociological patterns also contributed to the creation of an intellectual vacuum in which
bardic poets, freed from the restrictive inheritance of convention, were
enabled to privilege new modes of political assessment. The bardic institution, finely interwoven within the fabric of élite Gaelic culture, was evidently
subject to the fortunes of the seigneurial polity. Progressively denuded of the
validatory function which provided its *raison d'être* and confronted by deeply
unsympathetic colonial administrative and jurisdictional arrangements, the
corporate institution decayed rapidly. Nevertheless as long as a modicum of
patronage remained available, it encouraged sufficient bardic dynamism to
permit the articulation of relevant interpretative strategies. It was from this
circumscribed trajectory of vocational continuity that bardic convention and,
to a lesser extent, bardic innovation drew support. If, as the evidence presented in this volume strongly suggests, initial bardic realisation of corporate
decline is to be traced to the middle years of Elizabeth's reign, then, paradoxically, the beginnings of institutional palsy coincide with the refocusing of
bardic political *mentalités*. In effect, contrasting currents of modernisation and
corporate retrenchment are concurrent in their appearance. Indeed, the protracted impact of institutional disarray facilitated the development of an intellectual environment conducive to experimentation. In other words,
modernisation and decline were structurally complementary, in so far as one
trend yielded to the other, allowing innovation to make good the lacuna left
in the wake of restrictive institutional modes.

This study is effectively confined in scope, both textually and chronolog-
ically, to discussion of the bardic corpus. While the case has been made for
the emergence and cultivation of a significant stock of coherent and revitalised themes in bardic poetry, it can also be demonstrated that the results of
innovative attitudes long outlived the parent institution which underpinned
their development and presentation. If the outmoded contractual focus of the
bardic apparatus in the context of alternative jurisdictional structures is self-
evident, it should not be assumed that bardic attitudes were correspondingly
obsolete. The central argument of this book has been that the contrary was in
fact the case. That argument will conclude with a summary appraisal of the
thematic innovation discussed in the preceding chapters and its continuity in
the context of a new generation of Gaelic gentlemen poets.

Before looking at the striking degree of post-bardic thematic continuity, it
is necessary to place these new poets in context by making some observations

about aspects of the work of the literary cohort who inherited so much stock-in-trade from bardic precursors. Clearly, these poets did not evolve in either an ideological or literary void and they cannot be considered to have suddenly appeared on a stage vacated by the *fileadha*. Their poetic development can be traced to the emergence of humanist littérateurs such as Uilliam Nuinseann, Eoghan Ó Dubhthaigh and Muiris Mac Gearailt during the course of Elizabeth's reign. While the new poets undoubtedly occupy a distinctive niche in the organic evolution of the Gaelic poetic tradition, it is also noteworthy that they operated untrammelled by the metrical, linguistic and contractual constraints previously borne by bardic poets. By reason of social position and formation, many of these poets formed an élite at least as select as that constituted by bardic poets. Importantly, this new group was appropriately representative, both ethnically and ideologically, of early modern Irish cultural diversity. Well-educated and relatively affluent poets of Anglo-Norman stock such as Céitinn, Feiritéar and Haicéad are remarkable not so much for their intellectual originality but for the eloquence with which they articulated themes incorporated from the bardic repertoire.[2] These new poets manifested a creative facility in the composition of poetry at once both intensely individualistic and yet characterised by a wider communal relevance.

The predication of an ethno-cultural amalgamation encompassing the historic Irish communities articulated in the work of bardic poets and their successors is of decisive social and political importance in the context of the evolution of an inclusive Irish national identity by way of reaction to colonial intervention. Given the high degree of cultural experience shared by both communities, it is emblematic that several prominent gentlemen poets are of Anglo-Norman ancestry: clerics like Céitinn, Haicéad and Déis, and minor gentry such as Piaras Feiritéar and Séamus Dubh Nuinseann. In fact, the level of conscious integration emboldened some Anglo-Norman families to go so far as to gaelicise their genealogies.[3] Evidently not subject to the unilateral priorities of the Gaelic literati, authors from Anglo-Norman backgrounds independently articulate the notion of a coalition of mutual interests and allegiances with their Gaelic Irish compatriots. Haicéad refers to the common fate of both historic communities and he stresses a collective Irish experience of social and political trauma.[4] Céitinn, too, interprets the relationship between *Gaoidhil* and *Gaill* in terms of a coalescence of interests. In the elegy, 'Mór antrom inse Banbha', which he composed *c.* 1642 in memory of Lord Dunboyne's sons, Céitinn contrasted the fraternal sentiments which existed between both communities and the external aggression directed against them by the *Nua-Ghoill* or New English. The Gaelic Irish and the Anglo-Normans stand united in amity by their shared kinship ties and common devotion to the Roman Catholic faith.[5] Indeed, such expressions of communal solidarity and benevolence are not exclusive to poets of Anglo-Norman pedigree. In a composition known as 'Tuireamh na hÉireann' (composed *c.* 1655–9), Seán Ó Conaill considers the shared fate of the two historic communities. Appalled by the ferocity of the Cromwellian onslaught, Ó Conaill appears surprised that both *Gaoidhil* and *Sean-Ghaoidhil* had fared equally badly under the new regime ('s iad do dhíbir seanGhaill tséimhe').[6] It seems that the indiscriminate nature of the tragedy of these years removed any lingering Gaelic doubts as to residual ambiguity in transcendent Anglo-Norman political loyalties. Nonetheless, it is evident from this process of ethnic harmonisation that unilateral expressions of historic communal pride were neither elided nor obscured by an integrational dynamic. If Anglo-Norman authors are happy to acknowledge Gaelic culture as an esteemed inheritance held in common with their Gaelic compatriots, an integral component in the articulation of their religious and political affinity with the Gaelic Irish, this is not to say that they were submerged completely by the dominant cultural idiom. Like the *Gaoidhil*, they too retained a fundamental awareness of their distinctive ethnic and cultural patrimony. On the whole, complementarity of outlook dominated, even a resolute Palesman such as the historian Richard Stanihurst (1547–1618), largely indifferent to Gaelic culture, has been shown to have manifested a positive developmental attitude to the Gaelic Irish. His writings, in fact, reveal a mindset working towards an inclusive notion of Irish identity held together by common allegiance to Roman Catholicism.[7]

Historically, the equation of Gaelic culture with the Catholic faith is undoubtedly one of the most potent and enduring of concepts to emerge from the intellectual ferment of early modern Ireland. During the floruit of the amateur poets in the 1640s and 1650s, the plights of Catholicism and Gaelic Ireland were effectively construed as synonymous. In 'Is buartha an cás so 'dtárlaig Éire' (composed *c.* 1654–7), Dáibhí Cúndún locates persecution of the Catholic church within a wider range of abuses perpetrated by the colonial oligarchy. Significantly, the degraded condition of the church is cited as a particularly galling aspect of Ireland's plight ('Is tinn an aithris dam eaglais Éireann, mar chím i n-easba a sagairt 's a cléirig').[8] In the anonymous poem beginning 'Do chuala scéal do chéas gach ló mé', the author bewails the violent Cromwellian assault on Irish civilisation. The chaotic state of the church is presented as a central aspect of a baneful schedule of attrition ('is Eaglais Dé dá claochlá is ordaibh').[9] Even a general reading of the work of the new poets confirms their awareness of Catholicism as an integral element in Irish national identity. The ideological combination of culture and religion so deftly propagated by the literati produced a concept which was both political and confessional in scope and effect. In fact, by the end of James's reign and arguably as early as the 1590s, Roman Catholicism constituted a lynch-pin of Irish national identity. The implicit corollary of this powerful image of a sacrosanct union of culture and faith encouraged popular identification of the reformed church as the religious ancillary of an alien and intrusive oligarchy. This unfavourable perception of Anglicanism was severely compounded by the unfortunate reluctance of a structurally-weak Church of Ireland to employ Irish as the medium of evangelisation on anything but a minutely ineffectual scale, and it underlined a generally denigratory colonial attitude among Protestant clerics to Gaelic culture. In this way, Protestantism became synonymous with the English conquest and ensuing settlement. An immediate objective of counter-reformation agents in Ireland and Louvain had been to unite Gaelic culture and Catholicism on a formal ideological basis and to present this alliance as the target of a campaign of externally-sourced vilification. This brilliantly shrewd strategy undermined the established church's claim to constitute an inclusive and representative national church in the tradition of Saint Patrick.[10]

By way of contrast, for example, in the introduction he appended to his catechism in Irish, published in Brussels in 1639, the Anglo-Norman priest Teabóid Gallduf (*anglice* Theobald Stapleton) urges that the vernacular be used as the language of devotional instruction. Crucially, while Gallduf's attitude to the Irish language is influenced by his desire to mould it as a medium of religious propaganda, he also adduces another less immediately utilitarian reason for employing 'our own natural native language' ('ar tteangain nduchais nadurtha féin').[11] Convinced of the intrinsic worth of the language, he notes that every nation is proud of its own vernacular and it is suggested that the Irish should take care to foster their native tongue. He criticises what he presents as the convoluted linguistic modes of the scholarly classes which he claims made the literary medium impenetrable for uneducated people. Gallduf's introduction is noteworthy for what it reveals of the mindset of a committed counter-reformation activist imbued with the renaissance idea of the cultural integrity of the vernacular. Taken as a paradigm of the transformation of Gaelic culture, his introduction presents a convincing picture of a cleric from an Anglo-Norman background at ease in his use and championship of the Irish language.[12] The preface represents in many ways the culmination of a literary and cultural revolution.

The concept of divine providence is central to the bardic explication of the Gaelic experience of subjugation and communal upheaval. Although the manifestation of providence enjoyed a general and widely-accepted currency in contemporary European intellectual and theological thought, its popularity among the new poets must largely stem from its repeated invocation in the bardic corpus. In this particular case again, integral thematic continuity links bardic poets and their successors. Indeed, a providentialist schema of causation suggested a variety of possible interpretative emphases. Céitinn, for instance, claims that the moral degeneracy of the Irish, and not foreign military intervention, had resulted in their downfall.[13] Donnchadh Mac an Chaoilfhiaclaigh in a poem he composed *c.* 1640, 'Do fríth, monuar, an uain si ar Éirinn', is equally emphatic in the attribution of Ireland's plight to divine retribution.[14] The manifestation of divine will is perceived as judgmental in quality and the retribution exacted from the Irish is presented as a severe censure of communal dissoluteness. While both bardic and gentlemen authors recognised and acknowledged the lamentable results of supposed negative providence, their dynamically reactive analytical strategy largely diffused the providentialist schema of its inherent passive acquiescence. The *fileadha*, and their successors in particular, supplemented and primed their presentation of the providentialist topos by means of a strategic codicil. Providence, of course, was not necessarily negative in manifestation and the omnipotent creator could at any moment beneficially redirect the course of events. If it were in accordance with divine purpose, communal deliverance might be tantalisingly close at hand. Seán Ó Conaill argues that only pious supplication to the Almighty and the saints promises relief of Irish distress ('Níl ár leigheas ag liaig i n-Éirinn acht Dia do ghuí 's na naoimh i n-aonacht'). Although he admits that the Gaelic Irish had transgressed divine ordinance and undoubtedly richly deserved their misfortune ('Sinn féin do thuill gach ní tá déanta'), Ó Conaill nonetheless prays for the remission of these sins and for the restoration of the faith and liberties of the *Gaoidhil*.[15] In a variation of this plea for divine forgiveness, Haicéad petitions the Virgin Mary to intercede on behalf of the Irish.[16] The evidence of this fairly common type of divine supplication highlights the passionate urgency of the Irish response to crisis.

The Gaelic/Hebrew comparison embodying provocative redemptive implications also appears in the *oeuvre* of the new poets. In a poem of comfort composed for the *Gaoidhil* banished to Connacht, 'In ainm an Athar go mbuaidh', Fear Dorcha Ó Mealláin (*fl. c.* 1650) invokes the parallel of the Israelites in their Egyptian bondage and emphasises that God who had succoured the Israelites at their hour of tribulation is the same God in whom the Irish must now place their confidence. Ó Mealláin exhorts the Gaelic Irish to wear the badge of their faith with pride and by way of symbolic defiance they are encouraged to welcome the denigratory appellation 'Papist' applied by their detractors ('Má ghoirthear dhaoibhse Páipis, cuiridh fáilte re bhur ngairm').[17] In the piece beginning 'Músgail do mhisneach, a Bhanbha', Haicéad strikes a similarly militant note when he too presents the plight of Ireland as historically evocative of the Israelites' predicament ('Clann Israel isí Éire; Éigipt eile a géibheann gann').[18] Inherently optimistic in so far as it held out the promise of dramatic divine intervention to liberate the Gaelic Irish from their contemporary equivalent of the Egyptian captivity, in a more immediate way this comparison also encouraged the cultivation of an outlook enshrining an active consciousness of general resistance to the new order. The potential for intellectual dissidence encapsulated in the Hebrew metaphor offers a specific rebuttal of the argument that Irish responses to crisis are characterised by fatalism and acquiescence.

A pervasive sense of national consciousness is discernible in the early modern bardic corpus and in the work of the gentlemen amateurs. This articulation of national identity is neither static nor purely rhetorical, rather it is evolutionary in quality and scope. The concept developed in expression and reference with the result that by the middle of the seventeenth century a remarkable formal consensus had been forged among the Gaelic and gaelicised Anglo-Norman literati with regard to the ethnic, cultural and religious determinants of Irish nationality. It is obvious from the material collated in the present study that the genesis of modern Irish national identity is to be traced to Elizabeth's time. Particularly explicit statements of this politicised national consciousness are evident in poems of the exile genre. Structured along paradigmatic lines, they are generally congruent in their presentation of the constituent elements of an ethnically-inclusive Irish nationality. Haicéad's 'Cuirim séad suirghe chum seise' embodies a pan-insular premise typical of the genre which is unmarked by overt provincialism. A utopian evocation of Ireland is complemented by a vivid sense of the physical texture of the island. Allied to the geographical integrity of the island, the poet discerns and elaborates on a distinct sense of communal identity. Haicéad's treatment of his compatriots is predicated on a tripartite division. He distinguishes between the great mass of the population, the literati and the clergy. His and other poets' emphasis on the literati and clergy highlights the extent to which religion and culture are integral to the contemporary delineation of Irish national identity.[19]

A marked consciousness of Gaelic cultural integrity also forms a vital constituent in the expression of politicised nationality. A transcendent loyalty to the Gaelic cultural idiom can be distinguished in manipulative bardic approaches to the accession of King James I and in bardic willingness to inculturate newcomers within a Gaelic representational schema. In both these examples of ameliorative stratagems developed in the midst of crisis, the literati undertake a process of mediation in order to conserve the socio-cultural base of their magisterium. Incidentally, in spite of ongoing Gaelic loyalty to the Stuart dynasty, it is instructive to note that in the work of the new poetic cohort James is not always portrayed in wholly uncritical terms ('Níor thuar faoiseamh do chríocha Fhéilim, an fear do thógaibh a bpór as a bhfréamhaibh').[20]

Together with a tenacious advocacy of Gaelic cultural integrity and the predication of Gaelic and Catholic mutuality, a third constituent element is contemporaneously adduced to form the conceptual triad which underpins contemporary expression of Irish nationality. Bardic and new poets were acutely conscious of the territorial integrity of the island of Ireland and of the violation of insular sovereignty by the intrusion of the culturally and ethnically-divergent New English. Traditionally, Ireland had been depicted in Gaelic literature in terms of a feminine embodiment of sovereignty. In the medieval period this topos had been deployed for largely conventional dynastic interests. However, bardic poets and their successors succeeded in regenerating the motif's relevance in the context of early modern conditions and they employed the topos to project a heightened and inevitably politicised awareness of historic insular integrity. The English conquest and settlement are implicitly mediated in terms of violation of pan-insular territorial sovereignty. The most potent and vivid expression of this perception centres on the portrayal of Ireland as a woman prostituted and debased by foreign intruders ('nuachar Chríomhthainn, Chuinn is Eóghain suas gach oíche ag luí le deóraibh').[21]

In his analysis of early modern poetry and politics mentioned in the introduction, Tom Dunne argues that the evidence of the poetry reveals a Gaelic response to conquest and colonisation which 'was highly pragmatic, deeply fatalistic, increasingly escapist and essentially apolitical'.[22] If by 'pragmatic' it is meant that the literati were solicitous only of short-term corporate advancement and indifferent to the configuration of long-term ideological strategies reflective both of communal and professional priorities, then, clearly his reading of the poetry is eloquently contradicted by the material assessed in this study. It is demonstrated in the present book that bardic attitudes are characterised by an innovative verve which flourishes in the intellectual space made available by a contracting corporate framework. The poems are animated by an ingrained sense of Irish national consciousness predicated on the mutual indivisibility of Gaelic cultural integrity, territorial sovereignty and the interlinking of Gaelic identity with profession of the Roman Catholic faith. In terms of this evolution of a politicised nationality by way of reaction to English expansionism, the response of the native literati is incontrovertibly forward-looking and resourceful. Of course, bardic appraisal of a contemporary evolving political climate is developmental in so far as poets are immediately influenced by and react variously to different prevailing political and social circumstances. For instance, the militant timbre of several poems composed in the 1590s accedes to a manipulative and optimistic avowal of the validity of James's dynastic pedigree while, in turn, the subsequent influx of settlers encourages the strategic bardic predication of inculturation. The responsive quality of the poetry negates Dunne's claim and correspondingly Michelle O Riordan's similar argument that it was essentially escapist and fatalistic. Moreover, the dynamic aspects of bardic ideology facilitated the emergence and articulation of two influential concepts. The combination of an ethnically-inclusive notion of identity embracing the two historic Irish communities with commitment to counter-reformation Catholicism laid the foundations of a modern Irish nationality conceptually defined in terms of culture, religion and insular sovereignty. The implications of a coherent expression of national sensibility such as this were so inherently politicised in the context of early modern crown aggrandisement that they conclusively rebut Dunne's charge that the bardic response was 'essentially apolitical' and O Riordan's theory of automatic bardic acquiescence in the *fait accompli*. Crucially, the compositional milieu in which bardic reaction evolved was not exclusively dominated by debilitating vocational paralysis. Although the corporate bardic structure was in decline, the ideological fabric of the bardic mindset experienced a transformation coloured by a telescoped amalgam of renaissance, counter-reformation and baroque influences. The last generation of professional bardic poets has been inaccurately dismissed as an archaic and self-obsessed caste incapable of negotiating the integration of the medieval

Gaelic world within the dynamic intellectual embrace of early modern Europe. This study has sought to redress such an historiographical misconception by demonstrating how careful investigation of bardic poetry reveals a very different picture indeed. In reality, the poets initiated a pioneering re-evaluation of traditional Gaelic modes of communal definition which culminated in the creation of the modern Irish national identity which was to prove an exceptionally potent and resilient influence in the ill-fated and troubled evolution of British and Irish relations over the coming centuries.

NOTES

Introduction

1. Barnard, 'Crises', p. 39.
2. For the accuracy of the term 'bardic' as applied to poetry composed by the *fileadha* in the period 1200–1650 see Murphy, 'Bards', p. 203.
3. See for example Canny, 'The ideology'; idem., 'Identity formation'; idem., *The Formation*; Bradshaw, 'Robe and sword'; Barnard, 'Cork settlers'.
4. Ó Tuathaigh, "Early modern Ireland", p. 157; Simms, 'Bardic poetry', pp. 58–75; O'Dowd, 'Gaelic economy', pp. 120–147; Morgan, 'Writing up', p. 702. A working introduction to the concept of the history of mentalities is provided by Darnton, *The great cat massacre*, pp. 11–15. Cf. Ginzburg, *The cheese and the worms*, pp. xiii-xxvi. A useful study of the value of poetry as a reflection of communal mores is to be had in Martines, *Society and history*.
5. Simms, *Kings to warlords*, p. 4.
6. Ó Cuív in Moody et al. (eds.), *A new history,* iii, p. 530.
7. A scribal note dating to 1620 in a manuscript containing poems for Philip O'Reilly (ob. 1596) of east *Bréifne* (Cambridge, University Library, MS.3082) sheds interesting light on one process by which poems were included in that collection. The scribe apologises for what he considers the poor state of preservation of some of the poems he has copied, stating that his only source was a blind old man who had memorised them some thirty years before: 'Acht ataim ag iarraidh air an leighoir gabhail agam fana danta sa nach fhuair me ughdar leo acht seanndhuine dall do cuir do mheabhair iad ata deich mbliaghna fithceat uadh'. Carney (ed.), *O'Reillys*, p. xiii. For family poem-books see Ó Cuív, *The Irish bardic duanaire*; idem., 'Ireland's manuscript heritage', p. 96.
8. For poets in the Old Irish linguistic period see Mac Mathúna, 'The designations'; Ó Tuama, *An grá i bhfilíocht na n-uaisle,* p. 6. The traditional role of the poet in Gaelic and other societies is discussed in Ó hÓgáin, *An file*; Bloomfield and Dunn, *The role of the poet*.
9. Breatnach, 'The chief's poet', pp. 55–6. I have loosely followed the editor's literal translation in my English version of the quatrain. Cf. O'Grady, *Catalogue*, pp. 474–6; Carney, *The Irish bardic poet*, pp. 23–5; Mhág Craith, *Studia Celtica*, iv (1969), pp. 133–6. For a general discussion of the *fileadha* and the bardic corpus see Williams, 'The court poet'.
10. Breatnach (ed.), 'Cú Chonnacht Ó Dálaigh's poem before leaving Aodh Ruadh', quatrain 16, p. 36.
11. MacCarthy (ed.), *The life and letters*, p. 362; O'Donovan (ed.), *The tribes of Ireland*, p. 24.
12. Some other instances of the quasi-diplomatic role of the *fileadha* may be found in Stafford, *Pacata Hibernia*, pp. 293, 360–1; Meehan, *Geraldines*, pp. 119–20; MacCarthy, ibid., p. 239; O'Rahilly, 'Irish poets, historians, and judges', p. 90, p. 93; O'Sullivan (ed.), 'Tadhg O'Daly', p. 31; Mhág Craith (ed.), *Dán na mbráthar*, i, p. 152.

13. Greene (ed.), *Duanaire*, no. IX, quatrains 6, 14, pp. 78–89.
14. For the modern quest for an heroic and untainted Celtic past see Ó Danachair, 'Oral tradition', pp. 31–2. Simms, *Kings to warlords*; Nicholls, *Land, law and society*; Bradshaw, 'The Elizabethans and the Irish'.
15. More generally, see Martin, 'Ireland, the renaissance and the counter-reformation'; Silke, 'Irish scholarship and the renaissance'. A pioneering account of a modernising Gaelic lord is provided in Bradshaw, 'Manus'. A case of Gaelic reception (*c.* 1599) of a translation from renaissance literature is documented in Harington (ed.), *Nugae antiquae*, pp. 248–9. Early seventeenth-century Irish architecture, an important cultural barometer, did not escape renaissance influence either. See Waterman, 'Some Irish seventeenth-century houses', p. 252.
16. Ó Dúshláine, *An Eoraip*; Mac Craith, 'Gaelic Ireland and the renaissance' and *Lorg na hiasachta*.
17. Mac Craith, *Lorg na hiasachta*, pp. 228–32; Curtis, 'The spoken languages', p. 239; Bliss, 'Language and literature'; Mac Niocaill (ed.), *Crown surveys*, pp. 312–14, pp. 355–6.
18. Joep Leerssen interprets native learning as being irredeemably medieval in focus: idem., 'On the edge of Europe', p. 97; Leerssen, 'Wildness', p. 36.
19. Ó Cróinín (ed.), 'A poet in penitential mood'.
20. Ó Caithnia, *Apalóga*, pp. 123–35; Stanford, *Ireland and the classical tradition*, pp. 73–89; Knott, *Irish syllabic poetry*, p. 90.
21. Mac Craith, 'Ovid, an macalla agus Cearbhall Ó Dálaigh'; idem., 'Cioth na Baoise'.
22. Brian Ó Corcráin (*fl.* 1607), a Fermanagh poet, recorded in a colophon how he had obtained the inspiration for his romantic tale entitled 'Eachtra Mhacaoimh an Iolair' from a nobleman who had heard a similar story told in French. Bruford, *Gaelic folk-tales*, n.8, p. 46, p. 52. A rare apparent instance of a sixteenth-century bardic scholar abroad is documented in Meyer, 'Ein irischer Barde in Oxford'. For an atypically renaissance-style Gaelic littérateur, Dáibhí Dubh Mac Gearailt, poet, philosopher, musician and craftsman, see O'Rahilly (ed.), *Dánta grádha*, p. xiv.
23. Scowcroft, 'Miotas na gabhála i Leabhar Gabhála'; Carey, *A new introduction*.
24. Knott (ed.), *Bardic poems*, i, no. 17, pp. 120–31. Regarding the Anglo-Normans and bardic poetry see Simms, 'Bards and barons', pp. 177–97. The use by an Anglo-Norman author of the validation by invasion theory is discussed by Cunningham, 'Seventeenth-century interpretation of the past', p. 127.
25. Mac Cuarta (ed.), 'Mathew De Renzy's letters', p. 129, pp. 153–4.
26. Ó Cuív, *Linguistic training*, p. 3, p. 4, p. 17. John Morrill's claim that supposed 'linguistic diversities that made for poor or non-existent communications' in sixteenth-century Ireland partly precluded the internal development of a sense of national consciousness fails to appreciate the linguistic and thematic standardisation of Gaelic literary discourse. Morrill, 'The fashioning of Britain', p. 12.
27. Slotkin, 'Folkloristics', pp. 214–5; cf. Ó Coileáin, 'Oral or literary?'.
28. For early modern print culture see Eisenstein, *Printing revolution*; Watt, *Cheap print*. Something of the complex and creative interchange between oral and literary material is evident in Stewart, *Boccaccio in the Blaskets*.

29. For the public delivery and communal reception of bardic poetry see Hore (ed.), 'Irish bardism in 1561', p. 166–7; Hughes (ed.), *Shakespeare's Europe*, p. 119, p. 238; Rich, *A new description*, p. 3; O'Brien (ed.), *Advertisements*, p. 44.

30. O'Rahilly, 'On the origin'; Herbert, 'Goddess and king'.

31. Carney, 'Society and the bardic poet', pp. 248–9.

32. Pollard, *Dublin's trade in books*, pp. 32–9; Gillespie, 'The book trade in southern Ireland'.

33. For non-professional poets in the medieval period see Watson (ed.), *Scottish verse*; Mac Niocaill (ed.), 'Dhá dhán'; idem., 'Duanaire Ghearóid iarla'.

34. Bradshaw, 'Native reaction', p. 72, p. 74.

35. Ó Buachalla, 'Na Stíobhartaigh', p. 119; *Aisling ghéar*, p. 61. Cf. Ó Buachalla, 'James our true king'.

36. 'Na Stíobhartaigh', p. 105, pp. 120–21. Cf. *Aisling ghéar*, chapters 1 and 2.

37. Dunne, 'Gaelic response', pp. 10–12, pp. 15–18, pp. 29–30.

38. 'Gaelic response', p. 12, p. 30.

39. Canny, 'Formation of the Irish mind', pp. 93–4.

40. 'Formation of the Irish mind', p. 94, pp. 98–9.

41. Cunningham, 'Native culture', p. 155, p. 159. Cf. Cunningham, 'Irish language sources'.

42. 'Native culture', pp. 163–4.

43. Ibid.

44. Ibid., pp. 165–6; 'Culture and ideology', p. 29.

45. Leerssen, *Mere Irish*, pp. 156–7, p. 179, pp. 189–190.Cf. Leerssen, 'Wildness'; *Contention of the bards*.

46. *Mere Irish*, pp. 156, p. 182, p. 197, p. 223.

47. Dooley, 'Literature and society', p. 514, p. 521, pp. 531–2.

48. O Riordan, *Gaelic mind*, pp. 5–6, p. 8, p. 48, p. 60, p. 69. O Riordan's work has been heavily criticised in Ó Buachalla, 'Poetry and politics'; Caball, 'An appraisal'; Bradshaw, 'Bardic response'. Cf. Mac Craith, 'Litríocht'; Simms, 'Literary sources'.

49. *Gaelic mind*, chapters 1 and 2.

50. *Gaelic mind*, chapter 4. In subsequent published work on early seventeenth-century Gaelic literature, Michelle O Riordan's interpretative approach has been less deterministic and rigid than that adopted in her monograph. See O Riordan, 'A seventeenth-century political poem'; 'Native Ulster'; '"Political" poems'.

51. Darnton, 'Symbolic element', p. 219, p. 223.

Continuity and Reaction in Two Poem-Books

1. Eagleton, *Marxism*, p. 6.

2. O Riordan, *Gaelic mind*; Cunningham, 'Native culture', pp. 150–51. The validatory power of tradition is discussed in the introduction to Hobsbawm and Ranger (eds.), *The invention*, pp. 1–14.

3. *Acts privy council, Ire., 1556–71*, p. 166; *Cal. S.P. Ire., 1509–73*, p. 317, p. 325; O'Donovan (ed.), *Annals of the Four Masters (A.F.M.)*, v, pp. 1608–9 (A.D.1566); *Cal. Carew MSS 1575–88*, p. 335; *Fiants Ire., Eliz.*, no. 1081. For Fermanagh in the medieval period see Simms, 'The medieval kingdom'; idem., 'Gaelic lord-

ships in Ulster', pp. 441–94; Livingstone, *Fermanagh story*; Walsh, *Irish chiefs*, pp. 1–57.

4. Ellis, *Tudor Ireland*, p. 255.

5. *Cal. S.P. Ire., 1509–73*, p. 353, p. 402, pp. 417–18, p. 445; *Acts privy council, Ire., 1556–71*, p. 219; *Cal. Carew MSS 1575–88*, p. 13, pp. 15–16, p. 30, p. 340; *Cal. S.P. Ire., 1574–85*, p. 85, p. 440; *Calendar of the manuscripts of the most hon. the marquis of Salisbury*, iii, p. 67.

6. *Sidney S.P.*, p. 75; *Cal. S.P. Ire., 1509–73*, p. 340, p. 351, p. 526; *Cal. Carew MSS 1515–74*, p. 445; *Cal. Carew MSS 1575–88*, p. 30; *Cal. S.P. Ire., 1574–85*, p. 85, p. 440. The similarly ambiguous position of the MacMahons is discussed in Duffy, 'Patterns of landownership', p. 316; and that of the O'Reillys of east *Bréifne* in Cunningham, 'O'Reillys'.

7. *A.F.M.*, v, pp. 1827–9 (A.D.1585); O'Grady, *Catalogue*, i, p. 430; Hardiman, *Tracts*, ii, pp. 139–43; Moody, 'The Irish parliament', pp. 41–81; Perrot, *Chron. Ire., 1584–1608*, pp. 41–3.

8. *Fiants Ire., Eliz.*, no. 4682; *Cal. Carew MSS 1575–88*, p. 473. Morgan, *Tyrone's rebellion*, chapter 3.

9. *Cal. S.P. Ire., 1586–88*, p. 11, p. 110, pp. 142–3; *Fiants Ire., Eliz.*, nos. 4809–10; Morley (ed.), *Ireland*, p. 347; *Cal. Carew MSS 1575–88*, p. 435.

10. *Cal. S.P. Ire., 1586–88*, p. 333, p. 335, p. 459; *Cal. pat. rolls Ire., Eliz.*, pp. 126–7. The term *uirrí* is discussed in Simms, *Kings to warlords*, p. 69.

11. *Fiants Ire., Eliz.*, nos. 5013, 5027.

12. E.C.S., *The government*, p. 117; *A.F.M.*, vi, p. 1874 (A.D.1589).

13. *Cal. S.P. Ire., 1509–73*, p. 355; *Cal. S.P. Ire., 1586–88*, p. 237; *Cal. Carew MSS, 1575–88*, p. 48. The Sligo O'Connors maintained a castle at Moymlough in the north-west of Leyney: see O'Dowd, 'Landownership', p. 468, p. 484. More generally for early modern Sligo see idem., *Power*. For an account of the O'Haras and their survival of the collapse of the Gaelic system see Bartlett, 'The O'Haras'.

14. *Cal. S.P. Ire., 1509–73*, p. 355; *Cal. S.P. Ire., 1574–85*, p. 102; O'Dowd, 'Land inheritance', p. 7.

15. McKenna (ed.), *Book*, pp. 40–3; Knott (ed.), *Bardic poems*, i, pp. 238–9; ibid., ii, pp. 157–8.

16. Hennessy (ed.), *Annals of Loch Cé*, ii, pp. 438–9.

17. *Fiants Ire., Eliz.*, nos. 3390, 3391.

18. McKenna, *Book*, pp. 70–3.

19. Freeman (ed.), *The compossicion*, p. 125, p. 132, pp. 137–8; Hayes-McCoy, *Index*; O'Flaherty, *Chorographical*, pp. 340–6; O'Dowd, 'Land inheritance', p. 6; Ellis, *Tudor Ireland*, pp. 288–90; Hayes-McCoy in Moody et al., *A new history*, iii, pp. 109–111.

20. *Fiants Ire., Eliz.*, no. 4873.

21. McKenna, *Book*, pp. 10–11; *A.F.M.*, vi, p. 2003 (A.D.1596); *Cal. S.P. Ire., 1592–96*, p. 333, p. 336.

22. *Cal. S.P. Ire., 1592–96*, p. 407, p. 511; *Cal. S.P. Ire., 1596–97*, p. 4, p. 11; Hayes-McCoy in Moody et al., *A new history*, iii, p. 123.

23. Ranger, 'Richard Boyle'; idem., 'The career of Richard Boyle', pp. 10–11; Canny, *The upstart earl*; O'Rorke, *The history of Sligo*, ii, pp. 69–80; O'Rorke, *History, antiquities*, pp. 312–37.

24. *Cal. pat. roll Ire., Jas I*, p. 23; *Fiants Ire., Eliz.*, no. 6633.
25. National Library of Ireland (NLI), Reports on Private Collections, no. 493, pp. 277–9. Mary O'Dowd, who has made a detailed study of landownership patterns in Sligo at this period, describes the legal document drawn up at Cormac's behest in 1611 to safeguard his sons' inheritance as follows: 'This document indicates that Cormac was well aware of the new legal requirements concerning the inheritance of land and was anxious to comply with them in order that his sons would enjoy their estates without involvment in any legal dispute. Indeed, it could be argued that Cormac adopted English habits in order to avoid the division of the family property among a larger number of men who might have had a claim under Irish law'. O'Dowd, 'Landownership', p. 474.
26. McKenna, *Book*, pp. 8–9.
27. Tadhg O'Hara represented Sligo in parliament between 1613 and 1615. He also served as sheriff of the county: *Cal. S.P. Ire., 1611–14*, p. 360. The details of the arrangements Tadhg made for continued O'Hara possession of the lands in Leyney are given in *Cal. pat. rolls Ire., Jas I*, pp. 589–90; O'Dowd, 'Landownership', p. 476. Tadhg was also concerned about the future security of his brother, Cormac Óg, and it is known that he transferred lands by deed to Cormac Óg on the same day as he dictated the terms of his will: *Cal. pat. rolls Ire., Jas I*, p. 425. For the date of Tadhg's death see NLI, Reports on Private Collections, no. 493, p. 282.
28. *Cal. S.P. Ire., 1615–25*, p. 203; *Cal. pat. rolls Ire., Jas I*, p. 339; O'Rorke, *History, antiquities*, p. 381; NLI, Reports on Private Collections, no. 493, p. 282.
29. For poem-books in general see Ó Cuív, *The Irish bardic duanaire*; idem., 'Ireland's manuscript heritage', p. 96.
30. The Royal Library, Copenhagen manuscript bears the pressmark *Ny Kgl. Saml. 268b in folio*. A full description of the manuscript, including the later paper portion, which also contains Maguire material, is given in Stern, 'Ueber eine'. The Cú Chonnacht Maguire poems have been edited by Greene, *Duanaire*.
31. No. V in Green (ed.), *Duanaire*, is a poem of apology while no. XIX is a poem of supplication.
32. This Cú Mhumhan was either the son or grandson of Giolla Riabhach Ó Cléirigh, a poet whose work is represented in this compilation. More likely his grandson, he was also the scribe of a copy of *Cáin Adamnáin*: Greene, *Duanaire*, p. xv, p. 15; Walsh, *The Ó Cléirigh family*, p. 39. Cf. Meyer (ed.), *Cáin*, p. 32. It is not clear whether the scribe of Killiney, Franciscan Library, MS. A.12, also a Cú Mhumhan Ó Cléirigh, is to be identified with the present subject. Dillon et al., *Catalogue*, p. 23.
33. McKenna, *Book*, pp. ix–x; Ó Cuív, *The Irish bardic duanaire*, p. 36; Greene, 'The O'Hara MS'; Williams, 'Y beirdd llys'.
34. 'Isam sgítheach aniu a nGleann Fhiadha a mBaoidhiollchaibh. Ag sin doid a Chormuic Í Eadhra ogus sgoth leis ód chaomh ód charoid Tuathal Ó hUigintt, agus ní fheadar cia do-ríne an dán beagsa ro sgríobhus daoibhsi go fóill'. Tuathal Ó hUiginn was the author of one poem addressed to Cormac in the O'Hara poem-book. In 'Díoghruis chomainn ar Chormac' Tuathal spoke of his relationship with Cormac, using terminology which suggests that he was O'Hara's *ollamh*. He may have replaced Cormac's original *ollamh*, Írial Ó hUiginn, when the latter lost his patron's favour. The name of at least one of the other scribes

of the original manuscript is known. Three notes on page two of the manuscript, including an obituary of Cormac, are by Dubhthach Óg Ó Duibhgheannain (McKenna, *Book*, pp. 242–3, pp. 244–9, pp. 8–9). For Ó Duibhgheannain see Walsh, *Irish men*, pp. 25–33.

35.   'Is an bhliadhoin ro sgriobhadh an leauarsa tangadar Goill agus maithe Connacht agus Muimhneach morshluaighiodh go Sidh Aodha Easa Rúaidh a gConallchaibh agus athchuirthear iad da n-aimhdheoin tar Duibh tar Drophais as sin go Sligeach tar a n-ais'. McKenna, *Book*, pp. 10–11; *Cal. S.P. Ire.*, 1596–97, p. 373. Work on the original manuscript took place at Gleann Fiadha in the barony of Boylagh, Donegal. (McKenna, ibid., pp. 10–11. Cf. pp. 242–3.) For the light marginalia generally shed on the date and provenance of Gaelic manuscripts see Plummer, *Colophons*.

36.   Details of the O'Haras to whom the remaining fifteen poems are dedicated are given in McKenna, *Book*, pp. xxi-xxvii, pp. 451–3.

37.   Brian O'Hara was executed in Galway in 1586 by order of Sir Richard Bingham, lord president of Connacht: ibid., pp. xxv-xxvi. Six poems are attributed to Tadhg Dall Ó hUiginn in the O'Hara manuscript. Two poems, those dedicated to Seaán Buidhe O'Hara, Brian O'Hara and Domhnall O'Hara are found only in the O'Hara collection. These two pieces were not available to Eleanor Knott when she prepared her definitive edition of the poet's *oeuvre*. The remaining four poems are dedicated to Cormac, the dedication of one of which Cormac shares with Brian O'Hara. Ibid., nos. II, III, IV, V, XXVII, XXIX.

38.   Ibid., no. V, quatrain 1.

39.   Ibid., no. V, quatrain 29.

40.   Greene, *Duanaire*, no. XIV. In Dublin, Royal Irish Academy, MS. H.4.20, written by Tadhg Ó Neachtain, between 1725 and 1729, a copy of 'Manchaigh riamh 'na Róimh oinigh' is attributed to a 'Mac an Bhaird'. See Abbott and Gwynn, *Catalogue*, p. 195. Cf. Ó Caithnia, *Apalóga*, p. 71.

41.   Greene, *Duanaire*, no. XIV, quatrain 4.

42.   Ibid., no. XIV, quatrain 14.

43.   Ibid., no. XIV, quatrain 8.

44.   Ibid., no. XIV, quatrain 9.

45.   Williams and Ní Mhuiríosa, *Traidisiún*, pp. 183–4.

46.   Giolla Riabhach Ó Cléirigh was a member of a prominent Gaelic learned family associated with the O'Donnells. The evidence indicates that Giolla Riabhach was an active scribe, although only one of his manuscripts appears to be extant (London, British Library, MS. Harley 5280). There are several interesting notes and jottings in the hand of Ó Cléirigh on the margins of this vellum manuscript. At one point, he describes himself as a *felmac* or an apprentice bardic student. He also made a copy of Manus O'Donnell's *Betha Colaim Chille* sometime after 1532. The original manuscript has been lost, but a copy made by Brian Mac-Nelis is in the Franciscan Library at Killiney, Co. Dublin. Walsh, *The Ó Cléirigh family*, pp. 4–5; Flower, *Catalogue*, ii, pp. 298–9; Walsh, *Irish men*, p. 174, p. 177. Cf. Ní Laoire (ed.), *Bás*, p. 17.

47.   Greene, *Duanaire*, nos. VII, VIII. 'Craobh eoluis teisd tigherna' is not ascribed to Giolla Riabhach Ó Cléirigh in the Copenhagen manuscript, its authorship being anonymous. However, Stern ascribed it and another anonymous poem in the collection to Ó Cléirigh ('augenscheinlich von demselben O'Clery'): Stern,

'Ueber eine' p. 339. Walsh assumed that Giolla Riabhach had composed the poems for Cú Chonnacht Comharba Maguire (ob. 1538). idem., *The Ó Cléirigh family*, p. 6.

48.   Cf. Williams (ed.), *The poems of Giolla Brighde*, no. VIII.

49.   Greene, *Duanaire*, no. VIII, quatrain 1.

50.   idem., no. VIII, quatrain 20.

51.   Canny, 'Hugh O'Neill'; Nicholls, *Gaelic and gaelicised Ireland*; Canny, 'Changing views', pp. 19–28; Nicholls, *Land, law and society.*

52.   Greene, *Duanaire*, no. V. Scion of a prominent northern bardic family, Fearghal Óg Mac an Bhaird's floruit belongs to the end of the sixteenth and the beginning of the seventeenth centuries. His father, Fearghal (ob. 1550), was described in his obituary as a learned poet and master of a bardic school. Fearghal Óg's brother, Eoghan Ruadh, was one of a number of poets hanged by order of the earl of Thomond in 1572. Mac an Bhaird was well-known to the O'Donnells. Poems he composed for Conn mac Calbhaigh (ob. 1583), Hugh Roe (ob. 1602), Aodh (Hugh) Óg mac Aodha Duibh (ob. 1618) and Rory O'Donnell (ob. 1608) and his son, Hugh, are extant. One of his earlier poems was written sometime after the inauguration of Toirdhealbhach Luineach O'Neill in 1567. From his habit of adding extraneous quatrains in their praise to his poems, it appears that Fearghal Óg was particularly devoted to two patrons, Conn O'Rourke (ob. 1577) and Hugh Maguinnes (ob. 1595). He appears to have had a tense relationship with the O'Donnells. In the poem, 'Ionnmhas ollaimh onóir ríogh', he complained of the indifference of Hugh Roe O'Donnell to his status as a *fileadh*. Rory also appears to have clashed with the poet, apparently resulting in Mac an Bhaird spending a period in Munster. Later he left for the continent, though it is difficult to determine precisely when. In 1618 Hugh Óg O'Donnell died and Fearghal Óg composed an elegy in his memory, either that year or shortly after. The composition of 'Ní tráth aithreachais d'fhuil Conaill' *c.* 1618 might be taken to imply that he was still in Ireland at that stage. He sought the help of Flaithrí Ó Maolchonaire on the continent. McKenna (ed.), *Aithdhioghluim*, i, pp. xxvii–xxviii; Ó Donnchadha (ed.), *Leabhar cloinne*, p. xxvi; Mhág Craith (ed.), *Dán na mbráthar*, ii, p. 153; Ó Cuív, 'The earl of Thomond'; Ó Concheanainn, 'A feature'; McKenna, 'Some Irish bardic poems', pp. 99–104. For Ó Maolchonaire see Ó Cléirigh, *Aodh Mac Aingil*, pp. 34–40; O'Rahilly (ed.), *Desiderius*.

53.   Greene, *Duanaire*, no. V, quatrain 6.

54.   Ibid., no. V, quatrain 8.

55.   Ibid., no. V, quatrain 11.

56.   Ibid., no. V, quatrain 12.

57.   Ibid., no. V, quatrain 11. For other examples of reconciliation/apology poems see Carney (ed.), *O'Reillys*, no. XX; Mac Airt (ed.), *Leabhar Branach,* no. 2; McKenna (ed.), *Leabhar Méig Shamhradhain*, no. 3. Examples of the equivalent Welsh genre of *dadolwch* are found in Morris-Jones and Parry-Williams (eds.), *Llawysgrif*, p. 150; Clancy, *Earliest*, pp. 29–30.

58.   The first reference to the Ó hEódhusa family in the annals is found under the year 1350. Although they seem to have enjoyed some prominence in the following centuries, it is not until the end of the sixteenth century that they emerge in Fermanagh as subjects of Maguire. By this time they were the chief bardic household in the area, having replaced the former bardic families of the

Maguires: the Ó Fialáin and the Mac Rithbheartaigh septs. Eochaidh was born sometime between 1565 and 1570. He was granted a crown pardon in 1586, around the time he was appointed *ollamh* to Maguire. He was also court poet to the latter's son Hugh (ob. 1600). He seems to have spent some time in Munster as a bardic student. He again obtained pardons in 1591 and 1592. In the relevant document, he is described as being a freeholder of Baile Uí hEódhusa, which is located at Castlehume Lough, Lower Lough Erne in the parish of Devenish. Soon after he succeeding his father in 1589, Hugh presented him with lands at Corrán near Ballinamallard. After Hugh's death in 1600, Ó hEódhusa appears to have been on close terms with his successor Cú Chonnacht Óg Maguire (ob. 1608). He was granted a pardon in 1607 and in 1611 was made a grant of land in the barony of Clanawley. He died in June 1612. McGrath, 'Í Eódhosa'; Ó Maolagáin, 'Eochaidh'; Carney, *The Irish bardic poet*; O'Grady, *Catalogue*, i, pp. 453–4, p. 476, p. 478, pp. 661–2; Ó Cléirigh, 'A poem book', p. 59; *Cal. pat. rolls Ire., Jas I*, p. 34, p. 91; *Fiants Ire., Eliz.*, no. 5716; *Cal. Carew MSS 1603–24*, p. 240; *Cal. S.P. Ire., 1611–14*, p. 210; Moody (ed.), 'Ulster plantation papers', p. 206; Walsh, *Irish chiefs*, pp. 64–5; Breatnach, 'Eochaidh Ó hEódhusa'.

59. Greene, *Duanaire*, no. XXIII, quatrain 18.
60. See Caball, 'Some notes'.
61. For events in Munster in the period 1579–83 see MacCurtain, 'The fall'; Sheehan, 'The killing'; Bagwell, *Ireland under the Tudors*, iii, pp. 1–115; Brady, 'Faction'. Fitzmaurice's political outlook may be glimpsed in some of his extant letters in Irish: O'Donovan (ed.), 'The Irish correspondence'.
62. Greene, *Duanaire*, no. XIX, quatrain 2.
63. Ibid., no. XIX, quatrain 3.
64. Ibid., no. XIX, quatrain 10.
65. Ibid., no. XIX, quatrain 25.
66. Ibid., no. XIX, quatrain 21.
67. Írial Ó hUiginn had been O'Hara's *ollamh*, but was replaced by Tuathal Ó hUiginn when he apparently fell from grace. Írial's appointment is probably to be dated to shortly after 1581, by which time O'Hara had finally managed to secure his grip over Leyney. In what must have been one of his earliest compositions for Cormac, 'Ceanglam re chéile, a Chormuic', Írial mentions Máire Nic Suibhne. If evidence from the poem-book is reliable, Máire had married Cormac by 1584 at the latest. Several quatrains in her honour are included by Tadhg Mac Bruaideadha in a poem he addressed to Cormac entitled 'Ciondus fríth fearand Luighne', which is relatively unusual in that the scribe recorded its date of composition ('Aois an Tigherna an uair do-rinniodh an dánsa 1584'): McKenna, *Book*, p. 102. For the Mac Bruaideadha family see McGrath, 'Materials'.
68. McKenna, *Book*, no. XII, quatrain 2. A similar poem is that beginning 'A Mharta ceanglum connradh' by Domhnall Ó hEachaidhéan: Ó Donnchadha (ed.), *Leabhar cloinne*, no. XXXIII.
69. McKenna, *Book*, no. XII, quatrains 10, 17.
70. Ibid., no. XII, quatrain 5.
71. Ibid., no. XIV, quatrain 1.
72. Ibid., no. XV, quatrain 18.

73. Ibid., no. XV, quatrain 11.
74. Ibid., no. XV, quatrain 9.
75. Ibid., no. XV, quatrain 12. In two poems in the Magauran poem-book, Giolla Pádraig Mac Naimhin requests a horse of Brian Magauran (ob. 1298). In another poem in that collection, Giolla Aonghuis Ó Clúmháin thanked Niall Magauran (ob. 1362) for the gift of a horse. McKenna, *Leabhar Méig Shamhradhain*, nos. VI, VII, XV. In a poem in *Leabhar cloinne Aodha Buidhe*, Cormac Mac Con Midhe sought a horse from Sir Henry O'Neill (ob. 1638) in return for a praise poem: Ó Donnchadha, *Leabhar cloinne*, no. XXVI.
76. O Riordan, *Gaelic Mind*.
77. Curiously, in the Copenhagen manuscript 'Brath lendáin ac Leic Lughaidh' is introduced by the phrase 'Athtogha Duaine an Fherghail chédna'. The meaning of 'athtogha duaine' is unclear. McKenna translated the line 'dual dh'fhilidh athtogha ort' (line 2261) as 'a poet should choose thee on two grounds' and *athtogha* is rendered 'additional choice' in his glossary to the O'Hara collection.
78. Greene, *Duanaire*, no. I, quatrains 1–3; Ó Concheanainn, 'Smacht rí'.
79. Greene, *Duanaire*, no. I, quatrains 12, 21, 22.
80. Ibid., no. I, quatrain 27. The Goidelic division of Ireland into five provinces (Ulster, Connacht, Munster, Leinster and the Midland province [Old Irish *Mide*]) is discussed in O'Rahilly, *Early*, pp. 171–83.
81. Ibid., p. 240.
82. Throughout the Maguire poem-book, the poets highlighted the valour of Maguire and his family. However, Sir John Davies (ob. 1626) provides a contrasting picture of the Maguires when he wrote of Hugh Maguire (ob. 1600): 'For albeit Hugh M'Guire that was slain in Munster were indeed a valiant rebel and the stoutest that ever was of his name, not withstanding generally the natives of this county are reputed the worst swordsmen of the north, being rather inclined to be scholars or husbandmen than to be kern or men of action, as they term rebels in this kingdom. And for this cause M'Guire in the late wars did hire and wage the greatest part of his soldiers out of Connaught and out of the Breny O'Reilly, and made his own countymen feed them and pay them; and therefore the jury inquiring of escheats found only two freeholders in this county, besides Hugh M'Guire himself, to have been slain in the late rebellion'. (Morley (ed.), *Ireland*, p. 370); Kenney, *Sources*, i, p. 34.
83. Greene, *Duanaire*, no. IV, quatrains 5, 9, 22.
84. Ibid., no. IV, quatrains 19, 24.
85. Ibid., no. I, quatrain 5; no. IV, quatrain 19.
86. Ibid., no. IV, quatrains 1, 5.
87. 'Bardic poets continued to address Irish chiefs by their ancestral title of *rí* or king, but it has been the main underlying argument of this book that the Gaelic lords of the sixteenth century were not seen by others, nor indeed did they see themselves, as kings in any meaningful sense of the word.' (Simms, *Kings to warlords*, pp. 38–40, p. 147.)
88. Bregia is the latinised form of *Brega*, an area which approximated to modern Co. Meath and north Co. Dublin. See Knott, *Bardic poems*, ii, p. 188 and *Dictionary of the Irish language*, s.v. *Brega*.
89. Greene, *Duanaire*, no. I, quatrain 18. Cf. Ó Concheanainn, 'Smacht rí'. I have emended Greene's translation of *tuatha* (line 2) as 'states' to 'territories'.

90.   O'Brien (ed.), *Corpus,* i, p. 130, p. 147.

91.   Greene, *Duanaire,* no. I, quatrains 9, 14, 28.

92.   'As iad na ceithre haibhne as uaisle a nUltuibh tóranna fheruinn chloinne na
       cColladh .i. Bóinn, Banna, an Éirni, agus an Fhionn': Knott, *Bardic poems,* ii, p.
       229; Skene, *Celtic Scotland,* iii, pp. 462–6.

93.   Greene, *Duanaire,* no. I, quatrain 2.

94.   Ibid., no. I, quatrains 3, 9; no. IV, quatrains 1, 15. For *Aileach* see Hogan, *Ono-
       masticon,* p. 17.

95.   The poem composed by Fearghal Óg Mac an Bhaird on the accession of James
       Stuart to the English throne ('Trí coróna i gcairt Shéamais') shows him to have
       been acquainted with the history of the Stuart dynasty. McKenna (ed.), *Aithdio-
       ghluim,* i, p. 205; Bannerman, 'Scots language', p. 10.

96.   Greene, *Duanaire,* no. II, quatrain 24.

97.   Ibid., no. II, quatrain 1.

98.   Stern, 'Ueber eine', p. 334; Gwynn, 'Ireland and the continent', pp. 196–7.

99.   Greene, *Duanaire,* no. II, quatrain 6.

100.   It is worth quoting Katharine Simms's remarks on Irish awareness of the con-
       cept of crowned kingship in the later middle ages: 'Interestingly, by the early fif-
       teenth century, the Irish themselves became conscious of a distinction between
       their own local 'kings' and the heads of evolving nation-states in the rest of
       Europe. Under the year 1418 in the Annals of Connacht it is carefully pointed
       out that the Hundred Years' War was being fought between the 'crowned kings'
       (etir na rigaib coronta) of England and France. If the Irish had wished to ape
       such great ones, there was nothing to prevent them from introducing a corona-
       tion-ceremony into their inauguration-rites.' Simms, *Kings to warlords,* p. 38.

101.   Greene, *Duanaire,* no. II, quatrains 8, 9, 10; Plummer (ed.), *Lives,* i, p. 325.

102.   McKenna, *Book,* no. IV, quatrain 5.

103.   Ibid., no. IV, quatrain 10.

104.   Ibid., no. IV, quatrains 15, 16, 17.

105.   Ibid., no. IV, quatrains 42, 43.

106.   Ibid., no. XXI. Nothing is known of Maol Muire Ó an Cháinte. He may be the
       Maoilín of the same name who composed a poem entitled 'Tobar fíreinigh Fir
       Mhanach' for Maguire (ob. 1589). idem., p. xii.

107.   McKenna, *Book,* no. XXI, quatrains 3, 6, 8.

108.   Ibid., no. XXI, quatrain 9.

109.   J. Fraser, P. Grosjean and J. G. O'Keeffe (eds.), *Irish texts,* iv, pp. 27–9; Ó
       Lochlainn (ed.), *Tobar,* p. 54–5. For biographical details of Ó Mailchonaire see
       Walsh, *Irish men,* p. 39; idem., *Irish chiefs,* pp. 285–97; Ó Cuív, 'Miscellanea',
       pp. 288–90.

110.   McKenna, *Book,* no. XXII. The scribe Tuathal Ó hUiginn recorded his lack of
       information on the authorship of 'Gabh mo chosaoid, a Chormuic' at the end
       of the poem ('Ní fheadar cia do-ríne an dán beagsa ro sgríobhus daoibhsi
       [namely, O'Hara] go fóill').

111.   McKenna, *Book,* no. XXII, quatrains 3, 4.

112.   Ibid., no. XXII, quatrains 5, 6.

113.   Ó Cuív, 'The earl of Thomond', p. 127. For an indication of the apparent ease
       with which patronage was obtained for élite Gaelic culture in Leinster *c.*1590
       see Walsh (ed.), *Gleanings,* pp. 125–9.

114. For instance, in 1563 Gerald, earl of Desmond, had been instructed by the English authorities to outlaw all 'rhymers, bards, and dice players' within his territory: *Cal. S.P. Ire., 1509–73*, p. 227; *Cal. Carew MSS 1575–88*, p. 389.

115. McKenna, *Book*, no. III; Knott, *Bardic poems*, i, p. xxx; Leerssen, *Mere Irish*, pp. 184–7; Breatnach, 'An appeal'.

116. McKenna, *Book*, no. III, quatrains, 9 11, 13.

117. Freeman, *The compossicion*, p. 131; Cunningham, 'Composition'.

118. McKenna, *Book*, no. III, quatrains 5, 6.

119. Ibid., no. III, quatrain 14.

120. 'Gedicht auf Cuchonnacht Maguire, den Gönner der Dichter, augenscheinlich von demselben O'Clery, 36 Strophen in Casbairdne. Das Stuck scheint bald nach Elisabeths Thronbesteigung (1558) verfasst zu sein.' Stern, p. 339. Greene considers Stern's dating of this poem to soon after the accession of Elizabeth to be impossible. As Greene cited no evidence for this statement, it must be assumed that he took into account the fact that the poem was addressed to Cú Chonnacht as lord of the Maguires, a position he did not occupy until 1566. (Greene, *Duanaire*, no. IX, p. 244.)

121. Ibid., no. IX, quatrains 11, 12, 22.

122. Ibid., no. IX, quatrain 32.

123. See the remarks of Gwyn Prins on the question of historical continuity: 'Continuity must be explained. Historical continuity, especially in oral cultures, requires more attention than change. Tradition is a process – it only lives as it is continually reproduced. It is effervescently vital in its apparent stillness.' Prins, 'Oral history', p. 137.

A Pattern Established: 1558–1603

1. Innes, for instance, refers to the 'bards' as 'ignorant and venal guides . . . famous for their flattering their patrons with ancient pedigrees, and whole nations with ancient successions of kings'. Innes, *A critical essay*, i, p. iv.

2. Hyde, *A literary history*, pp. 525–8; de Blácam, *Gaelic literature*, pp. 125–7; Edwards, *Church and state*, p. 97; Ó Cuív (ed.), 'A sixteenth-century political poem', pp. 261–76; Leerssen, *Mere Irish*, pp. 181–2.

3. Ó Cuív, 'A sixteenth-century political poem', quatrain 1, p. 272.

4. Ibid., quatrain 6, p. 273.

5. Ibid., quatrain 8, p. 273; Bradshaw, 'Manus', pp. 15–36.

6. Ó Cuív, 'A sixteenth-century political poem', pp. 265–6.

7. Ibid., quatrain 9, p. 273. Brian Ó Cuív mentions Carney's suggestion that the poet's use of *Béarla* is a form of ellipsis for *Béarla Féine*. Carney translated 'cúirt gan Bhéarla' as 'court without Irish law': ibid., p. 267. Ó Cuív's translation of *Béarla* (originally *bélrae* or 'speech, language') as 'English' sits oddly with the general sentiment of this quatrain. Doris Edel has suggested the possibility of another ellipsis: *Béarla* may stand for 'Béarla na bhFileadh' or the 'poetic language'. See Leerssen, *Mere Irish*, note 42, pp. 396–7. An anonymous poem entitled 'Ab an aonuigh caruid dé', preserved in the 'Book of O'Conor Don', fo27b (cf. Dublin, Royal Irish Academy, transcript MS. 625–43) is another early poem composed to the background of the reformation. Written in an obscure style, this piece appears

to be a satiric elegy in memory of Tadhg O'Meara, last prior of Tyone Priory in Nenagh, which was dissolved in 1551. I am grateful to Dr Katharine Simms for providing me with a transcript of the poem. See also Gwynn and Gleeson, *A history*, pp. 476–82; Gwynn and Hadcock, *Medieval religious houses*, pp. 214–5.

8. Ó Cuív, 'A sixteenth-century political poem', p. 267.

9. Hayes-McCoy in Moody et al., *A new history*, iii, pp. 96–9; Loeber, *Geography*, pp. 31–4; Brady, *Shane O'Neill*.

10. Ó Donnchadha (ed.), *Leabhar cloinne*, no. VIII, pp. 94–100.

11. Ibid., lines 1–2, p. 94.

12. Ibid., lines 25–8, p. 95.

13. Ibid., lines 33–80, pp. 95–6.

14. Ibid., lines 81–4, p. 96.

15. Ibid., line 109, p. 97; Ó Caithnia, *Apalóga*, p. 81.

16. Ibid., lines 101–2, p. 97.

17. Ibid., lines 201–12, p. 100. Muircheartach Ó Cobhthaigh in his 'Séd fine teisd Toirdhealbhaigh', composed *c*.1577, seems to advise O'Neill to pursue a policy of conciliation with the government, with the intention of using the time gained to prepare to strike more effectively against the crown at a later stage. Ó Cróinín (ed.), 'A poem to Toirdhealbhach Luinneach'.

18. Hayes-McCoy in Moody et al., *A new history*, iii, pp. 97–8. For Smith's colonial ideology and the activities of his son in Ulster see Quinn, 'Sir Thomas Smith' and Morgan, 'Colonial venture'.

19. Ó Donnchadha, *Leabhar cloinne*, no. VII, pp. 87–93. Ó Gnímh is most likely the 'Ogneiff' mentioned in a fiant of 18 May 1602 (no. 6633). Listed along with Ó Gnímh in this document are presumably his sons 'Ferflaha Ogneiffe' (Fear Flatha) and 'Bernard oge Ogneife' (Brian Óg). It is probable that Brian Ó Gnímh is also the author of the following poems: 'Mionn súl Éireann i nÁth Cliath', on the beheading in May 1586 of Alastar MacDonnell; the poems entitled 'Treisi an eagla ioná an andsacht' and 'Do loisceadh mise san Mhuaidh' which are attributed to a Brian Ó Gnímh in Killiney, Franciscan Library, MS. A. 25. Cunningham and Gillespie have argued that the poem beginning 'Cuimseach sin, a Fhearghail Óig' should be attributed to Brian and not to his son Fear Flatha. Ó Cuív, 'Some Irish items', pp. 152–3; Cunningham and Gillespie, 'East Ulster bardic family', pp. 106–114. Cf. Ó Buachalla, 'Aodh Eanghach'.

20. Ó Donnchadha, *Leabhar cloinne*, line 9, p. 87, line 49, p. 89.

21. Ibid., lines 37–40, p. 88.

22. In his obituary in the *Annals of the Four Masters* s.a. 1576, Uilliam Óg Mac an Bhaird's scholarship and support of the literati were acknowledged. He seems to have had a close association with the O'Donnells. In the heading to a poem he composed *c*.1572, Hugh O'Donnell (ob. 1600) is described as his *tighearna* or lord. Poems he composed for O'Donnell, Maguire (ob. 1589) and Seaán mac Uilliam do Búrc are extant. Ó Cuív, 'The earl of Thomond', pp. 125–45; Greene (ed.), *Duanaire*, p. xii; Walsh, *Irish men*, p. 154; Ó Cléirigh, 'A poem book', p. 59; McGrath, 'Eoghan Ruadh', p. 111.

23. Ní Dhomhnaill, *Duanaireacht*, no. 10, pp. 96–7.

24. Ibid., quatrains 10–13, p. 97.

25. Knott (ed.), *Bardic poems*, i, no. 17, pp. 120–31; Ó Corráin, 'Nationality and kingship', pp. 5–6.

26.	Knott, *Bardic poems*, i, quatrain 10, p. 121. The enduring quality of Anglo-Norman identity is discussed in Cosgrove, 'Hiberniores'.

27.	Knott, *Bardic poems*, i, quatrains 17–18, p. 122; Ibid., ii, quatrains 17–18, p. 81.

28.	Ibid., i, quatrain 20, p. 123.

29.	For instance, the eighteenth-century antiquarian Charles O'Conor wrote scathingly of the author's alleged treachery on the margin of the copy of the poem in 'The Book of O'Conor Don': 'Mo mallacht ort a thaidhg is nairech an dan é so do dhiaidh'. Ibid., i, p. 120; Leerssen, *Mere Irish*, p. 177. O'Conor's historical mindset is discussed in Hill, 'Popery', pp. 105–6.

30.	'T'aire riot, a Riocaird Óig' is ascribed to Ó hUiginn only in 'The Book of O'Conor Don'. In other manuscripts (for example Dublin, Royal Irish Academy, MS. 23. F. 16., MS. 23. L. 17.; Killiney, Franciscan Library, MS. A. 34.) the poem is credited to Brian Ó Domhnalláin (ob. 1582). See Knott, *Bardic poems*, ii, p. 266; MacKinnon, *A descriptive catalogue*, p. 23; O'Grady, *Catalogue*, i, p. 344, p. 401.

31.	Knott, *Bardic poems*, ii, p. 263; Leerssen, *Mere Irish*, pp. 174–5.

32.	Ibid., i, quatrain 2, p. 160.

33.	Ibid., i, quatrains 3, 5, p. 160.

34.	Ibid., i, quatrain 7, p. 161; ii, quatrain 7, p. 106.

35.	Ibid., i, quatrains 9, 12, p. 161, quatrain 19, p. 162.

36.	Ibid., i, no. 16, pp. 108–119; O'Grady, *Catalogue*, i, pp. 412–420; O Riordan, *Gaelic mind*, pp. 165–7.

37.	Hayes-McCoy in Moody et al., *A new history*, iii, p. 117; Morgan, 'Extradition'.

38.	Knott, *Bardic poems*, i, pp. 108–109, quatrains 3, 5, 6, 7. See also Proinsias Mac Cana's comments on Ó hUiginn's image of English troops in control of the very centre of Ireland ('na glémheadhón'): '<I>n other words the foreigner has established himself at the sacred spot which symbolises the unity of the country. The phrasing is eloquent in its brevity'. Mac Cana, 'Early Irish ideology', p. 77; A. and B. Rees, *Celtic heritage*, pp. 146–72.

39.	Ibid., i, quatrains 8, 9, p. 109.

40.	Ibid., i, quatrain 10, p. 109; ii, quatrain 10, p. 73.

41.	Ibid., i, quatrains 14, 28, 32, p. 110, p. 112, p. 113.

42.	Ibid., i, quatrains 49, 56, 65, pp. 115–6, p. 118.

43.	Ibid., i, quatrain 68, p. 118.

44.	For the O'Byrnes of *Gabhal Raghnuill* see Price, 'Notes' and 'The O'Byrnes' country'.

45.	Mac Airt (ed.), *Leabhar Branach*, no. 39, lines 3860–62, 3866, pp. 147–8. Tuileagna Ruadh Ó Maolchonaire is probably the 'Tullegne mc Torne O Mulconere' of Co. Kilkenny who was granted a pardon in 1584. He is also likely to be the Tuileagna mac Torna Uí Mhaoilchonaire who composed a poem entitled 'Labhram ar iongonntaibh Éireann' (Dublin, Royal Irish Academy, MS. 23 L. 17., fo152b) in praise of the Anglo-Irish judge, Sir Nicholas Walsh (ob. 1615). O'Rahilly, 'Irish poets', pp. 88–9; McKenna (ed.), *Aithdioghluim*, i, p. xxxvi; Ó Raghallaigh (ed.), *Filí*, pp. 264–9.

46.	Mac Airt, *Leabhar Branach*, lines 3881–6, p. 148; Bradshaw, 'Native reaction', p. 76.

47.	Maolmuire mac Con Uladh Mic an Bhaird was killed in 1597 while accompanying a military detachment led by Rory O'Donnell (ob. 1608) out of Connacht. He also composed 'A dhúin thíos atá it éanar' on Hugh Roe's demolition of Donegal Castle in 1595. In a poem entitled 'Créd fúarais oram, a Aoidh' Maolmuire complained to Hugh about his supposed failure to provide him with all requisite bardic privileges. O'Rahilly (ed.), *Measgra*, ii, no. 56, pp. 150–5; Breatnach (ed.), 'A poem of protest', pp. 91–100; Ó Dúshláine, *An Eoraip*, p. 166.

48. Breatnach (ed.), 'An address', quatrains 1, 6–8, pp. 205–6.
49. Ibid., quatrains 9, 35–7, p. 206, p. 210.
50. Ibid., quatrain 39, p. 211.
51. O'Rahilly, *Measgra*, ii, no. 56, pp. 150–5. In the eighteenth-century (?) Dublin, Royal Irish Academy, MS. A. v. 1. (fo75b) the poem is described as follows: 'An Maolmuire cédna do rinne an dán so eile ag éccaoíne caisléin Dhúin na nGall do briseadh le hÚa nDomhnaill iar ngabhail tighernais do agus iar mbriseadh cheithre ccaislén décc do chaislénaibh Contae Sligidh ar dhaigh ná ro aittreabhatais Goill inntip ag aidhmhilleadh na tíre iná [sic] nuirthimchioll. Anno Domini 1595'. Ó Raghallaigh (ed), *Duanta*, no. 19, pp. 268–81; Breatnach, 'Trí fhadhb', pp. 256–8; Ó Háinle, 'Notitiae', pp. 226–8. Cf. Walsh (ed.), *Beatha*, i, p. 110.
52. O'Rahilly, *Measgra*, ii, lines 77–9, p. 153.
53. Ibid., ii, lines 85–90, p. 153.
54. Ibid., ii, lines 125–6, p. 155.
55. Carney (ed.), *O'Reillys*, no. XIX, quatrain 14, p. 94.
56. Price, 'Notes' and 'The O'Byrnes' country'.
57. Mac Airt, *Leabhar Branach*, no. 32, line 3445, p. 131. Regarding Domhnall Ó hUiginn see Knott, *Bardic poems*, ii, p. 311.
58. Mac Airt, *Leabhar Branach*, no. 32, lines 3455, 3457–9, p. 131.
59. Ibid., no. 32, lines 3473–4, p. 132; Ó Caithnia, *Apalóga*, p. 81; Ó Cuív, 'Lugh'; Bradshaw, 'Native reaction', p. 75.
60. Mac Airt, *Leabhar Branach*, lines 3521–2, 3533–4, 3529–31, pp. 133–4.
61. Ibid., no. 35; Hardiman, *Irish minstrelsy*, ii, pp. 280–5; O'Grady, *Catalogue*, i, pp. 504–6; Ní Ógáin (ed.), *Duanaire*, iii, no. 9, pp. 32–3; Bradshaw, 'Native reaction', p. 77.
62. For Aonghus Ó Dálaigh see Mac Airt, *Leabhar Branach*, p. 434; Ó Tuathail, 'A poem'.
63. Mac Airt, *Leabhar Branach*, lines 3737–40, p. 142.
64. Ibid., lines 3741–4, p. 142.
65. Ibid., lines 3749–52, p. 142.
66. Ibid., lines 3761–4, p. 143.
67. Ibid., lines 3765–8, p. 143.
68. Ibid., lines 3771–2, 3775–6, p. 143.
69. Ibid., lines 3779–80, 3784, p. 143.
70. Ibid., lines 3787–8, 3791–2, pp. 143–4.
71. For Fearghal Mac Eochadha see Ibid., p. 433. The present analysis of poems from the *Leabhar Branach* supports Brendan Bradshaw's argument for the emergence of a self-conscious patriotism, characterised by a significant element of political insight, in several of the O'Byrne poems.
72. Ibid., no. 57, line 5335, p. 203, lines 5370–71, p. 205, lines 5452–3, p. 207.
73. Ibid., lines 5458–60, 5473, 5474–7, p. 208.

74. Ibid., lines 5519–20, 5524–5, p. 210.
75. Breatnach (ed.), 'Cú Chonnacht'; Caball, 'Some notes'.
76. Breatnach, 'Cú Chonnacht', quatrain 7, p. 35, quatrain 7, p. 39.
77. Ibid., quatrains 10, 12, p. 35.
78. Ibid., quatrains 15–6, p. 36, quatrain 16, p. 39.
79. Ibid., quatrain 17, p. 36, quatrain 17, p. 39.
80. Ibid., quatrains 18–9, p. 36.
81. Ibid., quatrain 20, p. 36.
82. Ibid., quatrains 29, 31, p. 38.
83. McKenna (ed.), *Dioghluim*, no. 92, pp. 302–6. Conor MacDermot succeeded to
     the lordship of Moylurg in 1595, thus providing the earliest possible date for
     the composition of 'Fód codarsna críoch Bhanbha'. A feature of Ó hEódhusa's
     poetry is the supplementary stanza he included in poems in honour of his
     patron Hugh Maguire (ob. 1600). He first declared his intention to follow this
     practice in what was, apparently, his inaugural composition as court poet to
     Maguire (ob. 1589) ('Do gheallus d'Aodh, aigneadh grind, rann as gach dán dá
     ndingnind'). In the poem for MacDermot, he appended the customary codicil
     for Hugh ('A-tá im chunnradh re a chéibh dtigh rann do ghnáth d'Aodh Mhág
     Uidhir'). Maguire was killed near Cork city in March, 1600, providing a *termi-
     nus ante quem* for the poem. Walsh, *Irish men*, p. 19; Greene (ed.), *Duanaire*,
     lines 2897–8; McKenna, ibid., no. 92, quatrain 46, p. 306.
84. McKenna, *Dioghluim*, quatrain 4, p. 302.
85. Ibid., quatrains 2, 3, 11, pp. 302–3.
86. Mac Airt, *Leabhar Branach*, no. 49, lines 4514, 4520–1, 4534–7, p. 173. Giolla
     Íosa Ó Dálaigh is probably the 'Gillyse O Daly, of Templeglantan, in Limerick
     co., yeoman' granted a pardon in 1603. Mac Airt proposed to identify him with
     a poet of the same name who composed a poem for Theobold Butler (ob.
     1596), lord of Cahir. Carney (ed.), *Butlers*, p. xvii.
87. Mac Airt, *Leabhar Branach*, lines 4538–9, p. 173.
88. Ibid., lines 4554–5, p. 174, line 4606, p. 176; Ó Caithnia, *Apalóga*, p. 76.
89. Price, 'Notes', pp. 174–5.
90. Mathghamhain Ó hUiginn's biographical details are far from clear. Edward
     O'Reilly mentioned him under the year 1584 and described him as a retainer of
     the O'Byrnes. He is not to be confused with Mathghamhain (ob. 1585), father
     of Tadhg Dall Ó hUiginn (ob. 1591). O'Reilly, *Irish writers*, p. cxliii; Knott,
     Bardic poems, i, p. xiv.
91. Mac Airt, *Leabhar Branach*, lines 4674, 4685, 4698, pp. 178–9.
92. Ibid., lines 4722–53, pp. 180–1; Ó Caithnia, *Apalóga*, p. 197.
93. Ibid., lines 4754–7, p. 181.
94. Ibid., lines 4758–9, p. 181.
95. Bergin (ed.), *Irish bardic poetry*, no. 3, 31–4. No detailed information survives
     about Mac an Bhaird's career. In 1603 an 'Owen roe McAward' of Donegal was
     granted a pardon and in an inquisition taken that year at Donegal, 26 Novem-
     ber 1603, an 'Owen roe Mc Award of Kilbarron, cronicler' was mentioned. Ó
     Raghallaigh in his edition of Mac an Bhaird's poems suggested, on the basis of
     an entry in the *Annals of the Four Masters*, that he died in 1609. There is, how-
     ever, firm evidence to assume that he joined the O'Donnells in their continen-
     tal exile, and he is probably the 'Irish nobleman Don Eugenio Bardeo'

mentioned in contemporary documents as the recipient of a Spanish pension. On the continent, Mac an Bhaird appears to have been associated with Nuala O'Donnell and Hugh, son of Rory O'Donnell (ob. 1608). Fifteen poems in the 'Book of O'Donnell's Daughter' are ascribed to Mac an Bhaird. This collection of work dedicated to members of the O'Donnell family may have been put together in Spanish Flanders for Nuala, who is recorded as living in Louvain from 1613 onwards. Ó Raghallaigh, *Duanta,* pp. 49–53; McGrath, 'Eoghan Ruadh'; Jennings (ed.), *Wild geese,* p. 139. Cf. Walsh, 'Last years', p. 122, p. 125, p. 241, p. 299; Mhág Craith, *Dán na mbráthar,* ii, pp. 147–8; Kerney Walsh, '*Destruction*', p. 324; Ó Buachalla, 'Na Stíobhartaigh', p. 121; Cunningham, 'Native culture', p. 161. For the 'Book of O'Donnell's Daughter' see Meyer, 'A collection'; Walsh, *Irish men,* pp. 179–205; de Brún, *Lámhscríbhinní,* p. 11.

96.   Bergin, *Irish bardic poetry,* quatrain 10, p. 32, quatrain 10, p. 223. (I have replaced Bergin's translation, 'O Aodh', with 'Hugh'.)

97.   Ibid., quatrain 12, p. 32, quatrain 16, p. 33, quatrain 16, p. 223. I have modernised the language of Bergin's translation here and below for the sake of clarity.

98.   Ibid., quatrain 18, p. 33, quatrain 24, p. 34, quatrain 24, p. 224. Ó Buachalla, 'Na Stíobhartaigh', p. 121; Ó Raghallaigh, *Duanta,* no. 21, pp. 302–12.

99.   Breatnach (ed.), 'Marbhna'; Ó Concheanainn, 'A feature', p. 241. The apparently natural death of Hugh Roe at the age of 29 is discussed in Mooney, 'The death'.

100.   Ibid., quatrain 3, p. 35, quatrain 38, p. 42, quatrain 12, p. 36, quatrain 64, p. 47. (In the editor's translation I have replaced 'Gael' with *Gaoidhil.*)

101.   Ibid., quatrain 51, p. 44, quatrain 14, p. 37, quatrain 61, p. 46.

102.   This account of Nuinseann's revolt is largely based on Coburn Walshe, 'Rebellion of William Nugent'; *Cal. S.P. Ire., 1574–85,* p. 301, p. 314, p. 346, p. 492, p. 540; *Cal. S.P. Foreign, 1582,* p. 415. For Nuinseann generally see Ó Tuathail, 'Nugentiana'; Murphy (ed.), 'Poems of exile'; Ua Brádaigh, 'Na Nuinnsionnaigh', pp. 215–9; Mathew, *Celtic peoples,* pp. 184–207; Bradshaw, *Constitutional revolution,* pp. 285–8. For Christopher Nugent's Irish primer see Gilbert, *Facsimiles,* iv, plate XXII. Concerning Anglo-Irish nationalism see Bradshaw, 'Beginnings' and *Constitutional revolution,* pp. 258–88. Regarding the concept of faith and fatherland see Corish, 'Origins'; Morgan, 'Faith and fatherland'.

103.   Murphy, 'Poems of exile', quatrain 5, p. 12; de Brún et al., *Nua-dhuanaire,* i, no. 4, p. 6; Ní Ógáin, *Duanaire,* ii, no. 56, pp. 99–100; Hardiman, *Irish minstrelsy,* ii, pp. 227–9; Foster, *Alumni Oxonienses,* iii, p. 1082. For Hart Hall and its recusant tradition see Williams, 'Elizabethan Oxford', p. 413.

104.   Murphy, 'Poems of exile', quatrain 7, p. 15.

105.   Mac Airt, *Leabhar Branach,* no. 5, pp. 20–3; Bradshaw, 'Native reaction', p. 72; Leerssen, *Mere Irish,* p. 183–4. For Ó Dálaigh see Mac Airt, *Leabhar Branach,* p. 435.

106.   Ibid., lines 499–500, p. 20, lines 521–8, p. 21.

107.   Ibid., lines 543–4, 547–8, 551–2, p. 22.

108.   Ibid., lines 553–6, p. 22.

109.   Ibid., lines 561–3, p. 22.

110.   O'Rahilly, *Measgra,* i, no. 26, pp. 41–4. Mac Bruaideadha came from a family who traditionally provided chroniclers for the O'Briens of Thomond. According

to the *Annals of the Four Masters*, he died in 1602. In 1585 a 'Miellien oge Mc
Brodie of the Synnganagh (Co.Clare)' was granted a pardon. Maoilín Óg may be
identical with a person of the same name who was associated with Nehemias Ó
Domhnalláin and Uilliam Ó Domhnuill in translating the New Testament to
Irish. Ó Domhnuill described this Mac Bruaideadha as 'duine iúlmhar sa tean-
guidh Ghaoidheilge, sa gColáisde nuadh láimh ré Baile Atha Cliath' (namely,
Trinity College, Dublin). O'Rahilly, 'Irish poets', p. 96; McGrath, 'Materials', p.
51; Ó Cuív in Moody et al., *A new history*, iii, p. 524; Leerssen, *Mere Irish*, p.
327, pp. 471–42 and Leerssen, *The contention*, pp. 38–40; Williams, *I bprionta*,
p. 29.

111. O'Rahilly, *Measgra*, i, lines 37, 43, p. 42; see p. 80 for the editor's dating of
'Bráthair don bhás an doidhbhreas'. In 1572 Conor O'Brien (ob. 1581) allegedly
hanged three poets, an action which was bitterly condemned by Uilliam Óg
Mac an Bhaird; see Ó Cuív, 'The earl of Thomond'.

112. O'Rahilly, *Measgra*, i, lines 45–72, pp. 42–3. A similar list of exactions levied by
the late earl of Desmond and compiled in 1587 is reproduced by Hore and
Graves, *Social state*, pp. 266–7. For a contemporary account of indifferent or
lacklustre conformity to the established church in Thomond around 1591 see
Cunningham (ed.), 'A View'.

113. Bergin, *Irish bardic poetry*, no. 9, pp. 49–50; Ní Dhomhnaill, *Duanaireacht*, p.
122. The poem is preserved in only one manuscript, the seventeenth-century
Dublin, Royal Irish Academy, MS. A. iv. 3., p. 778. Laoiseach Mac an Bhaird
may be the person of the same name, resident in Farney, Co.Monaghan, who
was pardoned in 1601. O'Rahilly, 'Irish poets', p. 104; Ó Dúshláine, *An Eoraip*,
pp. 119–120.

114. Bergin, *Irish bardic poetry*, quatrains 1–4, p. 49.

115. Ibid., quatrains 5–8, pp. 49–50.

116. Ibid., quatrains 9–11, p. 50, quatrain 11, p. 232. The adoption of English dress
in Gaelic Ireland is discussed in Morgan, 'The end of Gaelic Ulster', pp. 23–4.

117. Walsh (ed.), *Gleanings,* p. 186. Regarding the date of Harrington's appointment
as seneschal see Price, 'Notes', p. 140. Already in 1571 in the adjoining district
of Kildare, a commission was bestowed on Gerald, earl of Kildare, and Piers fitz
James of Ballysonnon, to exercise martial law: 'They are also to punish by death,
or otherwise as directed, harpers, rhymers, bards, idlemen, vagabonds and such
horseboys as have not their master's bill to show whose men they are'. Walsh
(above) p. 186. Cf. Watt, *Cheap print*, p. 15, pp. 24–5.

118. Mac Airt, *Leabhar Branach*, no. 8, lines 797–820, pp. 31–2. An edition of 'Cia
cheannchus adhmad naoi rann?' is also available in Walsh, *Gleanings*, pp.
182–93. Its author is probably identical with the Seaán mac Ruaidhrí Óig Uí
Uiginn who composed a poem beginning 'Rogha an chuaine Cú Chonnacht' for
Maguire (ob. 1589); Greene, *Duanaire*, p. xiii.

119. Ibid., lines 821–8, p. 32.

120. Walsh (ed.), *Irish chiefs*, quatrains 1, 3, 9, pp. 72–4; Cunningham and Gillespie,
'East Ulster bardic family', p. 110.

121. Ibid., quatrain 23, p. 78; I have emended Walsh's translation for the sake of clarity. A normalised version of quatrain twenty-three and a commentary on the Ó
Gnímh genealogies is provided by Ó Cuív, 'Some Irish items', pp. 152–6.

122. Mhág Craith, *Dán na mbráthar,* i, no. 5, pp. 25–7 and *Dán na mbráthar,* ii, pp.

116–7; Knott (ed.), 'A poem', pp. 241–5; Hyde (ed.), *Abhráin*, i, p. 54. For a comprehensive account of Ó hEódhusa see Mhág Craith, *Dán na mbráthar*, ii, pp. 108–14; Ó Maonaigh, 'Scríbhneoirí', pp. 192–213; Silke, 'Irish scholarship', pp. 196–7; Ó Dúshláine, *An Eoraip*, pp. 8–10.

123. Mhág Craith, *Dán na mbráthar*, i, quatrains 2–3, pp. 25–6.

124. Ibid., quatrain 5, p. 26; Mhág Craith, *Dán na mbráthar*, ii, quatrain 5, p. 11.

125. Bergin, *Irish bardic poetry*, no. 37, quatrain 7, pp. 145–6; Dunne, 'Gaelic response', p. 15; Leerssen, *Mere Irish*, pp. 199–200. Mathghamhain Ó hIfearnáin is most likely the 'Mahon O Hifernan, rimer' of Co. Cork, who was pardoned in May, 1585. He also composed 'A mhic, ná meabhraigh éigse' in which he advised his son against becoming a poet. Ní Ógáin, *Duanaire*, iii, no. 4, pp. 16–17; O'Grady, *Catalogue*, i, pp. 392–3; O'Rahilly, 'Irish poets', p. 92; McKenna (ed.), *Iomarbhágh*, i, p. xi.

126. Bergin, *Irish bardic poetry*, quatrains 2–3, p. 145.

127. Ibid., quatrains 4–5, p. 146.

128. Ibid., quatrains 11–21, pp. 38–40.

129. Bradshaw, 'Sword'; Ford, *Protestant reformation*; Mac Craith, 'Gaelic reaction'.

130. For Ó Cearnaigh (ob. *c.* 1600) see Williams, *I bprionta*, pp. 21–6; de Bhaldraithe, 'Leabhar Charswell', pp. 61–7; Ó Cuív (ed.), *Aibidil*. Significantly, the first piece to be printed in Irish, as a trial exercise for the subsequent production of Ó Cearnaigh's catechism, was a bardic poem entitled 'Tuar ferge foighide Dé' by Pilib Bocht Ó hUiginn (ob. 1487). See Lynam, *Irish character*, pp. 5–6. For Sir William Herbert see Keaveney and Madden (eds.), *Croftus sive de Hibernia liber*; Canny, 'Why the reformation failed', p. 448; Bradshaw, 'Robe and sword'; de Brún, 'Dhá bhlogh', p. 56. Poems composed by Domhnall Óg Ó hUiginn for Tadhg O'Hara (ob. 1616) of Leyney are extant. He is probably the 'Donell Oge O Higgen of Kilclony, gent' granted a pardon in 1590. Kilcloney (*Ceall Cluaine*) was a bardic school run by the Uí Uiginn, possibly near Ballinasloe, Co. Galway. Uilliam Ó Domhnuill mentioned Ó hUiginn in his introduction to the Irish New Testament and spoke of linguistic assistance received from the poet: 'air ar chuir mé úalach na coda eile dho sgríobhadh do réir óghuim agus chirt na Gaoidheilge'. McKenna (ed.), *The Book*, p. 447; Knott, *Bardic poems*, ii, p. 312; Ó Domhnuill (trans.), Tiomna Nuadh, preface.

131. One Gaelic scholar was sufficiently incensed by liturgical and theological reform to include comments in the margins of a medical manuscript he was copying in the home of Brian Kavanagh of Carlow in 1578. Corc Óg Ó Cadhla ventured some acerbic observations on the Protestant claim to religious supremacy. Interestingly, Kavanagh was married to Eisibél, a sister of Feagh O'Byrne of *Gabhal Raghnuill*. Ó Cadhla acquiesced in the crown's claim to dominion but he rejected Elizabeth's ecclesiastical stance: 'Et is i is prinsa Saxan agus Erend ann i. Quene Elizabeth, agus aderid moran go bfuil rioghachd Alban agus na Fraince [aice] agus ni bfuil a commor agus ataid sin. Agus ataid Saxanaigh ag a radh gurob aice ata airdchennus an chreidimh. Agus is breg doibh oir is dearbhtha linn gurob e an Papa cenn na hegailsi naomhtha catholgdha. Agus is fior do Shaxanachaibh aní aderid fein, oir is í is cenn ar an droichcreidemh co huilidhi an med ata fa na smachd. Oir ni connaimhther aoine ná corghus na cataoir ina an tsaeire do ordaigh Dia do chonnmhail, fa na smachd, agus ni mo berther anoir na cion dh'arus naoimh iná ré, agus fos is iad is mo

do ní dunmharbhadh agus is uaibhrighe san roinn Eorpa co huilidhi.' (Walsh, *Gleanings,* pp. 158–9.)

132. Mhág Craith, *Dán na mbráthar,* i, no. 27, quatrain 25, p. 133; *Dán na mbráthar,* ii, quatrain 25, p. 61; Ó Muirgheasa (ed.), *Dánta diadha,* no. 51, pp. 284–306. For Ó Dubhthaigh see Ó Cléirigh, *Aodh Mac Aingil,* pp. 100–5; O'Rahilly, 'Irish poets', p. 116.

133. Mhág Craith, *Dán na mbráthar,* i, quatrains 21, 26, 27, 42, 67, 69, 89c, pp. 133–51. Ó Dubhthaigh's description of Protestantism as a perversion of historical development finds its counterpoint in the Protestant view of history as a cumulative struggle towards the establishment of true religion, a view graphically expressed in Foxe's 'Book of Martyrs': Watt, *Cheap print,* p. 91.

134. Ibid., no. 28, quatrains 1–6, pp. 151–3. Ó Buachalla has suggested that 'A Bhanbha is truagh do chor!' was composed by an Eoghan Ó Dubhthaigh other than the Franciscan who died in 1590 and he interprets the reference to 'sluagh Saxan . . . is fir Alban' as an allusion to the Ulster plantation. However, Mhág Craith took it to refer to the attempted plantations in east Ulster in 1572–3. Mhág Craith, *Dán na mbráthar,* ii, p. 186; Ó Buachalla, 'Na Stíobhartaigh', p. 105.

135. Knott, *Bardic poems,* i, p. xvi; O'Grady, *Catalogue,* i, pp. 442–3.

136. O'Rahilly, *Measgra,* ii, no. 52, line 45, lines 53–6, 75–6, pp. 140–1. Cf. Bergin (ed.), *Trí bior-ghaoithe,* p. 168. The contemporary European currency of the concept of divine wrath is discussed in Bossy, *Christianity,* p. 36; Muchembled, *Popular culture,* pp. 26–7.

137. O'Rahilly, *Measgra,* ii, no. 53, pp. 143–4.

138. McKenna (ed.), *Aithdioghluim,* i, quatrains 4, 7, 18, 21, no. 53, pp. 204–7; Ó Concheanainn, 'A feature', pp. 249–50. Regarding Mac an Bhaird's presence in Scotland in 1581 see Bannerman, 'Scots language', p. 10. The traditionalism of Mac an Bhaird's religious beliefs is evident in his 'Slán uaim ag oileán Pádraig', composed following a pilgrimage to Lough Derg. Leslie (ed.), *St Patrick's purgatory,* pp. 172–3. The Thomond poet Domhnall Mac Bruaideadha composed a piece entitled 'Raghad d'éisteacht Aifrinn Dé', similarly in defence of the Mass. Cuallacht Cholm Cille, *Mil na mbeach,* pp. 35–7. The liturgical pre-eminence and communal public focus of the Mass in pre-reformation Europe is emphasised in Bossy, 'Mass as a social institution'.

139. Mhág Craith, *Dán na mbráthar,* i, no. 21, quatrains 11, 12, 13, 14, 16, 17, pp. 107–110; McKenna, *Dioghluim,* no. 122, pp. 423–5. For Lochluinn Ó Dálaigh see *Dán na mbráthar,* ii, p. 151. The importance of the friars' pastoral role in Gaelic Ireland is stressed in Corish, *Catholic community,* p. 22.

140. The poem beginning 'I n-ainm an áirdmhic doghnídh grása', supposedly dedicated to Queen Elizabeth *c.* 1588(?), has been excluded from consideration in this chapter. Its uncertain authorship, preservation in a late manuscript (1725), and ironic tone undermine its integrity as a credible historical document. It is not improbable that it is a piece of Elizabethan black propaganda. For instance, Sir John Perrot, lord deputy between 1584 and 1588, paid 6s. 8d. 'to O'Neill's rhymer for making a rhyme of the Queen'. Mac Erlean (ed.), *Duanaire Dháibhidh,* iii, no. XII, pp. 64–75; Carney, *Butlers,* p. 137; O'Grady, *Catalogue,* i, pp. 544–5; Canny, *Kingdom,* p. 21.

141. Mac Niocaill, *Irish population,* p. 4.

142. For instance, Patrick Crosbie, who was the son of O'More's *ollamh*, Mac an Chrosáin, was an active agent in the service of the crown. In 1601 Crosbie was said to be hated by the Irish because he was 'a continual worker of means for their overthrow'. O'Donovan (ed.), *The tribes*, p. 25; Kenney, *Sources*, i, p. 32; Caball, 'Pairlement'. As early as 1571, a lawyer named 'James O'Scingin' had written a Latin statement on *cin comhfhocuis* (a family's corporate legal responsibility) for Sir Edward Fitton, lord president of Connacht. Regarding other Gaelic legal scholars who took service with the English authorities see Patterson, 'Brehon law', p. 48.

Conquest and Evaluation: 1603–1612

1. Canny, 'The treaty of Mellifont'; idem., 'Hugh O'Neill'.
2. Curtis, *A history*, pp. 219–20.
3. Meyer, 'A collection'; Walsh, *Irish men*, pp. 179–205; Ó Raghallaigh (ed.), *Duanta*, p. 27; Ó Cuív in Moody et al., *A new history*, iii, p. 530. This manuscript is now in Brussels, Bibliothèque royale, MS. 6131–3.
4. Hyde, 'The book of the O'Conor Don', pp. 78–99; Murphy (ed.), *Duanaire Finn*, iii, pp. ix-xi, pp. 217–19; Ó Cuív in Moody et al., *A new history*, iii, p. 530; de Brún, *Lámhscríbhinní*, p. 41. In a note on fo149 of the manuscript Ó Dochartaigh sheds some light, admittedly perfunctory, on his rationale for selecting poems for inclusion: 'Do sgriobhas do réir mar fuaras do chaiptín Samhuirle mise Aodh'. Walsh, *Irish chiefs*, p. 139. See also Gillespie, *Conspiracy*, pp. 33–5.
5. O'Rahilly, *Catalogue*, i, pp. 6–18; Ó Cuív in Moody et al., *A new history*, iii, p. 530.
6. Roderick O'Flaherty in his *Ogygia* (London, 1685) outlined the most scholarly case for Gaelic allegiance to the Stuart dynasty and its claim to the kingdom of Ireland on the basis of descent from the ancient kings of Munster: 'For all the sovereign rights of the ancient British, Anglo-Saxon, Norman, and Saxon kings, have devolved hereditarily, to your (namely, James, Duke of York and Albany) royal family; besides Ireland primarily claims your paternal line of ancestry, time immemorial, as Scotland does from her.' O'Flaherty, *Ogygia*, i (Dublin, 1793), p. xiv, translated from the original Latin by James Hely. See also Hugh Reily, *Ireland's case briefly stated* (1695); Murphy, 'Royalist Ireland', pp. 592–3; Millett in Moody et al., *A new history*, iii, p. 574; Hill, 'Popery', p. 100; Ó Ciardha, 'A voice'.
7. Tomás Ó Concheanainn dates the composition of 'Trí coróna i gcairt Shéamais' to sometime between 1577 and 1595. Breandán Ó Buachalla argues, however, that the latter's identification of a reference in the poem ('éinríoghan dá gclaon coill') with Elizabeth I is incorrect, preferring to read it as a reference to Mary, queen of Scots and he dates the poem to *c.* 1603. Ó Concheanainn, 'A feature', p. 249; Ó Buachalla, 'Na Stíobhartaigh', p. 85. For the poem's text see McKenna (ed.), *Aithdioghluim*, i, no. 44, pp. 177–180; and translation in *Aithdioghluim*, ii, pp. 104–6. See also O Riordan, *Gaelic mind*, pp. 173–7.
8. McKenna, *Aithdioghluim*, i, quatrains 1–5, p. 177.
9. Ibid., quatrains 6–15, pp. 177–8.
10. Ibid., quatrains 16–20, p. 179.

11. Ibid., quatrains 21–2, p. 179; *Aithdioghluim*, ii, quatrains 21–2, p. 105. (I have emended slightly the editor's translation of quatrain 21.)

12. Ibid., i, quatrain 23, p. 179. For Gaelic pedigrees of James VI and I see 'Geinealaighe', pp. 68–70; Comyn (ed.), *Foras feasa*, i, p. 208; Ó Donnchadha (ed.), *Leabhar cloinne*, pp. 52–3. Cf. Williams (ed.), *Pairlement*, p. 23; Ó Cuív, 'A seventeenth-century criticism', pp. 123–4; Silke, 'Primate Lombard and James I', p. 126; Mac Aingil, *Scáthán*, edited by Ó Maonaigh, p. ix.

13. Breatnach (ed.), 'Metamorphosis', quatrain 3, p. 171, quatrains 5, 7, p. 172, quatrain 13, p. 174. Ó Buachalla, 'Na Stíobhartaigh', pp. 83–4; Ó Caithnia, *Apalóga*, p. 194.

14. Breatnach, 'Metamorphosis', quatrain 14, p. 174, quatrain 16, p. 175.

15. Ibid., quatrain 11, p. 173, quatrain 12, p. 174.

16. Ibid., quatrain 19, p. 175; Breatnach (ed.), 'Anarchy', quatrain 2, p. 58; p. 61.

17. Bergin (ed.), *Irish bardic poetry*, no. 2, quatrains 1–3, 7, pp. 27–8; Ó Raghallaigh, *Duanta*, no. 6, pp. 64–9. In 'The Book of O'Donnell's Daughter', 'Dána an turas tríalltar sonn' was transcribed by the poet himself and he appended an historical gloss to the poem: 'Dán do rinniodh diarla Tíre Conuill an tráth tug umhlucht do choróin Shaxan ar tús: Eoghan Ruadh Mac an Bhaird do rinne agus do sgríobh an dán so' (fo28). Walsh, *Irish men*, p. 199; Ó Buachalla, 'Na Stíobhartaigh', p. 83; Falls, 'Neill Garve', pp. 2–7.

18. Bergin, *Irish bardic poetry*, quatrains 12–14, p. 29.

19. Ibid., quatrains 18, 20, p. 30.

20. Ó Raghallaigh, *Duanta*, no. 2, pp. 58–63; no. 18, pp. 258–67.

21. Eoghan Ruadh Mac an Bhaird also composed a poem ('Ionmhuin sgríbhionn sgaoilter sonn') for Hugh (ob. *c*. 1642) on his arrival in Louvain. Its date of composition is not immediately clear. Mac an Bhaird speaks of Hugh having arrived in Louvain in his seventh year ('gan daois sunn acht seacht mbliadhno'), yet if a date of birth in 1606 is correct, Hugh was about two years old when he reached Louvain with other Gaelic exiles. Brendan Jennings's researches show that Hugh was subsequently entrusted to the care of the Dames Blanches and later the Irish Franciscans in Louvain. Therefore, it is not immediately obvious why Mac an Bhaird should compose a poem of welcome in 1613, when his subject had been in Louvain since 1607. Walsh, *Irish men*, pp. 183–6; Walsh (ed.), *Beatha Aodha*, ii, p. 124; Jennings, 'The career of Hugh'. Regarding Bridget Fitzgerald see Ó Háinle, 'Flattery rejected'.

22. Ó Raghallaigh, *Duanta*, quatrain 11, p. 62.

23. Ibid., quatrains 2–3, p. 58; quatrain 3, p. 314.

24. Ibid., quatrain 4, p. 58; quatrain 8, p. 60.

25. 'Rob soraidh an séadsa soir' is of uncertain authorship. The earliest extant copy in the 'Book of O'Gara' (Dublin, Royal Irish Academy, MS. 23. F. 16, p. 65) is attributed to S[eán] Mhá Colgan (Cf. London, British Library, MS. Egerton III, fo70). Mhág Craith suggested that S. Mhá Colgan and John Colgan, O.F.M., (1592–1685) were the same person. The likelihood, however, of a teenager from a non-bardic family composing such a poem seems doubtful. O'Reilly repeated the ascription to Mhág Colgan, while noting that the piece was sometimes attributed to Eoghan Ruadh Mac an Bhaird. Mhág Craith, 'Seaán Mhág Colgan cct.', pp. 60–9; O'Reilly, *Irish writers*, p.clxiii; Ó Raghallaigh, *Duanta*, no. 18, pp. 258–67; Walsh, *The will*, pp. 72–4; Canny, 'Hugh O'Neill', p. 16;

Ó Buachalla, 'Na Stíobhartaigh', p. 119. An anonymous poem entitled 'Rug cabhair ar chlár Banba' was composed on Turlough's return from England: O'Grady, *Catalogue*, i, pp. 387–8, pp. 484–5.

26. Ó Raghallaigh, *Duanta*, quatrain 3, p. 258.

27. Ibid., quatrain 24, p. 264, quatrains 5–6, pp. 258–60, quatrains 5–6, p. 390.

28. Canny, 'Hugh O'Neill', p. 16; *Cal. S.P. Ire., Jas. I, 1603–1606*, p. 319; *Cal. S.P. Ire., Jas. I, 1606–1608*, p. 281.

29. Bardic confidence is discernible in Giolla Brighde Ó hEódhusa's decision to leave Ireland for the continent at the beginning of James's reign to begin his studies for the priesthood. Apparently assured of the future of Gaelic society, he vowed that he would certainly return home. Mhág Craith (ed.), *Dán na mbráthar*, i, no. 6, quatrain 13, p. 30; *Dán na mbráthar*, ii, no. 6, quatrain 13, p. 13; Knott (ed.), 'A poem by Giolla Brighde Ó Heoghusa', pp. 10–15.

30. Canny, 'The flight'; Mooney, 'A noble shipload'; McCavitt, 'The flight of the earls, 1607'; Walsh (ed.), *The flight of the earls by Tadhg Ó Cianáin*.

31. Bergin, *Irish bardic poetry*, no. 30, quatrain 2, p. 127, quatrain 6, p. 128.

32. Ní Ógáin (ed.), *Duanaire Gaedhilge*, iii, no. 4, quatrains 1, 12, pp. 16–17; O'Grady, *Catalogue*, i, pp. 392–3; Black, 'The genius of Cathal MacMhuirich', p. 338; Leerssen, *Mere Irish*, pp. 199–200.

33. Bergin, *Irish bardic poetry*, no. 28, quatrains 1, 2, 6, 8, 13, pp. 120–23; Walsh, *The will*, pp. 38–9; Cunningham and Gillespie, 'East Ulster bardic family', p. 108.

34. Fear Feasa Ó an Cháinte's 'Gluais a litir go Lunndain' is undated. Both Ó an Cháinte and his wife ('Katherine Ny Daly') are mentioned in a fiant of 1601, where his place of residence is given as Curravordy, north of Bandon, Co. Cork. Florence MacCarthy (*c.* 1562–*c.* 1641) of Carbery experienced a varied career which centred on several periods of imprisonment in the Tower of London. Given the nature of Ó an Cháinte's complaints about a decline in patronage, it is quite possible this poem was composed either in the early or middle years of James's reign. For Ó an Cháinte see O'Rahilly, 'Irish poets', p. 109; McKenna, *Aithdioghluim*, i, p. xxxvi; Ó Dúshláine, *An Eoraip*, pp. 121–22; Bergin, *Irish bardic poetry*, no. 39, quatrain 10, pp. 151–3. For Florence MacCarthy see Mac-Carthy, *Life and letters*; O'Donovan (ed.), *The tribes of Ireland*, p. 24; Ó hInnse (ed.), *Miscellaneous*, pp.vii–ix; de Brún, 'Litir ó thor Londain', pp. 49–53.

35. O'Grady, *Catalogue*, i, pp. 555–7; Ó Dúshláine, *An Eoraip*, pp. 121–2; Black, 'The genius of Cathal MacMhuirich', p. 360.

36. Williams, *Pairlement*, p. 40.

37. O'Grady, *Catalogue*, i, p. 556.

38. P. de Brún, B. Ó Buachalla and T. Ó Concheanainn, *Nua-dhuanaire*, i, no. 1, pp. 1–2, p. 91; Ní Ógáin, *Duanaire*, iii, no. 5, pp. 18–19; Mac Cionnaith (ed.), *Dioghluim*, no. 115, pp. 398–9; Ní Dhomhnaill, *Duanaireacht*, no. 14, pp. 103–104; Ó Buachalla, 'Na Stíobhartaigh', n. 26, p. 120; Cunningham and Gillespie, 'East Ulster bardic family', p. 108; Leerssen, *Mere Irish*, p. 200.

39. De Brún et al., *Nua-dhuanaire*, i, lines 8, 37–40, pp. 1–2.

40. Ní Ógáin, *Duanaire*, iii, quatrains 4, 7, pp. 16–17.

41. Cunningham and Gillespie, 'East Ulster bardic family', p. 113; O'Sullivan (ed.), 'Tadhg O'Daly'; Cunningham, 'Native culture', pp. 155–6; MacCarthy, *Life and letters*, p. 362.

42.   Gillies (ed.), 'A poem on the downfall', quatrain 3, p. 204; Ó Buachalla, 'Na Stíobhartaigh', p. 91; Ó Dúshláine, *An Eoraip*, p. 183.
43.   Gillies, 'A poem on the downfall', quatrains 6, 8, p. 205. I have replaced the editor's translation of *Albonaigh* as Scotch with Scots.
44.   Mac Cionnaith (ed.), *Dioghluim*, no. 107, quatrains 2, 5, 37, pp. 363–7; Ó Caithnia, *Apalóga*, p. 133.
45.   Mac Cionnaith, *Dioghluim*, quatrain 8, p. 364.
46.   Ibid., quatrains 4, 7, p. 364.
47.   Walsh (ed.), *Beatha*, ii, pp. 118–125; Ní Dhomhnaill, *Duanaireacht*, no. 8, pp. 91–3.
48.   Walsh, *Beatha*, ii, quatrains 6–9, pp. 118–121. In quatrain seven cited above, I have altered Walsh's translation of *oireachus* from supremacy to sovereignty.
49.   Walsh (ed.), *The flight of the earls by Tadhg Ó Cianáin*, p. 238, pp. 240–3; Meehan, *The fate and fortunes*, pp. 275–6, p. 279.
50.   Bergin, *Irish bardic poetry*, no. 4, quatrains 9, 11, 13, 16, pp. 35–7.
51.   Walsh, *Beatha*, ii, p. 14, pp. 126–31; Walsh (ed.), *Gleanings*, pp. 108–10; Bergin, *Irish bardic poetry*, no. 8, pp. 46–8.
52.   Bergin, *Irish bardic poetry*, quatrain 14, p. 48, quatrain 14, p. 231.
53.   Extracts from 'Beag mhaireas do mhacraidh Ghaoidheal' have been published by O'Grady and Ní Dhomhnaill. O'Grady, *Catalogue*, i, pp. 471–4; Ní Dhomhnaill, *Duanaireacht*, no. 12, pp. 99–101; Breatnach, 'Metamorphosis', p. 169. For Sir Brian MacMahon (ob. 1622) see Walsh, *The will*, pp. 40–41.
54.   Ní Dhomhnaill, *Duanaireacht*, quatrains 1, 6, 7, pp. 99–100.
55.   Knott, *Irish classical poetry*, p. 60.
56.   Bergin, *Irish bardic poetry*, no. 1, pp. 25–7. Bergin surmised that this poem was composed for Hugh, son of Cathbharr O'Donnell (ob. 1608). However, in an eighteenth-century manuscript (Dublin, National Library of Ireland, MS. G. 167, pp. 300–1) containing an extensive collection of O'Donnell poems, the following heading was appended to the poem indicating Hugh's identity: 'Leabhar ar riaghlachaibh et ar inneall an chogaidh ar a ndearna Eoghan Ruadh translation et tionntudh i nGaoidheilg air. Et do rinne a dhedication i ndán don Iarla óg cheanda .i. Aodh mac Rudhraighe.' Breandán Ó Buachalla argues that the poem was composed *c.* 1627, possibly to accompany a Gaelic translation of Justus Lipsius's famous military commentary on Polybius, *De militia Romana libri quinque*. Ó Buachalla, 'Cúlra'; Ní Shéaghdha (ed.), *Catalogue*, v, p. 13; Ó Cléirigh, 'A poem book', p. 134; Ó Raghallaigh, *Duanta*, no. 3, pp. 64–9.
57.   See Ní Shéaghdha, *Catalogue*, v, p. 13; Dunne, 'The Gaelic response', p. 16; Ó Buachalla, 'Annála', pp. 80–1.
58.   Bergin, *Irish bardic poetry*, quatrain 14, p. 26, quatrain 14, p. 220 (I have made changes to the editor's translation here and below.)
59.   Ibid., quatrains 8–15, pp. 26–7.
60.   Mac Cionnaith, *Dioghluim*, no. 93, quatrain 30, p. 310, quatrain 50, p. 312; Ó Raghallaigh, *Duanta*, no. 20, pp. 282–301; Ó Caithnia, *Apalóga*, p. 133. Breandán Ó Buachalla attributes the composition of 'Fogus furtacht don tír thuaidh' to Eoghan Ruadh Mac an Bhaird as opposed to Fearghal Óg. It must be remembered, however, that the two earliest manuscript copies of the poem in the 'Book of O'Donnell's Daughter' (fo20) and the 'Book of O'Conor Don' (fo197b) cite Fearghal Óg as the author. Ó Buachalla, 'Cúlra', n.10, p. 407;

McGrath, 'Eoghan Ruadh', p. 110.

61. O'Rahilly (ed.), *Measgra*, ii, no. 55, p. 206; Bergin, *Irish bardic poetry*, no. 26, quatrain 9, pp. 115–17; Dunne, 'The Gaelic response', p. 16; Cunningham and Gillespie, 'East Ulster bardic family', p. 108. In the late eighteenth and early nineteenth-century Dublin, Royal Irish Academy, MS. 23. E. 15, p. 160, Mícheál Óg Ó Longáin ascribed 'Beannacht ar anmain Éireann' to Ó Gnímh and dated the poem to 1609. An earlier manuscript (Dublin, Royal Irish Academy, MS. 23. N. 12, p. 30) written by Mícheál Ó Longáin *c.* 1763 also attributed this work to Ó Gnímh. Cf. Ó Háinle, 'Flattery rejected', n. 42, p. 26.

62. Ó Raghallaigh, *Duanta*, no. 13, pp. 170–205; Ó Buachalla, 'Na Stíobhartaigh', pp. 105–6. While it is generally assumed that 'Maith an sealad fuair Éire' was composed shortly after the death of O'Donnell in 1608, a reference in the poem suggests otherwise. Presumably alluding to the coming of the Anglo-Normans to Ireland, the poet speaks in quatrain eight of this event having taken place 460 years ago ('Acht seascad bliadhain amháin 's ceithre chéad, tús ar dtochráidh, ó theacht slóigh Lunndan tar lear'). If the poet took 1169 as his date for the arrival of the Anglo-Normans, it might be inferred that he was composing in 1629. Moreover, the authorship of the poem in the two earliest extant copies, those in the 'Book of O'Donnell's Daughter' and the 'Book of O'Conor Don', is anonymous. In a table of contents added to the 'Book of O'Donnell's Daughter' not earlier than 1637, it is ascribed to Eoghan Ruadh Mac an Bhaird, though according to Paul Walsh the entry was subsequently 'stroked through with a pen': *Irish men*, pp. 199–200, p. 203. It appears that the first unqualified attribution to Mac an Bhaird occurs in a late seventeenth-century manuscript (Dublin, Royal Irish Academy, MS. 24. P. 27, p. 164m). On this basis, it is prudent to assign the poem a strictly tentative date of composition *c.* 1608.

63. Ó Raghallaigh, *Duanta*, quatrains 18, 19, 20, 22, p. 178, p. 362.

64. Ibid., quatrain 83, p. 202, p. 369.

65. Simms, *Kings to warlords*, p. 170. For the social focus of the medieval church in Gaelic Ireland see Corish, *Irish catholic experience*, pp. 63–95.

66. Ó Maonaigh, 'Scríbhneoirí', pp. 192–3; Silke, 'Irish scholarship', pp. 196–7; Wall, 'The catechism'; Ó Fachtna, 'Cúig teagaisg chríostaidhe'; Ó Lochlainn (ed.), *Tobar*, pp. 98–9. Regarding the influence of catechisms at this period see Bossy, 'The counter-reformation and the people of catholic Europe', pp. 66–7.

67. McGrath (ed.), 'Three poems', pp. 175–96; Vendryes (ed.), 'Le poème'; Ó Muirgheasa (ed.), *Dánta diadha*, no. 52, pp. 320–38; Lynam, *Irish character in print*, p. 8; Mhág Craith, *Dán na mbráthar*, i, no. 9, pp. 38–51; *Dán na mbráthar*, ii, pp. 16–23, pp. 126–31; Ó hEódhasa, *An teagasg críosdaidhe*, edited by Mac Raghnaill.

68. 'Dán do rinne an bráthair bocht d'órd S. Proinsias, Bonabheantúra Ó hEódhasa, Gáirdian Bhráthar nÉirionnach Lobháin, d'fhíorcharaid áiridhe dhó, do thuit i n-eiriceacht lé mearghrádh an tsaoghail agus ainmhian a cholna.' Mhág Craith, *Dán na mbráthar*, i, p. 38.

69. Ibid., i, quatrain 24, p. 42, quatrain 49, p. 45; Mhág Craith, *Dán na mbráthar*, ii, quatrain 49, p. 20. Cf. Mac Raghnaill (ed.), *An teagasg críosdaidhe*, p. 32.

70. Mhág Craith, *Dán na mbráthar*, ii, quatrains 35, 43, pp. 43–4; O'Rahilly (ed.), *Desiderius*, pp. 125–6.

71. Mhág Craith, *Dán na mbráthar*, i, quatrain 60, p. 47.

72. In the notes to his 1927 edition of 'Mo thruaighe mar táid Gaoidhil!' O'Rahilly concluded that it was composed c. 1612. Subsequently, in 1950, he revised his earlier conclusion and, citing no evidence for an emendation, he dated it to around 1622. O'Rahilly (ed.), *Measgra*, ii, no. 54, lines 12, 33, 40, pp. 144–7, p. 206. O'Rahilly, 'Ó Gnímh's alleged visit to London', p. 331; Ní Ógáin, *Duanaire*, iii, no. 7, pp. 23–5; Hardiman (ed.), *Irish minstrelsy*, ii, pp. 102–13; Ó Buachalla, 'Na Stíobhartaigh', p. 120; Leerssen, *Mere Irish*, p. 199.

73. Silke in Moody et al., *A new history*, iii, pp. 608–11.

74. Mac Cionnaith, *Dioghluim*, no. 93, quatrain 7, pp. 307–12.

75. O'Rahilly, *Measgra*, ii, line 84, p. 147.

76. Bergin, *Irish bardic poetry*, no. 43, quatrains 13, 14, 18, pp. 161–6; Bergin (ed.), 'Address to Sémas mac Aonghais', pp. 136–49; Ó Caithnia, *Apalóga*, pp. 75–6.

77. Mac Neill (ed.), *Duanaire Finn*, i, no. XXXIV, p. 85; Murphy (ed.), *Duanaire Finn*, iii, pp. 72–5; J. Fraser, P. Grosjean and J. G. O'Keeffe (eds.), *Irish texts*, iv, pp. 43–4.

78. Ó Caithnia, *Apalóga*, p. 169.

79. Walsh, *Beatha*, ii, quatrain 12, pp. 138–48; Knott, 'The flight of the earls (1607)'; Ní Ógáin, *Duanaire*, iii, no. 2, pp. 13–14; Ó Raghallaigh, *Duanta*, no. 16, pp. 242–51; Ó Buachalla, 'Na Stíobhartaigh', p. 121; Leerssen, *Mere Irish*, p. 193–3. 'Anocht is uaigneach Éire' is ascribed to Eoghan Ruadh Mac an Bhaird in the 'Book of O'Donnell's Daughter' (fo42), while in the 'Book of O'Conor Don' (fo413b) it is attributed to Ainnrias Mac Marcuis. In a fiant of 1601 there is reference to an 'Henrias Mc Marcas', while a fiant of 1602 mentions 'Enrias Mc Marchais'. No place names are given in either fiant and O'Rahilly suggested that on the basis of the personal names they both belonged to north-east Antrim. Knott and O'Grady took 'mac Marcuis' to be a patronymic rather than a family name and they both concluded that the poet was a Mág Craith. Walsh identified him as a member of the Ó Gnímh family of Antrim. O'Rahilly, 'Irish poets', p. 105; Leerssen, *Mere Irish*, n. 48, p. 398.

80. Ó Raghallaigh, *Duanta*, no. 14, quatrain 8, pp. 206–21; Ní Ógáin, *Duanaire*, iii, no. 3, pp. 14–15; Ó Buachalla, 'Na Stíobhartaigh', p. 90; Leerssen, *Mere Irish*, pp. 191–2; Ó Dúshláine, 'Ionmholta', pp. 43–4. In the O'Gara manuscript (Dublin, Royal Irish Academy, MS. 23. F. 16, p. 49i) and in London, British Library, MS. Egerton III 'Frith an uainsi ar Inis Fáil' is ascribed to Eochaidh Ó hEódhusa.

81. O'Rahilly, *Measgra*, ii, no. 54, lines 85–8, pp. 144–7; Ó Caithnia, *Apalóga*, pp. 168–9.

82. Ó Raghallaigh, *Duanta*, no. 16, quatrain 11, pp. 242–51. Quatrain eleven of Eoghan Ruadh Mac an Bhaird's (?) 'Anocht is uaigneach Éire' also appears as quatrain nineteen of Lochlainn Ó Dálaigh's 'Cáit ar ghabhadar Gaoidhil?'. It is unlikely that either poet borrowed from each other's work. Given that the earliest manuscript copies of 'Cáit ar ghabhadar Gaoidhil?' ('Book of O'Conor Don', fo412a; Dublin, Royal Irish Academy, MS. 23. F. 16, p. 26) are of anonymous authorship, this parallel suggests that the poem's ascription to Ó Dálaigh must be taken as tentative. Moreover, Breandán Ó Buachalla's suggestion that there may have been a workshop producing poems with a national slant and ascribing them to prominent bardic poets is worth bearing in mind in this case of duplication. Another example of such repetition occurs between quatrain eight of Mac an Bhaird's 'Fríth an uainse ar Inis Fáil' and quatrain twelve of his

'Anocht is uaigneach Éire'. Gillies, 'A poem on the downfall', p. 208, quatrain 19; Ó Buachalla, 'Na Stíobhartaigh', p. 120.

83. Ní Ógáin, *Duanaire*, iii, no. 3, quatrain 11, pp. 14–15, p. 97 (I have emended O'Grady's translation as reproduced by Ní Ógáin.)

84. Ó Cuív (ed.), 'A poem on the Í Néill', quatrains 21, 23, pp. 245–51; Ó Caithnia, *Apalóga*, pp. 204–5; Cunningham and Gillespie, 'East Ulster bardic family', p. 107; Bergin (ed.), *Trí bior-ghaoithe*, p. 168.

85. Gillies, 'A poem on the downfall', quatrain 26, p. 209.

86. Knott (ed.), 'Mac an Bhaird's elegy', quatrains 33, 38, pp. 161–71 (I have modernised the language of Knott's translation); Ní Ógáin, *Duanaire,* iii, no. 52, pp. 88–92; Ó Raghallaigh, *Duanta,* no. 11, pp. 136–51; O'Rahilly (ed.), *Five seventeenth-century political poems*, p. 13; Ó Tuama, 'Téamaí iasachta', p. 202; Hale, 'Sixteenth-century explanations'.

87. Caball, 'Providence and exile'; Worden, 'Providence and politics'; Thomas, *Religion*, pp. 90–132. Regarding the Gaelic apocryphal tradition see McNamara, *The apocrypha.*

88. Walsh, *Beatha*, ii, quatrains 17–18, pp. 142–3.

89. Quatrain twenty in 'Anocht is uaigneach Éire', with its reference to the Tower of Nimrod, also appears (as do quatrains 6, 8–18) in Mac an Bhaird's 'Fríth an uainsi ar Inis Fáil' (quatrain 15). While the allusion is obscure, it may concern the pride of Holofernes and his downfall at the hands of Judith. Ó Caithnia, *Apalóga*, p. 138; Macalister (ed.), *Lebor gabála*, i, quatrain 51, p. 192.

90. Gillies, 'A poem on the downfall', quatrains 21–22, p. 208.

91. O'Rahilly, *Measgra*, ii, lines 65–6, p. 146.

92. Ó Raghallaigh, *Duanta*, no. 14, quatrain 23, pp. 216–17, quatrain 23, p. 374.

93. Walsh, *Beatha*, ii, quatrain 28, p. 146.

94. Ibid., ii, quatrain 26, p. 144.

95. O'Rahilly, *Measgra*, ii, line 79, p. 147.

96. O'Rahilly, 'Irish poets'.

97. Ó Raghallaigh, *Duanta*, p. 49, p. 53; de Brún et al., *Nua-dhuanaire*, i, p. 182.

98. Davies, *Historical tracts*, pp. 217–71; Morley (ed.), *Ireland*, pp. 364–6. Regarding the date of Davies's northern tour see Hayes-McCoy, 'Sir John Davies in Cavan', n. 24, p. 181.

99. Morley, *Ireland*, pp. 368–9; Kenney, *Sources*, i, pp. 32–4.

100. 'Original letter from Sir John Davys', p. 195.

101. Leslie, *Derry clergy*, p. 102, p. 110, p. 117, p. 177, p. 219, pp. 247–8.

102. *Cal. pat. rolls Ire., Jas I*, p. 32; Ua Duinnín (ed.), *Me Guidhir Fhearmanach*, p. 105.

103. O'Rahilly, 'Irish poets', p. 95; Moody (ed.), 'Ulster plantation papers', p. 207; *Cal. Carew MSS 1603–24*, p. 240; *Cal. pat. rolls Ire., Jas I*, p. 34, p. 185; *Inquisitionum*, ii, p. xxxii; Hill, *An historical account*, p. 179, p. 333; Flower, *Catalogue*, ii, p. 353; Bruford, *Gaelic folktales*, p. 52, n. 8; Breathnach (ed.), 'Dánta Bhriain Í Chorcráin', pp. 35–50.

104. *Cal. pat. rolls Ire., Jas I*, p. 91; *Cal. Carew MSS 1603–24*, pp. 239–40; *Cal. S.P. Ire., 1611–14*, p. 210; Moody, 'Ulster plantation papers', p. 206; Hill, *An historical account*, p. 333.

Faith and Fatherland: 1612–1625

1. Davies, *Discovery*, p. 286.
2. Carney (ed.), *O'Reillys*, no. XXV, quatrain 2, pp. 121–7; Carney, *Studies*, p. 264; Carney, *The Irish bardic poet*, pp. 35–7; Flower, *Catalogue*, ii, p. 166.
3. Carney, *O'Reillys*, quatrains 7, 13, 25, 26, pp. 122–5; Ó Caithnia, *Apalóga*, p. 126.
4. Falls, 'Black Tom', pp. 10–22; Brady, 'Thomas Butler', pp. 49–59.
5. Regarding the *caithréim* device in prose and poetry see O'Sullivan and Ó Riain (eds.), *Poems on marcher lords*, pp. xxv-xxvi; Mac Airt (ed.), *Leabhar Branach*, no. 18, pp. 61–73; Nic Ghiollamhaith, 'Dynastic warfare', pp. 73–89.
6. Carney (ed.), *Butlers*, no. XV, quatrains 6, 8, 30, 46, pp. 67–73. For an earlier poem ('Taghaim Tómás ragha is róghrádh') on the earl of Ormond (ob. 1614) see no. XVI in the above collection. Mac Erlean credited Flann Mac Craith with the authorship of 'I n-ainm an áirdmhic doghnídh grása', a eulogy to Elizabeth supposedly composed *c.* 1589. Carney has demonstrated the unreliability of this ascription, unfortunately, his caveat has been neglected in Leerssen's discussion of the poem. Mac Erlean (ed.), *Duanaire Dháibhidh*, iii, no. XII, pp. 64–75; Murphy, 'Royalist Ireland', p. 593; Carney, *Butlers*, pp. 136–7; O Riordan, *Gaelic mind*, pp. 140–151; Leerssen, *Mere Irish*, p. 223.
7. Carney, *Butlers*, quatrains 41, 43, 44, p. 73.
8. Dublin, Royal Irish Academy, MS. F. V. 5 (p. 289), written by Henrí Mac an tSaoir in Dublin in 1787; Carney, *Butlers*, p. xv.
9. O'Grady, *Catalogue*, i, p. 380; O'Rahilly, *Catalogue*, i, p. 15. For a critical edition of 'Iomdha éagnach ag Éirinn' see McKenna (ed.), *Aonghus Fionn*, no. LIII, pp. 73–5. Cf. Ó Buachalla, 'Na Stíobhartaigh', p. 112.
10. Ó Donnchadha (ed.), *Leabhar cloinne*, no. XXIII, lines 105–116, pp. 166–71; Cunningham and Gillespie, 'East Ulster bardic family', p. 113; Gillespie, *Colonial Ulster*, p. 151.
11. Ó Donnchadha, *Leabhar cloinne*, lines 129–32, p. 170.
12. Ibid., lines 141–56, p. 171. In 1601 Sir Francis Stafford considered the natives of Ulster 'perfidious, ungrateful and apt to wind with every innovation'. Gillespie, *Colonial Ulster*, p. 108; *Cal. S.P. Ire., 1601–3*, p. 118.
13. Ó Donnchadha, *Leabhar cloinne*, pp. xxvi-xxvii.
14. Ibid., lines 9–28, pp. 203–4.
15. Ibid., line 41, lines 57–60, 63–4, 66–8, pp. 204–5.
16. Ibid., lines 89–92, p. 206.
17. Ibid., lines 73–6, p. 205.
18. Ibid., no. XXXIII, lines 6–7, 15–16, pp. 215–17. Bloomfield and Dunn, *The role of the poet*, pp. 26–8.
19. Other poems dedicated to Martha Stafford include no. XXXI ('A Lámh dar bhean an béim súl') and no. XXXII ('Mór loitios lot na láimhe') and appendages in her honour are found in nos. XXII, XXIII, XXIV, XXV, XXVI, XXVII, XXVIII, XXIX in Ó Donnchadha, *Leabhar cloinne*.
20. For Tadhg (mac Diarmada Óig?) Ó Dálaigh see O'Grady, *Catalogue*, i, pp. 445–6; O'Donovan (ed.), *Miscellany of the Celtic Society*, pp. 340–51; O'Rahilly, *Catalogue*, i, p. 18.
21. Hayes-McCoy in Moody et al., *A new history*, iii, pp. 128–30.

22. O'Sullivan, 'Tadhg O'Daly', pp. 28–9; Hayes-McCoy in Moody et al., *A new history*, iii, p. 89; O Riordan, *Gaelic mind*, pp. 203–214; O'Curry, *Lectures*, p. 635.
23. O'Sullivan, 'Tadhg O'Daly', quatrains 2, 4, 5, 7, 8, 20, pp. 33–5, p. 37.
24. Ibid., quatrains 11, 13, 15, pp. 34–5.
25. Ibid., quatrains 18, 25, pp. 35–6. Ó Dálaigh's use of 'Gabh mo gherán, a Sheóirse' as a means of highlighting personal tenurial difficulties corresponds to an earlier series of three poems composed by Eochaidh Ó hEódhusa in which he recounts to Hugh Maguire his dissatisfaction with the lands the latter had assigned him. Ó hEódhusa also claims that his position as *ollamh* was not receiving the respect it merited. Carney, *The Irish bardic poet*, pp. 22–6; Bergin (ed.), *Irish bardic poetry*, no. 33, pp. 136–8.
26. O'Sullivan, 'Tadhg O'Daly', quatrains 24, 25, 26, pp. 36–8.
27. Ibid., quatrain 27, pp. 36, 38.
28. Ibid., quatrain 28, p. 36.
29. Carew, for instance, owned copies of Uilliam Ó Domhnuill's Gaelic translations of the New Testament (1602–3) and the *Book of Common Prayer* (1608). He appears to have had an antiquarian interest in Ireland's history and he acquired several manuscripts of Irish origin. Two of his manuscripts in particular (Oxford, Bodleian Library, Laud misc. 610 and Laud misc. 615) contain material in Irish. James, 'The Carew manuscripts', pp. 261–3; O'Sullivan, 'Ussher as a collector of manuscripts', pp. 40–2; Dillon, 'Laud misc. 610', pp. 67–8; Ní Shéaghdha, 'Collectors of Irish manuscripts', pp. 2–3; Ó Cuív, 'Some Irish items', pp. 139–41; de Brún, *Lámhscríbhinní*, p. 23, p. 30.
30. 'Gabh mo gherán, a Sheóirse' is extant in London, Lambeth Palace Library, MS. 605 (fo239). On it Carew has written 'A rhyme in Irish touching the Lord Carew 1618'. O'Sullivan, 'Tadhg O'Daly', p. 27; de Brún, *Lámhscríbhinní*, p. 23; Stafford (ed.), *Pacata Hibernia*, pp. 293–4; O'Grady (ed.), *Pacata Hibernia*, ii, p. 159, p. 161; Dudley Edwards and O'Dowd, *Sources*, pp. 104–5.
31. Ó Cuív (ed.), 'The earl of Thomond', p. 127; Carney, *Butlers*, pp. 131–2; Ellis, *Tudor Ireland*, p. 262.
32. Tadhg Dall Ó hUiginn composed 'Aoibhinn an lása i Lonnainn' to celebrate the presence in London of five young Gaelic aristocrats, one of whom included Donnchadh O'Brien. Knott (ed.), *The bardic poems*, i, no. 36, pp. 257–9; McGrath, 'Materials', p. 62.
33. In fiants from the years 1586 and 1602 Mac Bruaideadha is described as a resident of Knockanalbie (*Cnoc an Albannaigh*) in Kilmurry parish, west Clare. Father Anthony Brody (*fl.* 1672), who wrote about the Mac Bruaideadha family in the seventeenth century, says that Donnchadh O'Brien was fostered by Tadhg Mac Bruaideadha's sister Phinola (Fionnuala?). Brody also claimed that Mac Bruaidheadha had accompanied the young Donnchadh during his stay in England in the 1570s and it seems that previously he had been O'Brien's tutor. Apparently thanks to O'Brien's influence, he was appointed a district sheriff in Clare sometime after their return home. Mac Bruaideadha is best remembered as a contributor to *Iomarbhágh na bhfileadh* (1616–24). He was on the continent by 1625. McKenna (ed.), *Aithdioghluim*, i, p. xxx; O'Grady, *Catalogue*, i, pp. 388–92; McGrath, 'Materials', pp. 61–3, p. 65; Gwynn, 'An unpublished work', p. 11; Kelly (ed.), *Audacht Morainn*, p. xiv; Ó Cuív, 'A fragment', p. 83; Leerssen, *Mere Irish*, n. 59, pp. 398–9; Ó Dúshláine, *An Eoraip*, p. 121, p. 174. Regarding

Anthony Brody (alias Bruodin) see Millett in Moody et al., *A new history*, iii, p. 580.

34. The earliest copy of 'Eascar Gaoidheal éag aoinfhir' is in the O'Gara manuscript (*c.* 1655–9) (Dublin, Royal Irish Academy, MS. 23. F. 16, p. 32).

35. Ó Cuív (ed.), 'An elegy', quatrains 1, 3, p. 91; O'Grady, *Catalogue*, i, pp. 389–90. The notion of a nobleman's death spelling disaster for Ireland is also found in the poem entitled 'Bean do lámhaigeadh leith Cuinn'. This is an elegy for Niall Garbh O'Donnell, who died in a London prison in 1625. Its author may have been Tuileagna Ó Maolchonaire. Walsh (ed.), *Gleanings*, pp. 27–52. For Ó Maolchonaire see Walsh, *The O'Neills in Spain*, pp. 30–1; Mac Aogáin (ed.), *Graiméir*, pp. xi–xii; Leerssen, *Mere Irish*, p. 261.

36. Ó Cuív, 'An elegy', quatrain 4, p. 91.

37. Ibid., quatrains 12, 13, 18, pp. 93–4.

38. McKenna (ed.), *Iomarbhágh*, ii, no. XVIII, quatrains 55–6, p. 184.

39. Ó Cuív, 'An elegy', quatrains 34, 53, 54, p. 97, p. 101. Regarding the theme of a grieving poet seeking to join his patron in death see Simms, 'The poet as chieftain's widow', pp. 404–5.

40. Ó Cuív, 'An elegy', quatrain 59, p. 102.

41. Ibid., quatrains 4, 17, p. 91, p. 94.

42. Gillespie, *Colonial Ulster*, pp. 87–9; Cunningham and Gillespie, 'East Ulster bardic family', pp. 108–9, p. 113.

43. Mac Cionnaith (ed.), *Dioghluim*, no. 89, pp. 290–3; Cunningham and Gillespie, 'East Ulster bardic family', n. 14, p. 109.

44. Knott (ed.), *The bardic poems*, ii, p. 231; Ó Cuív, 'Some Irish items', p. 149.

45. Mac Cionnaith, *Dioghluim*, quatrains 5, 6, 22, pp. 290–2.

46. Gillespie, *Colonial Ulster*, p. 85; Ó Cuív, 'Some Irish items', pp. 140–1.

47. Regarding Ussher and Gaelic culture see Leerssen, 'Archbishop Ussher and Gaelic culture', pp. 50–8; Ní Shéaghdha, 'Collectors of Irish manuscripts', pp. 5–6. Cf. Trevor-Roper, 'James Ussher'. Fynes Moryson declared that Irish 'would never be missed either for pleasure or necessity'. Litton Falkiner (ed.), *Illustrations*, p. 317.

48. Canny, *The upstart earl*, pp. 126–8; Grosart (ed.), *The Lismore papers*, (2nd series), i, pp. 39–40.

49. Canny, *The upstart earl*, p. 126; *The present state of Ireland*, p. 122; Barnard, 'Crises of identity', p. 70.

50. Grosart, *The Lismore papers*, (2nd series), ii, pp. 201–2; Abbott, 'On the history of the Irish bible', p. 31; Barnard, *Cromwellian Ireland*, pp. 177–8; Bottigheimer, 'The failure of the reformation in Ireland'; Ford, *The protestant reformation*; Ford, 'The protestant reformation in Ireland'; Ellis, 'Economic problems of the church'; Salmon, 'Missionary linguistics'; Morgan, 'Writing up early modern Ireland', p. 708; Williams, *I bprionta*.

51. Mac Cuarta, 'Newcomers', pp. 19–23, p. 28; Loeber, 'Civilization through plantation'; Mac Cuarta, 'Conchubhar Mac Bruaideadha'.

52. Mac Cuarta, 'Newcomers', p. 74.

53. Ibid., p. 76; Ó Maonaigh, 'Scríbhneoirí', p. 193; English, 'The Sir Mathew De Renzi memorial in Athlone'; Mac Cuarta, 'A planter's interaction with Gaelic culture'.

54. Mac Cuarta, 'Newcomers', p. 37, p. 41, p. 171.

55.   Ibid., pp. 53–5; Mac Cuarta (ed.), 'Mathew De Renzy's letters', p. 120.
56.   Mac Cuarta, 'Mathew De Renzy's letters', p. 125.
57.   Bradshaw, 'The Elizabethans and the Irish', pp. 239–40. For the anglicisation of the Gaelic élite see Clarke, 'Ireland and the general crisis', pp. 81–4.
58.   Evidence for the date of Mac Giolla Phádraig's ordination is extant in a colophon in a medical manuscript mainly written in upper Ossory between 1596 and 1610 (Dublin, Royal Irish Academy, MS. 23. N. 16, fo102v): 'Dar nail is ama-rach aderaidh Brian mac Toirrdhealbhaidh a ced-aithfrinn . . . an 10 la do Iunius 1610'. The Tinnakill MacDonnell poem-book is now Dublin, Trinity College, MS. H. 3. 19. Mac Giolla Phádraig entered his poem on the recto of fo30 (p. 57) and gave an old style date (11 January, 1614). Abbott and Gwynn, Catalogue, p. 164; O'Grady, Catalogue, i, p. 653; O'Sullivan, 'The Tinnakill dua-naire', p. 214, pp. 216–17.
59.   Mac Airt (ed.), Leabhar Branach, p. xiv; O'Sullivan, 'The Tinnakill duanaire', pp. 216–17.
60.   Mhág Craith, Dán na mbráthar, i, no. 6, pp. 28–31.
61.   Bradshaw, 'The Elizabethans and the Irish', p. 241; Mac Craith, 'Gaelic Ireland and the renaissance', p. 68. The evidence of Gaelic exile poems composed in the late sixteenth and early seventeenth centuries, testifying to an unambiguous articulation of Ireland's territorial integrity, contradicts Oliver MacDonagh's claim that modern Irish nationalism originally acquired the concept of Ireland's territorial sovereignty from the thought of eighteenth-century Anglo-Irish patri-ots: MacDonagh, States of mind, p. 18. For the early modern concept of patria see Elliott, 'Revolution and continuity', pp. 47–50.
62.   Mhág Craith (ed.), 'Brian Mac Giolla Phádraig', no. VII, quatrains 3, 4, p. 115.
63.   Ibid., quatrains 13–14, p. 117.
64.   Ibid., quatrains 16–29, pp. 117–18.
65.   Ibid., quatrain 30, p. 119.
66.   Ibid., quatrain 32, p. 119; no. VIII, pp. 120–78; O'Sullivan, 'The Tinnakill dua-naire', p. 216.
67.   Mhág Craith, 'Brian Mac Giolla Phádraig', quatrains 32–5, p. 119.
68.   Mac Craith, 'Gaelic Ireland and the renaissance', p. 68; Iske, The green cockatrice, pp. 30–2.
69.   Murphy (ed.), 'Poems of exile', quatrain 7, p. 15; de Brún et al. (eds.), Nua-dhuanaire, i, no. 14, p. 17.
70.   For the authorship and manuscript copies of 'Och! mo chreach-sa fasion Chláir Éibhir!' see de Brún et al., Nua-dhuanaire, i, p. 97; Mhág Craith, 'Brian Mac Giolla Phádraig', no. II, p. 106; Leerssen, Mere Irish, pp. 203–4.
71.   Carrigan, The history and antiquities of the diocese of Ossory, i, pp. 113–14.
72.   McGrath, 'Materials', p. 49. Flaithrí Ó Maolchonaire was similarly scathing in his assessment of this famous debate: 'Lughaidh, Tadhg agus Torna, ollaimh oir-rdheirce ar dtalaimh, coin iad go n-iomad feasa, ag troid fa an easair fhalaimh!'. Mhág Craith, Dán na mbráthar, i, no. 26, p. 126; Ó Cuív in Moody et al., A new history, iii, p. 539. More generally see Dooley, 'Literature and society'; Leerssen, Contention.
73.   McKenna (ed.), Iomarbhágh na bhfileadh, i, no. XI, quatrains 10–14, pp. 114–17.
74.   Ní Ógain (ed.), Duanaire, iii, no. 4, pp. 16–17; Bergin, Irish bardic poetry, no. 37, pp. 145–6.

75. The earliest extant copy of 'San Sbáinn do toirneadh Teamhair' is in the O'Gara manuscript (Dublin, Royal Irish Academy, MS. 23. F. 16, p. 160). Breatnach (ed.), 'Elegy on Donal O'Sullivan Beare'; O'Grady, Catalogue, i, p. 362; D.N.B., art. Donall O'Sullivan Beare.

76. Breatnach, 'Elegy on Donal O'Sullivan Beare', quatrains viii, ix, xxix, p. 168, p. 174.

77. Ibid., quatrains xviii-xix, p. 170; Breatnach (ed.), 'Donal O'Sullivan Beare to king Philip III', pp. 314–15.

78. Breatnach, 'Elegy on Donal O'Sullivan Beare', quatrain xxxi, pp. 174–5.

79. Ibid., quatrains xxxii-xxxiii, pp. 174–5.

80. Ibid., quatrains xxxv, xxxvii, pp. 174–6.

81. Ibid., quatrain xviii, p. 170.

82. Ibid., quatrain xxx, pp. 174–5. I have replaced the editor's 'Gaels' with Gaoidhil in his translation.

83. Ibid., quatrain xl, p. 176.

84. In the early seventeenth century, Protestant clerics identified their New English flock with the Israelites, a chosen people surrounded by Irish Catholic heathens. In the same vein, many Irish Protestants sought to account for the 1641 rebellion by attributing its cause to divine retribution for communal moral degeneracy. Caball, 'Providence and exile'; Mac Cuarta, 'Newcomers in the Irish midlands', p. 56; Ford, 'The Protestant reformation in Ireland', pp. 69–70; Barnard, 'Crises of identity', p. 53; Morgan, 'Writing up early modern Ireland', p. 708; Elliott, Watchmen in Sion, p. 8. For examples of continued Gaelic use of these motifs in the eighteenth century see Ó Maonaigh (ed.), Seanmónta, p. 37, p. 102.

85. Breatnach, 'Donal O'Sullivan Beare to king Phillip III', pp. 318–23.

86. O'Rahilly, 'Irish poets', p. 103; McKenna, Iomarbhágh, i, p. xii; Flower, Catalogue, i, p. 13. The earliest extant copy of 'Soraidh slán ler saoithibh saoidheachta' appears to be in Dublin, Royal Irish Academy, MS. 23. M. 29 (p. 328), written in west Munster between 1684 and 1707 by Eoghan Ó Caoimh. O'Rahilly, Catalogue, i, p. 63.

87. Ní Dhomhnaill (ed.), Duanaireacht, no. 20, quatrains 11–13, pp. 115–16.

88. Ó hEódhasa, An teagasg críosdaidhe, edited by Mac Raghnaill.

89. Ó Cuív, 'Flaithrí Ó Maolchonaire's catechism'; O'Rahilly (ed.), Desiderius; Ó Cléirigh, Aodh Mac Aingil, pp. 34–40; Kearney, 'Ecclesiastical politics', p. 204; Ó Fiaich, 'Republicanism'; Ó Buachalla, 'Na Stíobhartaigh', pp. 97–101.

90. Mac Aingil, Scáthán, edited by Ó Maonaigh; Ó Cléirigh, Aodh Mac Aingil, pp. 41–89; Ó Dúshláine, An Eoraip, pp. 82–115; Cregan, 'Social and cultural background', p. 93, p. 106, p. 109; Giblin, 'Hugh McCaghwell'; Mac Giolla Chomhaill, Bráithrín bocht.

91. Walsh (ed.), Gleanings, pp. 96–107; Mhág Craith, Dán na mbráthar, i, nos. 30–6. For a linguistic aspect of the influence of counter-reformation ideology on continental Irish clerics see Cunningham and Gillespie, "Persecution".

92. Canny, 'The formation of the Irish mind', pp. 94–5.

93. Mac Aingil, Scáthán, pp. 4–5, p. 171; Williams, 'A note', p. 436. When Roibeard Mhac Artúir (ob. 1636) entered the Franciscan order in Louvain in 1610, he directed that his wealth be used for the provision of a Gaelic typeface, which he hoped would contribute to the glory of God and raise the profile of the Irish

'nation' and that of the Franciscans: 'Fágaim an mhéid atá agam ar an rígh (namely, of Spain) re h-aghaidh an Clódh-Gaoidhilge agus neithe do chur i ccló do rachas an onóir do Dia, a cclú dár násion agus d'Órd San Froinsias'. Ó Lochlainn (ed.), *Tobar,* p. 97.

94.   O'Rahilly, *Desiderius,* p. 2.

95.   Mac Aingil, *Scáthán,* p. 5.

96.   Ó hEódhasa, *An teagasg críosdaidhe,* p. 2; Canny, 'The formation of the Irish mind', pp. 94–8; Mac Craith, 'Gaelic Ireland and the renaissance', pp. 74–6. For an early eschewal of the bardic idiom in favour of a more general style see John Carswell (ob. 1572) in the introduction to his Gaelic translation of the *Book of Common Order* in 1567. Thomson (ed.), *Foirm,* pp. 11–12.

97.   Mac Raghnaill, *An teagasg críosdaidhe,* p. xi; Ó Maonaigh, *Scáthán,* p. xi. For a list of contraband Roman Catholic devotional books and images seized aboard a French ship off the Cork coast in 1617 see Grosart, *The Lismore papers,* (2nd series), ii, pp. 116–17. Cf. Pollard, *Dublin's trade in books,* pp. 33–4. Regarding the oral reception of printed material see Robert Darnton's characteristically succinct commentary: '. . . for the common people in early modern Europe, reading was a social activity. It took place in workshops, barns, and taverns . . . for most people throughout most of history, books had audiences rather than readers. They were better heard than seen'. Darnton, 'History of reading', p. 150.

98.   Céitinn, *Eochair sgiath an aifrinn,* edited by O'Brien; Cronin, 'Sources'; Ó Dúshláine, 'More about Keating's use of the simile of the dung-beetle'; Cunningham, 'Geoffrey Keating's Eochair sgiath an aifrinn'.

99.   Mhág Craith, *Dán na mbráthar,* i, nos. 27, 28; Bradshaw, 'The reformation in the cities', p. 471.

100.   Black, 'The genius of Cathal MacMhuirich', pp. 332–3.

101.   When the compiler of the *Leabhar Muimhneach* recorded the pedigree of the anglicised James Butler (ob. 1688), first duke of Ormond, he ruefully noted Butler's indifference to the subject in hand: 'Agus triallfad anois go Buitléarachaibh; agus ní móide cion an Diúic so ann anois orm bheith 'na chúram'. Carney, *Butlers,* p. xiii.

102.   Morgan, 'Writing up early modern Ireland', pp. 705–6.

103.   Ní Dhomhnaill, *Duanaireacht,* quatrain 3, p. 115.

104.   Regarding the date and authorship of 'Cuimseach sin, a Fhearghail Óig' see Cunningham and Gillespie, 'East Ulster bardic family', p. 111; Ó hÓgáin, *An file,* pp. 108–10; Bergin, *Irish bardic poetry,* no. 27, quatrains 1–2, pp. 118–19.

105.   Ó Donnchadha, *Leabhar cloinne,* no. XXVII, lines 73–6, pp. 190–3; Cunningham and Gillespie, 'East Ulster bardic family', p. 112; Gillespie, *Colonial Ulster,* p. 151.

106.   'Sona do cheird, a Chalbhaigh' is found in MacMhuirich's autograph in Dublin, Royal Irish Academy, MS. A. V. 2, fo75B, which is of Irish provenance. An allusion to 'earl' in stanza ten may refer to Raghnall MacDonnell (ob. 1634), created first earl of Antrim in 1620. Coming after his own poem MacMhuirich has copied in two other pieces concerning bardic difficulties ('Mór do-níd daoine díobh féin' and 'A mhic, ná meabhraigh éigse', fos76A-77B). Greene (ed.), 'A satire by Cathal Mac Muireadhaigh'; Thomson, 'Three seventeenth century bardic poets', p. 233, p. 237; Black, 'The genius of Cathal MacMhuirich', p. 337, p. 360; Thomson (ed.), *The companion to Gaelic Scotland,* pp. 185–6.

107. Greene, 'A satire by Cathal Mac Muireadhaigh', quatrains 1–2, p. 52.
108. Ibid., quatrains 14–15, p. 54.
109. The latest certain date in Mac an Bhaird's life is 1618 when Hugh Óg O'Donnell died and was elegised by Mac an Bhaird. Two of his three Louvain poems are addressed to Flaithrí Ó Maolchonaire, who probably left Spain in 1615–6 to travel to Louvain to oversee the publication of his *Sgáthán an chrábhaidh* (1616). On this basis, these poems may be tentatively assigned to the period 1616–18. Cuthbert Mhág Craith has suggested that a fourth poem entitled 'Th'aire, a chumthaigh, réd chomhrádh!' was also addressed by Mac an Bhaird to Ó Maolchonaire. Ó Concheanainn, 'A feature', n. 20, pp. 239–40; O'Rahilly, *Desiderius*, p. xii; Mhág Craith, *Dán na mbráthar*, ii, p. 156.
110. Mhág Craith, *Dán na mbráthar*, i, no. 23, quatrains 3, 5, pp. 117–121; no. 24, quatrain 6, pp. 121–4; Mac Cionnaith, *Dioghluim*, no. 46, quatrains 28, 29, pp. 139–44. All three of Mac an Bhaird's Louvain poems are recorded in the 'Book of O'Conor Don'.
111. Mhág Craith, *Dán na mbráthar*, i, quatrains 1, 5, 7, pp. 121–2.
112. Mac Erlean, *Duanaire Dháibhidh*, iii, no. II, quatrain 1, pp. 4–5; de Brún et al., *Nua-dhuanaire*, i, no. 42, p. 55.
113. Campbell, 'Edward Lhuyd in Ireland', p. 221; O'Sullivan and O'Sullivan, 'Edward Lhuyd's collection of Irish manuscripts', pp. 61–2; Campbell and Thomson, *Edward Lhuyd*, p. xvi.

The Bardic Corpus and National Identity

1. Mac Craith, 'Gaelic Ireland and the renaissance', p. 61.
2. Bardic poetry continued to be composed informally throughout the seventeenth century, although on a greatly reduced scale and in social and political circumstances quite different from those of the classical phase of bardic activity: see for example Hughes, 'The seventeenth-century Ulster/Scottish contention'. Regarding Feiritéar's landed status see Grosart, *The Lismore papers*, (1st series), ii, p. 46; Ua Duinnín (ed.), *Dánta Phiarais Feiritéir*, p. 12. The emergent poets were neither exclusively upper class in origin nor male in gender. For an apparently lower class poet see Ó Ciardha (ed.), 'The lament for Eoghan Mac Criostail'. The elusive Caitlín Dubh is known for her extant elegies on the earl of Thomond (ob. 1624) among others. See Ó Fiannachta, *Lámhscríbhinní*, iv, p. 26.
3. Ua Brádaigh (ed.), 'Dhá dhán le Tomás Déis'; Brockliss and Ferté, 'Irish clerics in France', p. 569; Ua Brádaigh, 'Na Nuinnsionnaigh', pp. 219–21; Ó Cuív, 'Bunús mhuintir Dhíolún'; Simms, 'Bards and barons', p. 194.
4. Ní Cheallacháin (ed.), *Filíocht Phádraigín Haicéad*, no. XXXIX, lines 29–32, p. 46. Cf. Canny, 'Pádraigín Haicéad'; Hartnett (trans.), *Haicéad*.
5. Mac Giolla Eáin (ed.), *Dánta amhráin is caointe Sheathrúin Céitinn*, no. XIV, quatrain viii, p. 63. More generally regarding Céitinn's political outlook see Bradshaw, 'Geoffrey Keating: apologist of Irish Ireland'.
6. O'Rahilly (ed.), *Five seventeenth-century political poems*, no. IV, line 382, p. 76.
7. Lennon, *Richard Stanihurst*.
8. O'Rahilly, *Five seventeenth-century political poems*, no. III, lines 186–7, pp. 39–49.

9.   De Brún et al. (eds.), *Nua-dhuanaire,* i, no. 26, line 104, p. 33.

10.   James Ussher sought to 'nativise' the Church of Ireland by tracing its historical and theological pedigree to the early Irish church: Ford, 'Standing one's ground', pp. 2–3. For the contrasting successful inculturation of Protestantism in other Celtic territories see respectively Roberts, 'The union with England and the identity of 'Anglican' Wales' and Dawson, 'Calvinism and the Gaidhealtachd'.

11.   Teabóid Gallduf/Theobald Stapleton, *Catechismus,* 'Oraid don leaghthoir', section 31.

12.   Gallduf's *Catechismus* is also remarkable for being the first Gaelic book printed in Roman typeface. *D.N.B.,* art. T. Stapleton.

13.   Ó Cuív (ed.), 'Mo thruaighe mar tá Éire', quatrain 10, p. 304.

14.   O'Rahilly, *Five seventeenth-century political poems,* no. 1, line 149, p. 10; cf. Ní Cheallacháin, *Filíocht Phádraigín Haicéad,* no. XLI, line 5, p. 47; de Brún et al., *Nua-dhuanaire,* i, no. 26, lines 28, 44, 76, pp. 31–3.

15.   O'Rahilly, *Five seventeenth-century political poems,* no. IV, lines 439–40, 456, 487–8, pp. 79–81.

16.   Ní Cheallacháin, *Filíocht Phádraigín Haicéad,* no. XXXIX, lines 45–8, p. 46.

17.   De Brún et al., *Nua-dhuanaire,* i, no. 28, lines 45–6, p. 37.

18.   Ní Cheallacháin, *Filíocht Phádraigín Haicéad,* no. XXXVI, lines 65–6, 129ff, pp. 40–3.

19.   Ibid., no. XI, pp. 8–9.

20.   O'Rahilly, *Five seventeenth-century political poems,* no. II, lines 90–1, p. 21; Ibid., no. I, line 109, p. 8; no. IV, line 285ff, p. 72.

21.   De Brún et al., *Nua-dhuanaire,* i, no. 26 lines 62–3, p. 32. Cf. O'Rahilly, *Five seventeenth-century political poems,* no. I, line 9, p. 3. Regarding the topos of sacred espousal see Herbert, 'Goddess and king'.

22.   Dunne, 'The Gaelic response', p. 11.

BIBLIOGRAPHY

Primary Sources

Acts of the privy council in Ireland, 1556–1571 (Fifteenth report, Historical Manuscripts Commission, London, 1897).

Abbott, T.K., and E.J. Gwynn (eds.), *Catalogue of the Irish manuscripts in the library of Trinity College, Dublin* (Dublin, 1921).

Anon., *The present state of Ireland: together with some remarques upon the antient state thereof* (London, 1673).

Bergin, Osborn (ed.), *Trí bior-ghaoithe an bháis* (Dublin, 1931).

—— (ed.), 'Address to Sémas mac Aonghuis', *Scottish Gaelic Studies* IV, pt. 2 (1935), 136–47.

—— (ed.), *Irish bardic poetry*, edited by David Greene and Fergus Kelly (Dublin, 1970).

Black, Ronald (ed.), 'Poems by Maol Domhnaigh Ó Muirgheasáin', *Scottish Gaelic Studies* XII, pt. 2 (1976), 194–208.

Breathnach, Pól (ed.), 'Dánta Bhriain Í Chorcráin', *Irisleabhar Muighe Nuadhad* (1929), 35–50.

Breatnach, Pádraig A. (ed.), 'Marbhna Aodha Ruaidh Uí Dhomhnaill (+1602)', *Éigse* XV, pt. 1 (1973), 31–50.

—— (ed.), 'Metamorphosis 1603: dán le hEochaidh Ó hEódhasa', *Éigse* XVII (1977–8), 169–80.

—— (ed.), 'A poem of protest', *Celtica* XVII (1985), 91–100.

—— (ed.), 'An address to Aodh Ruadh Ó Domhnaill in captivity, 1590', *Irish Historical Studies* XXV, no. 98 (1986), 198–213.

—— (ed.), 'Cú Chonnacht Ó Dálaigh's poem before leaving Aodh Ruadh', in *Sages, saints and storytellers: Celtic studies in honour of Professor James Carney*, edited by Donnchadh Ó Corráin, Liam Breatnach and Kim McCone (Maynooth, 1989), 32–42.

—— (ed.), 'An appeal for a guarantor', *Celtica* XXI (1990), 28–37.

—— 'Eochaidh Ó hEódhusa (c.1560–1612)', *Éigse* XXVII (1993), 127–9.

Breatnach, R.B. (ed.), 'Donal O'Sullivan Beare to king Philip III, 20th February, 1602', *Éigse* VI (1948–52), 314–23.

—— (ed.), 'Elegy on Donal O'Sullivan Beare (+1618)', *Éigse* VII (1954), 162–81.

Breatnach, R.A., 'Trí fhadhb théaxúla', *Celtica* VI (1963), 256–8.

—— (ed.), 'Anarchy in west Munster', *Éigse* XXIII (1989), 57–66.

Calendar of state papers relating to Ireland, vols. I–XVI (London, 1860–80).

Calendar of the Carew manuscripts preserved in the archiepiscopal library at Lambeth, 6 vols. (London, 1867–73).

Calendar of the manuscripts of the most hon. the marquis of Salisbury pt. 3 (Historical Manuscripts Commission, London, 1889).

Calendar of state papers, foreign series, of the reign of Elizabeth, May–December 1582 (London, 1909).

Calendar of the patent and close rolls of chancery in Ireland, of the reigns of Henry VIII., Edward VI., Mary and Elizabeth, 2 vols. (Dublin, 1861–2).

'Calendar to fiants of the reign of Henry VIII . . .' [etc.] in *P.R.I. rep.D.K.* 7–22 (Dublin, 1875–90).

Carew, George, *Pacata Hibernia*, 2 vols., edited by Standish O'Grady (London, 1896).

Carney, James (ed.), *Poems on the Butlers of Ormond, Cahir and Dunboyne (A.D. 1400–1650)* (Dublin, 1945).

—— (ed.), *Poems on the O'Reillys* (Dublin, 1950).

Comyn, D. and P.S. Dinneen (eds.), *Foras feasa ar Éirinn le Seathrún Céitinn, D.D.*, 4 vols. (London, 1902, 1908, 1914).

Cronin, Anne, 'Sources of Keating's Forus feasa ar Éirinn: I the printed sources', *Éigse* IV (1943–4), 234–79.

Cuallacht Cholm Cille, *Mil na mbeach* (Maynooth, 1911).

Cunningham, Bernadette (ed.), 'A view of religious affiliation and practice in Thomond, 1591', *Archivium Hibernicum* XLVIII (1994), 13–24.

Davies, Sir John, *Discovery of the true causes why Ireland was never entirely subdued* (London, 1612) (reprint, Shannon, 1969).

—— 'A letter to the earl of Salisbury, on the state of Ireland, in 1607', *Historical tracts* (Dublin, 1787), 217–71.

—— 'Original letter from Sir John Davys giving an account of the inquisition on the forfeited lands in the county of Colerain, A.D. 1609', *The Ulster Journal of Archaeology* 4 (1856), 192–7.

De Brún, Pádraig, Myles Dillon and Canice Mooney (eds.), *Catalogue of Irish manuscripts in the Franciscan library, Killiney* (Dublin, 1969).

De Brún, Pádraig, Breandán Ó Buachalla and Tomás Ó Concheanainn (eds.), *Nua-dhuanaire*, 3 vols. (Dublin, 1971, 1976, 1978).

De Brún, Pádraig (ed.), 'Litir ó thor Londain', *Éigse* XXII (1987), 49–53.

—— (ed.), 'Dhá bhlogh de theagasc críostaí – ó ré Éilíse I (?)', *Celtica* XIX (1987), 55–8.

—— *Lámhscríbhinní Gaeilge: treoirliosta* (Dublin, 1988).

Dillon, Myles, 'Laud misc. 610', *Celtica* V (1960), 64–76.

English, N.W., 'The Sir Mathew De Renzi memorial in Athlone', *Old Athlone Society Journal* 2, no. 5 (1978), 1–2.

Falkiner, C. Litton, *Illustrations of Irish history and topography* (London, 1904).

Foster, Joseph, *Alumni Oxonienses: the members of the university of Oxford, 1500–1714*, 4 vols. (Oxford, 1891–2).

Fraser, J., P. Grosjean and J.G. O'Keeffe (eds.), *Irish texts* IV (London, 1934).

Freeman, A. Martin (ed.), *The compossicion booke of Conought* (Irish Manuscripts Commission, Dublin, 1936).

'Geinealaighe Fearmanach', *Analecta Hibernica* 3 (1931), 62–150.

Gilbert, John Thomas, *Facsimilies of national manuscripts of Ireland*, 4 vols. (Dublin, 1874–84).

Gillies, William (ed.), 'A poem on the downfall of the Gaoidhil', *Éigse* XIII (1969–70), 203–10.

Greene, David (ed.), 'A satire by Cathal Mac Muireadhaigh', in *Celtic Studies*, edited by David Greene and James Carney (London, 1968), 51–5.

—— (ed.), *Duanaire Mhéig Uidhir the poembook of Cú Chonnacht Mág Uidhir, lord of Fermanagh 1566–1589* (Dublin, 1972).

Grosart, Alexander B. (ed.), *The Lismore papers (first series)*, 5 vols. (London, 1886).

—— (ed.), *The Lismore papers (second series)*, 5 vols. (London, 1887–8).

Gwynn, Aubrey (ed.), 'An unpublished work of Philip O'Sullivan Beare', *Analecta Hibernica* 6 (1934), 1–11.

—— and R. Neville Hadcock, *Medieval religious houses in Ireland* (London, 1970).

Hardiman, James (ed.), 'Statute of Kilkenny', *Tracts relating to Ireland* II (Irish Archaeological Society, Dublin, 1843), 1–143.

—— (ed.), *Irish minstrelsy*, 2 vols. (London, 1831).

Harington, Henry (ed.), *Nugae antiquae*, 2 vols. (London, 1804).

Hartnett, Michael (trans.), *Haicéad* (Oldcastle, 1993).

Hayes-McCoy, G.A. (ed.), *Index to the compossicion booke of Conought, 1585* (Irish Manuscripts Commission, Dublin, 1942).

Hennessy, William M. (ed.), *The annals of Loch Cé*, 2 vols. (London, 1871).

Herbert, Sir William, *Croftus sive de Hibernia liber*, edited by W. E. Buckley (London, 1887).

—— *Croftus sive de Hibernia liber*, edited by Arthur Keaveney and John A. Madden (Irish Manuscripts Commission, Dublin, 1992).

Hogan, Edmund, *Onomasticon Goedelicum* (Dublin, 1910).

Hore, Herbert J. (ed.), 'Irish bardism in 1561', *The Ulster Journal of Archaeology* 6 (1858), 165–7, 202–12.

Hore, Herbert J. and James Graves (eds.), *The social state of the southern and eastern counties of Ireland in the sixteenth century* (Dublin, 1870).

Hyde, Douglas (ed.), *Abhráin diadha chúige Connacht*, 2 vols. (London/Dublin, 1906).

—— 'The book of the O'Conor Don', *Ériu* VIII (1916), 78–99.

Innes, Thomas, *A critical essay on the ancient inhabitants of the northern parts of Britain, or Scotland*, 2 vols. (London, 1729).

Inquisitionum in officio rotulorum cancellariae Hiberniae asservatum, repertorium II (Dublin, 1829).

James, M.R., 'The Carew manuscripts', *The English Historical Review* XLII (1927), 261–7.

Jennings, Brendan (ed.), *Wild geese in Spanish Flanders 1582–1700* (Irish Manuscripts Commission, Dublin, 1964).

Kelly, Fergus (ed.), *Audacht Morainn* (Dublin, 1976).

Kenney, James F. (ed.), *The sources for the early history of Ireland* I (New York, 1929).

Kew, Graham (ed.), *The Irish sections of Fynes Moryson's unpublished itinerary* (Irish Manuscripts Commission, Dublin, 1998).

Knott, Eleanor (ed.), 'A poem by Giolla Brighde Ó Heoghusa', *Gadelica* I (1912–3), 10–15.

—— (ed.), 'A poem by Giolla Brighde Ó Heoghusa', *Miscellany presented to Kuno Meyer*, edited by Osborn Bergin and Carl Marstrander (Halle, 1912), 241–5.

—— (ed.), 'The flight of the earls (1607)', *Ériu* VIII (1916), 191–4.

—— (ed.), *The bardic poems of Tadhg Dall Ó Huiginn (1550–1591)*, 2 vols. (London, 1922, 1926).

—— (ed.), *Irish syllabic poetry* (Dublin, 1957).

—— (ed.), 'Mac an Bhaird's elegy on the Ulster lords', *Celtica* V (1960), 161–71.

Leslie, Shane (ed.), *St Patrick's purgatory* (London, 1932).

Mac Aingil, Aodh, *Scáthán shacramuinte na haithridhe* (Louvain, 1618), edited by Cainneach Ó Maonaigh (Dublin, 1952).

Mac Airt, Seán (ed.), *Leabhar Branach* (Dublin, 1944).

Macalister, R.A.S. (ed.), *Lebor Gabála Érenn*, 5 vols. (Dublin, 1938–56).

Mac Aogáin, Parthalán (ed.), *Graiméir Ghaeilge na mbráthar mionúr* (Dublin, 1968).

MacCarthy, Daniel (ed.), *The life and letters of Florence MacCarthy Reagh* (London, 1867).

Mac Cionnaith, Láimhbheartach (ed.), *Dioghluim dána* (Dublin, 1938).

Mac Cuarta, Brian (ed.), 'Mathew De Renzy's letters on Irish affairs 1613–1620', *Analecta Hibernica* 34 (1987), 107–82.

—— (ed.), 'Conchubhar Mac Bruaideadha and Sir Matthew de Renzy (1577–1634)', *Éigse* XXVII (1993), 122–6.

Mac Erlean, J.C. (ed.), *Duanaire Dháibhidh Uí Bhruadair*, 3 vols. (London, 1910, 1913, 1917).

Mac Giolla Eáin, Eoin Cathmhaolach (ed.), *Dánta, amhráin is caointe Sheathrúin Céitinn* (Dublin, 1900).

McGrath, Cuthbert, 'Materials for a history of Clann Bhruaideadha', *Éigse* IV (1943–44), 48–66.

—— (ed.), 'Three poems by Bonabheantura Ó hEódhasa, O.F.M.', *Éigse* IV (1943–4), 175–96.

McKenna, Lambert (ed.), *Iomarbhágh na bhfileadh*, 2 vols. (London, 1918).

—— (ed.), *Dánta do chum Aonghus Fionn Ó Dálaigh* (Dublin, 1919).

—— (ed.), *Philip Bocht Ó Huiginn* (Dublin, 1931).

—— (ed.), *Aithdioghluim dána*, 2 vols. (Dublin, 1939–40).

—— (ed.), *Leabhar Méig Shamhradhain* (Dublin, 1947).

—— (ed.), *The Book of O'Hara Leabhar Í Eadhra* (Dublin, 1951).

—— (ed.), 'Some Irish bardic poems', *Studies* XLI (1952), 99–104.

MacKinnon, D. (ed.), *A descriptive catalogue of Gaelic manuscripts in the Advocates' library Edinburgh, and elsewhere in Scotland* (Edinburgh, 1912).

McNamara, Martin, *The apocrypha in the Irish church* (Dublin, 1975).

Mac Neill, Eoin and Gerard Murphy (eds.), *Duanaire Finn*, 3 vols. (London/Dublin, 1908–1953).

Mac Niocaill, Gearóid (ed.), 'Dhá dhán le Risteard Buitléir', *Éigse* IX (1958–61), 83–8.

—— (ed.), 'Duanaire Ghearóid iarla', *Studia Hibernica* 3 (1963), 7–59.

—— (ed.), *Crown surveys of lands 1540–41 with the Kildare rental begun in 1518* (Irish Manuscripts Commission, Dublin, 1992).

Manning, Conleth, 'Revealing a private inscription', *Archaeology Ireland* 8, no. 3 (1994), 24–6.

Meyer, Kuno (ed.), *Cáin Adamnáin* (Oxford, 1905).

—— 'A collection of poems on the O'Donnells', *Ériu* 4 (1910), 183–90.

—— 'Ein irischer Barde in Oxford', *Zeitschrift für Celtische Philologie* VIII (1912), 181.

Mhág Craith, Cuthbert (ed.), 'Brian Mac Giolla Phádraig', *Celtica* IV (1958), 103–205.

—— (ed.), 'Seaán Mhág Colgan cct.', *Father John Colgan O.F.M. 1592–1658*, edited by Terence O'Donnell, O.F.M., (Dublin, 1959), 60–9.

—— (ed.), *Dán na mbráthar mionúr*, 2 vols. (Dublin, 1967, 1980).

Morley, Henry (ed.), *Ireland under Elizabeth and James the first* (London, 1890).

Morris-Jones, J. and T.H. Parry-Williams (eds.), *Llawysgrif Hendregadredd* (Cardiff, 1933).

Moryson, Fynes, *Shakespeare's Europe unpublished chapters of Fynes Moryson's itinerary*, edited by Charles Hughes (London, 1903).

Murphy, Gerard (ed.), 'Poems of exile by Uilliam Nuinseann mac barúin Dealbhna', *Éigse* 6 (1949), 8–15.

—— (ed.), *Duanaire Finn III* (Dublin, 1953).

National Library of Ireland, 'Reports on private collections', no. 493.

Ní Cheallacháin, Máire (ed.), *Filíocht Phádraigín Haicéad* (Dublin, 1962).

Ní Dhonnchadha, Máirín (ed.), 'The poem beginning "A Shláine inghean Fhlannagáin"', *Ériu* XLVI (1995), 65–70.

Ní Dhomhnaill, Cáit (ed.), *Duanaireacht* (Dublin, 1975).

Ní Laoire, Siobhán (ed.), *Bás Cearbhaill agus Farbhlaidhe* (Dublin, 1986).

Ní Ógáin, Róis (ed.), *Duanaire Gaedhilge*, 3 vols. (Dublin, 1921–).

Ní Shéaghdha, Nessa (ed.), *Catalogue of Irish manuscripts in the National Library of Ireland*, fasc.1 (Dublin, 1967–).

O'Brien, George (ed.), *Advertisements for Ireland* (Dublin, 1923).

O'Brien, Patrick (ed.), *Eochair-sgiath an aifrinn: an explanatory defence of the mass* (Dublin, 1898).

O'Brien, M.A. (ed.), *Corpus genealogiarum Hiberniae* I (Dublin, 1962).

Ó Ciardha, Padhraic (ed.), 'The lament for Eoghan Mac Criostail', *The Irish Sword* XIII (1979), 378–81.

Ó Cléirigh, Tomás (ed.), 'A poem book of the O'Donnells', *Éigse* I (1939–40), 51–61, 130–42.

Ó Cróinín, D.I. (ed.), 'A poem to Toirdhealbhach Luinneach Ó Néill', *Éigse* XVI (1975–6), 50–66.

—— (ed.), 'A poet in penitential mood', *Celtica* XVI (1984), 169–74.

Ó Cuív, Brian (ed.), 'Flaithrí Ó Maolchonaire's catechism of christian doctrine', *Celtica* I (1950), 161–206.

—— (ed.), 'Lugh Lámhfhada and the death of Balar Ua Néid', *Celtica* II (1954), 64–6.

—— (ed.), 'A poem on the Í Néill', *Celtica* II (1954), 245–51.

—— (ed.), 'Mo thruaighe mar tá Éire', *Éigse* VIII (1956–7), 302–8.

—— 'A seventeenth-century criticism of Keating's "Foras Feasa ar Éirinn"', *Éigse* XI (1965), 119–40.

—— (ed.), 'Bunús mhuintir Dhíolún', *Éigse* XI (1964–6), 65–6.

—— 'Miscellanea: a poem by Seán Ó Maolchonaire', *Éigse* XI (1964–66), 287–95.

—— (ed.), 'A sixteenth-century political poem', *Éigse* XV (1973–4), 261–76.

—— (ed.), 'The earl of Thomond and the poets, A.D. 1572', *Celtica* XII (1977), 125–45.

—— (ed.), 'A fragment of Irish annals', *Celtica* XIV (1981), 83–104.

—— *The linguistic training of the mediaeval Irish poet* (Dublin, 1983).

—— (ed.), 'Some Irish items relating to the MacDonnells of Antrim', *Celtica* XVI (1984), 139–56.

—— (ed.), 'An elegy on Donnchadh Ó Briain, fourth earl of Thomond', *Celtica* XVI (1984), 87–105.

—— (ed.), *Aibidil Gaoidheilge & caiticiosma Seaán Ó Cearnaigh's Irish primer of religion published in 1571* (Dublin, 1994).

Ó Domhnuill, Uilliam (trans.), Tiomna nuadh ar dtighearna agus ar slanaightheora Iosa Criosd (Dublin, 1602).

—— *Leabhar na n-urnaightheadh gcomhchoidchiond agus mheinisdraldacha na sacrameinteadh* (Dublin, 1608).

Ó Donnchadha, Tadhg (ed.), *Leabhar Cloinne Aodha Buidhe* (Dublin, 1931).

O'Donovan, John (ed.), 'Documents relative to the O'h-Eidirsceoils (O'Driscolls)', *Miscellany of the Celtic Society*, edited by John O'Donovan (Dublin, 1849), 340–51.

—— (ed.), *The tribes of Ireland* (Dublin, 1852).

—— (ed.), *Annals of the kingdom of Ireland, by the four masters, from the earliest period to the year 1616*, 7 vols. (Dublin, 1856).

—— (ed.), 'The Irish correspondence of James Fitz Maurice of Desmond', *The Journal of the Kilkenny and South-East of Ireland Archaeological Society* II, N.S. (1858–9), 354–69.

Ó Fiaich, Tomás (ed.), 'Richard Weston agus "Beir mo bheannacht go Dundalk"', *Seanchas Ard Mhacha* 5, no. 2 (1970), 269–88.

O'Flaherty, Roderic, *Ogygia, or a chronological account of Irish events, collected from very ancient documents: written originally in Latin by R. O'Flaherty; transl. by the rev. J. Hely*, 2 vols. (Dublin, 1793).

—— *A chorographical description of west or h-Iar Connaught, written in A.D. 1684* (Irish Archaeological Society, Dublin, 1846).

Ó Fiannachta, Pádraig (ed.), *Lámhscríbhinní Gaeilge choláiste Phádraig Má Nuad*, fascúl IV (Maynooth, 1967).

O'Grady, Standish Hayes, and Robin Flower (eds.), *Catalogue of Irish manuscripts in the British Museum*, 3 vols. (London, 1926, 1953).

Ó Háinle, Cathal (ed.), 'Flattery rejected: two seventeenth-century Irish poems', *Hermathena* CXXXVIII (1985), 5–27.

Ó hEodhasa, Bonabhentura, *An teagasg críosdaidhe* (Antwerp, 1611), edited by Fearghal Mac Raghnaill (Dublin, 1976).

Ó hInnse, Séamus (ed.), *Miscellaneous Irish annals (A.D. 1114–1437)* (Dublin, 1947).

Ó Laidhin, Tomás (ed.), *Sidney state papers, 1565–70* (Irish Manuscripts Commission, Dublin, 1962).

Ó Lochlainn, Colm (ed.), *Tobar fíorghlan Gaedhilge deismireachta na teangadh 1450–1850* (Dublin, 1939).

Ó Macháin, Pádraig Carthach (ed.), 'Poems by Fearghal Óg Mac an Bhaird' (unpublished Ph.D. dissertation, University of Edinburgh, 1988).

Ó Maolagáin, P. (ed.), 'Eochaidh Ó hEoghusa, file Fhear Manach', in *St Macartan's Seminary Centenary Volume* (1940), 165–70.

Ó Maolchonaire, Flaithrí, *Sgáthán an chrábhaidh* (Louvain, 1616), edited by Thomas F. O'Rahilly (Dublin, 1941).

Ó Maonaigh, Cainneach (ed.), *Seanmónta chúige Uladh* (Dublin, 1965).

Ó Muireadhaigh, Réamonn (ed.), 'Aos dána na Mumhan, 1584', *Irisleabhar Muighe Nuadhat* (1960), 81–4.

Ó Muirgheasa, Énrí (ed.), *Dánta diadha Uladh* (Dublin, 1936).

Ó Raghallaigh, Tomás (ed.), *Duanta Eoghain Ruaidh Mhic an Bhaird* (Galway, 1930).

—— (ed.), *Filí agus filidheacht Chonnacht* (Dublin, 1938).

O'Rahilly, Cecile (ed.), *Five seventeenth-century political poems* (Dublin, 1952).

O'Rahilly, T.F., 'Irish poets, historians, and judges in English documents, 1538–1615', *Proceedings of the Royal Irish Academy* XXXVI, C, no. 6, (1922), 86–120.

—— (ed.), *Danta grádha* (Cork, 1926).

—— (ed.), *Measgra dánta*, 2 vols. (Dublin/Cork, 1927).

O'Rahilly, T.F., et al. (eds.), *Catalogue of Irish manuscripts in the Royal Irish Academy*, 28 fasciculi (Dublin, 1926–70).

Ó Raithbheartaigh, Toirdhealbhach (ed.), *Genealogical tracts I* (Irish Manuscripts Commission, Dublin, 1932).

O'Sullivan, Anne (ed.), 'Tadhg O'Daly and Sir George Carew', *Éigse* XIV (1971), 27–38.

—— 'The Tinnakill duanaire', *Celtica* XI (1976), 214–28.

O'Sullivan, Anne and Pádraig Ó Riain (eds.), *Poems on marcher lords* (London, 1987).

Ó Tuathail, Éamonn (ed.), 'Nugentiana', *Éigse* II (1940), 4–14.

—— (ed.), 'A poem for Felim O'Toole', *Éigse* III (1941–42), 261–71.

Perrott, James, *The chronicle of Ireland, 1584–1608*, edited by Herbert Wood (Irish Manuscripts Commission, Dublin, 1933).

Perrot, *The government of Ireland under Sir John Perrot, 1584–8*, by E.C.S. (London, 1626).

Plummer, Charles (ed.), *Lives of Irish saints*, 2 vols. (Oxford, 1922).

—— *On the colophons and marginalia of Irish scribes* (London, 1926).

Quinn, David B. (ed.), 'Calendar of the Irish council book, 1581–1586', *Analecta Hibernica* 24 (1967), 91–180.

Reily, Hugh, *Ireland's case briefly stated* (n.p., 1695).

Rich, Barnabe, *A new description of Ireland* (London, 1610).

Skene, William Forbes, *Celtic Scotland: a history of ancient Alban*, 3 vols. (Edinburgh, 1876–80).

Stafford, Thomas (ed.), *Pacata Hibernia, Ireland appeased and reduced: or, an historie of the late warres of Ireland, especially within the province of Mounster, under the government of Sir George Carew* (London, 1633).

Stapleton, Theobald, *Catechismus, seu doctrina christiana, Latino-Hibernica, per modum dialogi, inter magistrum et discipulum* (Brussels, 1639) (reflex facsimile, Irish Manuscripts Commission, Dublin, 1945).

Stern, L.C., 'Ueber eine Sammlung irischer Gedichte in Kopenhagen', *Zeitschrift für Celtische Philologie* II (1899), 323–72.

Thomson, R.L. (ed.), *Foirm na n-urrnuidheadh* (Edinburgh, 1970).

Ua Brádaigh, Tomás (ed.), 'Dhá dhán le Tomás Déis, easbog na Mí, 1622–1652', *Ríocht na Midhe* 3, no. 2 (1964), 99–104.

Ua Duinnín, Pádraig (ed.), *Me Guidhir Fhearmanach* (Dublin, 1917).

—— (ed.), *Dánta Phiarais Feiritéir* (Dublin, 1934).

Vendryes, Joseph (ed.), 'Le poème "Truagh liomsa, a chompáin, do chor", par Bonaventura O'Hussey: variantes d'un manuscrit du 18e siècle', *Éigse* V (1945–47), 290–93.

Walsh, Micheline Kerney, *'Destruction by peace': Hugh O Neill after Kinsale* (Armagh, 1986).

Walsh, Paul (ed.), *The flight of the earls by Tadhg Ó Cianáin* (Dublin, 1916).

—— *The will and family of Hugh O'Neill, earl of Tyrone* (Dublin, 1930).

—— (ed.), *Gleanings from Irish manuscripts* (2nd edition, Dublin, 1933).

—— (ed.), *Beatha Aodha Ruaidh Uí Dhomhnaill*, 2 vols. (Dublin, 1948, 1957).

—— (ed.), 'Worth and virtue unrequited', in *Irish chiefs and leaders* (Dublin, 1960), 67–81.

Watson, W.J. (ed.), *Scottish verse from the Book of the Dean of Lismore* (Edinburgh, 1937).

Williams, N.J.A. (ed.), *Dánta Mhuiris Mhic Dháibhí Dhuibh Mhic Gearailt* (Dublin, 1979).

—— (ed.), *The poems of Giolla Brighde Mac Con Midhe* (Dublin, 1980).

—— (ed.), *Pairlement Chloinne Tomáis* (Dublin, 1981).

Secondary Sources

Abbott, T.K., 'On the history of the Irish Bible', *Hermathena* XVII (1913), 29–50.

Bagwell, Richard, *Ireland under the Tudors*, 3 vols. (London, 1885–90) (reprint ed. London, 1963).

Bannerman, John, 'The Scots language and the kin-based society' in *Gaelic and Scots in harmony*, edited by Derick S. Thomson (Glasgow, 1990), 1–19.

Barnard, T.C., *Cromwellian Ireland: English government and reform in Ireland 1649–1660* (Oxford, 1975).

—— 'Crises of identity among Irish protestants 1641–1685', *Past & Present* 127 (1990), 39–83.

—— 'The political, material and mental culture of the Cork settlers, c.1650–1700', in *Cork history & society*, edited by Patrick O'Flanagan and Cornelius G. Buttimer (Dublin, 1993), 309–65.

—— 'Protestants and the Irish language, c.1675–1725', *Journal of Ecclesiastical History* 44, no. 2 (1993), 243–72.

Bartlett, Thomas, 'The O'Haras of Annaghmore c.1600–c.1800: survival and revival', *Irish Economic and Social History* IX (1982), 34–52.

Binchy, Daniel, *Celtic and Anglo-Saxon kingship* (Oxford, 1970).

Black, Ronald, 'The genius of Cathal MacMhuirich', *Transactions of the Gaelic Society of Inverness* L (1976–78), 327–66.

Bliss, Alan, 'Language and literature', in *The English in medieval Ireland*, edited by James Lydon (Dublin, 1984), 27–45.

Bloomfield, Morton W. and Charles W. Dunn, *The role of the poet in early societies* (Cambridge, 1989).

Bossy, John, 'The counter-reformation and the people of catholic Europe', *Past & Present* 47 (1970), 51–70.

—— 'The counter-reformation and the people of catholic Ireland, 1596–1641', *Historical Studies* VIII, edited by T. D. Williams (Dublin, 1971), 155–69.

—— 'The mass as a social institution 1200–1700', *Past & Present* 100 (1983), 29–61.

—— *Christianity in the west 1400–1700* (Oxford, 1985).

Bottigheimer, K., 'The failure of the reformation in Ireland: une question bien posée', *Journal of Ecclesiastical History* 36, no. 2 (1985), 196–207.

Bradshaw, Brendan, 'The beginnings of modern Ireland', in *The Irish parliamentary tradition*, edited by Brian Farrell (Dublin, 1973), 68–87.

—— *The dissolution of the religious orders in Ireland under Henry VIII* (Cambridge, 1974).

—— 'The Elizabethans and the Irish', *Studies* LXVI (1977), 38–50.

—— 'Sword, word and strategy in the reformation in Ireland', *The Historical Journal* XXI, no. 3 (1978), 475–502.

—— 'Native reaction to the westward enterprise: a case-study in Gaelic ideology', in *The westward enterprise: English activities in Ireland, the Atlantic and America 1480–1650*, edited by K.R. Andrews, N.P. Canny and P.E.H. Hair (Liverpool, 1978), 65–80.

—— 'Manus "the magnificent": O'Donnell as renaissance prince', in *Studies in Irish history*, edited by Art Cosgrove and Donal McCartney (Dublin, 1979), 15–36.

—— *The Irish constitutional revolution of the sixteenth century* (Cambridge, 1979).

—— 'The Elizabethans and the Irish: a muddled model', *Studies* LXX (1981), 233–44.

—— 'The reformation in the cities: Cork, Limerick and Galway, 1534–1603', in *Settlement and society in medieval Ireland*, edited by John Bradley (Kilkenny, 1988), 445–76.

—— 'Robe and sword in the conquest of Ireland', in *Law and government under the Tudors,* edited by Claire Cross, David Loades and J.J. Scarisbrick (Cambridge, 1988), 139–62.

—— 'Nationalism and historical scholarship in modern Ireland', *Irish Historical Studies* XXVI, no. 104 (1989), 329–51.

—— 'Geoffrey Keating: apologist of Irish Ireland', in *Representing Ireland: literature and the origins of conflict, 1534–1660,* edited by Brendan Bradshaw, Andrew Hadfield and Willy Maley (Cambridge, 1994), 166–90.

—— 'The bardic response to conquest and colonisation', *Bullán* 1, no. 1 (1994), 119–22.

—— 'The English reformation and identity formation in Wales and Ireland', in *British consciousness and identity: the making of Britain, 1533–1707*, edited by Brendan Bradshaw and Peter Roberts (Cambridge, 1998), 43–111.

Brady, Ciaran, 'Faction and the origins of the Desmond rebellion of 1579', *Irish Historical Studies* XXII, no. 88 (1980–81), 289–312.

—— 'The O'Reillys of east Breifne and the problem of "surrender and regrant"', *Bréifne* VI (1985), 233–62.

—— 'Thomas Butler, earl of Ormond (1531–1614) and reform in Tudor Ireland', in *Worsted in the game: losers in Irish history*, edited by idem. (Dublin, 1989), 49–59.

—— *The chief governors the rise and fall of reform government in Tudor Ireland, 1536–1588* (Cambridge, 1994).

—— *Shane O'Neill* (Dublin, 1996).

Breatnach, Pádraig A., 'The chief's poet', *Proceedings of the Royal Irish Academy* 83, C, 3 (1983), 37–79.

Breatnach, R.A., 'The lady and the king: a theme of Irish literature', *Studies* XLII (1953), 321–36.

Brockliss, L.W.B., and P. Ferté, 'Irish clerics in France in the seventeenth and eighteenth centuries: a statistical study', *Proceedings of the Royal Irish Academy* 87, C (1987), 527–72.

Bruford, Alan, *Gaelic folktales and romances* (Dublin, 1969).

Burke, Peter, *Popular culture in early modern Europe* (reprint, Aldershot, 1988).

—— (ed.), *New perspectives on historical writing* (reprint Cambridge, 1995).

Byrne, F.J., 'Senchas: the nature of Gaelic historical tradition', *Historical Studies* IX, edited by J.G. Barry (Belfast, 1974), 137–59.

Caball, Marc, 'Notes on an Elizabethan Kerry bardic family', *Ériu* XLIII (1992), 177–92.

—— 'Pairlement Chloinne Tomáis I: a reassessment', *Éigse* XXVII (1993), 47–57.

—— 'The Gaelic mind and the collapse of the Gaelic world: an appraisal', *Cambridge Medieval Celtic Studies* 25 (Summer 1993), 87–96.

—— 'Providence and exile in early seventeenth-century Ireland', *Irish Historical Studies* XXIX, no. 114 (1994), 174–88.

—— 'Bardic poetry and the analysis of Gaelic mentalities', *History Ireland* 2, no. 2 (1994), 46–50.

—— 'Aspects of sixteenth-century élite Gaelic mentalities: a case-study', *Études Celtiques* XXXII (1996), 203–16.

—— 'Faith, culture and sovereignty: Irish nationality and its development, 1558–1625', in *British consciousness and identity: the making of Britain, 1533–1707,* edited by Brendan Bradshaw and P.R. Roberts (Cambridge, 1998), 112–139.

Campbell, J.L. and Derick Thomson, *Edward Lhuyd in the Scottish highlands 1699–1700* (Oxford, 1963).

—— 'The tour of Edward Lhuyd in Ireland in 1699 and 1700', *Celtica* V (1960), 218–28.

Canny, Nicholas, 'The treaty of Mellifont', *The Irish Sword* 9 (1969–70), 249–62.

—— 'Hugh O'Neill, earl of Tyrone and the changing face of Gaelic Ulster', *Studia Hibernica* 10 (1970), 7–35.

—— 'The flight of the earls, 1607', *Irish Historical Studies* XVII, no. 67 (1971), 380–99.

—— 'The ideology of English colonisation: from Ireland to America', *William and Mary Quarterly* XXX (1973), 575–98.

—— *The formation of the Old English elite* (O'Donnell Lecture, Dublin, 1975).

—— *The Elizabethan conquest of Ireland: a pattern established 1565–76* (Hassocks, 1976).

—— 'Early modern Ireland: an appraisal appraised', *Irish Economic and Social History* IV (1977), 56–65.

—— 'Why the reformation failed in Ireland: une question mal posée', *Journal of Ecclesiastical History* 30, no. 4 (1979), 423–50.

—— 'The formation of the Irish mind: religion, politics and Gaelic Irish literature, 1580–1750', *Past & Present* 95 (1982), 91–116.

—— *The upstart earl: a study of the social and mental world of Richard Boyle first earl of Cork 1566–1643* (Cambridge, 1982).

—— 'Pádraigín Haicéad: an sagart agus an file i gcomhthéacs a aimsire', *Dúchas 1983–1984–1985* (Dublin, 1986), 8–20.

—— 'Identity formation in Ireland: the emergence of the Anglo-Irish', in *Colonial identity in the Atlantic world, 1500–1800,* edited by Nicholas Canny and Anthony Pagden (Princeton, 1987), 159–212.

—— *From reformation to restoration: Ireland 1534–1660* (Dublin, 1987).

—— *Kingdom and colony: Ireland in the Atlantic world, 1560–1800* (Baltimore, 1988).

Carey, John, *A new introduction to Lebor Gabála Érenn* (Irish Texts Society, London, 1993).

Carrigan, William, *The history and antiquities of the diocese of Ossory*, 4 vols. (Dublin, 1905).

Carney, James, *Studies in Irish literature and history* (Dublin, 1955).

—— *The Irish bardic poet* (Dublin, 1967).

—— 'Society and the bardic poet', *Studies* LXII (1973), 233–50.

Clancy, P., *The earliest Welsh poetry* (London, 1970).

Clarke, Aidan, 'Ireland and the general crisis', *Past & Present* 48 (1970), 79–99.

—— 'Colonial identity in early seventeenth-century Ireland', in *Nationality and the pursuit of national independence*, edited by T.W. Moody (Belfast, 1978), 57–71.

Corish, Patrick J., 'The origins of catholic nationalism', in *A history of Irish catholicism* III, fasciculus 8, edited by Patrick J. Corish (Dublin, 1968).

—— *The catholic community in the seventeenth and eighteenth centuries* (Dublin, 1981).

—— *The Irish catholic experience: a historical survey* (Dublin, 1985).

Cosgrove, Art, 'Hiberniores ipsis Hibernis', in *Studies in Irish history*, edited by Art Cosgrove and Donal McCartney (Dublin, 1979), 1–14.

Cregan, Donal, 'The social and cultural background of a counter-reformation episcopate, 1618–60', in *Studies in Irish history*, edited by Art Cosgrove and Donal McCartney (Dublin, 1979), 85–117.

Cunningham, Bernadette and Raymond Gillespie, 'The east Ulster bardic family of Ó Gnímh', *Éigse* XX (1984), 106–14.

—— 'The composition of Connacht in the lordships of Clanricard and Thomond, 1577–1641', *Irish Historical Studies* XXIV, no. 93 (1984), 1–14.

—— 'Native culture and political change in Ireland, 1580–1640', in *Natives and newcomers*, edited by Ciaran Brady and Raymond Gillespie (Dublin, 1986), 148–70.

—— 'Seventeenth-century interpretation of the past: the case of Geoffrey Keating', *Irish Historical Studies* XXV, no. 98 (1986), 116–28.

—— and Raymond Gillespie, '"Persecution" in seventeenth-century Irish', *Éigse* XXII (1987), 15–20.

—— 'Natives and newcomers in Mayo, 1560–1603', in 'A various country': essays in Mayo history 1500–1900, edited by Raymond Gillespie and Gerard Moran (Westport, 1987), 24–43.

—— 'Geoffrey Keating's Eochair sgiath an aifrinn and the catholic reformation in Ireland', in The churches, Ireland and the Irish, edited by W.J. Sheils and Diana Wood (Studies in Church History, 25) (Oxford, 1989), 133–43.

—— 'The culture and ideology of Irish Franciscan historians at Louvain 1607–1650', in Ideology and the historians, edited by Ciaran Brady (Historical Studies, XVII), (Dublin, 1991), 11–30.

—— 'The anglicisation of east Breifne: the O'Reillys and the emergence of county Cavan', in Cavan: essays on the history of an Irish county, edited by Raymond Gillespie (Dublin, 1995), 51–72.

—— and Raymond Gillespie, ' "The most adaptable of saints": the cult of St Patrick in the seventeenth century', Archivium Hibernicum XLIX (1995), 82–104.

—— 'Irish language sources for early modern Ireland', History Ireland 4, no. 1 (1996), 44–8.

Curtin, Margaret, 'Daniel O'Daly, 1595–1662: an agent in seventeenth century diplomacy' (unpublished Ph.D. dissertation, N.U.I. (U.C.D.), 1962).

Curtis, Edmund, A history of Ireland (London, 1936).

—— 'The spoken languages of medieval Ireland', Studies VIII (1919), 234–54.

Darnton, Robert, The great cat massacre and other episodes in French cultural history (Harmondsworth, 1988 ed.).

—— 'History of reading', in New perspectives on historical writing, edited by Peter Burke (reprint ed. Cambridge, 1995), 140–67.

—— 'The symbolic element in history', The Journal of Modern History 58, no. 1 (1986), 218–34.

Davis, Natalie Zemon, Society and culture in early modern France (Stanford, 1975).

Dawson, Jane, 'Calvinism and the Gaidhealtachd in Scotland', in Calvinism in Europe, 1540–1620, edited by Andrew Pettegree, Alastair Duke and Gillian Lewis (Cambridge, 1994), 231–53.

De Bhaldraithe, Tomás, 'Leabhar Charswell in Éirinn', Éigse IX, pt. 1 (1958–61), 61–7.

De Blácam, Aodh, Gaelic literature surveyed (Dublin, 1929).

Dooley, Ann, 'Literature and society in early seventeenth-century Ireland: the evaluation of change', in Celtic languages and Celtic peoples: proceedings of the second north American congress of Celtic studies, edited by Cyril J. Byrne, Margaret Harry and Pádraig Ó Siadhail (Halifax, 1992), 513–34.

Duffy, Patrick J., 'Patterns of landownership in Gaelic Monaghan in the late sixteenth century', Clogher Record X, no. 3 (1981), 304–22.

Dunne, T.J., 'The Gaelic response to conquest and colonisation: the evidence of the poetry', Studia Hibernica XX (1980), 7–30.

Eagleton, Terry, *Marxism and literary criticism* (London, 1976).

Edwards, R. Dudley, *Church and state in Tudor Ireland* (Dublin, 1935).

—— 'Ireland, Elizabeth I and the counter-reformation', in *Elizabethan government and society*, edited by S.T. Bindoff, Joel Hurstfield and C.H. Williams (London, 1961), 315–39.

Edwards, R. W. Dudley and Mary O'Dowd, *Sources for early modern Irish history, 1534–1641* (Cambridge, 1985).

Eisenstein, Elizabeth L., *The printing revolution in early modern Europe* (Cambridge, 1993 ed.).

Elliott, J.H., 'Revolution and continuity in early modern Europe', *Past & Present* 42 (1969), 35–56.

Elliott, Marianne, *Watchmen in Sion: the protestant idea of liberty* (Derry, 1985).

Ellis, Steven G., *Tudor Ireland: crown, community and the conflict of cultures, 1470–1603* (London, 1985).

—— 'Nationalist historiography and the English and Gaelic worlds in the late middle ages', *Irish Historical Studies* XXV, no. 97 (1986), 1–18.

—— 'Economic problems of the church: why the reformation failed in Ireland', *The Journal of Ecclesiastical History* 41, no. 2 (1990), 239–65.

Falls, Cyril, 'Neill Garve: English ally and victim', *The Irish Sword* 1, no. 1 (1949–53), 2–7.

—— 'Black Tom of Ormonde', *The Irish Sword* 5 (1961–2), 10–22.

Ford, Alan, *The protestant reformation in Ireland, 1590–1641* (Frankfurt am Main, 1985).

—— 'The protestant reformation in Ireland', in *Natives and newcomers*, edited by Ciaran Brady and Raymond Gillespie (Dublin, 1986), 50–74.

—— '"Standing one's ground": religion, polemic and Irish history since the reformation', in *As by law established the church of Ireland since the reformation*, edited by Alan Ford, James McGuire and Kenneth Milne (Dublin, 1995), 1–14.

—— 'The reformation in Kilmore before 1641', in *Cavan: essays on the history of an Irish county*, edited by Raymond Gillespie (Dublin, 1995), 73–98.

Giblin, Cathaldus, 'Hugh McCaghwell, O.F.M., archbishop of Armagh (+1626) – aspects of his life', *Seanchas Ard Mhacha* 11, no. 2 (1985), 259–90.

Gillespie, Raymond, *The settlement of east Ulster 1600–1641* (Cork, 1985).

—— *Conspiracy: Ulster plots and plotters in 1615* (Belfast, 1987).

—— 'The book trade in southern Ireland, 1590–1640', in *Books beyond the Pale: aspects of the provincial book trade in Ireland before 1850*, edited by Gerard Long (Dublin, 1996), 1–17.

—— *Devoted people: belief and religion in early modern Ireland* (Manchester, 1997).

Ginzburg, Carlo, *The cheese and the worms* (Harmondsworth, 1992 ed.).

Greene, David, 'The O'Hara MS.', *Hermathena* LX (1942), 81–6.

Gwynn, Aubrey, 'Ireland and the continent in the eleventh century', *Irish Historical Studies* VIII, no. 31, 193–216.

—— and D.F. Gleeson, *A history of the diocese of Killaloe* (Dublin, 1962).

Hale, J.R., 'Sixteenth-century explanations of war and violence', *Past & Present* 51 (1971), 3–26.

Hammerstein, Helga, 'Aspects of the continental education of Irish students in the reign of Elizabeth I', *Historical Studies* VIII, edited by T.D. Williams (Dublin, 1971), 137–53.

Harrison, Alan, *An chrosántacht* (Dublin, 1979).

Hayes-MacCoy, G.A., 'Sir John Davies in Cavan in 1606 and 1610', *Bréifne* 1, no. 3 (1960), 177–91.

—— 'Gaelic society in Ireland in the late sixteenth century', *Historical Studies* IV, edited by G.A. Hayes-MacCoy (London, 1963), 45–61.

—— 'Conciliation, coercion, and the protestant reformation, 1547–71', in *A new history of Ireland* III, edited by T.W. Moody, F.X. Martin and F.J. Byrne (Oxford, 1976), 69–93.

—— 'The completion of the Tudor conquest and the advance of the counter-reformation, 1571–1603', in *A new history of Ireland* III, edited by T.W. Moody et al. (Oxford, 1976), 94–141.

Henry, Gráinne, *The Irish military community in Spanish Flanders, 1586–1621* (Dublin, 1992).

Herbert, Máire, 'Goddess and king: the sacred marriage in early Ireland', in *Women & Sovereignty*, edited by L.O. Fradenburg (Edinburgh, 1992), 264–75.

Hill, George, *An historical account of the plantation in Ulster at the commencement of the seventeenth century 1608–1620* (Belfast, 1877) (reprint ed. Shannon, 1970).

Hill, Jacqueline R., 'Popery and protestantism, civil and religious liberty: the disputed lessons of Irish history, 1690–1812', *Past & Present* 118 (1988), 96–129.

Hobsbawm, Eric and Terence Ranger, *The invention of tradition* (Cambridge, 1983).

Hore, Herbert F., 'The Munster bards', *The Ulster Journal of Archaeology* 7 (1859), 93–115.

Hughes, A.J., 'The seventeenth-century Ulster/Scottish contention of the red hand: background and significance', in *Gaelic and Scots in harmony*, edited by Derick S. Thomson (Glasgow, 1990), 78–94.

Hyde, Douglas, *A literary history of Ireland* (London, 1899).

Iske, Basil, *The green cockatrice* (Dublin, 1978).

Jackson, Donald, *Intermarriage in Ireland 1550–1650* (Montreal, 1970).

Jennings, Brendan, 'The career of Hugh, son of Rory O Donnell, earl of Tirconnel, in the Low Countries, 1607–1643', *Studies* XXX (1941), 219–34.

Kearney, H.F., 'Ecclesiastical politics and the counter-reformation in Ireland, 1618–1648', *The Journal of Ecclesiastical History* XI, no. 2 (1960), 202–12.

Knott, Eleanor, *Irish classical poetry* (Dublin, 1957).

Knox, R. Buick, *James Ussher archbishop of Armagh* (Cardiff, 1967).

Leerssen, J.Th., 'Archbishop Ussher and Gaelic culture', *Studia Hibernica* 22–23 (1982–3), 50–58.

—— *The contention of the bards (Iomarbhágh na bhfileadh) and its place in Irish political and literary history* (Irish Texts Society, London, 1994).

—— 'Wildness, wilderness, and Ireland: medieval and early-modern patterns in the demarcation of civility', *Journal of the History of Ideas* 56, no. 1 (1995), 25–39.

—— *Mere Irish & fíor-Ghael: studies in the idea of Irish nationality, its development and literary expression prior to the nineteenth century* (2nd ed., Cork, 1996).

Lennon, Colm, *Richard Stanihurst the Dubliner 1547–1618* (Dublin, 1981).

Leslie, J.B., *Derry clergy and parishes* (Enniskillen, 1937).

Livingstone, Peadar, *The Fermanagh story* (Enniskillen, 1969).

Loeber, Rolf, 'Civilization through plantation: the projects of Mathew De Renzi', in *Irish Midland Studies*, edited by Harman Murtagh (Athlone, 1980), 121–35.

—— *The geography and practice of English colonisation in Ireland from 1534 to 1609* (Belfast, 1991).

Lynam, E.W., *The Irish character in print 1571–1923* (London, 1924) (reprint Shannon, 1968).

Mac Cana, Proinsias, 'Early Irish ideology and the concept of unity', in *The Irish mind*, edited by Richard Kearney (Dublin, 1985), 56–78.

McCavitt, John, 'The flight of the earls, 1607', *Irish Historical Studies* XXIX, no. 114 (1994), 159–73.

McCone, K.R., 'Fírinne agus torthúlacht', *Léachtaí Cholm Cille* XI (1980), 136–73.

Mac Craith, Mícheál, 'Ovid, an macalla agus Cearbhall Ó Dálaigh', *Éigse* XIX, pt. 1 (1982), 103–120.

—— 'Cioth na baoise', *Béaloideas* 51 (1983), 31–54.

—— *Lorg na hiasachta ar na dánta grádha* (Dublin, 1989).

—— 'Gaelic Ireland and the renaissance', in *The Celts and the renaissance: tradition and innovation*, edited by Glanmor Williams and Robert Owen Jones (Cardiff, 1990), 57–89.

—— 'The Gaelic reaction to the reformation', in *Conquest & union fashioning a British state 1485–1725*, edited by Steven G. Ellis and Sarah Barber (Harlow, 1995), 139–61.

—— 'Litríocht an 17ú haois: tonnbhriseadh an tseanghnáthaimh nó tonnchruthú an nuaghnáthaimh', *Léachtaí Cholm Cille* XXVI (1996), 50–82.

Mac Cuarta, Brian, 'Newcomers in the Irish midlands, 1540–1641' (unpublished M.A. dissertation, N.U.I. (U.C.G.), 1980).

—— (ed.), *Ulster 1641 aspects of the rising* (Belfast, 1993).

—— 'A planter's interaction with Gaelic culture: Sir Matthew De Renzy, 1577–1634', *Irish Economic and Social History* XX (1993), 1–17.

MacCurtain, Margaret, *Tudor and Stuart Ireland* (Dublin, 1972).

—— 'The fall of the house of Desmond', *Journal of the Kerry Archaeological and Historical Society* 8 (1975), 28–44.

MacDonagh, Oliver, *States of mind: a study of Anglo-Irish conflict 1780–1980* (London, 1983).

Mac Giolla Chomhaill, Anraí, *Bráithrín bocht ó Dhún: Aodh Mac Aingil* (Dublin, 1985).

McGrath, Cuthbert, 'Eoghan Ruadh Mac Uilliam Óig Mhic an Bhaird', in *Measgra i gCuimhne Mhichíl Uí Chléirigh*, edited by Sylvester O'Brien (Dublin, 1944), 108–16.

—— 'Ollamh Cloinne Aodha Buidhe', *Éigse* VII (1953–55), 127–8.

—— 'Í Eodhosa', *Clogher Record* 2, no. 1 (1957), 1–19.

Mac Mathúna, Liam, 'The designations, functions and knowledge of the Irish poet', *Österreichische Akademie der Wissenschaften Philosophisch-historische Klasse Veröffentlichungen der Keltischen Kommission* 2 (Anz. ph. 1982, Nr.11), 225–38.

Mac Niocaill, Gearóid, *The medieval Irish annals* (Dublin, 1975).

—— *Irish population before Petty: problems and possibilities* (O'Donnell Lecture, Dublin, 1981).

Martin, F.X., 'Ireland, the renaissance and the counter-reformation', *Topic* 13, 7 (1967), 23–33.

Martines, Lauro, *Society and history in English renaissance verse* (Oxford, 1985).

Mathew, David, *The Celtic peoples and renaissance Europe* (London, 1933).

Meigs, Samantha, *The reformations in Ireland tradition and confessionalism, 1400–1690* (Dublin, 1997).

Meehan, C.P., *The fate and fortunes of Hugh O'Neill, earl of Tyrone, and Rory O'Donel, earl of Tyrconnel* (Dublin, 1868).

—— (trans.), *The rise, increase, and exit of the Geraldines, earls of Desmond, and persecution after their fall* (Dublin, 1878).

Meek, Donald E., 'John Carswell, superintendent of Argyll: a reassessment', *Records of the Scottish Church History Society* 19 (1975), 1–22.

Millett, Benignus, 'Irish literature in Latin, 1550–1700', in *A new history of Ireland* III, edited by T.W. Moody, F.X. Martin and F.J. Byrne (Oxford, 1976), 561–86.

Moody, T.W. (ed.), 'Ulster plantation papers 1608–13', *Analecta Hibernica* 8 (1938), 179–297.

—— 'The Irish parliament under Elizabeth and James I: a general survey', *Proceedings of the Royal Irish Academy* XLV, C, no. 6 (1939–40), 41–81.

Moody, T.W., F.X. Martin and F.J. Byrne (eds.), *A new history of Ireland* III (Oxford, 1976).

Mooney, Canice, 'The death of Red Hugh O'Donnell', *The Irish Ecclesiastical Record* LXXXI, Fifth Series (1954), 328–45.

—— 'A noble shipload', *The Irish Sword* II (1955), 195–204.

—— 'Father John Colgan, O.F.M., his work and times and literary milieu', in *Father John Colgan O.F.M. 1592–1658*, edited by Terence O'Donnell (Dublin, 1959), 7–40.

—— 'The first impact of the reformation', in *A history of Irish catholicism* III, edited by Patrick J. Corish (Dublin, 1967).

Morgan, Hiram, 'The colonial venture of Sir Thomas Smith in Ulster, 1571–1575', *Historical Journal* 28, no. 2 (1985), 261–78.

—— 'The outbreak of the nine years war: Ulster in Irish politics, 1583–96' (unpublished Ph.D. dissertation, Cambridge University, 1987).

—— 'Extradition and treason – trial of a Gaelic lord: the case of Brian O'Rourke', *The Irish Jurist* XXII, N.S., pt. 2 (1987), 285–301.

—— 'The end of Gaelic Ulster: a thematic interpretation of events between 1534 and 1610', *Irish Historical Studies* XXVI, no. 101 (1988), 8–32.

—— 'Writing up early modern Ireland', *Historical Journal* 31, no. 3 (1988), 701–11.

—— *Tyrone's rebellion: the outbreak of the nine years war in Tudor Ireland* (Dublin, 1993).

—— 'Hugh O'Neill and the nine years war in Tudor Ireland', *Historical Journal* 36, no. 1 (1993), 21–37.

—— (ed.), 'Faith and fatherland or queen and country?', *Dúiche Néill: Journal of the O Neill Country Historical Society* 9 (1994), 9–65.

Morrill, John, 'The fashioning of Britain', in *Conquest & union fashioning a British state 1485–1725*, edited by Steven G. Ellis and Sarah Barber (Harlow, 1995), 8–39.

Muchembled, Robert, *Popular and élite culture in France 1400–1750* (Baton Rouge and London, 1985).

Murphy, Gerard, 'Royalist Ireland', *Studies* XXIV (1935), 589–604.

—— 'Bards and filidh', *Éigse* II (1940), 200–207.

Nic Ghiollamhaith, Aoife, 'Dynastic warfare and historical writing in north Munster, 1276–1350', *Cambridge Medieval Celtic Studies* 2 (1981), 73–89.

Nicholls, Kenneth, *Gaelic and gaelicised Ireland in the middle ages* (Dublin, 1972).

—— *Land, law and society in sixteenth-century Ireland* (O'Donnell Lecture, Dublin, 1976).

Ní Shéaghdha, Nessa, 'Collectors of Irish manuscripts: motives and methods', *Celtica* XVII (1985), 1–28.

O'Brien, W.P., 'Two sixteenth century Munster primates: Donnchadh Ó Taidhg (1560–62) & Richard Creagh (1564–85)', *Seanchas Ard Mhacha* 14, no. 1 (1990), 35–57.

Ó Buachalla, Breandán, 'Annála ríoghachta Éireann is Foras feasa ar Éirinn: an comhthéacs comhaimseartha', *Studia Hibernica* 22–23 (1982–83), 59–105.

—— 'An mheisiasacht agus an aisling', in *Folia gadelica aistí ó iardhaltaí leis a bronnadh ar R.A. Breatnach*, edited by Pádraig de Brún, Seán Ó Coileáin and Pádraig Ó Riain (Cork, 1983), 72–87.

—— 'Na Stíobhartaigh agus an t-aos léinn: cing Séamas', *Proceedings of the Royal Irish Academy* 83, C, 4 (1983), 81–134.

—— Foreword to 1987 reprint of *Foras feasa ar Éirinn* (Irish Texts Society, London, 1987).

—— 'Aodh Eanghach and the Irish king-hero', in *Sages, saints and scholars*, edited by Donnchadh Ó Corráin et al. (Maynooth, 1989), 200–32.

—— 'Cúlra is tábhacht an dáin *A leabhráin ainmnighthear d'Aodh*', *Celtica* XXI (1990), 402–16.

—— 'Poetry and politics in early modern Ireland', *Eighteenth-Century Ireland Iris an Dá Chultúr* 7 (1992), 149–75.

—— 'James our true king: the ideology of Irish royalism in the seventeenth century', in *Political thought in Ireland since the seventeenth century*, edited by D. George Boyce, Robert Eccleshall and Vincent Geoghegan (London, 1993), 7–35.

—— *Aisling ghéar na Stíobhartaigh agus an t-aos léinn 1603–1788* (Dublin, 1996).

Ó Caithnia, Liam P., *Apalóga na bhfilí 1200–1650* (Dublin, 1984).

Ó Ciardha, Éamonn, 'A voice from the Jacobite underground: Liam Inglis (1709–1778)', in *Radical Irish priests,* edited by Gerard Moran (Dublin, 1998), 16–38.

Ó Coileáin, Seán, 'Oral or literary: some strands of the argument', *Studia Hibernica* 17–18 (1977), 7–35.

Ó Cléirigh, Tomás, *Aodh Mac Aingil agus an scoil nua-Ghaeilge i Lobháin* (Dublin, 1936) (2nd ed., Dublin, 1985).

Ó Concheanainn, Tomás, 'A feature of the poetry of Fearghal Óg Mac an Bhaird', *Éigse* XV (1973–74), 235–251.

—— 'Smacht rí agus ruire', *Celtica* XVI (1984), 86.

Ó Corráin, Donnchadh, 'Nationality and kingship in pre-Norman Ireland', *Historical Studies* XI, edited by T.W. Moody (Belfast, 1978), 1–35.

—— 'Seathrún Céitinn (c.1580–c.1644): an cúlra stairiúil', *Dúchas 1983–1984–1985* (Dublin, 1986), 56–68.

Ó Cuív, Brian, *The Irish bardic duanaire or 'poem-book'* (Dublin, 1973).

—— 'The Irish language in the early modern period', in *A new history of Ireland* III, edited by T.W. Moody et al. (Oxford, 1976), 509–45.

—— 'Ireland's manuscript heritage', *Éire-Ireland* XIX, no. 1 (1984), 87–110.

O'Curry, Eugene, *Lectures on the manuscript materials of ancient Irish history* (Dublin, 1878).

Ó Danachair, Caoimhín, 'Oral tradition and the printed word', *Irish University Review* 9, no. 1 (1979), 31–41.

O'Dowd, Mary, 'Landownership in the Sligo area, 1585–1641' (unpublished Ph.D. dissertation, N.U.I. (U.C.D), 1979).

—— 'Land inheritance in early modern county Sligo', *Irish Economic and Social History* X (1983), 5–18.

—— 'Gaelic economy and society', in *Natives and newcomers*, edited by Ciaran Brady and Raymond Gillespie (Dublin, 1986), 120–47.

—— *Power, politics and land: early modern Sligo 1568–1688* (Belfast, 1991).

Ó Dúshláine, Tadhg, 'Athléamh ar Aodh Mac Aingil', *Irisleabhar Mhá Nuad* (1975–76), 9–25.

—— 'Ionmholta malairt bhisigh', *Léachtaí Cholm Cille* VIII (1977), 40–54.

—— 'More about Keating's use of the simile of the dung-beetle', *Zeitschrift für Celtische Philologie* 40 (1984), 282–5.

—— 'Seathrún Céitinn agus an stíl bharócach a thug sé go hÉirinn', *Dúchas 1983–1984–1985* (Dublin, 1986), 43–55.

—— *An Eoraip agus litríocht na Gaeilge 1600–1650* (Dublin, 1987).

Ó Fachtna, Anselm, 'Cúig teagaisg chríostaidhe de'n seachtmhadh aois déag: compráid', in *Measgra i gcuimhne Mhichíl Uí Chléirigh*, edited by Sylvester O'Brien (Dublin, 1944), 188–9.

Ó Fiaich, Tomás, 'Republicanism and separatism in the seventeenth century', *Léachtaí Cholm Cille* II (1971), 74–87.

—— *The Irish colleges in France* (Dublin, 1990).

Ó Háinle, Cathal, 'Notitiae', *Éigse* XVII, pt. 2 (1977–8), 221–35.

—— *Promhadh pinn* (Maynooth, 1978).

Ohlmeyer, Jane H. (ed.), *Ireland from independence to occupation 1641–1660* (Cambridge, 1995).

Ó hÓgáin, Dáithí, *An file: staidéar ar osnádúrthacht na filíochta sa traidisiún Gaelach* (Dublin, 1982).

Ó Madagáin, Breandán, *An Ghaeilge i Luimneach 1700–1900* (Dublin, 1974).

Ó Maonaigh, Cainneach, 'Scríbhneoirí Gaeilge oird san Froinsias', *Catholic Survey* I (1951), 54–75.

—— 'Scríbhneoirí Gaeilge an seachtú haois déag', *Studia Hibernica* 2 (1962), 182–208.

O'Rahilly, T.F., *Early Irish history and mythology* (Dublin, 1946).

—— 'On the origin of the names Érainn and Ériu', *Ériu* XIV (1946), 7–28.

—— 'Ó Gnímh's alleged visit to London', *Celtica* I (1950), 330–1.

O'Reilly, Edward, *Irish writers* (Dublin, 1820).

O Riordan, Michelle, *The Gaelic mind and the collapse of the Gaelic world* (Cork, 1990).

—— 'A seventeenth-century "political poem"', in *Aspects of Irish studies*, edited by Myrtle Hill and Sarah Barber (Belfast, 1990), 117–26.

—— 'The native Ulster "*mentalité*" as revealed in Gaelic sources, 1600–1650', in *Ulster 1641: aspects of the rising*, edited by Brian Mac Cuarta (Belfast, 1993), 61–91.

—— '"Political" poems in the mid-seventeenth-century crisis', in *Ireland from independence to occupation 1641–1660*, edited by Jane H. Ohlmeyer (Cambridge, 1995), 112–27.

O'Rorke, T., *History, antiquities and present state of the parishes of Ballysadare and Kilvarnet in the county of Sligo* (Dublin, 1878).
—— *The history of Sligo: town and county*, 2 vols. (Dublin, 1890).
O'Sullivan, Anne and William O'Sullivan, 'Edward Lhuyd's collection of Irish manuscripts', *Transactions of the Honourable Society of Cymmrodorion* (1962), 57–76.
O'Sullivan, William, 'Ussher as a collector of manuscripts', *Hermathena* LXXXVIII (1956), 34–58.
Ó Tuama, Seán, 'Téamaí iasachta i bhfilíocht pholaitiúil na Gaeilge (1600–1800)', *Éigse* XI, pt. 3 (1964–66), 201–13.
—— 'Dónal Ó Corcora agus filíocht na Gaeilge', *Studia Hibernica* 5 (1965), 29–41.
—— *An grá i bhfilíocht na n-uaisle* (Dublin, 1988).
Ó Tuathaigh, M.A.G., '"Early modern Ireland, 1534–1691": a re-assessment', *Irish Studies* I, edited by P.J. Drudy (Cambridge, 1980), 153–60.
Patterson, Nerys, 'Brehon law in late medieval Ireland: "antiquarian and obsolete" or "traditional and functional"?', *Cambridge Medieval Celtic Studies* 17 (1989), 43–63.
Perceval-Maxwell, M., *The Scottish migration to Ulster in the reign of James I* (London, 1973).
Pollard, Mary, *Dublin's trade in books 1550–1800* (Oxford, 1989).
Price, Liam, 'Notes on Feagh McHugh O'Byrne', *Journal of the County Kildare Archaeological Society* XI (1932), 134–75.
—— 'The O'Byrnes' country in county Wicklow in the sixteenth century', *The Journal of the Royal Society of Antiquaries of Ireland* LXIII, pt. 2 (1933), 224–42.
Prins, Gwyn, 'Oral history', in *New perspectives on historical writing*, edited by Peter Burke (reprint Cambridge, 1995), 114–39.
Quinn, David Beers, 'Sir Thomas Smith (1513–1577) and the beginnings of English colonial theory', *Proceedings of the American Philosophical Society* 89 (1945), 543–60.
—— *The Elizabethans and the Irish* (Ithaca, 1966).
Ranger, T.O., 'Richard Boyle and the making of an Irish fortune, 1588–1614', *Irish Historical Studies* X, no. 39 (1957), 257–97.
—— 'The career of Richard Boyle, first earl of Cork in Ireland, 1588–1643' (unpublished D.Phil. dissertation, Oxford University, 1958).
Rees, Alwyn and Brinley, *Celtic heritage* (London, 1961).
Roberts, P.R., 'The union with England and the identity of "Anglican" Wales', *Transactions of the Royal Historical Society*, fifth series, 22 (1972), 49–70.
—— 'The Welsh language, English law and Tudor legislation', *Transactions of the Honourable Society of Cymmrodorion* (1989), 19–75.
Robinson, Philip, *The plantation of Ulster* (reprint Belfast, 1994).
Salmon, Vivian, 'Missionary linguistics in seventeenth-century Ireland and a

north American analogy', *Historiographia Linguistica* XII, no. 3 (1985), 321–49.

Scowcroft, Mark, 'Miotas na gabhála i Leabhar Gabhála', *Léachtaí Cholm Cille* XIII (1982), 41–75.

Sheehan, Anthony J., 'The killing of the earl of Desmond, November 1583', *Journal of the Cork Historical and Archaeological Society* LXXXVIII, no. 247 (1983), 106–10.

Silke, John J., 'Later relations between primate Peter Lombard and Hugh O'Neill', *The Irish Theological Quarterly* XXII (1955), 15–30.

—— 'Primate Lombard and James I', *The Irish Theological Quarterly* XXII (1955), 124–50.

—— 'Irish scholarship and the renaissance, 1580–1673', *Studies in the Renaissance* XX (1973), 169–206.

—— 'The Irish Peter Lombard', *Studies* LXIV, no. 254 (1975), 143–55.

—— 'The Irish abroad, 1534–1691', in *A new history of Ireland* III, edited by T.W. Moody et al. (Oxford, 1976), 587–633.

Simms, Katharine, 'Gaelic lordships in Ulster in the later middle ages' (unpublished Ph.D. dissertation, Dublin University, 1976).

—— 'The medieval kingdom of Lough Erne', *Clogher Record* IX (1977), 126–41.

—— *From kings to warlords: the changing political structure of Gaelic Ireland in the later middle ages* (Woodbridge, 1987).

—— 'Bardic poetry as a historical source', in *The writer as witness: literature as historical evidence*, edited by Tom Dunne (Historical Studies, XVI) (Cork, 1987), 58–75.

—— 'Bards and barons: the Anglo-Irish aristocracy and the native culture', in *Medieval frontier societies*, edited by Robert Bartlett and Angus Mackay (Oxford, 1989), 177–97.

—— 'The poet as chieftain's widow: bardic elegies', in *Sages, saints and story-tellers,* edited by Donnchadh Ó Corráin et al. (Maynooth, 1989), 400–411.

—— 'The brehons of later medieval Ireland', in *Brehons, serjeants and attorneys: studies in the history of the Irish legal profession,* edited by Daire Hogan and W.N. Osborough (Dublin, 1990), 51–76.

—— 'Literary sources for the history of Gaelic Ireland in the post-Norman period', in *Progress in medieval Irish studies,* edited by Kim McCone and Katharine Simms (Maynooth, 1996), 207–15.

Slotkin, Edgar M., 'Folkloristics and medieval Celtic philology: a theoretical model', in *Celtic folklore and christianity*, edited by Patrick K. Ford (Los Angeles, 1983), 213–225.

Stewart, James, *Boccaccio in the Blaskets* (Galway, 1988).

Thomas, Keith, *Religion and the decline of magic* (London, 1971).

Thomson, Derick S., 'Three seventeenth-century bardic poets: Niall Mór, Cathal and Niall MacMhuirich', in *Bards and makars: Scottish language and literature*, edited by A.J. Aitken, M.P. McDiarmid and Derick S. Thomson (Glasgow, 1977), 221–46.

—— (ed.), *The companion to Gaelic Scotland* (Oxford, 1983).

Trevor-Roper, Hugh, 'James Ussher, archbishop of Armagh', in *Catholics, anglicans and puritans seventeenth century papers* (London, 1987), 120–165.

Stanford, W.B., *Ireland and the classical tradition* (Dublin, 1984).

Ua Brádaigh, Tomás, 'Na Nuinnsionnaigh, mór-theaghlach Gall-Ghaelach, agus an cultúr Gaelach', *Ríocht na Midhe* 3, no. 3 (1965), 211–21.

Wall, Thomas, 'The catechism in Irish: Bonaventure O'Hussey, O.F.M.', *The Irish Ecclesiastical Record* LIX, Fifth Series (1942), 36–48.

Walshe, Helen Coburn, 'The rebellion of William Nugent, 1581', in *Religion, conflict and coexistence in Ireland*, edited by R.V. Comerford, Mary Cullen, Jacqueline R. Hill and Colm Lennon (Dublin, 1990), 26–52.

Walsh, Micheline, *The O'Neills in Spain* (O'Donnell Lecture, Dublin, 1957).

—— 'The last years of Hugh O'Neill', *The Irish Sword* 8 (1967–8), 120–9, 230–41, 294–303.

Walsh, Paul, *The Ó Cléirigh family of Tír Conaill* (Dublin, 1938).

—— *Irish men of learning* (Dublin, 1947).

—— *Irish chiefs and leaders* (Dublin, 1960).

Waterman, Dudley M., 'Some Irish seventeenth-century houses and their architectural ancestry', in *Studies in building history*, edited by E.M. Jope (London, 1961), 251–74.

Watt, Tessa, *Cheap print and popular piety, 1550–1640* (Cambridge, 1991).

Williams, J.E. Caerwyn, 'Y beirdd llys yn Iwerddon', *Llên Cymru* 3 (1954), 1–11.

—— 'The court poet in medieval Ireland', *Proceedings of the British Academy* LVII (1971), 85–135.

Williams, J.E. Caerwyn and Máirín Ní Mhuiríosa, *Traidisiún liteartha na nGael* (Dublin, 1979).

Williams, N.J.A., 'A note on Scáthán shacramuinte na haithridhe', *Éigse* XVII, pt. 4 (1977–9), 436.

—— *I bprionta i leabhar: na protastúin agus prós na Gaeilge 1567–1724* (Dublin, 1986).

Williams, Penry, 'Elizabethan Oxford: state, church and university', in *The history of the university of Oxford* 3, edited by James McConica (Oxford, 1986), 397–440.

Worden, Blair, 'Providence and politics in Cromwellian England', *Past & Present* 109 (1985), 55–99.

INDEX OF FIRST LINES

INDEX